Recent years have witnessed a substantial development of global macroeconomic modelling in which researchers have applied techniques developed to consider the industrialized countries to analyse North–South interactions in the world economy. This collection of papers uses these advances to examine the implications for the South of macroeconomic developments in the North, to examine international policy questions in a genuinely global context, and to consider the design of policy packages for the Third World (aid versus trade, growth-oriented adjustment) in an empirical context.

The book begins with papers that model trade linkages and look at recent progress in the 'elasticities debate', specifically in the context of the dynamic economies of the Asian Pacific Rim. It goes on to consider linkages through trade in commodities and the impact of commodity prices on the performance of the world economy; and growth linkages and convergence between North and South, with an examination of the speed and scale of the transfer of technology and knowledge between North and South. A further section presents two rather different ways of modelling macroeconomic adjustment in the South in response to external shocks emanating from the North. The final and largest section contains a number of exercises in global scenario analysis, where the interactions are both from North to South and from South to North. These include an examination of global responses to: a US deficit reduction package, a reduction in global military spending, and a rise in world real interest rates.

This book provides a useful overview of the flourishing and important research area relating to interactions between North and South, and also highlights areas where future research is needed.

North–South linkages and international
macroeconomic policy

Centre for Economic Policy Research

The Centre for Economic Policy Research is a network of over 250 Research Fellows, based primarily in European universities. The Centre coordinates its Fellows' research activities and communicates their results to the public and private sectors. CEPR is an entrepreneur, developing research initiatives with the producers, consumers and sponsors of research. Established in 1983, CEPR is a European economics research organization with uniquely wide-ranging scope and activities.

CEPR is a registered educational charity. Institutional (core) finance for the Centre is provided through major grants from the Economic and Social Research Council, under which an ESRC Resource Centre operates within CEPR; the Esmée Fairbairn Charitable Trust; the Bank of England; 15 other central banks; and 33 companies. None of these organizations gives prior review to the Centre's publications, nor do they necessarily endorse the views expressed therein.

The Centre is pluralist and non-partisan, bringing economic research to bear on the analysis of medium- and long-run policy questions. CEPR research may include views on policy, but the Executive Committee of the Centre does not give prior review to its publications, and the Centre takes no institutional policy positions. The opinions expressed in this volume are those of the authors and not those of the Centre for Economic Policy Research.

1 February 1995

North–South linkages and international macroeconomic policy

Edited by

DAVID VINES

and

DAVID CURRIE

CAMBRIDGE
UNIVERSITY PRESS

Published by the Press Syndicate of the University of Cambridge
The Pitt Building, Trumpington Street, Cambridge CB2 1RP
40 West 20th Street, New York, NY10011–4211, USA
10 Stamford Road, Oakleigh, Melbourne 3166, Australia

First published 1995

Printed in Great Britain at the University Press, Cambridge

A catalogue record for this book is available from the British Library

Library of Congress cataloguing in publication data

North–South linkages and macroeconomic policy / edited by David Currie
and David Vines.
   p. cm.
Papers presented at an international conference organized by the Centre for
economic Policy Research and held Apr. 23–24, 1993 at the University of
Oxford.
ISBN 0 521 46234 7
1. International economic relations – Congresses.
2. International trade – Congresses.
3. Economic development – Congresses.
4. Macroeconomics – Congresses.
I. Currie, David A.   II. Vines, David.
III. Centre for Economic Policy Research (Great Britain)
HF 1359.N673   1995
337–dc20   94–47635   CIP

ISBN 0 521 46234 7 hardback

Contents

Figures

Tables

Preface

This volume contains the proceedings of the international conference 'North-South Linkages and International Macroeconomic Policy', organised by the Centre for Economic Policy Research (CEPR), held at the University of Oxford on 23–24 April 1993. This conference was a sequel to the earlier CEPR conference held in 1987. It drew on the fruits of a series of international conferences held since 1989 in London, Rio de Janeiro and Seoul. These conferences were funded by the Rockefeller Foundation, as well as by the United Nations Development Programme, the OECD and the Korea Development Institute.

Financial support was provided by the Rockefeller Foundation and the Brookings Institution. We express our thanks for this support. We are grateful to CEPR for the efficient organisation of the conference, and especially to Kate Millward for her help in preparing this book for publication and to John Black for all his efforts as Production Editor. We should also thank the authors and discussants of papers, and all participants in the conference for making it such a stimulating event.

David Vines and David Currie   *February, 1995*

Conference participants

Chris Allen, *London Business School*
George Alogoskoufis, *Athens School of Economics and CEPR*
Beatriz Armendariz de Aghion, *LSE*
Premachandra Athukorala, *La Trobe University and Australian National University*
Ray Barrell, *National Institute for Economic and Social Research, London*
Tamim Bayoumi, *IMF*
Ralph C. Bryant, *Brookings Institution*
W. Max Corden, *Johns Hopkins University, Washington DC*
David Currie, *London Business School and CEPR*
David Fielding, *Institute of Economics and Statistics, Oxford*
Christopher L. Gilbert, *Queen Mary and Westfield College, London, and CEPR*
John F. Helliwell, *University of British Columbia*
Jaime Marquez, *Federal Reserve Board, Washington DC*
Jimmy McHugh, *St Antony's College, Oxford*
Warwick J. McKibbin, *Brookings Institution*
Vito Antonio Muscatelli, *University of Glasgow*
Christian E. Petersen, *World Bank*
Andrew Powell, *University of Warwick*
James Riedel, *Johns Hopkins University, Washington DC*
Klaus Schmidt-Hebbel, *World Bank*
Luis Serven, *World Bank*
Peter Smith, *University of Warwick*
Charles C. Soludo, *UN Economic Commission for Africa, Addis Ababa*
T. G. Srinivasan, *World Bank*
Nicholas Vanston, *OECD*
David Vines, *Balliol College, Oxford, and CEPR*
Peter Warr, *Australian National University*
Fabrizio Zilibotti, *LSE*

1 North–South linkages and international macroeconomic policy: an overview

DAVID CURRIE and DAVID VINES

The concern of this book is with the macroeconomic linkages between the developed North and less developed South countries in the world economy. It is based on papers presented at a conference held in Oxford in 1993 as part of a programme of workshops and conferences funded by the Rockefeller Foundation under the auspices of the Centre for Economic Policy Research. This book may be regarded as a companion and follow up to the book which we published in 1988, also under the auspices of the Centre for Economic Policy Research (Currie and Vines, 1988).

At the time of that earlier book, while the theory of interactions between North and South was well articulated (as summarized in our introduction to that book), empirical modelling of these interactions was little advanced. None of the international macroeconometric models had an adequate representation of the South, which usually entered as a shadowy set of trade relationships to ensure a representation of the international world trade matrix intended to be complete and consistent. The key additional interactions through commodity prices and supply, capital flows, debt and technology transfer were almost entirely neglected. Reflecting that, the few papers in the earlier volume that attempted an empirical orientation were generally based on rather shaky foundations.

The aim of this book is to provide a much more substantial empirical basis to the study of North–South macroeconomic linkages, and it reflects the progress that has been made in this area over the past six years or so. This is not to say that we know enough: the nature of empirical work is that our understanding and knowledge is always incomplete. But it is a good deal more advanced than at the time of the earlier volume. Thus almost all of the papers in this book are empirically oriented or used for purposes of policy analysis models that are empirically grounded.

This empirical grounding is most evident in the papers of the final section of the book, which examine global scenarios using some of the main international macroeconometric models, for example the IMF's Multimod, the McKibbin/Sachs global model and the London Business School/NIESR's GEM. The incorporation of adequate empirical models of the South into the main global models has two main advantages. First, it means that it is possible routinely to examine the implications for the South of macroeconomic developments in the North. Second, it makes it possible to examine international policy questions in a genuinely global context. Finally, it offers the way to consider the design of international policy packages (aid versus trade, growth-oriented adjustment) in an empirical context.

The structure of the book is as follows. The first section is concerned with the modelling of trade linkages, specifically in the context of the dynamic economies of the Asian Pacific Rim, though the relevance may be wider. The second section considers linkages through trade in commodities and the impact of commodity prices on the performance of the world economy. The third section considers growth linkages and convergence between North and South, examining the speed and scale of the transfer of technology and knowledge between North and South. The fourth section considers macroeconomic adjustment in the South in response to external shocks emanating from the North; since this section neglects possible feedbacks from the South back to the North, it may be considered as part of the literature on open economy macroeconomics adapted to the South. The final and most substantial section focuses on global scenarios, where the interactions are both from North to South and from South to North. In the rest of this introduction, we provide a summary of and commentary on the subsequent chapters of the book.

The first two papers, by Muscatelli and by Riedel and Athukorala are devoted to the controversy surrounding the export demand elasticities of Asia's Newly Industrialized Economies (NIEs): whether their remarkable economic performance can be explained by high income elasticities of demand, high price elasticities or both. Muscatelli's empirical model of export demand draws heavily upon recent theories of international trade that emphasize product innovation and imitation as well as the growth of productive capacity. His estimations using cointegration techniques over quarterly data for 1973–89 indicate that the traditional view that the NIE's income elasticities of demand are high proves quite robust, once demand and supply effects are properly isolated, while their price elasticities of demand were quite low in a number of cases.

Riedel and Athukorala provide a thought-provoking and plausible counterview. They maintain that economies like Hong Kong must be

Singapore, South Korea and Taiwan (the ANIEs), and on Indonesia, Malaysia, the Philippines and Thailand (the ASEAN 4). While a gradual but credible deficit reduction programme of the type announced by the Clinton administration will dampen the negative impact of US and other industrialized economies' government spending cuts and reduce world interest rates, Asia will experience a more sustained negative shock. McKibbin and Sundberg find that this will hurt the ANIEs more than the ASEAN 4; the latter rely more on trade with Japan rather than the US, and they will benefit more from the fall in interest rates since their debt burden is greater. In the longer term, the US deficit reduction and higher savings rate yield a permanent rise in the global capital stock and raise output across all economies. The ASEAN 4 will also benefit more than the ANIEs from a Japanese fiscal expansion. Switching the global fiscal policy mix to contract in the US and expand in Japan will therefore benefit low-income economies within the Asia-Pacific region far more than their high-income neighbours.

Bayoumi, Hewitt and Symansky use the IMF Multimod model to examine the consequences of major cuts in defence expenditure. Treating cuts in military expenditure as transfers to consumption expenditure, they find that a 20 per cent world-wide cut in military expenditure will raise developing countries' welfare by $1.45 trillion. This also has important consequences for trade, since cuts in military imports allow increases in non-military imports, which in turn raise export ratios and real commodity prices. Countries with close bilateral trade links with the US gain the most, as US demand for their exports rises considerably. Of the various regions, Africa gains the most, even though it has lower current military expenditure than some others.

Using the World Bank version of GEM, Petersen and Srinivasan find that an adverse interest rate shock is particularly serious for lower-middle-income countries because of their high indebtedness. For a five-year rise in real interest rates of 100 basis points, growth rates fall by 0.3 per cent per year in the medium term. Latin America is hurt the most, with reductions in national growth rates of more than 0.5 per cent, while North and West Africa suffer reductions in growth rates of around 0.4–0.5 per cent. Asia seems more robust towards such shocks. When secondary effects stemming from terms-of-trade losses are incorporated, the debt stock of the lower-middle-income economies increases by almost $100 billion over ten years. Without policy adjustments to increase the less-developed countries' savings ratios, this situation could become unsustainable.

Marquez uses the Fed's Multi-Country Model (MCM) to examine monetary and fiscal linkages between developed and developing countries, focusing on the example of Mexico and the US during 1982–7. His analysis suggests that Mexico's economic performance is sensitive to changes in US policy: a US fiscal contraction with M2 targeting lowers US interest rates and hence Mexico's external debt servicing, which stimulates GDP even though exports to the US fall with US real GDP. Implementing the same US fiscal contraction with pegged US interest rates eliminates these beneficial effects and accentuates the reduction in US real GDP, which in turn reduces Mexico's income. Marquez stresses that the effects of policy changes in the North and South vary across countries in both sign and magnitude, which illustrates the dangers of treating developing countries as a single bloc.

Bryant and Soludo examine the effects of shocks emanating from the North on the South and also their effects within their countries of origin and cross-border transmission to other industrialized countries. They report simulations of a fiscal contraction in the North and a shock mimicking an external debt-forgiveness programme, under different assumptions about fiscal closure rules in North and South. Their results indicate that a US fiscal contraction would encourage greater medium- and long-run growth, for both the US and the rest of the world including the developing economies. Debt forgiveness also encourages substantial medium- and long-term growth, but the alternative closure rules concerning developing countries exchange rate policies significantly affect its impact.

These papers provide a useful overview of the flourishing and important research area concerned with interactions between North and South. They also highlight areas where future research is needed. It is to be hoped that empirical macromodelling on this area develops as fast over the next five years as in the recent past.

REFERENCE

Currie, D.A. and D. Vines (1988) *Macroeconomic Interactions between North and South*, Cambridge: Cambridge University Press.

Part One
Trade linkages: the elasticities debate

2 NIE export performance revisited: the estimation of export demand elasticities, and the role of product differentiation and growth

VITO ANTONIO MUSCATELLI

1 Introduction

This paper has two aims. First, to provide a brief survey of some recent empirical work on the export performance of the Asian Newly Industrializing Economies (NIEs), which has brought into sharp focus many of the debates surrounding the magnitude of trade elasticities. The second objective of the paper is to begin to answer some of the questions which my own earlier empirical work in this area raised. The particular models I estimate in this paper provide an initial attempt to bridge the gap between traditional approaches to modelling trade equations, and some of the recent theoretical developments which seek to link theories of international trade and growth.

Even though detecting an empirical link between growth and export performance at the aggregate macroeconomic (as opposed to a sectoral) level raises problems of data limitations, some of my results are supportive of those trade theories which emphasize the linkages between a country's resource base, product development (due to both innovation and imitation activity) and the demand for its exports.

The paper is divided as follows: in Section 2 I provide a brief survey of some of the key results and debates which have emerged from earlier work in this area. In Section 3 I consider how the 'new' theories of international trade can shed light on part of the elasticities debate. In Section 4 I conclude the paper by considering some of the policy implications of my results.

2 Unravelling the NIE export elasticities puzzle: a brief survey

The central question addressed in much of my own earlier empirical work was the following: why have the Asian NIEs confounded the predictions of theorists who viewed developing countries as facing a

9

secular deterioration in their terms of trade due to low price and income elasticities of export demand? Early empirical studies of LDC export demand[1] focusing only on relative price and income variables, seemed to show that, although price elasticities were relatively low, rapid export growth in the NIEs was explicable in terms of high income elasticities.

These results have been challenged by some observers (see, for example, Riedel, 1988; Athukorala and Riedel, 1990), who instead argue that, once one takes account of both export demand and supply functions, the data points to NIEs facing highly price-elastic demand curves. Consequently, the 'small country assumption' is valid, and world income growth does not play an important part in explaining the Asian NIEs' export performance: export growth is determined primarily by supply-side factors. This alternative perspective on the NIEs' performance is obtained by adopting an alternative normalization for the export demand and supply model, with export demand normalized as a price equation and export supply as a quantity equation, in contrast to the more conventional approach of estimating export demand as a quantity equation and export supply as a price equation. This choice of normalization is defended purely on the grounds that the results conform with the authors' prior views of what the export demand elasticities should be.

One should, however, be able to do better than this and explain why the two alternative normalizations yield diametrically opposite results. In Muscatelli *et al.* (1992), we set out to investigate the validity of these two alternative interpretations of the data by constructing export demand and supply models for a number of Asian NIEs using data from the Riedel (1988) study.[2] The specification of the *long-run* export demand and supply models tends to vary only marginally between different studies, and may be characterized as follows. Export demand is given by

$$X^d = f_1(P^x, P^w, Y^w) \tag{1}$$

where X represents the volume of export goods, P^x represents the prices of export goods of the exporting NIE, P^w are world export prices, and Y^w is a scale variable which captures world demand conditions. Typically, we would expect price homogeneity to hold in the long run such that demand depends only on relative prices and the scale variable.

Modelling the supply side of the export market is not a simple matter in the absence of perfect competition in export markets, given the resulting absence of a conventional supply curve. Normally, in imperfect competition, we would expect the price of NIE exports P^x (relative to the price of goods sold on the domestic markets, P^d) to be determined as a mark-up on NIE domestic costs, where the mark-up depends on the price elasticity of world demand for NIE exports. Whilst one would expect the price elasticity of export demand to vary pro-cyclically with export sales[3], for simplicity it is conventional to treat the mark-up as constant, so that there exists a unique relationship between the quantity supplied and the price of exports

$$X^s = f_2((P^x/P^d), K(C/P^d)) \tag{2}$$

where K represents the stock of fixed capital, and C is an index of variable costs (imported raw materials and wage costs).

So why does the 'normalization paradox' emerge from such an export demand and supply model? Elementary econometrics tells us that least-squares estimation methods will yield different results if the regression equation is renormalized with one of the regressors as the dependent variable, but that the differences will tend to disappear as the goodness of fit improves (i.e., as the R^2 statistic tends to unity). All this does not matter in a single-equation context, but the problem becomes acute in the case of a simultaneous model: in the case of equations (1) and (2) there is no a priori way of selecting the price and volume equation. In addition, with the use of modelling techniques which appeal to the well-known property of cointegration, the contrast becomes even more stark, as the estimation of static versions of equations (1) and (2) using the two alternative normalizations may yield wildly differing results (depending on the goodness of fit).

The diagnosis of the problem is very simple, but the cure is not: although the specification and estimation of simultaneous cointegrated models (SCMs) has received considerable attention in recent years[4] numerous problems arise in small samples, especially when dealing with models with large numbers of explanatory variables. In theory, one can resolve the normalization issue by proceeding as follows: consider the following reparameterization of a multivariate VAR (see Johansen, 1988)

$$\Delta Y_t = c + D_t + \sum_{i=1}^{k-1} \Gamma_i \Delta Y_{t-i} + \Pi Y_{t-k} + e_t \tag{3}$$

where the vector Y_t contains *all* the n variables in the system defined by equations (1) and (2). The Π matrix captures the long-run properties of the system, and may be decomposed by defining (nxr) matrices α and β such that $\Pi = \alpha\beta'$. The matrix β then contains the r significant $(nx1)$ cointegrating vectors between the variables, and α are the weights with which each cointegrating vector enters each equation in (3). The estimation of the system in (3) is straightforward, applying the maximum likelihood procedure suggested by Johansen, and hopefully one should find two significant vectors ($r = 2$) corresponding to the two behavioural relationships of interest.

The key issue is how one might *identity* the two vectors which represent the long-run demand and supply relationships (equations 1 and 2). Essentially this involves imposing identifying restrictions (typically exclusion restrictions) on the matrix Π such that the β matrix contains the two vectors

$$X = \underline{\beta}'_1 \underline{Z}_1 \quad \underline{Z}_1 \equiv (P^x \ P^w \ Y^w) \tag{4a}$$

$$X = \underline{\beta}'_2 \underline{Z}_2 \quad Z_2 \equiv (P^x \ P^d \ KC) \tag{4b}$$

The identifying restrictions which have to be imposed on the Π matrix in order to identify the two relationships in (4) are akin to those which have to be imposed on a reduced-form in order to make the transition to the structural model, and have to satisfy a similar rank condition (see Park, 1990). Naturally, one has to test the validity of these restrictions using appropriate likelihood ratio (LR) tests (hypothesis H6 in Johansen and Juselius, 1990).

This resolves the normalization issue as far as the long-run cointegrating vectors are concerned in that the two estimated long-run demand and supply relationships in (4) are obtained using a systems estimator.

Whilst such an approach is ideal in theory, in practice one encounters several practical difficulties in small samples, as is usually the case with system estimators. The first problem is that *both* the trace and determinant test statistics used to determine the order of cointegration (r) *and* the estimates of the long-run elasticities in β are very sensitive to the choice of lag length for the VAR, k. The second problem is that, particularly when dealing with VARs of a reasonable size (for instance equations (1) and (2) already contain seven variables, and with quarterly data $k = 4$ is sometimes required to obtain white noise residuals), severe collinearity may emerge between some of the regressors[5] which may render the estimated long-run elasticities so imprecise as to prevent a verification of the two rival hypotheses on trade elasticities.

Given these difficulties, other estimators may be preferable, such as the 'fully-modified estimate' proposed by Phillips and Hansen (1990), which is essentially a modification of the standard Engle–Granger OLS estimator for cointegrating vectors to take account of heterogeneity in the residuals *and* simultaneity between the series, using non-parametric corrections.

The key point here is that, unlike the Johansen method, we do not rely on parametric methods to account for the short-run dynamics and simultaneity, which in this case is a positive advantage given the imprecise estimates these are likely to yield. But of course, as the Phillips–Hansen method is a least-squares based estimation method it merely *alleviates* and does not resolve the differences in the estimates obtained for different normalization of the long-run cointegrating vector. The approach is *asymptotically* equivalent to systems procedures, and in some cases (e.g., the Muscatelli *et al.*, 1992, estimates for Hong Kong) it can be shown that the choice of normalization of the two cointegrating vectors does not matter too much; in other cases (e.g., the estimates presented by Riedel and Athakorala in their chapter of this volume) the Phillips–Hansen method may not reconcile the two normalizations.

Fortunately, however, estimating the long run is not the end of the story: one can obtain further insights into the appropriate normalization by focusing on the unrestricted reduced form (URF) having obtained (possibly rival) long-run estimates using least-squares based methods. This is in fact the second stage of the procedure described by Muscatelli *et al.* (1991a, 1992), which involves estimating a structural simultaneous error-correction model (ECM) for ΔX_t and ΔP_t^x, which contains both the demand and supply error-correction terms derived from the first stage of the procedure. In both these studies we find that, starting out from a standard URF such as equation (3), the particular structural interpretation found in all cases is one where:

(i) The demand and supply relationships as obtained from the first stage of the procedure by normalizing the demand equation as a volume equation and the supply equation as a price equation are imposed on the long-run matrix Π, and found to be data-acceptable using an LR test. This procedure, discussed in Bagliano *et al.* (1992), involves imposing the identifying restrictions on the SCM by estimating each error-correction term, and testing the validity of the resulting restricted reduced form against the URF[6] and is equivalent to testing the H6 hypothesis in Johansen and Juselius (1990) in the context of the Johansen estimation framework.

(ii) The demand-side ECM only enters the export volume equation and the supply-side ECM only enters the export price equation. In addition, the export volume equation exclusively contains demand-side variables, and the export price equation exclusively contains supply-side variables. The 'normalization' is not imposed, but is tested through an LR test of the overidentifying restrictions on the URF.

The evidence we have found in Muscatelli *et al.* (1991a, 1992) regarding the normalization issue, and the estimation of trade elasticities generally supports the traditional view as far as the Asian NIEs are concerned: the price elasticities of demand are quite low in a number of cases, whilst the income elasticities of demand are uniformly high. The above discussion should also illustrate the absurdity of any discussion of normalization issues except in the context of the full system: i.e., *one must examine the performance of any suggested normalization against the URF.*[7]

Of course, it would be foolish for us to claim that this is the final word on the issue of trade elasticities or even on the normalization debate. What if, for instance, one had omitted relevant I(1) demand- or supply-side variables in estimating the long-run relationships? Of course serious biases in the estimated long-run elasticities may then result, and indeed the outcome of the tests of the identifying restrictions on the URF may be affected with consequent implications for the normalization debate.

Indeed, in our previous work we have argued that misspecification of the long-run demand and supply[8] equations may be an important cause of the large income and rather small price elasticities which are obtained in most traditional studies. The rest of this paper examines one possible misspecification on the export demand side, which might help to explain some of the large income elasticities obtained for these countries.

3   Allowing for other demand-side factors

In our view, one must seriously question the adequacy of standard empirical models of trade flows as explanations of the economic forces determining trade patterns. Can one simply attribute the NIEs' remarkable export performance to a large income elasticity of export demand?

There are some basic points to be noted here. First, aggregate export models by their very nature do not address the effects which transformations in the productive capacity of a country over time have on the *types and quality* of goods produced. The omission of a 'compositional' effect may in part explain the large estimated income elasticities of export demand obtained for fast-growing countries, insofar as the movement by NIEs to export more income-elastic products is collinear with world growth.

In addition, there appears to be an empirical regularity present in most estimated trade equations (and this applies both to the Asian NIEs and OECD countries), whereby the size of countries' income elasticities of export demand seems to be directly related (whilst the size of countries' income elasticities of import demand is inversely related) to their economic growth (see Houthakker and Magee, 1969; Bushe *et al.*, 1986; Krugman, 1989) – this trend has occasionally been dubbed the '45-degree rule'. It does seem likely that such a pattern in income elasticities has to be due to some systematic underlying economic forces.

3.1   Allowing for growth and product innovation and imitation

An early explanation for the empirical pattern described above has been suggested by Krugman (1989), using a Dixit–Stiglitz-type model of product differentiation. His argument is that, as product differentiation in an economy is directly related to the size of its resource base, as a country's resource base grows *vis-à-vis* the rest of the world, there will be an increase in the proportion of world income devoted to the country's exports, as consumers in all countries respond to brand proliferation by spreading their consumption over the greater number of varieties now available. Thus, growth in a country's resource base relative to the resource base of the rest of the world will result in a larger income elasticity of world demand for the country's exports. This model can, with small modifications, be extended to allow for endogenous technical change (see Romer, 1990; Grossman and Helpman, 1992), where knowledge capital plays a public good role, and a similar result is found to hold.

Such a model can only provide a highly stylized account of the linkage between economic growth and trade in industrialized economies, given the limited applicability of the Dixit–Stiglitz notion of product differentiation, and is therefore of limited use at the aggregate empirical level. Furthermore, horizontal product differentiation does not sit well as an explanation of the NIE's export success. These countries have successfully penetrated world markets by flexibly switching their production facilities to products of increasing technological content. In addition, within any given product range, they have climbed the quality ladder by offering products of increasing quality[9] at low cost. Fortunately, however, the linkage between a country's resource base and the demand for its products emerges from a wide variety of new trade models.

The possibility of vertical differentiation, where product innovation involves an improvement in quality, is considered by Grossman and Helpman (1991a), who suggest a model where firms can invest effort in innovative activity and demonstrate that, once again, an economy's rate of innovation depends upon its total resource base.

All this suggests that the resource base is a determinant of product innovation activity and hence affects the demand for a country's exports. This approach is followed in Owen and Wren-Lewis's (1992) model of UK manufactured exports, and Muscatelli and Stevenson's (1992) NIE models, which allow the *relative* capital stock (as a proxy for the relative resource base) to determine long-run export demand. However, the situation is rendered a little more complex once one allows for *imitation* activity on the part of countries.

As 'product cycle' type accounts of the NIE miracle demonstrate, the diffusion of knowledge from developed to developing economies owes less to the 'public good' nature of knowledge capital than to actual effort employed in imitation activity, as the South assimilates and adapts Northern inventions. Essentially, this leads to two-country North–South versions of the models described above (see Grossman and Helpman, 1991b, 1992), where feedback effects are present between innovation activity in the North and imitation activity in the South.

Not surprisingly, a number of different results are possible. First of all, an expansion in the resource base of the North increases innovative activity, and may increase imitation activity in that it gives a greater incentive to Southern imitators to erode Northern monopoly profits. The opposite result is also possible: an increase in Northern innovation can discourage Southern imitation because certain products tend to become more rapidly obsolete. Second, an increase in the resource base of the South may either encourage or discourage Northern product innovation: it encourages it insofar as the profitability of Northern firms is increased as unsuccessful Northern firms which succumb to Southern imitators release resources; it discourages it insofar as the returns from innovation or quality upgrading are less.

The key point here is that models of imitation suggest that growth in one country may have positive (or negative) spillover effects on the other. Thus, the growth of a country's resource base *relative* to that of other countries may be a poor measure of the growth in its potential market. Instead, measures of the domestic and foreign resource base should enter as separate determinants in an export demand model.

3.2   The empirical modelling of product innovation and imitation

What would be an appropriate proxy for a country's resource base? This is not without its problems, given that some factors of production (e.g., the stock of human capital) are not amenable to measurement, and that each of the elements composing the resource base has an input into R&D or imitation activity.[10]

Thus, following Owen and Wren-Lewis (1992) and Muscatelli and Stevenson (1992), I resorted to looking at the accumulation of physical capital as a useful approximate measure of product innovation and imitation activity in the NIEs (which may consist of either horizontal product differentiation or improvements in product quality, and which may arise from domestic R&D activity or through technology transfer and imitation). My approach here differs from previous ones mainly in that I choose not to use a *relative* measure of accumulated investment, partly because of the unknown sign of the spillover effects, and partly because with many factors of production involved in the innovation process, country size may not be a good predictor of growth prospects. A corollary of this is that an investment rate of x per cent can produce very different effects from country to country depending on the sectors in which it takes place and on the degree of innovative activity which it embodies.

Of course, I am not suggesting that capital accumulation is the main driving force behind innovation and imitation activity, but *it may be the direct result of it* (for some empirical evidence on the causal linkages between R&D expenditures and investment, see Lach and Schankerman, 1989). The main reason for this is that, unlike theoretical models of innovation which examine the accumulation of 'disembodied knowledge', in practice product innovation will require a corresponding investment in physical capital in order for the product to be realized. This will always be the case where existing capital equipment cannot be adapted to produce new products.

Therefore, the long-run relationship I posit for export demand is as follows (all variables are in logs)

$$X_t^d = \alpha_0 + \alpha_1 Y_t^w - \alpha_2 (P^x - P^w)_t + \alpha_3 K_t^d + \alpha_4 K_t^w \quad \alpha_1, \alpha_2, \alpha_3 > 0 \qquad (5)$$

where in addition to the usual specification adopted in most empirical studies (see Section 2), I introduce a measure of the capital stock in the NIEs and their main competitors, which is described below.

I estimate a dynamic version of the above model for three of the NIEs (Korea, Singapore and Taiwan) on quarterly data over the period 1971 Q1–1989 Q2. I did not estimate a model for Hong Kong because of problems in obtaining up-to-date quarterly series. The series employed in this study were as follows:

X = Export volume index

P^x = Export unit value index; where available (Korea, and for part of the sample Singapore), I used export price series published in *IFS* which were obtained by survey methods.

P^w = Index of world prices constructed by trade-weighting G7 wholesale price indices.

K^d = Capital stock index measure constructed by accumulating a series for real gross domestic capital formation in the NIE. The exact method employed is described in the text.[11] I interpolate annual data to obtain a quarterly series.

K^w = The same method was employed here as for K^d using series for business investment for each of the G7 countries.

Y = Index of NIE export market potential constructed by trade-weighting total imports for the G7 countries.

$R = K^d - K^w$.

All the series on export volumes, export prices and NIE investment were obtained from *IFS* and *World Tables* (various issues), whilst the G7 series were obtained from OECD *Main Economic Indicators* (various issues). Taiwanese data were obtained from *IFS* pre-1980, and the special supplement to *IFS* post-1980.

There are some points to note about the series employed. First, although I make partial use of UVIs as measures of export prices, these have well-known drawbacks (see Leamer and Stern, 1970; Lipsey *et al.*, 1990). Where these were available (only for Korea and Singapore, for part of our total sample period), I also collected direct measures of export prices. These are typically obtained by survey methods and may more accurately reflect the movement of actual export prices. However, the differences between these series and the UVI series were found to be generally small. Second, as in most of our previous studies, I use world imports (in this case G7 imports) as a scale variable instead of GNP. Here I appeal to a separability assumption whereby consumers in importing countries first determine total expenditure on imports and secondly how to distribute this expenditure amongst various import sources (see Winters, 1984). Whilst this assumption is clearly extreme, using rest of the world GNP as a measure of export potential also has its disadvantages, as NIE exports are likely to be poor substitutes for non-tradable goods and services.

Finally, in constructing the capital stock variable from data on investment, an initial value has to be found for the capital stock for the first period of the sample.[12] This involves making the conventional assumption that at the beginning of the sample period the economy is in a steady state, such that the long-run desired capital–output ratio, γ is being maintained

$$\Delta K = \gamma \Delta Y \tag{6}$$

It then follows that

$$\frac{I}{Y} = \left(\frac{K}{Y}\right) g_y \tag{7}$$

where g_y is the growth rate of income.

In order to minimize errors which arise from sudden shifts in income growth, I took an average growth rate for GNP for three years prior to the start of the sample to compute the relationship between the investment–output and the capital–output ratios. In addition, in computing the final net capital stock series, I assumed an average life of seven years for capital. Obviously such a measure of accumulated investment will only provide us with a rough indicator of the relative capital stock, especially in the early years of the sample. However, as we shall see below, despite the data limitations, the results below do nonetheless suggest a significant growth-innovation effect for the three NIEs selected.

In what follows, I shall not focus on the normalization debate discussed in the survey in Section 2, although it is worth bearing in mind that by not focusing on a fully specified SCM, a key weak exogeneity assumption may be violated. However, previous work shows that the URF can be simplified to a simple structural form in which only the demand-side error-correction term enters the volume equation (see Muscatelli *et al.*, 1991a, 1992). Whether this is still the case using the modified demand model will be considered in future work.

In estimating the modified export demand model, I first of all estimate the long-run cointegrating vector, after checking that all the series employed in our study are I(1). This was done using ADF tests, which are reported in Table 2.1.[13]

As can be seen from Table 2.1, all the series which are employed in estimating the model for export demand seem to be I(1), with the exception of R for Taiwan. On closer inspection, this series appears to be a borderline I(1)–I(2) case. However, the two components of the R series have been generated by calculating the cumulative sum of investment series, and therefore they are likely to contain an MA element which, as discussed in Schwert (1989), is likely to affect the results of the ADF test. In the case of all the individual cumulated investment series, as well as the relative measure, R, it proved difficult to discriminate between the two possibilities. In the circumstances I proceed with caution on the assumption that K^d, K^w and R are indeed I(1), which validates the use of the estimation procedures employed.

Applying the Johansen estimation procedure to the three data sets, I found support for the existence of a single significant cointegrating vector between the series.[14] The estimated long-run income and capital stock effects were not very well determined, and as anticipated previously, were very sensitive to the choice of parameterization.

Turning to the non-parametric estimation procedures, the estimated cointegrating vectors obtained using the Phillips–Hansen method are reported in Table 2.2. The Wald tests reported are those described by Phillips and Hansen (1990).

Table 2.1   Integration tests for series employed

Series	ADF Test for I(0)			ADF Test for I(1)		
	Korea	Sing.	Taiwan	Korea	Sing.	Taiwan
X	−2.37	0.55	−0.54	−3.01*	−3.52*	−3.91*
P^x	−1.90	−2.27	−2.80	−4.62*	−4.66*	−4.33*
P^w	−2.42	−2.40	−1.59	−4.80*	−3.36	−4.59*
$P^x − P^w$	−1.97	−2.01	−0.66	−3.41*	−3.41*	−4.61*
Y^w	−0.29	−0.10	−0.35	−4.47*	−4.62*	−4.50*
$K^d − K^w$	−1.36	−1.38	−1.78	−3.45*	−3.04*	−1.52

Note: (1) * indicates rejection of the null hypothesis of non-stationarity at the 5 per cent significant level. (2) The number of lags used in the ADF tests was chosen by checking whether the residuals were white noise, and a trend was included if it proved to be significant.

The most clear-cut results emerge for South Korea. The income and price elasticities are correctly signed, and, interestingly, the addition of the capital stock terms has significantly lowered the income elasticity and made the price elasticity significant, compared to a conventional specification which excludes innovation effects. The income elasticity in fact becomes insignificantly different from one, suggesting that, but for the innovation effect, Korea's share of world trade would have remained constant over the sample period. Furthermore, the cointegration tests indicate that the series are cointegrated only when these additional terms are included. The data also reject a unit restriction on the capital stock terms, as indicated by the Wald test statistic $\chi^2(1)R$, but accept homogeneity, at the 5 percent level (the Wald statistic is given by $\chi^2(1)(HOM)$). The positive sign on K^d is as expected, and the positive sign on K^w supports the positive spillover hypothesis discussed in the previous section.

The results for Taiwan are also supportive of the modified model. The income elasticity is considerably lower (in this case it becomes less than unity), whilst the price elasticity becomes significant and negative. Interestingly, in the case of Taiwan, only the domestic capital stock effect is significant. Capital accumulation in competitor countries has a negative sign (recall that this is a theoretical possibility), but it is not significant. Homogeneity is found to be data-acceptable, but a unit restriction on the capital stock variables is rejected by the Wald test.

The case of Singapore is less straightforward. Estimating a conventional demand equation yields an income elasticity greater than two and a significant price effect, although homogeneity cannot be imposed. The

Table 2.2   Results from Phillips–Hansen estimation procedure

Korea:
Estimated cointegrating vector

$X = 0.354 + 0.941\,Y^w - 0.435\,(P^x - P^w) + 0.565K^d + 1.349K^w$
$(0.597)\quad(0.131)\qquad(0.111)\qquad\qquad\quad(0.058)\qquad(0.102)$

$R^2(PH) = 0.988 \qquad \chi^2(1)(HOM) = 3.13 \qquad \chi^2(1)(R) = 28.1$

$Z(t\alpha^*) = -4.14$

Estimated cointegrating vector excluding R

$X = -10.32 + 3.27\,Y^w - 0.151\,(P^x - P^w)$
$(1.34)\quad(0.316)\qquad(0.575)$

$R^2(PH) = 0.861 \qquad Z(t\alpha^*) = -1.87$

Singapore:
Estimated cointegrating vector

$X = -6.34 + 2.178\,Y^w + 0.388R + 0.174\,(P^x - P^w)$
$(0.911)\quad(0.171)\qquad(0.134)\qquad(0.114)$

$R^2(PH) = 0.974 \qquad \chi^2(1)(R) = 0.00 \qquad Z(t\alpha^*) = -3.63$

Estimated cointegrating vector excluding R

$X = -7.820 + 0.523P^w - 0.127P^x + 2.06\,Y^w$
$(0.317)\quad(0.107)\qquad(0.076)\qquad(0.103)$

$R^2(PH) = 0.986 \qquad Z(t\alpha^*) = -4.62$

Taiwan:
Estimated cointegrating vector

$X = 2.351 + 0.605\,Y^w - 0.609\,(P^x - P^w) + 0.839K^d - 0.158K^w$
$(0.504)\quad(0.112)\qquad(0.156)\qquad\qquad\quad(0.071)\qquad(0.163)$

$R^2(PH) = 0.984 \qquad \chi^2(1)(HOM) = 1.572 \qquad \chi^2(1)(R) = 17.72$

$Z(t\alpha^*0) = -5.89$

Estimated cointegrating vector excluding R

$X = -5.77 + 2.40\,Y^w + 0.658\,(P^x - P^w)$
$(1.16)\quad(0.274)\qquad(0.597)$

$R^2(PH) = 0.864 \qquad Z(t\alpha^*) = -3.60$

addition of the capital stock terms leads to an equation where homogeneity and a unit restriction on the capital stock terms can be imposed, but where the income elasticity is still as large, and where the price effect has become insignificant. In addition, the Z-test indicates that the null of no cointegration is not rejected. On balance, I chose to fit an error-correction model for Singapore based on the conventional long-run export demand equation.

Next, I estimated the dynamic models for export demand for the three

NIEs (see Table 2.3). These were obtained by employing a standard general to specific model selection procedure[15] where $DIF = (P^x - P^w)$, and where the numbers in brackets are Newey–West adjusted standard errors, using Bartlett weights. The models have a reasonable fit, the error-correction terms are all significant and correctly signed, and the stability of the estimated equations was verified using CUSUM-squared statistics for the three dynamic equations.[16] We also applied standard weak exogeneity tests, and these did not seem to show any problems due to the omission of supply-side influences.

Obviously, these models only represent preliminary results. It is conceivable that by obtaining better measures of investment in new lines of production or alternative proxies such as R&D expenditures one could obtain further insights into the role played by product innovation and technological change. One matter which warrants further investigation is the fact that, even with our modified model the 'problem' of low estimated price elasticities of demand persists. Whether improvements in the measurement of price series holds the key to solving this problem is a matter for debate. Our own view is that there may be other, more profitable, avenues of research. The first is to consider a richer specification of the export supply-side or price-setting equation, which might enable us to disentangle long-run demand and supply-side influences and may lead to a different view on price elasticities. As noted earlier, in a systems context the estimate of any one cointegrating vector is conditional on the correct specification of the system as a whole. The second possibility would be to look in greater detail at the issue of functional form and possible non-linear responses to price changes.

Of course, it is entirely possible that one may reach the conclusion that low price elasticities of demand are not a problem at all in a general-equilibrium sense, once one takes into account the supply side: even with low price elasticities a devaluation can still have a powerful effect with our modified export demand model by improving export profitability and encouraging export supply, thereby boosting export demand through product innovation and non-price competition.

4   Conclusions and policy issues

In this paper I have reviewed the elasticities debate in LDC trade models, and sought to extend existing work on the empirical modelling of NIE exports by establishing a role for technological change and product innovation in determining the demand for NIE exports. Our contention in most of our earlier work has been that, once one properly isolates demand and supply effects in models of export volumes and prices, the

Table 2.3 Estimated ECM models for export demand

Korea

$$\Delta X_t = 0.04 - 0.13Q1 + 0.15Q2 - 0.00Q3 + 0.18\Delta_2 X_{t-1} + 0.50\,(\Delta Y_t^w + \Delta Y_{t-2}^w)$$
$$\quad\quad (0.02)\quad (0.03)\quad\;\; (0.03\quad\;\; (0.02)\quad\;\;\; (0.08)\quad\quad\quad\;\;\; (0.19)$$

$$\quad\quad + 0.82\Delta DIF_{t-1} + 8.06\,(\Delta K_t^d - \Delta K_{t-1}^d) - 0.67 ECM_{t-1}$$
$$\quad\quad\quad\; (0.22)\quad\quad\quad\;\; (2.25)\quad\quad\quad\quad\quad\quad\; (0.11)$$

$\bar{R}^2 = 0.82$ $\quad \hat{\sigma} = 0.062$ $\quad\quad SC\,(F(4,58)) = 0.78$ $\quad\quad$ Func $(F(1,61)) = 0.01$

ARCH $(F(4,58)) = 0.85$ $\quad\quad$ H $(F(1,69)) = 1.05$ $\quad\quad$ NORM $(\chi^2(2)) = 4.68$

Sample: 1973 Q1–1989 Q2

Singapore

$$\Delta X_t = -0.01 - 0.03Q1 + 0.07Q2 + 0.03Q3 - 0.33\Delta_3 X_{t-1} + 1.26\Delta Y_t^w$$
$$\quad\quad\;\; (0.02)\quad\; (0.04)\quad\;\; (0.02)\quad\;\; (0.03)\quad\;\; (0.06)\quad\quad\quad (0.26)$$

$$\quad\quad + 0.74\Delta Y_{t-1}^w + 0.50\Delta Y_{t-3}^w + 3.28\Delta R_t$$
$$\quad\quad\quad\; (0.20)\quad\quad\quad\; (0.19)\quad\quad\quad\;\; (1.50)$$

$$\quad\quad - 3.96\Delta R_{t-2} - 0.28 ECM_{t-1}$$
$$\quad\quad\quad\; (1.37)\quad\quad\quad (0.13)$$

$\bar{R}^2 = 0.59$ $\quad \hat{\sigma} = 0.04$ $\quad\quad SC\,(F(4,51)) = 0.01$ $\quad\quad$ Func $(F(1,54)) = 0.36$

ARCH $(F(4,51)) = 0.90$ $\quad$ H $(F(1,64)) = 0.11$ $\quad\quad$ NORM $(\chi^2(2)) = 0.14$

Sample: 1973 Q1–1989 Q2

Taiwan

$$\Delta X_t = -0.02 - 0.03Q1 + 0.17Q2 + 0.08Q3 - 0.59\Delta P_{t-3}^w$$
$$\quad\quad\;\; (0.02)\quad\; (0.02)\quad\;\; (0.02)\quad\;\; (0.02)\quad\;\; (0.22)$$

$$\quad\quad + 0.35\Delta P_t^w - 0.62 ECM_{t-1}$$
$$\quad\quad\quad\; (0.14)\quad\quad\quad (0.11)$$

$\bar{R}^2 = 0.65$ $\quad \hat{\sigma} = 0.06$ $\quad\quad SC\,(F(4,53)) = 0.67$ $\quad\quad$ Func $(F(1,56)) = 0.01$

ARCH $(F(4,53)) = 0.49$ $\quad$ H $(F(1,62)) = 0.63$ $\quad\quad$ NORM $(\chi^2(2)) = 0.76$

Sample: 1973 Q2–1988 Q4

---

result that the NIEs appear to have benefited from relatively large income elasticities is a reasonably robust one. However, I have also argued that some of the high income elasticities probably reflect hidden non-price factors. These influences cannot be tested directly given data limitations, but I would argue that the results presented here go at least some way to detecting the underlying role played by product innovation and technological change.

At a fundamental level, the different positions on the elasticities debate, as it has developed in Riedel (1988), Athukorala and Riedel (1990) and Muscatelli *et al.* (1991a, 1992) can be reconciled as follows: in both these approaches what distinguishes the NIEs is their remarkable ability to expand their productive capacity and hence their export supply. Where we part company with 'flat demand curve science' is in arguing that such a strategy could be employed by *any* LDC at *any* *point in time* (see Cline, 1982), no matter what their productive structure and position on the quality ladder, and regardless of their ability to improve their products and production processes. To deny the importance of non-price effects on export demand would be to suggest that for any one LDC expanding export supply is all that matters, regardless of whether they are expanding their capacity to export the same old goods they have always exported (be they pineapples and plimsoll shoes) or whether they are improving the quality of their products or moving into other areas of production.

What are the policy conclusions from this study? Of course, as is well known from theoretical models of endogenous technological innovation, the policy prescriptions which derive from such models are by no means straightforward and unambiguous: they critically depend upon the theoretical framework adopted. Nevertheless, if we choose to believe that innovation does play an important part in determining trade flows, this adds another North–South linkage which may be of some importance in macromodelling. In addition to suggesting that government policies aimed at encouraging R&D and imitation activity could potentially alter trade patterns on a permanent basis if comparative advantage evolved endogenously, our modified model also suggests that macroeconomic policies in any one country bloc can affect other regions.[17]

The empirical evidence in this paper also sheds some light on the nature of the product cycle. Traditionally the North–South product-cycle model has been viewed as follows: Northern innovations are imitated by Southern firms, and it appears from standard models of the product cycle that the North will suffer a deterioration in its terms of trade if the rate of imitation rises relative to the rate of innovation in the North. However, Grossman and Helpman (1991b) illustrate how this result *may* be turned on its head with endogenous innovation, as an increase in the rate of imitation in the South may actually increase the profitability of surviving Northern firms and hence may boost innovative activity in the North. Vice versa, rapid innovation in the North may or may not improve the South's performance. The empirical evidence above suggests that, where such an effect is present (Korea), the sign of the spillover is positive.

The strong export performance of the Asian NIEs and their penetration of world markets has caused considerable debate and has generated a certain degree of anxiety in OECD economies. Whilst policy issues cannot be discussed profitably in the absence of a consensus theoretical framework, and there have been remarkable advances in trade theory in recent years, empirical work on aggregate flows has arguably lagged behind these new theoretical developments. Perhaps the time has come for applied economists to do some product innovation of their own to correct this trend.

NOTES

I gratefully acknowledge financial support by the Commission of the European Communities under grant no. ERBSPECS-0007-UK. I would like to thank (but not implicate) Chandra Athukorala, Jaime Marquez, Warwick McKibbin, T.G. Srinivasan, Andrew Stevenson, David Vines, Alan Winters and participants at the SPES Evaluation Conference 1992 held at the European University Institute, Florence, and at seminars held at the Universities of Brescia and Manchester for useful comments on material contained in this paper.

1 See for example Goldstein and Khan (1978), Dornbusch (1985), Bond (1985), and Marquez and McNeilly (1988).
2 See also the work on exports of manufactured goods by Muscatelli *et al.* (1991a, 1994) using annual data.
3 See Rotemberg and Saloner (1986) and Bils (1989).
4 See Park (1990) for a useful analysis of SCMs, and Muscatelli and Hurn (1992) and Banerjee *et al.* (1993) for recent surveys on cointegration.
5 This collinearity may be particularly severe in the case of series which tend to move together over the cycle as well as in the long run (e.g., the income and capital stock series in the models considered later in this paper).
6 Note the similarity with the approach discussed in Hendry and Mizon (1992).
7 The simple estimates presented by Riedel in his chapter of this volume patently ignore this issue, which would allow one to test the validity of the contrasting long-run elasticity estimates from the two rival normalizations.
8 One key area where much work remains to be done is the supply side, by allowing for both endogenous export prices *and* wage determination. This may not be an easy task, however, especially given the lack of data on some key supply-side variables.
9 Note that 'quality' is an aspect of a product which may be real or perceived, and may play a public good role: a country's success and reputation in certain lines of production may produce a spillover in the form of greater custom for a country's other industries as it acquires a good standing for quality and reliability.
10 Of course one possibility would be to focus directly on R&D activity where such data are available. R&D expenditures may provide a useful proxy for innovation activity, but these series may not provide a reliable indicator, as there are a number of process and product innovations, such as changes in organization at the plant level, small changes in technical specification achieved outside the research laboratory, and a whole range of imitation activities which do not appear in R&D expenditure figures. That R&D expenditures do not provide the key to explaining trade performance should be apparent when one considers that industrial R&D intensity in the UK has matched that of Japan, and exceeded that of France and Italy in the last twenty years or so!

11 In finding a real measure of investment for the NIEs, I used domestic absorption deflators. Warwick McKibbin noted at the conference that the capital stock measure might be affected by changes in the terms of trade as the NIEs tended to rely on imports of investment goods. Whilst this may be a problem, its importance may be less over our sample period (post-1973) during which the share of investment goods in total NIE imports from the G7 declined.

12 An alternative (see Owen and Wren-Lewis, 1992), if sufficient data points are available, is to collect data for a number of years prior to the beginning of the sample used.

13 The Phillips Z-tests generally gave very similar indications to those provided by the ADF tests.

14 For reasons of space I do not report the Johansen results here, but they are available from the author on request.

15 The diagnostic tests reported are as follows: SC(n,m) is a test for nth order serial correlation, Func(n,m) is a test for functional misspecification, ARCH(n,m) is a test for an nth-order ARCH process in the residuals, H is a test for heteroscedasticity, and NORM is a test for normality of the residuals.

16 These are not reported here for reasons of space, but are available from the author on request.

17 If relative innovation plays a part in determining NIE import penetration in the North, it is arguable that major differences are likely to emerge in the rates of penetration by NIEs of different Northern economies. This is certainly a pattern which has been evident in the 1980s (see Muscatelli *et al.* 1991b).

REFERENCES

Athukorala, P. and J. Riedel (1990) 'How valid is the small country assumption?' Johns Hopkins University, mimeo.

Bagliano, F.C., C.A. Favero and V.A. Muscatelli (1992) 'Cointegrazione, simultaneita' ed. errata specificazione: un applicazione alla domanda di moneta in Italia', in Banca d'Italia, *Ricerche Applicate e Modelli per la Politica Economica* 1, 91–122.

Banerjee, A., J. Dolado, J.W. Galbraith and D.F. Hendry (1993) *Cointegration, Error-Correction and the Econometric Analysis of Non-Stationary Data*, Oxford: Oxford University Press.

Bils, M. (1989) 'Pricing in a customer market', *Quarterly Journal of Economics* 104, 699–718.

Bond, M. (1985) 'Export demand and supply for groups of non-oil developing countries', *IMF Staff Papers* 32, 56–77.

Bushe, D.M., I.B. Kravis and R.G. Lipsey (1986) 'Price, activity and machinery exports: an analysis based on new price data', *Review of Economics and Statistics* 68, 248–55.

Cline, W.R (1982) 'Can the East Asian model of development be generalized?' *World Development* 10, 81–90.

Dornbusch, R. (1985) 'Policy performance links between LDC debtors and industrial nations', *Brookings Papers on Economic Activity*, 303–66.

Goldstein, M. and M. Khan (1978) 'The supply and demand for exports: a simultaneous approach', *Review of Economics and Statistics* **60**, 275–86.

Grossman, G. and E. Helpman (1991a) 'Quality ladders in the theory of growth', *Review of Economic Studies* **58**, 43–61.

(1991b) 'Endogenous product cycles', *Economic Journal* **101**, 1214–29.

(1992) *Innovation and Growth in the Global Economy*, Cambridge MA: MIT Press.

Hendry, D.F. and G. Mizon (1992) 'Evaluating dynamic models by encompassing the VAR', in P.B.C. Phillips (ed.), *Models, Methods and Applications of Econometrics*, Oxford: Blackwells.

Houthakker, H. and S. Magee (1969) 'Income and price elasticities in world trade', *Review of Economics and Statistics* **51**, 111–25.

Johansen, S. (1988) 'Statistical analysis of cointegration vectors', *Journal of Economic Dynamics and Control* **12**, 111–25.

Johansen S. and K. Juselius (1990) 'Maximum likelihood estimation and inference on cointegration with applications to the demand for money', *Oxford Bulletin of Economics and Statistics* **52**, 169–209.

Krugman, P. (1989) 'Income elasticities and real exchange rates', *European Economic Review* **33**, 1031–54.

Lach, S. and M. Schankerman (1989) 'Dynamics of R&D and investment in the scientific sector', *Journal of Political Economy* **97**, 880–904.

Leamer, E.E. and R.M. Stern (1970) *Quantitative International Economics*, Boston: Allyn and Bacon.

Lipsey, R.E., L. Molineri and I.B. Kravis (1990) 'Measurement of prices and price competitiveness in international trade in manufactured goods', NBER Working Paper No. 3442.

Marquez, J. and C. McNeilly (1988) 'Income and price elasticities for exports of developing countries', *Review of Economics and Statistics* **70**, 306–14.

Muscatelli, V.A. and A.S. Hurn (1992) 'Cointegration and dynamic time series models', *Journal of Economic Surveys* **6**, 1–44.

Muscatelli, V.A. and A.A. Stevenson (1992) 'NIE export performance: an empirical investigation', paper presented at the SPES Evaluation Conference, Florence, 27 and 28 November 1992.

Muscatelli, V.A., T.G. Srinivasan and D. Vines (1992) 'Demand and supply factors in the determination of NIE exports: a simultaneous error-correction model for Hong Kong', *Economic Journal* **102**, 1467–77.

Muscatelli, V.A., A.A. Stevenson and C. Montagna (1991a) 'Modelling aggregate manufactured exports for some Asian NIEs', University of Glasgow Discussion Paper No. 9118 (forthcoming in *Review of Economics and Statistics*).

(1991b) 'An analysis of the disaggregated manufacturing exports of the Asian NIEs to the EC, USA and Japan', University of Glasgow Discussion Paper No. 9119 (forthcoming in *Applied Economics*).

(1994) 'Intra-NIE competition in exports of manufactures', *Journal of International Economics* **37**, 29–47.

Owen, C. and S. Wren-Lewis (1992) 'Variety, quality and UK manufacturing exports', mimeo, University of Strathclyde, July.

Park, J.Y. (1990) 'Maximum likelihood estimation of simultaneous cointegrated models', Institute of Economics, University of Aarhus memo, No. 1990–18.

Phillips P.C.B. and B.E. Hansen (1990) 'Statistical Inference in instrumental variables regression with I(1) processes', *Review of Economic Studies* **57**, 99–125.

Riedel, J. (1988) 'The demand for LDC exports of manufactures: estimates from Hong Kong', *Economic Journal* **98**, 138–48.

Romer, P.M. (1990) 'Endogenous technical change', *Journal of Political Economy* **98**, S71–102.

Rotemberg, J. and G. Saloner (1986) 'A super-game theoretic model of price wars during booms', *American Economic Review* **76**, 390–407.

Schwert G.W. (1989) 'Tests for unit root: a Monte Carlo investigation', *Journal of Business and Economic Statistics* **7**, 147–59.

Winters, L.A. (1984) 'Separability and the specification of foreign trade functions', *Journal of International Economics* **17**, 239–63.

3 Export growth and the terms of trade: the case of the curious elasticities

JAMES RIEDEL and
PREMACHANDRA ATHUKORALA

A country whose exports grow faster than world income will experience falling terms of trade, unless the income elasticity of demand for its exports is proportionately as high as its export growth rate. This is evident from the conventional export demand equation

$$q_x = \epsilon(p_x - p_w) + \eta y_w \tag{1}$$

where all variables are expressed as rates of change, and q_x is the quantity of exports, p_x is the price of exports, p_w is the price of competing goods in world markets, y_w is real world income, and where $\epsilon\,(<0)$ is the price elasticity and $\eta\,(>0)$ is the income elasticity of export demand. It follows that a condition for stable terms of trade $(p_x - p_w = 0)$ is

$$\eta = q_x/y_w \tag{2}$$

Econometric estimates of income elasticities of export demand indicate that, by and large, this condition holds empirically (Houthakker and Magee, 1969). Countries whose export growth rates are relatively high are shown to have correspondingly high income elasticities of demand for their exports. The one-to-one relationship between estimates of the income elasticity of export demand (η) and the rates of growth of exports relative to world income (q_x/g_w), dubbed by Krugman (1989) the '45-degree rule', is illustrated for samples of developed and developing countries in Figures 3.1(a) and (b) respectively.[1]

The correspondence across countries between export growth rates and income elasticity estimates is too close to be purely coincidental. This curious empirical regularity demands an explanation. There are two possibilities: either (i) the income elasticity of export demand influences the rate of growth of exports, or (ii) the rate of export growth influences, or is systematically related to a bias in, estimates of the income elasticity of export demand.

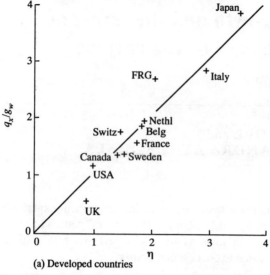

(a) Developed countries

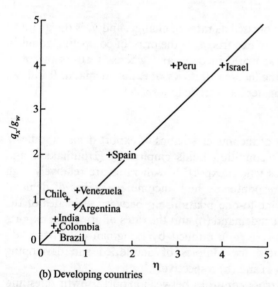

(b) Developing countries

Figure 3.1   The '45-degree rule' for samples of developed and developing countries

1   Hypothesis A: income elasticity of demand influences the rate of export growth

The income elasticity of export demand could determine, or at least influence, export growth in several ways, all of which require that export demand be price inelastic. A low price elasticity of export demand is, in fact, an empirical regularity as robust as the so-called '45-degree rule'. Goldstein and Khan's (1985) exhaustive survey of the literature found a 'consensus view' that the price elasticity of export demand is generally between -0.5 and -1.0, whether the estimate was for geographically and economically large or small countries, for developed or for developing countries, for primary or for manufactured exports.

The rate of growth of export volume (q_x) may become dependent on the income elasticity of export demand (η) if:

(i)   policymakers restrict exports to avoid terms-of-trade losses;
(ii) real wages are fixed, eliminating the possibility of real devaluations;
(iii) the supply of exports depends on balance-of-payments constrained imports of investment goods.

However, there is no evidence that the first two mechanisms obtain in practice, while the third mechanism implies a stable income elasticity of export demand for which there is little empirical support (Riedel, 1984). Indeed, it is the non-uniformity of the income elasticity of export demand that we seek to explain. On the face of it, therefore, it would seem that it is export growth that influences estimates of the income elasticity, rather than the other way around.

2   Hypothesis B: export growth influences estimates of the income elasticity of demand

What is suggested is not that export growth influences the elasticity *per se*, but instead that it is systematically related to a bias in conventional estimates of the income elasticity of export demand. Clearly, something is amiss when estimates of the income elasticity of export demand take values which vary so widely for countries at similar levels of development, exporting similar bundles of goods.

Three possible sources of bias in conventional estimates have been suggested: (1) that ordinary-least-squares (OLS) estimates, such as those of Houthakker and Magee, may be biased because they ignore the simultaneous interaction of export supply and demand; (2) that the income elasticity estimates may be biased because they ignore changes in product quality and other forms of non-price competition; and (3) that for a small, price-taking country the conventional estimation procedure is inappropriate and, not surprisingly, yields misleading results. We consider each of these in turn.

2.1   Simultaneous equation bias

An indication of the relevance of simultaneity bias in OLS estimates of export demand equations is revealed by comparing Houthakker and Magee's estimates with those of Goldstein and Khan (1978), who simultaneously estimate export supply and demand equations using full-information-maximum-likelihood (FIML) techniques for a similar sample of countries and similar time period.[2] As shown in Figures 3.2(a) and (b), comparing the two sets of results, the income elasticity estimates are broadly consistent with one another. The '45-degree rule' seems to hold whether the income elasticities are estimated by OLS or by simultaneous equation techniques.

The two sets of price elasticity estimates, on the other hand, differ significantly, with Goldstein and Khan obtaining generally better results in the sense that there are fewer instances of a perverse (i.e., positive) sign. The fact that both price and income elasticity estimates very widely among the countries in the sample, all of which have broadly similar economic structures and face the same world economy, suggests that something other than simultaneity bias is amiss.

2.2   Product quality bias

The argument that estimates of the income elasticity of export demand are biased by the failure to account for changing product quality was revived recently by Krugman (1989), whose reasoning runs as follows:

> Fast growing countries expand their share of world markets, not by reducing the relative prices of their goods, but by expanding the range of goods that they produce as their economies grow. What we measure as exports and imports are not really fixed sets of goods, but instead aggregates whose definitions change over time as more goods are added to the list. What we call 'Japanese exports' is a meaningful aggregate facing a downward-sloping demand curve at any point in time; but as the Japanese economy grows over time, the definition of that aggregate changes in such a way as to make the apparent demand curve shift outward. The result is to produce apparently favorable income elasticities that allow the country to expand its economy without the need for secular depreciation. (p. 1039)

Krugman illustrates this argument in the context of his well-known increasing returns model of intra-industry trade. In that model there are

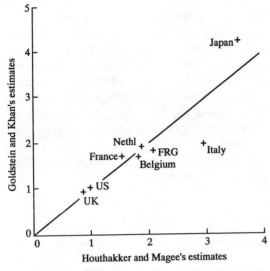

(a) Income elasticities

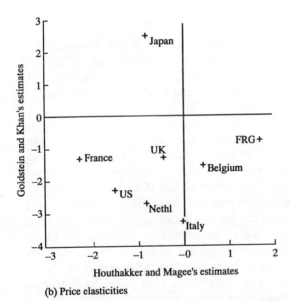

(b) Price elasticities

Figure 3.2   Houthakker and Magee's *versus* Goldstein and Khan's estimates of export demand elasticities

no relative price effects; input growth results in a country producing a greater number of goods, not a larger quantity of any good it already produces. Obviously, in such a model of terms-of-trade effect from export growth is ruled out by assumption. Unfortunately, Krugman offers no empirical support for this explanation of the '45-degree rule'. Instead, he suggests (p. 1031) that 'this empirical regularity lends support to a particular view of international trade', which rather confuses whether it is his model of international trade that explains the empirical regularity, or the other way around.

There have, however, been attempts to test the hypothesis that inordinately high income elasticity estimates are due to a bias resulting from the omission of product quality in export demand models. Perhaps the first to examine this hypothesis was Sato (1977), who anticipated Krugman (1989) by a dozen years. Sato contended that the conventional export demand function (e.g., equation (1)) is misspecified by its exclusion of a role for non-price competition, the main form of which, he argued, is product differentiation. Sato suggested that the proper specification of the export demand function is

$$q_x = \epsilon(p_x - p_w) + \eta y_w + \gamma z_x \tag{3}$$

where z_x is an index of the rate of change in the quality of exports relative to competing goods in world markets, and γ is the elasticity of demand with respect to product quality change. It follows that estimation of (1) yields a strongly biased estimate of η if y_w and z_x are closely correlated.

Sato hypothesized that 'non-price competitiveness is significantly associated with an exporting country's growth performance' (p. 456). As a proxy for growth performance, and hence export quality change, Sato used the growth of industrial capacity, which he showed to be closely correlated across countries with conventional estimates of the income elasticity of export demand. This would be fine if we had evidence that the rate of growth of industrial capacity was indeed correlated with product quality change or with the proliferation of product varieties. Unfortunately, we do not. Hence, the association between the two is purely a matter of conjecture. These findings, therefore, do no more than to illustrate, again, the empirical regularity of the '45-degree rule'.

A similar approach was taken more recently by Helkie and Hooper (1988) who introduce a measure of foreign countries' capital stock into the import demand equation that they estimate for the US, their premise being that such a measure can 'capture the price effects of the introduction of significant new product lines' (p. 20). As they anticipated, inclusion of this proxy variable for changing product variety had the effect of lowering the estimated income elasticity of import demand in the US.

A similar finding is reported by Feenstra (1994), who incorporates a measure of product variety directly into the import price index used in estimating import demand parameters for six disaggregated manufactured goods imported into the US from developing countries over the period 1964–87. Feenstra finds that 'allowing for quality change in the imports from developing countries generally resulted in a price index that rose more slowly than conventional measures'. On the other hand, techniques used by the US Department of Labor to correct for quality change, he notes, 'result in an import price index that rises faster than conventional measures'. Feenstra finds that for two of the six products – men's leather athletic shoes and colour television receivers – the estimated income elasticity of import demand declined when adjustment was made for product quality, as he defines it. In the other cases the adjustment had no significant effect on the income elasticity estimates.

2.3   The small country case

It is curious that those who argue that conventional income elasticity estimates are biased are not equally suspicious of the price elasticity estimates that come from the same regression equations. Krugman (1989), for example, goes to great lengths to explain why the conventional estimates of income elasticities of export demand are biased upward, but accepts without question the empirical evidence that price elasticities are low, perhaps because it accords with his model which emphasizes product differentiation and monopolistic competition. However, a price elasticity of -0.5 to -1.0, which is the 'consensus view' in the econometrics literature, suggests far more than product differentiation – it suggests that goods produced in different countries are not even close substitutes. Taken at face value, the conventional estimates of the price elasticity of export demand indicate that most countries have significant market power, implying a potentially important role for optimal export taxes, though this implication is rarely drawn.

Suppose, however, that the export demand equation being estimated is for a small country, one that is a price taker in world markets, exporting goods which are very close, if not perfect, substitutes for those which are produced by its competitors in world markets. In this case, using least-squares techniques to estimate the conventional export demand equation, with quantity as the dependent variable and relative prices and world income as explanatory variables (i.e., equation (1)) is inappropriate, either as a single equation or as part of a simultaneous system of export supply and demand equations. The reason is very simple: for a small country, export quantity is determined exclusively by supply, and export price by the world price.

Estimation of equation (1) for a small, price-taking country yields meaningless results. Indeed, if the export price and world price are identical, estimation of (1) would be impossible since the variable matrix would be singular in that case. If, however, there is variance in relative prices due to measurement errors and other 'noise' factors, an estimate may be obtainable, but little explanatory power would be likely to be claimed by relative price. Instead, world income would generally turn out to be the more statistically significant explanatory variable in estimates of equation (1), even for a small country, since it has been shown by Sato that world income is highly correlated with key export supply variables, such as industrial output. In the case of a small, price-taking country, therefore, the 45-degree rule is a likely, and highly misleading, outcome.

There is, however, a very easy way around this problem. It is simply to estimate the inverse, rather than the standard form, of the export demand equation. If there is any doubt about whether the country being investigated is indeed small, the estimation should be done as part of a system of simultaneous equations. The inverse of (1) is

$$p_x = p_w + (1/\epsilon)q_x - (\eta/\epsilon)y_w \qquad (4)$$

which allows for the possibility that ϵ is infinite, something the regular form of the export demand equation does not do. In estimating (4), if it is found that the coefficient on p_w is not significantly different from one, and the coefficients on q_x and y_w are not significantly different from zero, the small country case is confirmed. For such a country, exports can, of course, grow at any rate without affecting the terms of trade.

Two case studies have been published which estimate both the standard form and the inverse export demand equation as part of a simultaneous supply and demand system (Riedel, 1988 and Athukorala and Riedel, 1991). The first was a study of Hong Kong's manufactured exports, using quarterly data for the period 1972 to 1984 (Riedel, 1988); the second was a study of Korean exports of machinery and transport equipment, using quarterly data for the period 1977 to 1988 (Athukorala and Riedel, 1991). Both studies took special care with data collection and with the specification of an export supply equation which was estimated simultaneously by the two-stage least-squares technique. Following previous work, both adopted the partial adjustment mechanism to capture the short-run dynamics, though the focus of the two studies was the long run.

Table 3.1 Published case studies of two small countries: Hong Kong and Korea

	Standard form Dep. var.: Q_x			Inverse form Dep. var.: P_x	
Explanatory var.	P_x/P_w	Y_w	P_w^a	Q_x	Y_w
Parameters	ϵ	η		$1/\epsilon$	$-\eta/\epsilon$
Estimates for					
Hong Kong	−0.70	4.03	1.00	−0.05	0.14
	(−3.78)	(27.00)		(−0.83)	(0.63)
Korea	−0.84	7.22	1.00	−0.002	−0.96
	(−2.15)	(7.93)		(−0.005)	(−1.00)

Notes: The price homogeneity restriction was imposed and tested, and in both cases passed. *t*-statistics in parentheses.
Variable definitions and data sources: see Riedel (1988) and Athukorala and Riedel (1991).

Table 3.1 presents the estimates of the long-run price and income elasticities of export demand derived from estimating both the standard form and the inverse of the export demand equation.

The results, in both cases, for the standard form of the export demand equation and for its inverse present very different pictures. The standard form suggests that both countries face a price-inelastic demand in world markets, but both are favoured by high income elasticities of export demand. The inverse form suggests that both are price takers, facing an infinitely elastic demand in world markets. There is little to choose between the two sets of results on the basis of goodness-of-fit criteria; both yield values for $\bar{R}^2$ above 0.95.

Is an income elasticity value between 4 and 7 reasonable for the kinds of goods Hong Kong and Korea export, indeed for any kind of exports? Is it possible that the optimal tax on exports in these two countries is greater than 100 per cent? On the face of it, this is what the conventional price elasticity estimates imply. How were Hong Kong and Korea able to avoid falling terms of trade, since both experienced exceptionally high export growth rates? (The volume of Hong Kong's manufactured exports grew at an annual rate of 26 per cent over the period of estimation, while the volume of Korea's machinery exports grew at a rate of 23 per cent.) One possibility is that they are small countries and do not influence the prices of their exports, no matter how much they export. Another is that export expansion took the form of increasing the number of varieties exported, rather than increasing the volume of any goods which were already being exported. We have econometric evidence in support of the small country hypothesis,[3] but nothing more than conjecture to support the product diversification hypothesis, which of course does not rule it out.

3   Methodological issues

The evidence cited above suggesting that Hong Kong and Korea are small countries in world trade has recently been challenged on methodological grounds (Muscatelli, Srinivasan and Vines (MSV), 1992). Using Riedel's data for Hong Kong, they argue that the small country results Riedel obtained from estimating the inverse export demand function are biased and invalid due to misspecification of the short-run dynamics.

MSV eschew the partial adjustment mechanism and instead apply cointegration techniques. After finding that the Hong Kong data series are I(1), i.e., integrated of order one, they employ the two-stage procedure for modelling separately long-run equilibrium relationships and short-run dynamics of export supply and demand. The long-run equilibrium relationships are first estimated using the fully modified ordinary least-squares method (FMOLS) proposed by Phillips and Hansen (1990).[4] Utilizing the residual estimates from these long-run equations to represent short-run deviations from the steady-state situation, parsimoniously parameterized error-correction models (ECMs) for export demand and supply were then simultaneously estimated using the full-information maximum likelihood (FIML) method.

MSV's estimation results for the long-run export demand equation are very similar to those Riedel (1988) obtained by applying two-stage least-squares (TSLS) techniques to a partial adjustment specification of these equations. However, their long-run export demand elasticities estimated for the price-dependent export demand function (with the zero price homogeneity restriction imposed) diverge markedly from Riedel's estimates for the inverse demand function. From this evidence, MSV (p. 1475) argue that 'even an economy such as Hong Kong's may face a low price elasticity of demand for its exports and so be demand-constrained in its export markets'.

MSV's attempt to refute the small country findings of Riedel (1988) and Athukorala and Riedel (1991) is unconvincing, however, since MSV did not formally test the small country assumption by imposing a zero coefficient restriction on the export quantity variable (QX) and world income variable (YW) in estimating the inverse export demand equation. They did, however, impose the zero price homogeneity restriction, which potentially could bias the coefficient estimates of the other regressors, even when such a restriction is statistically accepted at a given probability level (Warner and Kreinin, 1983).[5]

A more appropriate way to test the small country assumption, using the Phillips–Hansen procedure, is to estimate the inverse export demand function in unrestricted form and then subsequently test zero coefficient restrictions, first, on the export quantity variable and, second, on the export quantity and world income variables jointly. Going a step further, one could employ Johansen's (1988) maximum likelihood estimation procedure, which also takes explicit account of short-run dynamics in estimating the cointegrating vector and has the added advantage of being a maximum likelihood procedure which, unlike Phillips–Hansen's OLS technique, is not sensitive to the method of normalization adopted.[6]

Table 3.2 reports the results of both of these approaches applied to the Hong Kong data used in Riedel (1988) and subsequently in MSV (1992). Using the Phillips–Hansen procedure to estimate the unrestricted equation, we find that the coefficients on QX and YW are not statistically significant (at least at the 10 per cent level), though they do have the expected signs. The zero coefficient restriction on QX is supported by the Wald test (equation (2)), and the coefficients of PW and YW show remarkable resilience to the imposition of this restriction. The joint zero restriction on the coefficients of QX and YW is also data acceptable (equation (3)), and interestingly the world price variable (PW) alone explains over 90 per cent of the total variation in the export price variable (PX). The coefficient of PW is less than unity, reflecting perhaps measurement errors (see note 5 above), but the magnitude of the difference from unity is well within two standard errors of the coefficient estimate. The results based on the Johansen procedure basically tell the same story. The zero coefficient restrictions on QX and jointly on QX and YW are data acceptable.

In short, the inference that Hong Kong is a price taker in world markets, based on OLS estimation of the inverse export demand function (Riedel, 1988) is equally supported by the more robust Phillips–Hansen and Johansen methods, contrary to what is argued in MSV (1992). The same holds as well for Korean exports of machinery and transport equipment. As is shown in Table 3.3, the findings presented in Athukorala and Riedel (summarized in Table 3.1) emerge even stronger when the model is estimated using the Phillips–Hansen and Johansen procedures with the appropriate coefficient restrictions imposed.[7] As these findings indicate, the choice between the price-dependent and quantity-dependent versions of export demand specifications is critically important, even when applying the Phillips–Hansen cointegration procedure.

Table 3.2   Phillips–Hansen and Johansen estimates of the price-dependent export demand function for Hong Kong†

(a) Phillips–Hansen estimates††

1   Unrestricted

$PX = 0.18 - 0.18QX + 0.82PW + 1.16YW$
    (3.22)**(0.98)   (5.49)*   (1.58)
$R^2 = 0.91$ DF $= 3.26$ PP $= 3.72$

2   With zero restriction on QX

$PX = 0.19 + 0.72PW + 0.81YW$
    (3.17)**(4.50)*   (1.19)
$R^2 = 0.92$ W(1) $= 1.77$ DF $= 3.10$ PP $= 3.53$

3   With joint zero restriction on QX and YW

$PX = 0.24 + 0.90PW$
    (4.70)*(12.87)*
$R^2 = 0.91$ W(2) $= 3.71$ DF $= 3.54$ PP $= 4.08$

(b) Johansen estimates†††

1   Unrestricted

$PX = 0.52PW + 0.53QX - 1.13YW$

2   With zero restriction on QX

$PX = 0.75PW + 0.51YW$
LR(1) $= 2.46$

3   With joint zero restriction on QX and YW

$PX = 0.86PW$
LR(2) $= 5.86$

Notes: See Appendix A.
Variable definitions and data sources: see Riedel (1988)

4. Implications

Price and income elasticities of export demand are central to many economic issues. They are a key consideration in adopting a strategy of economic development and in setting trade policy. Yet the consensus view about the values of these estimates is clearly open to challenge. Everyone seems to recognize that conventional income elasticity estimates are implausible, but many retain faith in conventional price elasticity estimates which come out of the same regression equations. It is our contention, however, that the conventional price elasticity estimates are equally implausible. They are entirely inconsistent with the experience

Table 3.3   Phillips–Hansen and Johansen estimates of export demand functions for Korean machinery and transport equipment

(a) Phillips–Hansen estimates

1   Unrestricted (quantity-dependent export demand function)

$$QX = 23.29 - 1.43PX + 1.53PW + 5.93YW$$
$$\quad\quad (9.02)\quad (2.01)\quad\quad (2.32)\quad\quad (10.22)$$
$$R^2 = 0.95 \quad\quad DF = -3.79 \quad\quad PP = -4.18$$

2   Unrestricted (price-dependent export demand function)

$$PX = 3.32 + 0.003QX + 1.01PW - 0.81YW$$
$$\quad\quad (2.16)\quad (0.06)\quad\quad (22.61)\quad\quad (1.94)$$
$$R^2 = 0.94 \quad\quad DF = -3.72 \quad\quad PP = -4.12$$

3   With zero restriction on QX

$$PX = 3.05 + 1.013PW - 0.69YW$$
$$\quad\quad (5.92)\quad (20.12)\quad\quad\quad (4.75)$$
$$R^2 = 0.93 \quad\quad W(1) = 3.13 \quad\quad DF = -3.27 \quad\quad PP = -3.48$$

4   With zero restriction on QX and YW jointly

$$PX = 0.96PW$$
$$R^2 = 0.88 \quad\quad DF\ 3.07 \quad\quad PP = 3.24$$

(b) Johansen estimates

1   Unrestricted

$$PX = 1.04PW - 0.01XD - 0.88YW$$

2   With zero restriction on QX

$$PX = 1.04PW - 1.01WY$$
$$LR(1) = 0.161$$

3   With zero restriction on QX and YW jointly

$$PX = 1.03PW$$
$$LR(1) = 3.42$$

Notes: See Appendix B.
Variable definitions and data sources: see Athukorala and Riedel (1991)

of countries which achieved very rapid export growth without suffering deteriorating terms of trade.

Export diversification and product quality upgrading are important and well-documented phenomena, especially in countries with rapid export growth, where comparative advantage and relative factor prices change rapidly. However, there is no empirical evidence to support the argument, put forward by Krugman and MSV among others, that countries can achieve rapid export growth, without suffering declining terms of trade, only by increasing the number of product varieties exported and not by increasing the volume of any existing varieties because of price-inelastic demand. The evidence presented here, for Hong Kong and Korea, suggests instead that the number of small countries in world trade is likely to be much greater than is indicated by previous econometric evidence.

Appendix A Notes to Table 3.2

†   The sample period is from 1977Q1 to 1984Q2.
     t-ratios of regression coefficients are given in brackets with significance levels (one-tailed test) denoted as: $* = 1\%$, and $** = 5\%$.
††   W = Wald test for coefficient restriction. Five per cent significant levels for the χ^2 test are W(1) = 3.84 and W(2) = 5.99. DF = Dickey–Fuller test for residual stationarity. PP = Phillips–Perron test for residual stationarity. In all cases, the residual non-stationarity hypothesis is rejected by both DF and PP at the 5 per cent level or better.
††† The cointegration likelihood ratio (LR) tests (based on the maximum eigenvalue and the trace of the stochastic matrix, respectively) suggested the existence of two cointegrating vectors. Only the one with the largest latent root is reported. Given that the estimates are based on quarterly unadjusted data, the VAR length was set at 4. LR = Likelihood ratio test statistic on coefficient restriction. The LR(n) statistics are asymptotically χ^2 variates under the null hypothesis. Five per cent critical values are, LR(1) = 3.84 and LR(2) = 5.99.

Appendix B Notes to Table 3.3

The Cointegration likelihood ratio (LR) tests (based on the maximum eigenvalue and the trace of the stochastic matrix respectively) suggested the existence of a unique cointegration vector. Given that the estimates are based on quarterly unadjusted data, the VAR length was set at 4. Definitions of test statistics are as explained in notes to Table 3.2.

Appendix C Unit root tests

Table 3A.1   Unit root tests for data series employed for the estimation of demand functions for Korean exports of machinery and transport equipment

Variable	Test for I(0)**		Test for I(1)**	
	DF	PP	DF	PP
PX	−1.66	−2.98	−5.76	−9.59
XD	−2.00	−0.55	−6.63	−5.83
PW	−1.20	−1.40	−5.65	−5.54
YW	−0.77	−0.82	−6.56	−7.21

Notes:
*   DF = Dickey–Fuller test; PP = Phillips–Perron test. For both tests the text statistic reported is the -t-ratio on a_1 in the following auxiliary regression

$$y_t = a_0 + a_1 y_{t-1} + a_2 t + \sum_{t=1}^{p} b_j \, y_{t-j} + e_t$$

where y is the variable under consideration, t, time trend, and e stochastic error term. In estimating the regression, the lag length (p) on the lag-dependent variable was determined to ensure residual whiteness of the estimated equation. Note that in all cases t was included in the auxiliary regression to allow for the possibility that for most economic time series the main competing alternative to the presence of unit root is a deterministic linear time trend (Phillips and Perron, 1988).

**   The null hypothesis of non-stationarity is not rejected at the 5 per cent level or better for any of the variables.
***   The null hypothesis of non-stationarity is rejected at the 5 per cent level or better in all cases.

NOTES

Thanks are due to Michael Lewin, Will Martin, Morris Morkre and an anonymous referee for helpful comments and suggestions.

1 The '45-degree rule' is observed even in estimates at a more disaggregated level. For example, Bushe *et al.* (1986) found wide variation in their estimates of n for machinery exports of the US, Germany and Japan (1.45, 2.46 and 4.93, respectively), which it turns out corresponds closely to differences in the rates of growth of their machinery exports over the period of estimation (5.6, 8.6 and 22.6 per cent, respectively).
2 Houthakker and Magee use annual data from 1951 to 1966, while Goldstein and Khan use quarterly data from 1955 to 1970.
3 The small country hypothesis has also been confirmed, using a different method of analysis, in the case of Taiwan exports of footwear. See Bee-Yan Aw (1993).
4 This is a single-equation semi-parametric least-squares and instrumental variable method which permits direct estimation of the long-run relationships through a two-step method, whereby the data are subjected in the first step to a non-parametric correction for serial correlation and endogeneity.
5 It is true that the small country cases imply a one-to-one correspondence between the prices received by a country for its exports and the world market prices of the same commodity. However, in practice it is difficult if not impossible to obtain actual price series, and instead proxies for the two series have to be used. Given the potential for measurement error, we argue against arbitrarily imposing the price-homogeneity restriction at the outset.
6 The small sample properties of estimates based on Johansen's method have not yet been systematically assessed. However, being a maximum-likelihood procedure, point estimates generated by this method may be biased for small samples. By contrast, the Phillips–Hansen procedure has been found to

perform adequately in small-scale models with as few as fifty sample observations. Therefore, we use the Johansen results only as a check on the more appropriate Phillips–Hansen results.

7 Before applying the Phillips–Hansen and Johansen procedures, we first examined the time-series properties of the Korean data, employing the Dickey–Fuller and Phillips–Perron tests. As shown in Appendix C, in terms of both tests, all the series in the Korea data set are likely to be I(1) processes; they are non-stationary in level form and stationary in first difference form.

REFERENCES

Athukorala, Premachandra and James Riedel (1991) 'The small country assumption: a reassessment with evidence from Korea', *Weltwirtschaftliches Archiv* **127**, 138–51.

Aw, Bee-Yan (1993) 'Price discrimination and markups in export markets', *Journal of Development Economics* **42**, 315–36.

Bushe, Dennis M., Irving B. Kravis and Robert E. Lipsey (1986) 'Prices, activity, and machinery exports: an analysis based on new price data', *Review of Economics and Statistics* **68**, 248–55.

Feenstra, Robert C. (1994) 'New product varieties and the measurement of international prices', *American Economic Review* **84**, 157–77.

Goldstein, Morris and Mohsin S. Khan (1978) 'The supply and demand for exports: a simultaneous approach', *Review of Economics and Statistics* **60**, 275–86.

—— (1985) 'Income and price effects in foreign trade', in R. W. Jones and P. B. Kenen (eds.), *Handbook of International Economics*, Amsterdam: Elsevier, pp. 1041–105.

Helkie, William H. and Peter Hooper (1988) 'The US external deficit in the 1980s: an empirical analysis', in R. C. Bryant, G. Holtham and P. Hooper (eds.), *External Deficits and the Dollar: The Pit and the Pendulum*, Washington DC: The Brookings Institution, pp. 10–56.

Houthakker, H. S. and Stephen P. Magee (1969) 'Income and price elasticities in world trade', *Review of Economics and Statistics* **51**, 111–24.

Johansen, S. (1988) 'Statistical analysis of cointegrating vectors', *Journal of Economic Dynamics and Control* **12** (2), 231–54.

Krugman, Paul (1989) 'Differences in income elasticities and trends in real exchange rates', *European Economic Review* **33**, 1031–54.

Muscatelli, V. A., T. G. Srinivasan and D. Vines (1992) 'Demand and supply factors in the determination of NIE exports: a simultaneous error-correction model for Hong Kong', *Economic Journal* **102**, 1467–77.

Phillips, P. C. B. and B. E. Hansen (1990) 'Statistical inference in instrumental variables regressions with I(1) processes', *Review of Economic Studies* **57**, 99–125.

Phillips, Peter C. B. and P. Perron (1988) 'Testing for a unit root in time series regression', *Biometrika* **75** (3), 335–46.

Riedel, James (1984) 'Trade as an engine of growth in developing countries, revisited', *Economic Journal* **94**, 56–73.

—— (1988) 'The demand for LDC exports of manufactures: estimates from Hong Kong', *Economic Journal* **98**, 138–48.

Sato, Kazuo (1977) 'The demand function for industrial exports: a cross-country analysis', *Review of Economics and Statistics* 55, 456–64.

Warner, D. and M. E. Kreinin (1983) 'Determinants of international trade flows', *Review of Economics and Statistics* 65(1), 96–104.

Part two
Trade linkages: commodities

4 Economic activity and commodity prices: theory and evidence

ANNALISA CRISTINI

1 Introduction

The 1970s oil shocks prompted several studies both on primary commodity price formation and on the impact of primary commodity prices on the economic activity of the industrialized countries. Typically the first kind of studies condition on industrialized country demand while the second take primary commodity prices as given.[1] This procedure, though correct in the small open economy case, cannot assess the two-way causality existing between primary commodity prices and industrialized country economic activity.

By considering the industrialized countries as a whole, the overall demand for primary commodities can easily be endogenized, thereby permitting a joint determination of industrialized country economic activity and primary commodity prices; consequently this approach emphasizes the difference between primary and manufactured commodity price formation. The model is completed by endogenizing other relevant world-wide macroeconomic variables, namely the real interest rate, LDC external debt, and LDC GDP. The layout of the paper is as follows. The theoretical model is outlined in the next section; Section 3 comments on the estimation results and the working of the model; Section 4 discusses simulation exercises and the final section concludes.

2 The model

The model (Cristini, 1989) views the OECD as a unified bloc, which interacts with the rest of the world via the primary commodity market and the capital market. The bloc approach suits this type of investigation since OECD imported inflation can thereby be fully accounted for by the variability of the aggregated primary commodity

49

price index as long this is a good approximation of the average import price.[2]

2.1   The economy of the OECD bloc

On the basis of expected demand the OECD firms set output prices, as a mark-up on marginal costs, and employment; actual output, on the account of which employment is chosen, always meets expected demand; consequently, realized demand may induce changes in inventories (Layard and Nickell, 1986). The following log-linear system summarizes the product market for any firm i

$$n_i = \alpha^{-1} q_i - a_i - (1 - \alpha) \alpha^{-1} k_i \tag{1}$$

$$q_i = q_i^e = y_i^e = -\epsilon (p_i - p^e) + (\phi^e + \bar{y}) - c \tag{2}$$

$$p_i = \mu + \alpha^{-1} + (1 - \alpha) \alpha^{-1} (q_i^e - k_i) - a_i + w_i^e + \beta r \tag{3}$$

Equation (1) is a log-linear value added production function specified in terms of labour, n, with constant returns to scale and labour-augmenting technical progress a; q is value added, k is capital and α is the share of labour in production. Equation (2) defines expected demand as a function of the firm's relative price $(p_i - p^e)$, where p is the GDP deflator, and of aggregate demand $y = \phi + \bar{y}$, where ϕ are deviations of real demand from potential output obtainable when employment equals the labour force l: i.e., $\bar{y} = \alpha (a + l) + (1 - \alpha) k$; ϵ is the elasticity of demand, c is a constant equal to the logarithm of the number of firms composing the economy. Equation (3) is the marginal revenue condition, μ is the potentially cyclical mark-up. The wage, w, times the inverse of the marginal product of labour gives marginal cost which is also an increasing function of the real interest rate r.[3] Superscript 'e' indicates expectations.

Since firms are identical and are given the same set of information, aggregate functions are simply the sum of the individual ones. The price equation is obtained by substituting (2) into (3) using the definition of potential output

$$\begin{aligned} p - w = {} & \mu + \alpha^{-1} - c - \epsilon (1 - \alpha) \alpha^{-1} (p - p^e) + (1 - \alpha) \alpha^{-1} \phi^e \\ & - \alpha a - (1 - \alpha)(k - l) - (w - w^e) + \beta r \end{aligned} \tag{4}$$

The employment equation is obtained by substituting (3) into (1)

$$n - k = -(1 - \alpha)^{-1}(\mu + \alpha^{-1}) - (1 - \alpha)^{-1}(w - p)$$
$$+ (1 - \alpha)^{-1}(w - w^e) + \alpha(1 - \alpha)^{-1}a - \beta(1 - \alpha)r \qquad (5)$$

The wage equation, derived on the assumption of bargaining between unions and firms,[4] is obtained, in a standard way, by rearranging the first-order conditions of the Nash maximand and log-linearizing (Cristini, 1989)

$$w - p = c + (1 - \alpha)[(k - l) + (1 - \theta)U_{t-1}] - \alpha a - \beta r$$
$$+ (1 - \sigma)\sigma^{-1}(w^e - w - \sigma_i U - \sigma_2 \rho) + \gamma_1 tax$$
$$+ \gamma_2 (p_o - p) + \gamma_3 (p_n - p) \qquad (6)$$

σ, σ_1 and σ_2 are positive parameters, ρ is the replacement ratio, tax are employer and employee taxes, p_o and p_n are oil and non-oil commodity prices, respectively, γ_1, γ_2, γ_3 are wage resistance parameters and θ, which can vary between 0 and 1, captures the weight of previous period unemployed within the insiders' group. Union power enters the wage equation via σ and is empirically approximated by the number of conflicts normalized to the number of employees. Industrial conflicts, in turn, are assumed to arise whenever the desired real wage turns out to be higher than the actual one by an amount greater than the flow cost of a strike. Therefore the conflict equation augments the labour market representation.

2.2   The world markets and the developing country bloc

Normal financial assets and primary commodities are traded in world-wide or inter-bloc markets. Since homogeneity and storability, which characterize primary commodities, could make them similar to financial assets,[5] we test the significance of the rate of interest in the primary commodity price function; the latter is derived from the reduced form of the structural model (Gilbert and Palaskas, 1989) in order to avoid some usual estimation problems[6]

$$\Delta p_{n,t} = a_0 + L(a_{1s}\Delta p_{n,t-s}) + L(a_{2s}\Delta \iota_{t-s}) + L(a_{3s}\Delta \zeta_{t-s})$$
$$+ L(a_{4s}\Delta \zeta_{t-s}) + \{a_5(p_n - p)_{t-1} - [a_6 r_{t-1} + a_7 \bar{\xi}_{t-1} + a_8 \bar{\zeta}_{t-1}]\} \qquad (7)$$

ι is the nominal interest rate, L indicates empirically chosen distributed lags and ξ and ζ are demand and supply indicators which may originate both from the North and the South. Equation (7) behaves according to an error correction model; the variables appearing in the curly brackets are expressed in real terms and represent the long-run equilibrium relationship. The complexity of the expectation processes, which often discourages the use of rational expectations even in a single commodity framework, amplifies when aggregating over commodities; hence back-ward-looking expectations are used and no theoretical coefficient restrictions are imposed.

The real interest rate is set in the financial market as the price which equates demand and supply of loanable funds. Demand originates from the private and public sectors to finance investment plans and out-standing debts. Supply comes from accumulated wealth, e.g., OPEC wealth and savings. Real primary commodity prices may enter the real interest rate equation as long as they are used as demand indicators and/or there is some substitutability between financial and commodity assets

$$ r = \mathbb{R}\Big((m-p),(s-p),(b-p),(f-p),U,Z,(p_n-p),(p_o-p),y^*\Big) \quad (8) $$

In the above equation m is money supply, b is OECD government debt, f is OPEC wealth, y^* is LDC GDP and s is LDC external debt. The representation of the financial market is completed by a function describing LDC external debt which has become particularly important since the early eighties debt crisis. Given the accumulation of debt over time, described by equation (9)[7]

$$ \frac{d(s-p)/dt}{(s-p)} = r + \phi/(s-p) \quad (9) $$

a long-run relationship is provided by the present value of the non-interest debt component, ϕ, which determines the level of sustainable debt (Dornbusch, 1986). ϕ, though partly affected by domestic policies, has been largely shaped by the developments of the world economy, the relevant indicators of which we take to be the terms of trade with OECD, with oil-exporting countries and the rate of OECD unemployment

$$ s - p = \mathbb{S}\Big(r,(p_n-p),(p_n-p_o),U,y^*\Big) \quad (10) $$

The empirical version of equation (10) allows the impact of each explanatory variable to change between the pre- and the post-default period in order to capture a possible change of regime.

Finally, an aggregated developing country GDP equation, which is a reduced form of an *IS–LM* type system, is added to the model

$$y^* = \Upsilon\Big(U, r, (p_n - p), (p_o - p), (s - p)\Big) \qquad (11)$$

3   The estimated model

The model is composed of equations (4), (5), (6), (7), (8), (10) and (11), plus the equation determining the number of industrial conflicts (*NC*). In addition the rate of unemployment is linearly linked to the log of employment and of the labour force by the relationship: $U = l - n$.[8] The system is estimated by three-stage least squares on annual data, described in Appendix B[9], from 1959 to 1988: Appendix A reports the estimated equations which have been obtained in accordance with the 'general to specific' methodological procedure.

3.1   The product and labour markets

The estimated links within the OECD bloc and between this and the outside markets define the propagation mechanism and the functioning of the model. Inside the OECD there exist some obvious links between the product and the labour markets; the level of employment depends on the real wage with a long-run elasticity of -0.78; in turn, the real wage, which is a combined outcome of the wage bargained in the labour market and the output price set by the employers, is influenced by the rate of unemployment with a long-run elasticity of -0.77. Those decisions which are regarded as unilaterally taken by the firms, i.e., the level of employment and the price of output, are affected by the real interest rate with a long-run coefficient of 0.59 for prices, which are also positively affected by the change of the rate of interest, and -0.71 for employment. Overall the influence of the rate of interest highlights the presence of important links between the OECD economy and the financial market through which monetary policy can also potentially convey its impulses; on the other hand, fiscal policy effects come through the demand index which appears in the employment equation.

The direct impulse from the primary commodity market reaches the OECD economy via the import price component of the wedge, in the wage equation. The response of wages to rising commodity prices is negative initially but positive afterwards and in the long run as well. The commodity price index that enters the wage equation is a time-varying weighted average of oil and non-oil prices; indeed, if the last two prices are entered separately (Gilbert, 1991), they are scarcely significant and their coefficients show opposite signs ($t = 1.30$ for $(p_o - p)_{t-2}$ and $t = -1.10$ for $(p_n - p)_{t-2}$); the use of the aggregated price index is also supported by the lower standard error of the relevant regression. Primary commodity prices do not appear in the final price equation ($t = -1.29$ for $(p_o - p)_{t-1}$ and -1.09 for $(p_n - p)_{t-1}$): their presence also introduces instability according to the Chow test and causes the equilibrium of the OECD bloc to be sustained by a long-run *downward*-sloping relationship between real non-oil commodity prices and U.[10] Taxes, the other component of the wedge, influence wages only through industrial conflicts which, in turn, are clearly pro-cyclical. Finally, the significance of wage and price forecasting errors, in the price and in the wage equation respectively, creates nominal inertia which produces a short-run gap between the price mark-up over wages and the real wage;[11] this gap is proportional to the rate of inflation present in the system which is consistent with the exogenously given level of real demand. The price mark-up over wages and the real wage coincide in the long run, when expectations are fulfilled.

3.2   World markets and the South bloc

The financial market reveals significant connections with the two blocs of economies and the primary commodity market. In particular, in the real interest rate equation, the oil price appears as a relevant indicator of the inflationary pressure which, by inducing restrictive policies, causes an interest rate increase.[12] As expected, accommodating monetary policies reduce the real interest rate whereas a positive change of debt brings on a rise of the real interest rate, irrespective, however, of the debtor country. Finally, the real interest rate depends on demand indicators: deviations of LDC GDP from its trend and the OECD rate of unemployment. The latter indicates that, in the long run, high levels of U are associated with high levels of the interest rate; it is only in the short run that the rate of unemployment can produce some depressive effects on the rate of interest.

These demand indicators also enter the estimated version of the LDC external debt equation which describes a positive relationship between poor OECD performance and high LDC external debt whereas the latter gets smaller if LDC GDP grows above its trend. The estimated debt equation also pictures a plain two-way relationship between LDC debt and the rise in interest rates after 1981. Again after 1981, a significant determinant of LDC debt is high non-oil commodity prices ($t = 0.79$ for the oil price).

Primary commodity prices, since they are usually set in competitive markets (Labys, 1980), tend to absorb the effects of variable economic conditions much more than cost-based manufactured goods prices do. Hence, primary commodity prices are expected to be highly and positively responsive to excess demand, at least in the short run. Indeed, the estimated relevant regression shows a negative influence of the rate of unemployment which is quite pronounced in the short run and smaller in the long run: in the latter case a 1 per cent fall in U raises real commodity prices by 4.9 per cent. The interest rate has only a short-run effect: the negative coefficient implies that an increase in ordinary financial asset returns determines a successive fall of the price of non-oil commodities in accordance with the arbitrage rule; alternatively, the rate of interest can be interpreted as a demand indicator additional to the rate of unemployment.[13] The significance of the oil price in the non-oil commodity price equation finds several explanations; the oil price is a determinant of the marginal cost curves of some non-oil primaries as well as of some of their petroleum-based synthetic substitutes; moreover, the effects of oil price hikes on international liquidity may induce purchases of primary commodities as stores of value and allow some countries to avoid sharp falls of non-oil commodity prices in the face of depressed demand conditions.

Finally, LDC GDP deviations from trend are negatively linked to changes in the OECD rate of unemployment.

3.3   The estimated long run

In the long run expectations are fulfilled and exogenous variables are fixed; the model solves for $(w-p)$, U, ϕ, (p_n-p), r, $(s-p)$, y^* and the number of conflicts normalized to the number of employees. The long-run system encloses two fundamental relationships linking commodity prices and the OECD rate of unemployment. One of these relationships underlines primary commodity market equilibrium (let us call it the South line), the other one equilibrium in the Northern economy (the North line). In a $(p_n-p)-U$ space, the intersection of the two lines determines the equilibrium real price of primary commodities and the equilibrium rate of unemployment.

The empirical North and South lines, derived using the steady-state solutions of the estimated equations, are depicted in Figure 4.1. The North line is obtained by equating the real wage with the price mark-up over wages and then replacing the real interest rate and the number of conflicts using the relevant equations; the South line reduces to the non-oil primary commodity equation. Together the two lines indicate, for the relevant sample period, an equilibrium rate of unemployment of 7.2 per

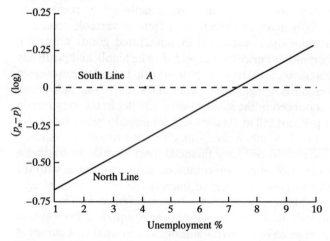

Figure 4.1   North and South equilibrium

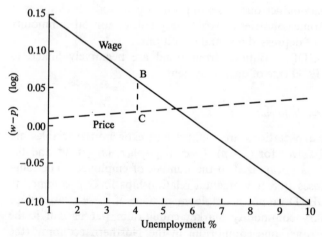

Figure 4.2   North equilibrium

cent, which falls to 5 per cent if the model excludes the feedbacks from both LDC debt and GDP. By further excluding the primary commodity market the equilibrium rate of unemployment falls to 6.7 per cent. This is illustrated, in Figure 4.2, by the intersection of the wage and price line in $(w-p)-U$ space; these lines would actually correspond to a vertical line in $(p_n-p)-U$ space.

A comparison between the North and South lines reveals the weak importance of the OECD demand for the long-run course of non-oil commodity prices relative to the effects that such prices produce on the long-run rate of unemployment. However, it remains true that, both in the short and in the long run, real primary commodity prices are much more responsive to demand than OECD goods prices. This is confirmed by the slope of the price equation in Figure 4.2, which implies an almost normal-cost pricing procedure.

3.4   How the model operates

All points on the North line are points of equilibrium for the North: the rate of inflation is constant and unemployment is at NAIRU. Above and below the North line the rate of inflation is, respectively, increasing and decreasing.

Suppose that the North follows an expansionary policy in order to lower the rate of unemployment below the equilibrium. Depending on the relative inertia of wages and prices, real wages will set at some new point between B and C, say, in Figure 4.2, thereby initiating a positive rate of inflation. In addition, since the expansionary policy creates extra demand for primary commodities, the price of the latter increases and reaches point A, in Figure 4.1. Such a rise, by moving the wage line rightwards, sharpens inflation which now becomes proportional to a segment longer than BC. If the expansion is 'once and for all' and money supply is not accommodating, real money balance effects are likely to bring the system back to equilibrium. Alternatively, one may think of preserving the lower rate of unemployment and decreasing inflation by moving the wage line leftwards towards point C. A well known way to achieve such an objective is by appreciating the OECD currency *vis-à-vis* the LDC currency; however this policy is detrimental for the non-OECD bloc[14] and likely to involve large balance-of-payments deficits in the North. If the demand or supply shock is a permanent one, then the North and possibly the South line, depending on the type of shock, may shift permanently and determine a new long-run equilibrium.

A permanent upsurge of the oil price, for example, shifts the North line downwards and the South line upwards: on the assumption of a twofold increase, the long-run rate of unemployment would actually rise by 0.14 percentage points.

4   Simulations

The short-run response of the model to a permanent doubling of the oil price is analysed on the basis of simulation exercises (for the analysis of different shocks using a similar model see Cristini, 1989). These exercises are performed using the dynamic version of the model, hence deviations of demand from trend are exogenous while wage and price forecasting errors are endogenous.

4.1   The oil shock

According to the propagation mechanism described in Sections 3.1 and 3.2, the OECD economy responds to an oil price shock by resisting real wage cuts and, indirectly, via the impacts of the shock on the real interest rate and on non-oil commodity prices. In turn, the OECD rate of unemployment has repercussions on both the LDC economy and the two inter-bloc markets which all transmit their impulses back to the North. In order to assess the relative weight of the international linkages and how they operate, the simulation is performed on three versions of the model: in one case only the OECD bloc and the real interest rate are allowed to operate (model 3); this version is successively extended to comprise the primary commodity market while still conditioning on LDC GDP and LDC debt (model 2); finally, by including both LDC equations, the original model (model 1) is recovered.

The impact of the shock on each endogenous variable is measured on the last ten years of the sample and the relevant multipliers are computed using the historical dynamic simulations as base runs.

The three multipliers of the rate of unemployment (Figure 4.3) are bell-shaped; in model 3 the maximum (0.5 p.p.) is reached four years after the shock; thereafter the multiplier declines to reach, by the end of the sample, 0.1 p.p., i.e., the virtual long-run change according to this version. The most evident effect of including the primary commodity market is to shift the plot of the multiplier rightwards; the change of the rate of unemployment is now increasing for the first six years after the shock, though in a more gradual manner; likewise the decline to the long-run value takes longer. Finally, according to the complete model, the maximum value of the multiplier reaches 0.7 p.p., though the fall thereafter is also steeper than in the previous case.

The increased persistence of the rate of unemployment that emerges with the inclusion of the primary commodity market, finds a plausible explanation in the real wage multipliers (Figure 4.4). According to model 3, the latter falls visibly after the third year, i.e., once the pressure from the lagged rate of unemployment present in the wage equation starts being effective. On the other hand, in models 2 and 1, the drop of the real wage multiplier, which, however, does not even reach -1 per cent, is postponed until the fifth-sixth year from the shock due to the

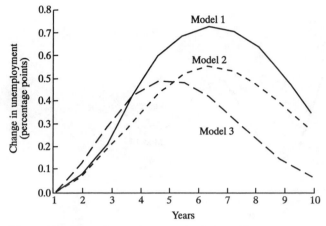

Figure 4.3   Rate of unemployment dynamic multipliers

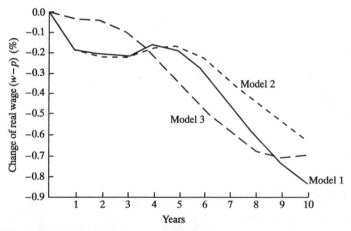

Figure 4.4   Real wage dynamic multipliers

stronger counter-balancing force of the wage resistance which is now augmented by the rise of non-oil prices (the latter multipliers are depicted in Figure 4.5).

As far as the multipliers of the real interest rate are concerned (Figure 4.6), the most evident difference is between the multiplier derived from the complete model and those obtained from the two restrictive versions. Indeed the inclusion of the primary commodity market, since not directly affecting the real interest rate, has a

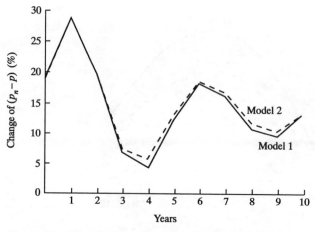

Figure 4.5 Non-oil commodity price dynamic multipliers

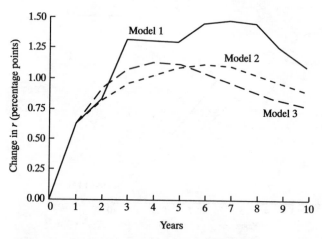

Figure 4.6 Real interest rate dynamic multipliers

significant impact only when the LDC debt equation is also endogenous. This extension causes an additional 0.25–0.5 p.p. rise on top of the 1 p.p. increase reached by the multipliers of the restricted versions. Indeed, as shown in Figure 4.7, the LDC nominal debt rises considerably as the only counter-balancing factor, the rise of LDC GDP above trend, becomes effective only towards the end the sample when the negative effect of the rising rate of unemployment ceases.

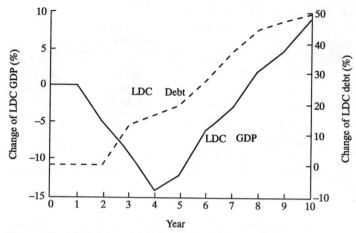

Figure 4.7   **LDC debt and LDC GDP dynamic multipliers**

5   Conclusions

This paper addressed the analysis and estimation of the two-way relationship linking OECD activity and primary commodity prices. The theoretical model views the OECD as a unified bloc which interacts with the Southern bloc via the capital and the primary commodity markets. The eight equations composing the system are simultaneously estimated on annual 1959–88 data and used to simulate oil price shocks. The main results can be summarized as follows.

A permanent two-fold rise of the oil price produces, during the first six years from the shock, a gradual increase in the rate of unemployment which, at most, rises by 0.72 p.p.; thereafter the rate of unemployment declines to its new long-run value which is 0.14 p.p. higher than the original one. To this dynamics the non-oil commodity market mainly contributes by augmenting the persistence of the higher rate of unemployment, since it strengthens wage resistance and thereby delays the wage fall which, however, is less than 1 per cent.

The evident contribution of the financial market is to raise the rate of unemployment increase, particularly because of the LDC external debt surge; the growth of the real interest rate is, at most, 1.5 p.p.

Beside higher external debts, the South also suffers a negative rate of GDP growth for at least eight years after the shock.

Appendix A: Estimated model

Method of estimation: three-stage least squares, 1959–88.

Table 4.1   Employment equation

Dependent variable: $(n-k)_t$			Diagnostic tests	
C	-3.643	(2.82)	s.e.	0.005789
$(n-k)_{t-1}$	0.805	(5.31)	R_c^2	0.9959
$(n-k)_{t-2}$	-0.145	(1.18)	D.W.	1.9020
a_t	-0.153	(4.68)	L.M. 't'	1.397
σ_t	0.637	(2.04)	$F(8,14)$	0.807
r_t	-0.241	(3.73)		
$(w-p)_t$	-0.396	(3.04)		
$(w-p)_{t-1}$	0.135	(1.02)		

Notes: t statistic in parenthesis.

The LM(1) test is a modified Lagrange Multiplier to test for first-order autocorrelation in the presence of a lagged dependent variable and IV. We perform the test by first running two-stage least squares and then regressing the dependent variable on the original explanatory variables plus the first lag of the residuals obtained from the initial regression; the set of instruments used is the same in the two regressions (see Breusch and Godfrey, 1981).

The Chow test for parameter stability (split 1972) is constructed as follows

$$\frac{(SSR_0 - SSR_1 - SSR_2)/k}{(SSR_1 + SSR_2)/(n + m - 2k)}$$

which is distributed as $F(k, T-2k)$,

where SSR_1, SSR_2, SSR_0 are the residuals sum of squares from the regression on the first T_1 observations, the second $(T-T_1)$ observations and the complete set of observations respectively.

Instruments include constant, trend, dummy, current and lagged exogenous variables and lagged endogenous variables.

Table 4.2   Price equation

Dependent variable: $(p-w)_t$			Diagnostic tests	
C	0.593	(1.99)	s.e.	0.006832
$(p-w)_{t-1}$	1.245	(8.49)	R_c^2	0.9998
$(p-w)_{t-2}$	-0.414	(3.71)	D.W.	1.8915
$(k-1)_t$	-0.150	(2.04)	L.M. 't'	0.777
Δr_t	0.090	(1.07)	$F(7,16)$	2.152
r_{t-2}	0.100	(1.59)		
$(w-w^0)_t$	0.221	(2.59)		

Notes: As Table 4.1.

Table 4.3 Wage equation

Dependent variable: $(w-p)_t$			Diagnostic tests	
C	-0.875	(4.03)	s.e.	0.005335
$(w-p)_{t-1}$	0.755	(13.3)	R_c^2	0.9999
$(k-l)_t$	0.218	(4.12)	D.W.	1.9575
$s(p_n-p)_{t-1}$	-0.049	(1.32)	L.M. 't'	-0.827
$s(p_n-p)_{t-2}$	0.666	(1.43)	$F(8,14)$	2.152
U_{t-3}	-0.190	(1.71)		
ncn_t	0.447	(3.92)		
$(p-p^0)_{t-1}$	-0.097	(1.32)		

Notes: As Table 4.1.

Table 4.4 Conflicts equation

Dependent variable: NC_t			Diagnostic tests	
$N_t\,C$	0.004	(0.49)	s.e.	1686
$N_t\,(NC/N)_{t-1}$	0.599	(5.96)	R_c^2	0.8295
$N_t\,U_{t-1}$	-0.451	(3.83)	D.W.	1.9695
$N_t\,tax_t$	0.098	(2.49)	L.M. 't'	-0.820
			$F(4,22)$	1.131

Notes: As Table 4.1.

Table 4.5 Real interest rate equation

Dependent variable: r_t			Diagnostic tests	
C	0.084	(7.70)	s.e.	0.006200
r_{t-1}	0.207	(2.58)	R_c^2	0.9555
$\Delta log[(B+S)/2]t$	0.059	(3.99)	D.W.	1.7766
$(y^*-\bar{y}^*)_t$	0.253	(2.14)	L.M. 't'	0.524
Δm_t	-0.831	(9.26)	$F(8,14)$	2.805
$(p_o-p)_{t-1}$	0.009	(2.50)		
U_{t-1}	1.243	(4.13)		
U_{t-2}	-0.830	(3.27)		

Notes: As Table 4.1.

Table 4.6　Commodity price equation

Dependent variable: $\Delta p_{n,t}$			Diagnostic tests	
C	0.975	(6.88)	s.e.	0.066616
$\Delta p_{n,t-1}$	0.720	(17.6)	R_c^2	0.97819
$\Delta p_{o,t}$	0.280	(6.57)	D.W.	1.7952
Δr_{t-1}	−1.717	(1.85)	L.M. 't'	0.604
ΔU_t	−6.565	(1.96)	$F(9,12)$	2.851
$(p_n-p)_{t-1}$	−1.096	(9.02)		
$(p_o-p)_{t-1}$	0.250	(5.11)		
U_{t-2}	−5.403	(2.63)		
dumcof	0.167	(3.32)		
time	−0.020	(5.00)		

Notes: As Table 4.1.

Table 4.7　LDC external debt equation

Dependent variable: Δs_t			Diagnostic tests	
C	−0.211	(1.06)	s.e.	0.072494
$d81\,\Delta r_t$	5.106	(3.37)	R_c^2	0.99718
$(s-p)_{t-1}$	−0.053	(1.81)	D.W.	2.3474
U_{t-1}	2.293	(1.89)	L.M. 't'	1.159
$(\bar{y}^*-y^*)_t$	−2.198	(1.68)	$F(6,18)$	0.774
$d81\,(p_n-p)_{t-1}$	0.494	(3.77)		

Notes: As Table 4.1.

Table 4.8　LDC GDP equation

Dependent variable: $(y^*-\bar{y}^*)_t$			Diagnostic tests	
C	0.002	(1.04)	s.e.	0.009489
ΔU_{t-1}	−0.676	(2.38)	R_c^2	0.9995
			D.W.	0.666
			$F(2,26)$	0.042

Notes: As Table 4.1.

Appendix B:　Data definitions and sources

The main sources of the data are IMF and OECD statistics; in addition we used some data collected by Grubb and explained in Grubb (1985). Since there is a slightly different country coverage between the IMF definition of 'Industrial

Countries', 'Total OECD' and the countries entering Grubb's data set, adequate corrections have been made; these are explained in Cristini (1989).

a **Index of technical progress.**
Note: The index is derived as follows

$$\Delta a = 1/s_l \Delta y - [(1 - s_l)/s_l]\Delta k - \Delta n$$

where s_l is the share of labour. The index of technical progress is obtained by assuming, arbitrarily, $a_t = 0$ at $t = 0$. Finally the index is smoothed by regressing a on a quintic and retaining the fitted values.
b **Direct total debt of central governments of industrialized countries.**
Source: IMF, *International Financial Statistics.*
f **Oil-exporting countries wealth.**
Source: IMF, *International Financial Statistics.*
k **Capital stock assuming a depreciation of 3.5 per cent.**
Source: OECD, *National Accounts* and elaborations.
Note: Aggregation has been made by summing over each country's capital stock. The latter was previously converted from national currency into dollars using the base-year exchange rate. The calculus of capital was made using TSP according to the formula $K_t = K_{t-1}(1-d) + I_{t-1}$, where d = depreciation rate and capital stock is assumed to be measured at the beginning of the year.
l **Total labour force.**
Source: OECD, *Labour Force Statistics Yearbook.*
m **Money + Quasi-Money.**
Source: IMF, *International Financial Statistics Yearbook*, 1986.
Note: The index refers to industrial countries. Data are linearly interpolated between 1950, 1955 and 1958.
n **Total employment.**
Source: OECD, *Labour Force Statistics Yearbook.*
nc **Number of conflicts.**
Source: see Grubb (1985).
p **GDP deflator.**
Source: IMF, *International Financial Statistics.*
p_n **Commodity price excluding petroleum.**
Source: UNCTAD, *Yearbook of International Trade and Statistics* 1979, 1984.
p_o **Crude petroleum price.**
Source: UN Statistical Papers series M No. 82 and UNMBS for update.
Pfe **Price forecasting errors.**
Source: Derived by regressing Δp on its lag values and retaining the residuals. The regression is restricted so that the coefficients on the left-hand side sum to one, i.e., inflation is neutral in the long run: $Pfe = \Delta p_t - 1.252\Delta p_{t-1} + 0.528\Delta p_{t-2} - 0.253\Delta p_{t-3}$.
r **Real long-term interest rate deflated by three-year expected inflation.**
Note: In order to maintain the original length of the sample, we use, for three-year expected inflation, the fitted values obtained from the following regression: $p_{t+3} - p_t = -0.10 + 1.45\Delta p_t - 0.94\Delta p_{t-1} + 1.84\Delta m_t + 0.81\Delta w_{t-2}$.
ι **Long-term nominal interest rate.**
Source: IMF, *International Financial Statistics.*
Note: Aggregation is computed by using GDP shares in 1980.

s **Developing countries external debt.**
Source: IMF, *World Debt Tables.*
$TAX = T1 + T2$ so defined:
T2 **Indirect taxes paid by households.**
Source: OECD, *National Accounts.*
Note: *T2* is defined as follows:
$T2 = (HSS + IT)/HTR$, where HSS = household contributions to social security,
IT = indirect taxes.
HTR = households' total current receipts.
HSS is not available for AL, hence only IT has been considered.
T1 **Tax on employment borne by the employer.**
Source: ILO, 'The cost of social security', various years; OECD *National Accounts.*
Note: *T1* is defined as follows:
$T1 = EC/(IE\text{-}EC)$, where $EC = SS + PE$. SS = Employers' contributions to social security.
PE = Employers' contributions to private pension schemes and welfare plans (not available for AU, BE, FN, NW). IE = Employment contribution to income (compensation to employees).
U **Rate of unemployment.**
Note: defined as $l - n$.
w **Hourly earnings.**
Source: OECD, *Main Economic Indicators* and elaborations.
Note: The total OECD has been obtained by weighted average; weights are the shares of employees in manufacturing in 1980.
Wfe **Wage forecasting errors.**
Note: Derived by regressing Δw on its lag values and retaining the residuals. The regression is restricted so that the coefficients on the left-hand side sum to one, i.e., inflation is neutral in the long run: $Wfe = \Delta w_t - 1.338\Delta w_{t-1} + 0.649\Delta w_{t-2} - 0.293\Delta w_{t-3}$.
y **GDP at constant prices.**
Source: IMF, *International Financial Statistics.*
ȳ **Potential output.**
Note: This variable is elaborated using the same formula as was applied to obtain the technical progress index, but replacing *n* with *l*.
y* **GDP of developing countries.**
Source: IMF, *International Financial Statistics.*
ȳ* **Trend GDP of developing countries.**
Note: defined as the fitted values obtained by regressing $log(Y^*)$ on a constant, a trend and a trend squared.
σ **Deviation of real demand from potential.**
Note: Real demand is defined as the sum of domestic (OECD) and foreign (LDC) demand; it is obtained as a reduced form of a classical open economy *IS-LM* system. The latter is briefly sketched in a log-linear form:

(i) $log Y = log C + log I + log G + log X - log IM$
(ii) $log C = c (log (Y - T), log (M/P))$
(iii) $log I = j (\Delta log Y)$
(iv) $log X = x (log Y^*)$
(v) $log IM = im (log Y)$

Table 4B.1   Output equation

Dependent variable $y - \bar{y}$, sample 1957–88
Method of estimation: Instrumental variables; instruments include constant and lagged values of the dependent and explanatory variables.

C	3.045	(4.69)	Tests:
$(y - \bar{y})_{t-1}$	0.470	(4.94)	se 0.002309
TAX_{t-1}	-0.066	(1.46)	
$(g - \bar{y})_t$	-0.067	(2.21)	$\bar{R}^2$ 0.9663
$(m - p - \bar{y})_t$	-0.123	(2.12)	DW 1.9801
$(m - p - \bar{y})_{t-1}$	0.157	(2.96)	
$(y^* - \bar{y}^*)_t$	-0.054	(2.78)	

where Y, I, C, G, X and IM are income, consumption, investment, government expenditure, exports and imports, all real; Y^* is real income abroad, M is nominal money supply, P is the price level. $c()$, $j()$, $x()$ and $im()$ indicate functions. The IS curve is obtained by substituting (ii), (iii), (iv) and (v) into (i); indicating logarithms with small letters the following function is obtained

$$y = f(T, m - p, g, y^*) \tag{D.1}$$

where f is a general function which will be dynamic thanks to (iii).
The system above does not include the LM curve: given Walras' law, money market equilibrium is assured by bond market equilibrium (described in the text). Finally, in terms of deviations from potential output (D.1) becomes

$$y - \bar{y} = f(T, g, m - p, y^*) - \bar{y} \tag{D.2}$$

σ is then given by the fitted values of the equation reported in Table 4B.1.

NOTES

The author is at the Università degli Studi di Bergamo.
This paper is based on an update of my Oxford D. Phil thesis, for help with which I am most grateful to my supervisor, Steve Nickell. Financial help from the Oxford Institute of Economics and Statistics, the Centre for Labour Economics, the London School of Economics, the Italian Ministry of Universities and Research and Bergamo 'Unione Industriali' is acknowledged. I also wish to thank David Grubb for providing some of the data. The usual caveats apply.
 1 On commodity prices see for example Enoch and Panić (1981), Winters (1987), Gilbert (1987, 1989b), Winters and Sapsford (eds.) (1990). An exception is Beenstock (1987a, b).
 2 Cristini (1989) shows that the real import unit value is directly proportional to an aggregated real primary commodity price index as long as: (i) the proportion of imported primary commodities relative to imported manufactured goods is greater than the proportion between the same class of goods in gross output and (ii) these proportions are constant. Although from 1970 to 1985 industrialized countries have increased their self-sufficiency in primary commodities while tending to import a larger percentage of manufactured

products from developing countries, the proportionality between the primary commodity price index and the import price index still holds (UNCTAD, 1987).

3 The real interest rate may enter the price equation for at least one of the following reasons:

(i) It proxies the cost of working capital which rises because production takes time; in this case it would appear as an additional regressor in the marginal cost function.

(ii) Through the discount rate it affects those firm decisions which involve a comparison of profits at different times; e.g., reputation models, limit pricing models, 'customers markets' models (Fitoussi and Phelps, 1986, 1988). In this case a function depending on the real interest rate would affect a given mark-up.

(iii) As a demand factor it may affect the elasticity of demand and hence change the profit-maximizing mark-up itself.

4 Other relevant wage setting mechanisms (market, efficiency wages) can be derived as special cases of the bargaining specification (Johnson and Layard, 1986).

5 In particular the equivalence with financial assets depends on the extent to which primary commodities are stored; at this regard, since the occurrence of stockouts is not allowed in linear models, the latter tend to yield an excessive degree of assimilability (Deaton and Laroque, 1990).

6 Unreliable storage data, unobservable future prices, inconsistent orders of integration of the series (see Gilbert, 1989b). We do not attempt to describe the oil price as it has been highly dependent on OPEC cartel decisions. The oil market recouped some competitiveness only from the mid-eighties.

7 Consider the level of real external debt and take time derivatives

$$\frac{d(S/P)}{dt} = \frac{dS/dt}{P} - \frac{S}{P}\left(\frac{dP/dt}{P}\right)$$

Distinguish the current-account deficit into its interest and non-interest components:

$$(s \dot{-} p) = (s - p) + \phi - (s - p)\dot{p}/p,$$

where $\imath$ is the nominal interest rate paid on the outstanding debt, $\phi = V/P$, where V is the non-interest debt component and a dot denotes time derivatives. Divide both sides by $(s-p)$ and use the definition of the real interest rate to obtain equation (9) in the text.

8 This relation is derived as follows

$$l - n = -log(N/L) = -log(N/L - 1 + 1) = -log[(1 + (N - L)/L] \cong$$
$$-(N - L)/L = U;$$ the approximation is good for small values of U.

9 Nominal variables are all expressed in OECD currency obtained from the basket of currencies of the countries entering the bloc; similarly, the interest rate is obtained by a GDP-shares-weighted average of national interest rates. In adopting this type of aggregation, rather than, for example, converting all nominal variables into US dollars, we follow the IMF, which is the main source of our data. However specified, currency aggregation may be limiting

in so far as the variability of the exchange rates of OECD currencies against the dollar may have distribution effects within the OECD. Similar effects may also be relevant to non-OECD economies.

10 Even in this case, however, the stability of the equilibrium is not invalidated.

11 Indeed the dynamic model solves for w and p separately.

12 Non-oil commodity prices, if included, show a negative coefficient but introduce serious stability problems for the long-run solution of the model.

13 The real interest rate effect was not significant in an earlier version of the paper updated to 1984; a similar result is found by other studies (Enoch and Panić, 1981; Winters, 1987; Gilbert and Palaskas, 1989; Vines and Ramanujam, 1988).

14 The South is out of equilibrium; $p_n - p$ is too low and this may induce, *ceteris paribus*, a fall of export revenues and finally of GDP.

REFERENCES

Beenstock, M. (1987a) 'An aggregate model of output, inflation and interest rates for industrialised countries', CEPR Discussion Paper No. 164.

(1987b) 'The balance of payments of oil-importing developing countries: an aggregate econometric analysis', CEPR Discussion Paper No. 165.

Breusch, T. and L. Godfrey (1981) 'A review of recent work on testing for autocorrelation in dynamic economic models', in D. Currie, R. Nobay and D. Peel (eds.), *Macroeconomic Analysis: Essays in Macroeconomics and Econometrics*, London: Croom Helm.

Cristini, A. (1989) 'OECD activity and commodity prices', D. Phil. thesis, Oxford.

Deaton, A. and G. Laroque (1990) 'On the behavior of commodity prices', Princeton, mimeo.

Dornbusch, R. (1986) *Dollar, Debts and Deficits*, Leuven University Press.

Enoch, C. and M. Panić (1981) 'Commodity prices in the 70s', *Bank of England Quarterly Bulletin*, 42–53.

Fitoussi, J-P. and E. Phelps (1986) 'Causes of the 1980s slump in Europe', *Brookings Papers on Economic Activity*, 487–520.

(1988) *The Slump in Europe*, Oxford: Basil Blackwell.

Gilbert, C. (1987) 'The impact of exchange rates and developing country debt on commodity prices', Applied Economics Discussion Papers, University of Oxford, No. 30.

(1989a) 'The impact of the exchange rate and developing country debt on commodity prices', *Economic Journal* **99**, 773–84.

(1989b) 'Modeling primary commodity prices under rational expectations', Report to the World Bank, International Commodity Division, mimeo.

(1991) 'Primary commodity prices and inflation', *Oxford Review of Economic Policy* **6**, 77–99.

Gilbert, C. and T. Palaskas (1989) 'Modeling expectation formation in primary commodity markets', Discussion Paper No. 192, Economics Department, Queen Mary College, University of London.

Grubb, D. (1985) 'The revised OECD data set', Centre for Labour Economics, Working Paper No. 781, London.

Johnson, G. and R. Layard (1986) 'The natural rate of unemployment:

explanation and policies', in O. Ashenfelter and R. Layard (eds.), *Handbook of Labor Economics*, Amsterdam: North-Holland.

Labys, W. C. (1980) *Market structure, bargaining power and resource price formation*, Lexington MA: Heath.

Layard, R. and S. Nickell (1986) 'Unemployment in Britain', *Economica*, (supplement) **53**, S121–S169.

UNCTAD (1987) *Handbook of International Trade and Development Statistics*, supplement.

Vines, D. and P. Ramanujam (1988) 'Commodity prices, financial markets and world income', mimeo.

Winters, A. (1987) 'Models of primary price indices', *Oxford Bulletin of Economics and Statistics* **49**, 307–27.

Winters, A. and D. Sapsford (eds.) (1990) *Primary Commodity Prices: Economic Models and Policy*, Cambridge University Press.

Discussion

VITO ANTONIO MUSCATELLI

Cristini's paper is of great interest because it represents one of the few current attempts to construct a highly aggregated empirical model of North–South interaction in which overall economic activity in the North and primary commodity prices are jointly determined. In discussing this paper I would like to highlight two major issues. First, I shall look at the nature of the linkages between North and South through commodity prices, and suggest that there is at least one important linkage which has been ignored in Cristini's model. Second, I would like to focus on the causal nexus between Northern macroeconomic policy and relative commodity prices.

1   The nature of the commodity price linkage

One linkage which seems to me to be paramount in describing the effects of commodity prices on Northern aggregate supply operates through the production function, and hence the marginal productivity condition, and the price-setting relationship. The impact of commodity prices on Northern production was one of the main issues confronted by Bruno and Sachs (1985), in their analysis of the effects of changing relative commodity prices on the factor price frontier.[1] The precise effects obtained by including primary commodities in the North's production function clearly depend upon the specification of the production technology and the separability assumptions made.

Nevertheless, it seems quite natural to conclude that an increase in the price of raw material inputs will shift the marginal product–labour demand relation, and that this effect will be analogous to a fall in productivity. This effect has not been explicitly tested for in Cristini's model. In contrast, the author prefers to focus solely on the effect of commodity prices on wage setting, through the impact of changes in relative commodity prices on the 'wedge' between consumer prices and producer prices.

It seems to me that the Bruno–Sachs production function linkage probably corresponds more closely to our intuition about the main first-round effect of a commodity price increase on Northern aggregate supply: the increase in commodity prices is important because it raises marginal costs (particularly in the short run with given production technology) and not because it raises consumer prices in the North relative to producer prices (after all, only some of these primary commodities are final consumer goods).

One could certainly argue that the effect of commodity prices on the price-setting relationship which I have just described will work in the same direction as the effect on the 'wedge' described by the authors, but I do think it is important to get the microfoundations right, because it will affect the model's quantitative predictions. This is easily demonstrated using a simple theoretical framework. Suppose that the North has the following separable production technology

$$Q = Q(J, N) \quad J = J(L, K) \tag{1}$$

where output Q is a function of raw material inputs, N, and a value added (or 'intermediate product') index J which is a function of capital (K) and labour (L). If we assume a CES technology for both $Q(.)$ and $J(.)$ with elasticities of σ_q and s_j respectively, we can write, in logs

$$q = k - \beta(w - p_j) - \sigma_q(p - p_j) \tag{2}$$

where lower-case letters indicate logs, and where w is the Northern wage, p is the price of Northern output, and p_j is a price index for value added, which can be defined as (see Bruno and Sachs, 1985)

$$p_j = (1/\eta_j)p - ((1 - \eta_j)/\eta_j)p_n \tag{3}$$

where p_n are commodity prices and where η_j represents the output elasticity of Q with respect to J. (Furthermore, it can also be shown that

$\beta = \sigma_j \eta_i / \eta_k$, where η_i and η_k are the relevant output elasticities of J). Using (2) and (3), we can derive an aggregate supply relationship for the North

$$q = -\beta(w - p) - \psi(p_n - p) + k \tag{4}$$

where $\psi = (\beta + \sigma_q)(1 - \eta_j)/\eta_j$.

Now, it should be apparent that the effect of increases in real commodity prices $(p_n - p)$ will have an effect on aggregate supply through its effect on real wages (the first term in (4) which *is* present in Cristini's model), but also directly through its effect on production costs (the second term in (4), which is absent from Cristini's account). The effect on the results will be to underpredict the impact of exogenous increases in commodity prices (e.g., through an oil shock) on Northern aggregate supply and hence on Northern unemployment. Admittedly, Cristini does not find commodity prices significant in the long-run price equation, but this result contrasts with previous empirical evidence (see Bruno and Sachs, 1985), and may be sensitive to the chosen empirical specification.

The production-function link is probably the most important omission from Cristini's paper. Another secondary linkage which is only partly recognized by the inclusion of the real interest rate in the price equation is the impact of 'competitiveness' on the mark-up[2], as changes in competitiveness may affect the elasticity of demand for a region's product.

Turning finally to the role of the 'wedge', which constitutes the main commodity price linkage in Cristini's paper, it should be noted that the effects of competitiveness on wage setting are not always clear-cut in every instance (see Bean *et al.*, 1986, Layard *et al.*, 1991). Interestingly, although Cristini finds a permanent effect for the wedge, she does report that the results are sensitive to a disaggregation between oil and non-oil commodity prices, and this might warrant further investigation.

2 Causal linkages between North and South

Two key conclusions emerge from Cristini's model about the causal linkages between North and South through commodity prices. First, OECD demand matters little for the long-run path of non-oil commodity prices (as may be gauged by the South line in her Figure 4.1), but commodity prices are highly responsive to short-run surges in OECD demand. This is an interesting conclusion, because it sheds some light on existing theoretical models of North–South interactions (see Alogoskoufis and Varangis, 1992).

Second, the quantitative impact of a sizeable oil shock on OECD unemployment is found to be rather small. We have already noted that the second of these conclusions may be rather overoptimistic because it ignores a key production function linkage. However, there is also a possible medium-run effect on productivity which cannot be captured by such an aggregate model, but which may be of some importance: the effect of high unemployment in the North in retarding the reallocation of resources between industrial sectors. Numerous economists (see for instance Lindbeck, 1983) have pointed to this as a source of productivity slowdown following the two OPEC shocks. Another issue which cannot be addressed in the context of the author's model, without providing a richer specification of the aggregate demand side, but which is surely important for our understanding of the North's reaction to the two oil shocks, is the effect of a different fiscal-monetary mix on commodity prices, and hence on Northern inflation and unemployment.

However, notwithstanding these qualifications, the paper by Cristini represents a useful attempt to characterize the North–South commodity price linkage at the empirical level. Many economists have mused about this link in theoretical models – this is a commendable attempt to assess its importance in practice.

NOTES

1 This built on earlier work by Bruno (1978).
2 See Bulow *et al.* (1985).

REFERENCES

Alogoskoufis, G. and P. Varangis (1992) 'OECD fiscal policies and the relative price of primary commodities', The World Bank, International Trade Working Paper No. 955.

Bean, C., R. Layard and S. Nickell (1986) 'The rise in unemployment: a multi-country study', *Economica* **53**: S1–22.

Bruno, M. (1978) 'Duality, intermediate inputs and value added', in M. Fuss and D. McFadden (eds.), *Production Economics: A Dual Approach to Theory and Applications*, Amsterdam: North-Holland.

Bruno, M. and J. Sachs (1985) *The Economics of Worldwide Stagflation*, Oxford: Basil Blackwell.

Bulow, J.I., J. Genakopoulos and P. Klemperer (1985) 'Multimarket oligopoly: strategic substitutes and complements', *Journal of Political Economy* **93**, 488–511.

Layard, R., S. Nickell and R. Jackman (1991) *Unemployment*, Oxford: Basil Blackwell.

Lindbeck, A. (1983) 'The recent slowdown in productivity growth', *Economic Journal* **93**, 13–34.

Part Three
Convergence and growth linkages

5 Convergence and growth linkages between North and South

JOHN F. HELLIWELL and ALAN CHUNG

In this paper we report some evidence on the longer-term growth linkages among countries, especially between the industrialized and developing nations. Our starting point will be the fairly well-established finding that there has been significant convergence in per-capita growth rates among the industrialized countries over the thirty years since 1960,[1] but little evidence of convergence between the industrialized and developing countries.[2] The central question we ask is: what are the conditions that appear to enable a country to enter a period of sustained growth that offers the prospect of convergence towards the income and productivity levels of the richer industrialized countries? Our tool for analysis will be an empirical framework explaining comparative growth performance over the 1960–85 period in a way that allows simultaneously for convergence in per-capita GDP, for possible returns to scale, and for international differences in investment rates in human and physical capital. We shall be especially on the look-out for evidence that the prospects for convergence differ by income level or region, or are characterized by possible threshold effects. We shall also try to assess whether convergence in the growth rates of GDP per capita, to the extent it is taking place, is due entirely to higher investment rates in the countries catching up,[3] or to international transfers of technology that permit faster growth of efficiency levels in the initially poorer countries.[4]

The next section sets the stage by reviewing previous studies. Section 2 then presents our new results on convergence by income class and region, while the subsequent section deals with the important ancillary linkage between per-capita GDP and real exchange rates. The concluding section sketches some possible implications of these results for analysing the lingages between North and South.

1   Some theory and previous results on convergence

Our empirical analysis starts with an extended form of the Solow (1956, 1957) growth model, as augmented by Mankiw *et al.* (1992) to include human capital accumulation, with real output determined as a Cobb–Douglas function of physical capital, human capital and efficiency units of labour

$$Y(t) = K(t)^\alpha H(t)^\beta (A(t)L(t))^{l-\alpha-\beta} \tag{1}$$

where H is the stock of human capital, L the stock of labour (growing at rate n), K the stock of physical capital, depreciating at rate δ, and A the level of technology, growing at the constant rate[5] g. The coefficients imply constant returns to all factors taken together, and hence diminishing returns to any combination of physical and human capital. If s_k is the fraction of output invested in physical capital and s_h the fraction invested in human capital, then in the steady state the log of output per capita is

$$ln[Y(t)/L(t)] = lnA(0) + gt - ((\alpha+\beta)/(1-\alpha-\beta))ln(n+g+\delta)$$
$$+ (\alpha/(1-\alpha-\beta))ln(s_k) + (\beta/(1-\alpha-\beta))ln(s_h) \tag{2}$$

This framework is extended to include the possibility of what Mankiw *et al.* call 'conditional convergence', that if each country starts at some level of output that differs from its steady-state value, there will be convergence towards the steady-state growth path for that country. This need not imply that all countries have the same equilibrium level of income per capita (they argue that the level of A can be different across countries, based on variations in natural resources, institutions and other factors unrelated to the stocks of human and physical capital) or even the same growth rate, since the equilibrium growth rate for each country will depend on its population growth and investment in human and physical capital. The Solow model augmented for human capital accumulation predicts that the rate of convergence of each country towards its steady-state growth path will be at the proportional rate λ, where

$$\lambda = (n + g + \delta)(1 - \alpha - \beta) \tag{3}$$

The log difference between current income per effective worker and that in any given earlier period 0 is thus given by

$$ln(y(t)) - ln(y(0)) = (1 - e^{\lambda t})[(\alpha/(1-\alpha-\beta))ln(s_k)$$
$$+ (\beta/(1-\alpha-\beta))ln(s_h) - ((\alpha+\beta)/(1-\alpha-\beta))$$
$$ln(n+g+\delta) - 1n(y(0))] \tag{4}$$

This equation, as applied by Mankiw *et al.* to a cross-sectional sample of the growth experience of ninety-eight countries from 1960 to 1985, seemed to fit the the experience of the developing as well as the industrial countries. There was evidence of conditional convergence for the whole sample of countries, as well as for the more restricted sample of industrial countries.[6] Their results also showed that allowing for the accumulation of human capital lowered the estimated coefficient on physical capital to a level that was consistent with capital's share in output, and hence the Cobb–Douglas assumption of constant returns to scale. Mankiw *et al.* interpreted their results as a vindication of the augmented Solow model, and an implicit rejection of the increasing number of models built on the assumption that knowledge spillovers created the likelihood of increasing returns to scale at the national level.[7]

The Mankiw *et al.* model differs in a fundamental way from the one we have used earlier[8] to study convergence. In the Mankiw *et al.* framework, the productivity index may have a different level in each country (to account for resource endowments, etc.), but has the same exogenous growth rate in each country. Although we used a similar production structure to Mankiw *et al.*,[9] we assumed that the efficiency indexes initially grow at different rates in each country, with convergence taking place in the rates of growth, and possibly in the levels, of the technology indexes. Thus international transfers to knowledge are given a central role in convergence, with the initially poorer countries able to have efficiency levels that grow faster than those in the initially richer countries. This is because the initially poorer countries are able to make use of current best practice procedures already in use in the more productive economies. If this approach is correct, it offers enhanced growth prospects for all countries that have the necessary conditions to be in the 'convergence club', since growth of per-capita incomes can be faster in the poorer countries without requiring higher levels of investment than in the richer countries, although of course that channel for convergence also remains available.

Since our earlier studies dealt with countries for which we were able to construct measures of the physical capital stock, we were able to obtain explicit measures of the 'Solow residuals',[10] and to see whether they showed evidence of convergence. In our combined time series and cross-section studies, the results for the industrial countries provided strong evidence of international convergence of the growth rates of the Solow residuals.[11] Thus our results rejected quite strongly the assumption of an unchanging rate of technical progress.[12] However, for the present paper, we shall concentrate on estimating cross-sectional equations of the sort used by Mankiw *et al.*, since they are also consistent with our preferred production structure. The difference lies in the interpretation of the constant term, which in the Mankiw *et al.* framework is just the logarithm of the ratio of equilibrium incomes. In our framework, the estimated constant term in a cross-sectional regression is a function of the equilibrium level differences as well as the speed of convergence of growth rates, and the initial level differences, of the productivity indexes. We shall also test more directly for convergence in the rates of growth of productivity indexes by using the more complete data available for the industrial countries.

An earlier paper (Helliwell, 1991) used a framework rather like that of Mankiw *et al.* to consider whether there were some threshold levels of education below which convergence could not take place. The results suggested that there were no material threshold effects for education, and that the Mankiw *et al.* log-linear specification was roughly appropriate. That paper also added a direct test for economies of scale, and found some evidence of a low degree of scale economies for the industrial countries, with some possibility of lesser effects for the world sample as a whole. In a companion paper to this one (Helliwell and Chung, 1991c), we extend the tests of economies of scale to see if they may apply over some range of country sizes, if not over the entire world sample, and compare the convergence process across countries with that applicable among regions within a given country.

2   Convergence results by income level and region

In this paper, we want to explore further the tentative conclusion that the above model of conditional convergence, augmented further by the possibility of some returns of scale, is equally applicable to countries at all income levels. Our tests of the applicability of the model of conditional convergence to the developing countries will be based on dividing the sample by region as well as ordering it by levels of initial income per capita. In this way we can see if it is true, as the Mankiw *et al.* global results seem to suggest, that the same model of convergence is equally applicable at all levels of development and in all parts of the world.

Our first result, as shown in Table 5.1, is a replication of the Mankiw *et al.* cross-sectional estimation of equation (4) explaining the 1960–85 growth in real GDP per adult for ninety-eight countries. The second equation imposes the parameter restrictions implied by equation (4), which are accepted quite easily, chiefly by means of shifting the weakly estimated coefficient on the final term. The third equation shows the

Table 5.1   Convergence tests using ninety-eight-country sample

	Mankiw/Romer/Weil Table V, Col. 1		Mankiw/Romer/Weil Table VI, Col. 1 (restricted estimates)	
No. of observations	98	98	98	98
Degrees of freedom	93	92	94	93
Constant	3.030	2.498	2.454	1.758
	(0.827)	(0.826)	(0.473)	(0.536)
Coefficients				
scale		0.065		0.0621
		(0.024)		(0.024)
cu	−0.288	−0.333	−0.298	−0.343
	(0.061)	(0.062)	(0.060)	(0.061)
invest	0.526	0.533		
	(0.087)	(0.084)		
school	0.231	0.189		
	(0.059)	(0.060)		
$n+g+\delta$	−0.503	−0.379		
	(0.288)	(0.283)		
invest			0.502	0.501
$-(n+g+\delta)$			(0.082)	(0.080)
school			0.235	0.196
$-(n+g+\delta)$			(0.059)	(0.059)
$\bar{R}^2$	0.464	0.497	0.466	0.495
S.E.E.	0.326	0.316	0.326	0.317

Notes: Standard errors are in parentheses. The data are from Mankiw, Romer and Weil (1992), with the addition of the *scale* variable, which is measured by the logarithm of average total GDP, 1960–85. *cu* is the logarithm of 1960 GDP per adult, *invest* is the logarithm of the average 1960–85 ratio of investment to DGP, and *school* is the logarithm of secondary school enrolment as a percentage of the working age population. The sum of $g+\delta$ is assumed to be 0.05, and *n* is the average 1960–85 proportionate growth rate of the working age population.

effects of adding a variable measuring the average scale of each of the countries, being the log of the mean of each country's average real GDP over the period from 1960 to 1985.[13] The final equation adds the parameter restrictions, once again with little loss in goodness of fit or change in the key parameter estimates. All four equations show strong convergence effects, even though the industrial countries, the group for which convergence has previously been shown, make up less than one-quarter of the sample.[14]

Mankiw *et al.* treat the empirical success of their model, which assumes constant returns to scale and which has an investment coefficient small enough to be consistent with the augmented Solow model, as evidence that increasing returns to scale are not required to explain international differences in growth rates. However, by adding the scale variable, we provide a more direct test of the returns to scale assumption. The results provide evidence of slight economies of scale, with each 10 per cent increase in size being associated with an increase in the annual growth rate of $0.062/25 = 0.0025$, or 0.25 per cent. Our estimate of 0.062 for economies of scale is only one-sixth as large as suggested by the sample calculations reported by Lucas (1990).

We shall return later to a direct test of the Mankiw *et al.* assumption of constant growth in the technical progress index. First we disaggregate the data sample by income class, to see if the new evidence of convergence applies equally to rich and poor countries. The results are shown in Table 5.2, where the basic cross-sectional equation is repeated for each of four quartiles, separated according to their 1960 levels of real GDP per adult. The model of conditional convergence fits better for the richest quartiles, in terms of the significance of coefficients and overall goodness of fit. Subsidiary tests were run to see if the differences among the coefficients for different income classes are individually or collectively significant, as for a smaller sample of countries by Dowrick and Gemmell (1991). As reported in Table 5.2, there are no significant differences of either constant terms or slope coefficients,[15] thus supporting the use of pooled data for countries of different initial income levels.

In Table 5.3, we examine the results by continent, to see whether geographic proximity is important in defining groups of countries among which convergence is expected to take place. For Latin America and the OECD, and to a slightly lesser extent Africa, convergence is significant and slightly larger than for the world sample, while there is no evidence of convergence in Asia. There appear to be no scale effects in any region except the OECD. Investment effects are largest and most significant in Asia, while schooling does not appear to have significant effects within any of the regions. More precise tests of regional differences are obtained by adding separate regional intercepts and slope coefficients to the ninety-eight country equation. Only the African and Latin American intercepts have *t*-values with absolute values greater than 1.0, and both show slower growth than the global equation would predict. None of the slope coefficients is significantly different by region.

Figure 5.1 shows the relatively weak partial relationship between initial GDP per adult and subsequent growth for Africa. South Africa is a clear

Table 5.2   Tests of convergence for rich and poor countries
(For these equations the ninety-eight observations are ranked by GDP per adult in 1960 and divided into quartiles)

Quartile samples	High income	2nd	3rd	Low income
No. of observations	24	24	24	26
Degrees of freedom	18	18	18	20
Constant	0.275	2.568	0.787	4.901
	(1.796)	(3.699)	(4.585)	(3.543)
Coefficients				
scale	0.036	0.066	0.133	0.044
	(0.032)	(0.071)	(0.061)	(0.060)
cu	−0.231	−0.216	−0.316	−0.641
	(0.159)	(0.430)	(0.396)	(0.308)
invest	0.560	0.776	0.457	0.476
	(0.159)	(0.294)	(0.197)	(0.157)
school	0.232	−0.013	0.186	0.158
	(0.140)	(0.278)	(0.148)	(0.125)
$n+g+\delta$	−1.075	0.002	−0.479	−0.253
	(0.314)	(0.278)	(1.206)	(0.921)
$\bar{R}^2$	0.645	0.423	0.448	0.336
S.E.E.	0.193	0.333	0.358	0.361

Note: Standard errors are in parentheses. Tests of parameter differences were performed by treating all ninety-eight countries as part of a single sample, and allowing for separate constant terms and intercepts for each of the four income groups. The constraint that all four income classes have the same constants and slope coefficients as the countries in the highest income class was easily accepted ($F = 1.073$ with 12 and 80 degrees of freedom, giving a probability value of 0.377).

outlier in having more growth than its high initial income would predict. The slow growers, relative to predicted, were Zaire, Ghana and Zambia, perhaps reflecting their dependence on primary exports.

The convergence model fits very badly for Asia, as shown by Figure 5.2. Hong Kong and Singapore grew much faster than convergence would suggest, and India much more slowly. Without those three countries, the remainder would support a negative relationship, once account was taken of differences in investment, education and scale effects.[16] Convergence applies fairly well to Latin America, with no major exceptions evident in Figure 5.3.

The convergence model fits best for the industrial countries, and inspection of Figure 5.4 shows that the strong convergence effect is not simply due to the experience of Japan, since there are countries spread over the range of growth rates and initial per-adult levels of real GDP. Two of the countries with the lowest growth rates, relative to the predicted

Table 5.3   Tests of convergence by region

Regions	Africa	Asia	Latin America	OECD	98-country sample*
No. of observations	38	13	18	22	98
Degrees of Freedom	32	7	12	16	90
Constant	2.826	2.665	5.050	1.864	3.454
Coefficients					
scale	0.076	−0.108	0.089	0.061	0.044
	(0.062)	(0.115)	(0.052)	(0.022)	(0.025)
cu	−0.402	0.095	−0.645	−0.437	−0.328
	(0.159)	(0.430)	(0.153)	(0.061)	(0.063)
invest	0.492	1.091	0.269	0.402	0.539
	(0.134)	(0.373)	(0.211)	(0.148)	(0.083)
school	0.129	−0.401	0.236	0.222	0.117
	(0.096	(0.339)	(0.224)	(0.122)	(0.063)
$n+g+\delta$	−0.223	−0.083	−0.048	−0.935	−0.106
	(0.849)	(2.353)	(0.537)	(0.286)	(0.308)
Africa					−0.300
					(0.107)
Latin America					−0.184
					(0.102)
$\bar{R}^2$	0.315	0.505	0.620	0.751	0.529
S.E.E.	0.370	0.337	0.223	0.124	0.306

Notes: Standard errors are in parentheses. * With regional dummies for Africa and Latin America (remainder includes OECD, Asia and residue).

values, are Australia and New Zealand. This is what we might expect, since both are countries which derived a large fraction of their 1960 incomes from pastoral and other land-intensive activities whose terms of trade and relative activity levels suffered over the subsequent twenty-five years. A similar natural resource effect, but with the opposite sign, is provided by Norway, whose oil wealth was discovered, developed, and brought into full production during the twenty-five year period.

It is apparent that convergence applies much more closely to the growth experiences of Latin America and the OECD than to Africa and Asia, even after allowing for differences in investment, education, and scale The need for additional explanatory factors is especially obvious in the case of Asia, where the correlation between the initial income and subsequent growth is not even of the expected sign.[17]

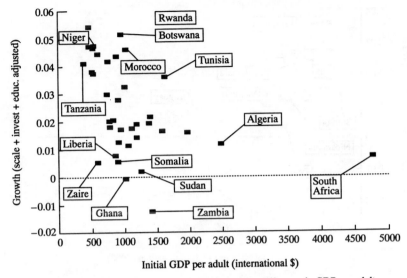

Note: Vertical axis measures average annual log difference in GDP per adult.

Figure 5.1   Growth and initial income per adult: Africa

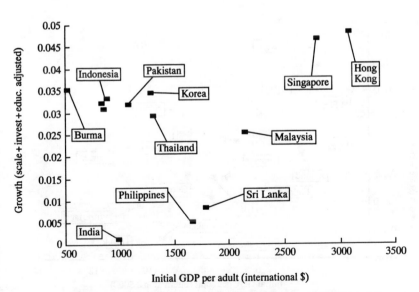

Note: Vertical axis measures average annual log difference in GDP per adult.

Figure 5.2   Growth and initial income per adult: Asia

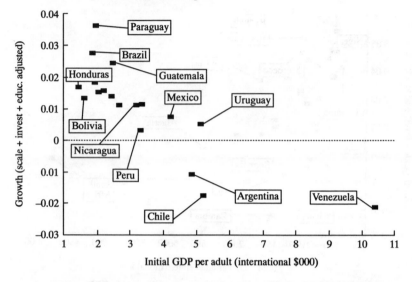

Note: Vertical axis measures average annual log difference in GDP per adult.

Figure 5.3   Growth and initial income per adult: Latin America

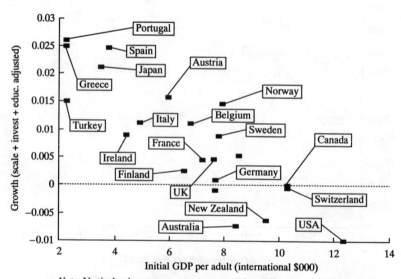

Note: Vertical axis measures average annual log difference in GDP per adult.

Figure 5.4   Growth and initial income per adult: OECD

Looking at the results from Tables 5.2 and 5.3 together, it would appear that the convergence results are more robust by region and income grouping than are those for education, investment, and scale. Conversely, it would appear that adding these latter variables, and especially education and investment, is important for explaining the growth variations among regions, and between the richest and the poorest countries.

We now turn, in Table 5.4, to attempt a more direct test of whether technical progress grows faster in the poorer countries, as suggested in our earlier work. In these experiments, we are limited to the group of nineteen OECD countries we studied in earlier papers, since that is the sample for which we have comparable data for employment and stocks of physical capital. The first equation repeats the OECD equation of Table 5.3, using the Mankiw *et al.* data, but with nineteen instead of twenty-two countries. The smaller sample makes no material difference to the results. The second equation continues with the nineteen country sample, but uses the OECD national accounts data instead of the Mankiw *et al.* data. This leads to some increase in the investment effect, and to some reduction in the overall explanatory power of the equation.

The third equation continues to use the OECD national accounts data, but changes the dependent variable from the growth of real GDP per adult to the growth of the Solow residual. If technical progress grows at the same constant rate in each country, then there should be no convergence effect apparent in the Solow residual, and hence the initial productivity level should drop out of the equation. The results show that this does not happen, and that the initial productivity level has a strong negative effect, even though the schooling variable remains in the equation to guard against the possibility that ignoring international differences in human capital had been responsible for our earlier finding.

The results also show no effect for investment. This is as one might expect in an equation for Solow residuals, since the effect of capital growth is already built into the dependent variable. However, if there were important capital embodiment effects in the implementation of technical progress, then one might expect to find that countries with higher investment rates had higher productivity growth rates. Similarly, if capital investment had important external effects, through the creation of knowledge spillovers at the national level, then one might also expect to find a positive effect from the investment rate. Neither of these influences appears to be important in this sample of industrial countries. Finally, the insignificance of the schooling variable may suggest that the secondary school enrollment rate is an inadequate measure of the differences in human capital among the industrial countries, where differences in higher education and research may be more important.

Table 5.4   Comparison of convergence results for the OECD using GDP per adult and Solow residuals, 1960–85

	(1) GDP per adult M/R/W data	(2) GDP per adult OECD SNA data	(3) Solow residuals using OECD SNA data
No. of observations	19	19	19
Degrees of freedom	13	13	13
Constant	3.246	1.606	26.620
Coefficients			
scale	0.054	0.061	0.069
	(0.023)	(0.023)	(0.024)
cu	−0.527	−0.426	−0.757
	(0.932)	(0.106)	(0.107)
invest	0.361	0.594	−0.005
	(0.162)	(0.251)	(0.255)
school	0.119	0.121	−0.110
	(0.154)	(0.154)	(0.161)
$n+g+\delta$	−0.665	−0.253	0.456
	(0.406)	(0.392)	(0.440)
$\bar{R}^2$	0.797	0.702	0.845
S.E.E.	0.129	0.123	0.128

Notes: Standard errors are in parentheses. The Mankiw–Romer–Weil data are mainly from the Penn World Table: (Mark 4) (Summers and Heston, 1988). GDP is measured in 1980 international dollars. The OECD SNA data are from the 1990 OECD National Accounts database. Purchasing power parities for 1985 are used to convert the GDP data into 1985 international dollars. For regressions (1) and (2), the dependent variable is defined as the log difference in GDP per adut over the period 1960–85, and cu is the logarithm of 1960 GDP per adult. For regression (3) the dependent variable is defined as the change in the logarithm of the Solow residual (as explained in Helliwell and Chung, 1991a), and cu is the logarithm of the 1960 Solow residual. The sample used in the above regressions contains the following nineteen countries: USA, Japan, Canada, France, Germany, Italy, United Kingdom, Australia, Austria, Belgium, Denmark, Finland, Ireland, Netherlands, New Zealand, Norway, Spain, Sweden and Switzerland.

3   Convergence and the real exchange rate

Is it still true, as pointed out earlier by Kravis and Lipsey (1983), Hill (1986) and Heston and Summers (1988), that there is a significant positive relationship between a country's real exchange rate and its relative GDP? Such a relationship has been rationalized by the possibility that productivity levels in services are relatively high in the poorer countries (Balassa, 1964; Kravis et al., 1983) or by the possibility of lower endowed K/L ratios in poorer countries (Bhagwati, 1984) combined with complete specialization in some products, with the poorer countries exporting labour-intensive commodities. The former explanation, when coupled with our evidence that productivity growth rates are faster in the poorer countries, would involve corresponding real appreciation of the currencies of the poorer countries, reflecting the implied changes in comparative advantage. If the empirical relationship between real exchange rates and real per-capita GDPs is maintained in a fairly stable way from one decade to the next, and if convergence of per-capita real GDPs is a powerful tendency, then we might expect to find some lessening of the cross-sectional variations of both real per-capita incomes and of real exchange rates from decade to decade.

In assessing the evidence we must distinguish, as Barro and Sala-i-Martín (1990) point out, what they call β convergence from what they call σ convergence. β convergence, which in the terminology that we have adopted for this paper should be referred to as λ convergence (as defined in equation (3)), relates to the partial convergence effect that we and others have found to be significant, as evidenced by the coefficients on the initial income variable. σ convergence relates to what happens to the cross-sectional variation in per-capita real incomes as time passes. There are several reasons why significant β or k convergence need not imply σ convergence. Barro and Sala-i-Martín emphasize the fact that different countries are likely to be subject to different disturbances, and that the variance of these disturbances may not be constant from decade to decade. In addition, since we are interested in the σ for real exchange rates as well as for real incomes, there is the question of disturbances to real exchange rates as well as to real incomes.

The correlations in Table 5.5 show that for the ninety-eight country sample as a whole there have been no noticeable decade-to-decade trends in σ for a cross-sectional variations of real exchange rates, real GDP per capita or real GDP per adult. Similarly, there has been little apparent trend in the correlation between real exchange rates and real per-capita GDPs. Disaggregating by average income, there appears to have been σ convergence for real incomes, but not for real exchange rates, within the richer two quartiles. There appears to be σ divergence for both real incomes and real exchange rates in the two poorer quartiles. As for the correlation between real exchange rates and real incomes, it is strong among the countries in the richest quartile[18] and effectively zero in the three other quartiles. This appears to contrast with the results in Helliwell and Chung (1993), where we found a consistently strong correlation between real incomes and real exchange rates for the industrial countries and for a group of Asian economies. To reconcile these two results, we

Table 5.5   Real exchange rates and real GDP per capita
Ranked by average GDP per adult and divided into quartiles

	High income	2nd	3rd	Low	98-country
Real exchange rate (log)					
Std dev: 1960–85	0.165	0.209	0.293	0.263	0.322
1960s	0.193	0.270	0.298	0.285	0.325
1970s	0.191	0.222	0.326	0.276	0.350
1980s	0.166	0.208	0.349	0.373	0.372
Real GDP per capita (log)					
Std dev's: 1960–85	0.255	0.313	0.262	0.272	1.05
1960s	0.359	0.387	0.270	0.308	0.995
1970s	0.255	0.325	0.290	0.282	1.07
1980s	0.262	0.295	0.345	0.289	1.15
Real GDP per adult (log)					
Std dev's: 1960–85	0.236	0.271	0.258	0.275	0.985
1960s	0.354	0.352	0.288	0.306	0.948
1970s	0.232	0.280	0.299	0.281	1.01
1980s	0.222	0.253	0.323	0.293	1.06
Correlations between real exchange rate and real GDP per capita					
1960–85	0.781	0.034	−0.023	0.040	0.587
1960s	0.662	0.021	0.019	−0.189	0.506
1970s	0.768	0.136	−0.039	0.183	0.589
1980s	0.524	−0.057	−0.017	0.058	0.558
Correlations between real exchange rate and real GDP per adult					
1960–85	0.763	−0.052	0.076	0.069	0.580
1960s	0.663	−0.036	0.085	−0.179	0.498
1970s	0.697	0.033	0.015	0.205	0.577
1980s	0.548	−0.051	0.083	0.069	0.560

turn now to consider the correlations on a regional basis, as reported on a decade-by-decade basis in Table 5.6.

The results summarized in Table 5.6, and displayed for 1985 in Figures 5.5 to 5.8, show strong correlations between real incomes and real exchange rates for Asia and for the OECD, thus confirming the earlier results, but relatively slight positive correlation in Africa and, for the 1980s, a negative correlation in Latin America. As for the international variability of real incomes, there is some evidence of σ convergence for the OECD and for Latin America, while there is σ divergence in Asia and Africa. Regressions using per-capita real GDP to explain cross-sectional variation in 1985 real exchange rates for the ninety-one countries in the four regions reveal that the data accept a common relationship applicable to Asia and the OECD countries, but strongly reject its applicability to

Table 5.6   Real exchange rates and real GDP per capita: regional evidence

	Africa	Asia	Latin America	OECD
Real exchange rate (log)				
Std dev's: 1960–85	0.240	0.258	0.159	0.219
1960s	0.279	0.218	0.216	0.222
1970s	0.246	0.297	0.167	0.227
1980s	0.286	0.395	0.199	0.257
Real GDP per capital (log)				
Std dev's: 1960–85	0.555	0.777	0.458	0.418
1960s	0.525	0.582	0.524	0.468
1970s	0.563	0.811	0.443	0.400
1980s	0.647	0.937	0.436	0.400
Real GDP per adult (log)				
Std dev's: 1960–85	0.547	0.742	0.426	0.395
1960s	0.519	0.593	0.497	0.464
1970s	0.553	0.790	0.411	0.384
1980s	0.633	0.877	0.397	0.371
Correlations between real exchange rate and real GDP per capita				
1960–85	0.269	0.762	0.179	0.877
1960s	0.131	0.513	0.230	0.752
1970s	0.326	0.736	0.325	0.857
1980s	0.311	0.865	−0.188	0.878
Correlations between real exchange rate and real GDP per adult				
1960–85	0.276	0.758	0.187	0.868
1960s	0.137	0.527	0.273	0.745
1970s	0.329	0.726	0.319	0.843
1980s	0.311	0.868	0.174	0.877

Latin America and Africa. For Asia and the OECD, the elasticity of the real exchange rate with respect to real per-capita GDP is 0.475 ($t=9.6$); this drops to 0.146 for Africa and is −0.295 for Latin America.[19] There is not space in this paper to dig much deeper into the reasons for these differences, but it seems likely that the relationship between real GDP and the real exchange rate is tighter for more open economies and weaker where national inflation rates are higher and uncertain.

4   Conclusions

What are the main features of our results? The evidence from all countries suggests that production structures ought to be modelled, especially for the developing countries, in a way that takes account of the

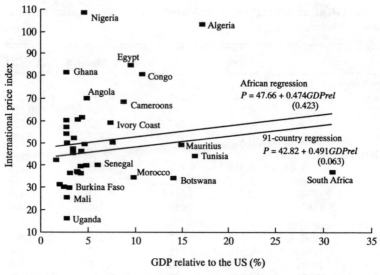

Figure 5.5   International price indices and real GDP per capita in 1985: Africa

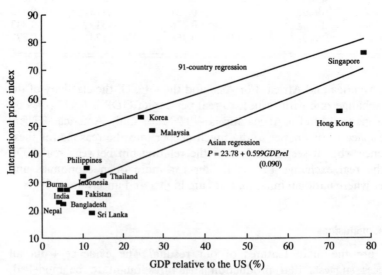

Figure 5.6   International price indices and real GDP per capita in 1985: Asia

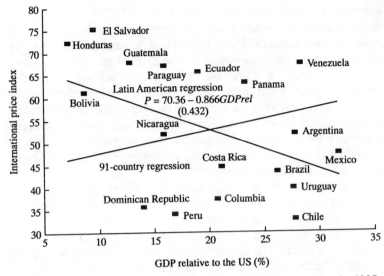

Figure 5.7 International price indices and real GDP per capita in 1985: Latin America

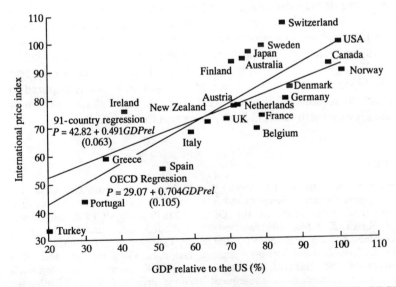

Figure 5.8 International price indices and real income per capita in 1985: OECD

accumulation of human as well as physical capital.[20] The evidence from the industrial countries, where there are fairly comparable measures of capital stocks, and hence of Solow residuals, also suggests that there is evidence of international convergence in the rates of technical progress. These results suggest, if they are subsequently supported for the developing countries when better data become available relating to capital stocks, that prospects for growth of real per-capita incomes in the poorer countries are thus brighter than they otherwise would have been. Earlier research for the industrial countries[21] also suggests that growth of Solow residuals has also been higher for countries that have had faster relative increases in their foreign trade.[22]

The applicability of the convergence model differs substantially by region, with its success being greatest for the OECD and Latin America, rather less for Africa, and non-existent for Asia. Thus it would appear that a fuller explanation for the diversity of Asian growth experiences will require more than the Solow model, even when augmented by human capital, technological convergence and scale effects.[23]

One surprise in our current results is that the linkage between real exchange rates and real per-capita incomes, which was found to be strong and sustained for the OECD and a sample of Asian economies, turns out to be of much less importance for Africa and Latin America. This may reflect differences in openness to trade, the prevalence of capital controls and restricted exchange rate regimes in Africa and Latin America, or some other factors. It may also be significant that average growth rates in Africa and Latin America have been below those in other regions, even after allowing for different rates of investment in human and physical capital. This may suggest that international involvements of the sort that lead to tighter linkages between real incomes and real exchange rates may also lead to higher average growth rates. More research is clearly required to spell out the reasons for the lesser real exchange rate linkages, as well as for the lower growth rates, in both Africa and Latin America.

NOTES

Alan Chung is at BC Hydro; formerly at University of British Colombia. We wish to thank the Social Sciences and Humanities Research Council for research support and participants of the OECD/KDI/Brookings/CEPR conference, Seoul, Korea, 27–8 May 1991, and especially Andrew Levin and Ralph Bryant, for comments on the first version of the paper. Thanks also to Giuseppe Bertola, Susan Collins, Richard Cooper, Elhanan Helpman, Greg Mankiw and other members of the Harvard, Princeton and NBER international economics seminars for comments on subsequent versions presented there. Finally, the paper was presented at the CEPR Oxford Conference on 23–4 April 1993, where helpful comments were made by several participants, and especially by Fabrizio Zilibotti.

1 For some discussion of the evidence, see Abramovitz (1979, 1990), Baumol (1986), Dowrick and Nguyen (1989) and Maddison (1982).
2 De Long (1988) suggests that the evidence for the richest countries may be due to sample selection bias. Other studies suggest that the evidence for the industrial countries is relatively robust to sample choice, but does not extend to the poorer countries, at least in terms of a simple negative correlation between starting values and subsequent growth of per capita incomes. See Baumol and Wolff (1988), Dowrick and Nguyen (1989), Baumol et al. (1989). Chenery et al. (1986) and Landes (1990). Factors advanced to explain the inability of many of the poorer countries to achieve the 'social capability' (Abramovitz, 1990) to 'take off' into sustained growth (Rostow, 1978) have included nutrition (Dasgupta, 1991), high inflation rates (Gylfason, 1990), poor macroeconomic policies (Fisher, 1991), unequal wealth distribution (Alesina and Rodrik, 1991) and education (Barro, 1991, Romer, 1989 and others). The evidence on the role of population growth is reviewed by Brander and Dowrick (1994).
3 This is what is implied by the augmented Solow model used by Mankiw et al. (1992), since in their model the technology index grows at the same rate in each country.
4 This possibility is central to the international convergence modelling in Helliwell and Chung (1991a, 1992, 1993), since the variable being explained, in part by convergence, is the 'Solow residual' that already takes account of international differences in the rate of accumulation of physical capital.
5 The assumption of a constant growth rate for the technology index marks an important distinction between the Mankiw et al. framework and the one we have employed earlier using a mixture of time-series and cross-sectional data to explain international differences in growth rates of productivity. In our framework (as developed and tested in Helliwell et al. 1985, Helliwell and Chung, 1991a, 1992, 1993, and Hansson and Helliwell, 1990) there is international convergence in the rate of growth of technical progress. We tested this assumption against the alternative of constant technical progress, especially in Helliwell and Chung (1991a, 1993) and Helliwell (1992b), and found significant rejection of the constant growth assumption.
6 The robustness of the conditional convergence result is confirmed by the sensitivity tests of Levine and Renelt (1992).
7 For examples, see Romer (1986, 1990a, 1990b) and Lucas (1988, 1990). Alternative endogenous growth models by Grossman and Helpman (1991) assume economies of scale and knowledge spillovers at the industry level, which has no necessary implications for returns to scale at the national level. See Helpman (1991) for a helpful survey.
8 In Helliwell et al. (1985) and Helliwell and Chung (1991b) for the G-7, in Helliwell and Chung (1991a) for nineteen industrial countries, and in Helliwell and Chung (1993) for nineteen industrial and eight Asian economies.
9 We have made use of a CES form, while they use Cobb–Douglas, but our elasticity of substitution is so close to 1.0 that our CES form has properties almost identical to the Cobb–Douglas. A potentially more important difference is that they account for international differences in human capital, while we did not do so in our earlier work.

10 The Solow residuals are obtained by inverting equation (1) to define a measured series for $A(t)$ using actual values for Y and K, and using the number of employees to represent the labour input HL.

11 Our results also showed rejection of long-term international equality of the levels of the efficiency indexes. Thus our experiments confirmed the Mankiw *et al.* hypothesis that there are likely to be continuing international differences in the levels of the efficiency index.

12 Our tests of the convergence model were against an alternative hypothesis of a country-specific constant rate of technical progress. The data reject even more strongly the assumption of an unchanging rate of technical progress that is the same in each country. We also found some evidence (in Helliwell and Chung, 1991a and Helliwell, 1992b) that the growth of productivity indexes was faster in countries which had the fastest rates of growth in their openness to international trade, as measured by the ratio of exports to GDP. Harrison (1991) and Ben-David (1991) also report evidence linking increased openness with faster growth.

13 An earlier paper (Helliwell, 1991) used the log of 1960 real GDP as the measure of scale, which gave smaller and less significant estimates of the scale effects. Backus *et al.* (1991) also use the log of initial GDP as their scale variable, and find no significant scale effects in the growth of GDP per capita (although they do find some scale effects in manufacturing). For an estimation covering a number of years, it makes a difference whether initial or average scale is used, and the theoretical preference must be for average scale, since it provides the appropriate discrete time analogue of a continuous time model in which the growth rate depends on the current relative scale. In addition, if there are errors of measurement in the initial scale, they will be correlated to some extent with initial real GDP per adult, which appears negatively in the dependent variable. This will cause the estimate of the scale effect to be biased downward. Using end-of-sample scale would have the opposite effect, so that using the sample average serves to eliminate this source of bias if the errors in measurement are of approximately the same relative size over the sample period.

14 Friedman (1992) and others have pointed out that measurement errors or reversible shocks affecting international differences in initial income could mean that some part of the significant negative coefficient on initial income could represent regression to a common mean rather than proving that even conditional average growth rates are higher in the poorer countries. Experiments designed to separate these two sources of convergence show that using instrumental variables or period-average values for income levels tends to reduce but not eliminate the evidence for conditional convergence. Evidence on the trends in the variances of per-capita GDP's is presented in Section III.

15 In an earlier version of this paper, distributed as NBER Working Paper No. 3948, the quartiles were defined by average rather than initial income, which gave rise to significantly lower constant terms in the poorer quartiles. Ranking by initial income, as is done here, avoids the potential sample selection bias that may arise from using average income.

16 If Hong Kong, Singapore and India are removed from the sample, the correlation between initial income and adjusted growth is -0.671 for the remaining countries.

17 The correlation between initial income and growth, after allowing for the estimated effects of other variables, is -0.417 for Africa, and 0.292 for Asia, compared to -0.823 for Latin America and -0.862 for the OECD.

18 Although the 1980s show some apparent lessening of the correlation between real incomes and real exchange rates.

19 The adjusted R^2 for the ninety-one-country equation is 0.531. The homogeneity of the slope coefficients and constant terms for Asia and the OECD is not rejected ($p = 0.33$), while similar restrictions are strongly rejected for Latin America ($p = 10^{-5}$) and for Africa ($p < 10^{-5}$).

20 De Long and Summers (1991) suggest that it may be important to separate the various types of investment, since they find equipment investment to have a much higher effect on growth than does other forms of fixed investment. They also note the importance of allowing for differences in the relative prices of investment goods. See also the results in Helliwell and Chung (1991a) comparing business, private and total capital.

21 As reported in Helliwell and Chung (1991a) and Helliwell (1992b).

22 Similar possibilities for productivity-enchancing trade growth are also noted by Rivera-Batiz and Romer (1991a, 1991b).

23 Growth differences among the Asian countries are considered further in Helliwell (1992), where several measures of openness are found to have explanatory power.

REFERENCES

Abramovitz, M. (1979) 'Rapid growth potential and its realization: the experience of capitalist economies in the postwar period', in E. Malinvaud (ed.), *Economic Growth and Resources*, London: Macmillan, 1–30.

—— (1990) 'The catch-up factor in postwar economic growth', *Economic Inquiry*: 1–18.

Alesina, A. and D. Rodrik (1991) 'Distributive polities and economic growth', CEPR Discussion Paper No. 565.

Backus, D. K., P. J. Kehoe and T. J. Kehoe (1991) 'In search of scale effects in trade and growth', Working Paper No. 451, Minneapolis, Federal Reserve Bank.

Balassa, B. (1964) 'The purchasing power parity doctrine: a reappraisal', *Journal of Political Economy* 72, 584–96.

Barro, R. J. (1991) 'Economic growth in a cross section of countries', *Quarterly Journal of Economics* 106, 407–44.

Barro, R. J. and X. Sala-i-Martín (1990) 'Economic growth and convergence across the United States', NBER Working Paper No. 3419.

Baumol, W. J. (1986) 'Productivity growth, convergence and welfare: what the long-run data show', *American Economic Review* 76, 1072–85.

Baumol, W. J., S. Blackman and E. N. Wolff (1989) *Productivity and American Leadership, The Long View*, Cambridge MA: MIT Press.

Baumol, W. J., and E. N. Wolff (1988) 'Productivity growth, convergence and welfare: reply', *American Economic Review* 78, 1155–9.

Ben-David, D. (1991) 'Equalizing exchange: a study of the effects of trade liberalization', NBER Working Paper No. 3706

Bhagwati, J. (1984) 'Why are services cheaper in poor countries?', *Economic Journal* 9, 279–86.

Brander, J. A. and S. Dowrick (1994) 'The role of fertility and population in economic growth', *Journal of Population Economics* 7, 1–25.

Chenery, H., S. Robinson and M. Syrquin (1986) *Industrialization and Growth: A Comparative Study*, Washington DC: The World Bank.

Dasgupta, P. (1991) 'Nutrition, non-convexities and redistribution policies', *Economic Journal* 101, 22–6.

De Long, J. B. (1988) 'Productivity growth, convergence and welfare: comment', *American Economic Review* 78, 1138–54.

De Long, J. B. and L. H. Summers (1991) 'Equipment investment and economic growth', *Quarterly Journal of Economics* 106, 445–502.

Dowrick, S. and D.-T. Nguyen (1989) 'OECD comparative economic growth 1950–85: catch-up and convergence', *American Economic Review* 79, 1010–30.

Dowrick, S. and N. Gemmell (1991) 'Industrialisation, catching up and economic growth: a comparative study across the world's capitalist economies', *Economic Journal* 101, 263–75.

Fischer, S. (1991) 'Growth, macroeconomics, and development', NBER Working Paper No. 3702.

Friedman, M. (1992) 'Do old fallacies never die?' *Journal of Economic Literature* 30, 2129–32.

Grossman, G. M. and E. Helpman (1991) *Innovation and Growth in the Global Economy*, Cambridge MA: MIT Press.

Gylfason, T. (1990) 'Inflation, growth and external debt: a review of the landscape', CEPR Discussion Paper No. 375.

Hansson, A., and J. Helliwell (1990) 'The evolution of income and competitiveness in the North Pacific Rim', in F. Langdon (ed.), *Canada and the Growing Presence of Asia*, Vancouver: Institute for Asian Research, pp. 17–40.

Harrison, A. (1991) 'Openness and growth: a time-series, cross-country analysis for developing countries', Policy Research Working Paper WPS809. Washington DC: World Bank.

Helliwell, John F. (1991) 'Are nations growing together or falling apart?' Mabel F. Timlin Lecture, University of Saskatchewan, Saskatoon, 8 April 1991.

—— (1992a) 'International growth linkages: evidence from Asia and the OECD', NBER Working Paper No. 4245, Cambridge: National Bureau of Economic Research.

—— (1992b) 'Trade and technical progress', NBER Working Paper No. 4226.

Helliwell, John F., and Alan Chung (1991a) 'Macroeconomic convergence: international transmission of growth and technical progress', in P. Hooper and J. D. Richardson (eds.), *International Economic Transactions: Issues in Measurement and Empirical Research*, Chicago: University of Chicago Press, pp. 388–436.

—— (1991b) 'Globalization, convergence, and the prospects for economic growth', in J. Cornwall (ed.), *The Capitalist Economies: Prospects for the 1990s*, London: Elgar.

—— (1991c) 'Are bigger countries better off?' in R. Broadway, T. Courchene and D. Purvis (eds.), *Economic Dimensions of Constitutional Change*, Kingston: John Deutsch Institute, pp. 346–67.

—— (1992) 'Aggregate productivity and growth in an international comparative setting', in B. G. Hickman (ed.), *International Productivity and Competitiveness*, New York: Oxford University Press, pp. 49–79.

(1993) 'Tri-polar growth and real exchange rates: how much can be explained by convergence?' in L. R. Klein (ed.), *A Quest for a More Stable Economic System*, New York: Kluwer, pp. 151–205.

Helliwell, John F., Peter Sturm and Gerard Salou (1985) 'International comparison of the sources of the productivity slowdown 1973–1982', *European Economic Review* **28**, 157–91.

Helpman, E. (1991) 'Endogenous macroeconomic growth theory', NBER Working Paper No. 3869.

Heston, A. and R. Summers (1988), 'What have we learned about prices and quantities from international comparisons: 1987', *American Economic Review* **78**(2), 467–73.

Hill, P. (1986) 'International price levels and purchasing power parities', *OECD Economic Studies* **6**, 133–59.

Kravis, I. B., A. Heston and R. Summers (1983) 'The share of services in economic growth', in F. G. Adams and B. G. Hickman (eds.), *Global Econometrics: Essays in Honour of Lawrence R. Klein*, Cambridge MA: MIT Press.

Kravis, I. B. and R. E. Lipsey (1983) *Toward an Explanation of National Price Levels*, Princeton Studies in International Finance No. 52, Princeton: International Finance Section.

Landes, D. (1990) 'Why are we so rich and they so poor?' *American Economic Review* **80**(2), 1–13.

Levine, R. and D. Renelt (1992) 'A sensitivity analysis of cross-country growth regression', *American Economic Review* **82**, 942–63.

Lucas, R. E. (1988) 'On the mechanics of economic development', *Journal of Monetary Economics* **22**, 3–32.

(1990) 'Why doesn't capital flow from rich to poor countries?' *American Economic Review* **90**(2), 92–6.

Maddison, A. (1982) *Phases of Capitalist Development*, Oxford: Oxford University Press.

Mankiw, G., D. Romer and D. Weil (1992) 'A contribution to the empirics of economic growth', *Quarterly Journal of Economics* **107**, 407–37.

Rivera-Batiz, L. A. and P. Romer (1991a) 'Economic integration and endogenous growth', *Quarterly Journal of Economics* **106**, 531–6.

(1991b) 'International trade with endogenous technical change', *European Economic Review* **34**, 971–1004.

Romer, P. M. (1986) 'Increasing returns and long-run growth', *Journal of Political Economy* **94**, 1002–37.

(1989) 'Human capital and growth: theory and evidence', NBER Working Paper No. 3173.

(1990a) 'Are non-convexities important for understanding growth?' *American Economic Review* **80**(2), 97–103.

(1990b) 'Endogenous technological change', *Journal of Political Economy* **98**, S71–S102.

Rostow, W. W. (1978) *The World Economy: History and Prospect*, Austin: University of Texas.

Solow, R. M. (1956) 'A contribution to the theory of economic growth', *Quarterly Journal of Economics* **70**, 65–94.

(1957) 'Technical change and the aggregate production function', *Review of Economics and Statistics* **39**, 312–20.

Summers, R. and A. Heston (1988) 'A new set of international comparisons of real product and prices: estimates for 130 countries, 1950 to 1985', *Review of Income and Wealth* **34**, 1–25.

Discussion

FABRIZIO ZILIBOTTI

The contribution of J. F. Helliwell and A. Chung (HC) is twofold. On the one hand, they perform a detailed sample stability test of the results of Mankiw *et al.* (1992) (MRW), by dividing the world sample by region and by groups of countries of similar income level. The results are interesting and self-explanatory, so we will not add anything to them. On the other hand, they introduce and test the hypothesis that a scale variable, measured by the absolute GDP, is a significant determinant of growth rates which is omitted in MRW analysis. My comments will focus on this aspect of the work.

I will discuss two issues. The first is about formal aspects of the estimation procedure. I will argue that the methodology used is correct under certain theoretical assumptions and will formulate a simple explicit model coherent with them. However, if we want to account for savings decisions which reflect a process of economic maximization and maintain the specific kind of technical change postulated by the authors, the estimation methodology becomes incorrect. In this aspect, the work of HC is less robust than MRW, to which my criticism does not apply. The second is about the economic implications of measuring the effects of increasing returns by GDP levels of countries and use of this variable for inference. My viewpoint is that the approach of HC takes too literally and naively the predictions of modern growth literature. The main reason is that they overemphasize the role of country borders in determining the size of markets and of potential exploitation of scale economies. I conclude by suggesting that the statistical relation between growth rates and the scale variable found by the authors may be explained by various types of deficiencies of the model used rather than the increasing returns effect postulated by HC.

1 On the robustness of the methodology

I start the analysis by briefly summarizing the basic model of MRW and HC. I consider, for the sake of simplicity, a version of the Solow–MRW model with physical capital only. The growth rate of population is n and the depreciation rate is δ. Capital letter terms denote absolute levels; lower case terms denote per-capita variables. The notation used is standard. Let the production function be

$$y_t = A_t k_t^\alpha, \alpha < 1 \tag{1}$$

The accumulation of capital is described by the following dynamic equation

$$\frac{\dot{k_t}}{k_t} = \left(\frac{I_t}{K_t} - (\delta + n) \right) = (\delta + n) \left(\frac{I_t}{Y_t} \frac{A_t}{\delta + n} k_t^{\alpha - 1} - 1 \right) \tag{2}$$

Then, define

$$k_t^* = \left(\frac{I_t}{Y_t} \frac{A_t}{\delta + n} \right)^{\frac{1}{1-\alpha}} \tag{3}$$

whence

$$\frac{\dot{k_t}}{k_t} = (\delta + n) \left(\frac{k_t}{k_t^*} - 1 \right) \tag{4}$$

Also, call $y_t^* = A_t(k_t^*)^\alpha$. Using MRW procedure, based on the linearization of (4) in the neighbourhood of k_t^*

$$logy_t - logy_0 = (1 - e^{-\lambda t})(logy_t^* - logy_0) \tag{5}$$

where $\lambda = (\delta + n)(1 - \alpha)$. (5) can be written as

$$logy_t - logy_0 = (1 - e^{-\lambda t})$$
$$\left(\frac{\alpha}{1 - \alpha} log \frac{I_t}{y_t} - \frac{\alpha}{1 - \alpha} log(\delta + n) - logy_0 + \frac{1}{1 - \alpha} log A_t \right) \tag{6}$$

Equation (6) is reconciled with MRW (p. 423, equation (16)) by assuming that (i) savings are a constant fraction of income (i.e., $\frac{I_t}{Y_t} = s$) and (ii) productivity grows according to an exogenous exponential law of motion (i.e., $A_t = A_0 e^{gt}$). Equation (6) plus (i) and (ii) is viable for OLS estimation, and the results are known from MRW.

HC (equation (4)) maintain (i) and modify (ii), by assuming that A_t is an increasing function of the absolute GDP. To illustrate the point, let us parametrize such relation as follows

$$log\ A_t = log\ A_0 + g\ log\ Y_t \qquad (7)$$

By plugging in (7) into (6) we obtain the equation that is estimated by HC using OLS. There is no objection to this methodology as far as we maintain the assumption (i) of exogenous saving rates. When savings decisions are treated as the result of a process of economic maximization, however, income and capital accumulation turn out to be simultaneously determined. The important difference between the two models is that the standard neoclassical model predicts long-run constant saving rates, where HC predicts a falling capital–output ratio and no long-run stationary equilibrium saving rate. So, MRW can justify the treatment of the saving rate as an exogenous regressor by appealing to the asymptotic result and assuming that observed $\frac{I}{Y}$s proxy long-run saving rates and legitimately treat them as exogenous regressors. The same is not true in HC, in which the use of OLS is not justified in the fully microfounded version of the model.

2   Is limited market size a problem for Luxembourg?

The second part of my comments will focus on the economic plausibility of the story which the authors implicitly tell us. Most of the endogenous growth literature ends up with identifying some source of economies of scale in the economy. In order for the growth process to be self-sustained in the presence of a fixed stock of non-reproducible resources, there must exist some economic force that prevents productivity from falling as the economy grows. There are plenty of theoretical considerations that motivate the attempt to assess empirically the effects of scale economies on growth. The first generation of models with externalities in the accumulation of physical capital (Romer, 1986, among the others) is the most obvious reference. Models with endogenous innovation (Romer, 1990; Rivera-Batiz and Romer, 1991) also exhibit non-convexities in the production function of designs. Fixed costs in opening markets for intermediation or financial market are a crucial feature of another cohort of endogenous growth models (Saint-Paul, 1992; Zilibotti, 1994).

However, I believe that two factors should be born in mind when moving from theory to empirical analysis:

(a) The adoption of national boundaries as the limit to the exploitation of the economies of scale is not a convincing choice. As the work of Rivera-Batiz and Romer (1991) correctly emphasizes, one should consider the degree of market integration of an economy in an international environment, in order to assess the real potential for the exploitation of economies of scale. The experiences of a number of medium-large semi-industrialized inward-oriented countries seems to be characterized by more severe market size constraints than those of many small export-oriented economies.

(b) Degree of openness apart, the scale variable that matters does not need to be the GDP level. The choice of the right state variable depends very much on what force we believe represents the engine of growth. If growth is driven by the production of ideas rather than of goods, and only human capital enters the production function of the activity of innovation, for instance, the relevant state variable is the size of the educated labour force. In this case absolute GDP can be relatively uninformative.

If we choose too literal an approach to accounting for economies of scale in empirical work, we run into some curious paradoxes. Let us consider data for the year 1985. I have grouped three sets of countries according to the criterion of similarity in income level, obtaining:

Group 1: Gabon, Ghana, Malawi, Mali, Niger, Cyprus, Luxembourg, Haiti, Honduras, Jamaica, Papua New Guinea;
Group 2: Burma, Ireland, Ecuador;
Group 3: Algeria, Egypt, Nigeria, Hong Kong, Iran, Austria, Denmark, Finland, Norway, Chile.

Is there any plausible story which suggests to us that there are some relevant structural similarities between countries within each different group that help make inferences about growth? We can hardly believe that there are interesting common features between Luxembourg and Haiti. Nor could we avoid paradoxes by looking at countries belonging to the same continent; think of the case of Iran and Hong Kong, or of Gabon and Niger. We could grant that GDP levels can capture something about the dimension of the internal market. However, in order to obtain a genuine market size effect, the authors should control in the regression for the degree of openness of the different economies.

Given our skeptical arguments, how do we interpret the finding that GDP levels are significantly correlated with average growth rates in HC regressions? We propose two explanations of the result, being aware that neither of them is conclusive:

(1) The scale variable captures the effect of omitted variables, whose explanatory power in growth regressions is known from the existing literature.
(2) The correlation is due to reverse causation. Countries with high growth rates in the last twenty-five years tend to have high income levels in the final year. Since HC use time-average GDP levels calculated throughout the period 1960–85, rather than, as one would expect, initial year estimates, they capture something of this type of correlation.

To check (1) we add to the explanatory variables the ratio of government consumption to GDP, Barro's index of political instability and the proxy for intermediation costs constructed in Zilibotti (1993). The role of the first two variables has been stressed by Barro (1991); the third variable is discussed in my referred work, which also provides a description of the data used. I suspect that the scale variable, which is negatively correlated with all three additional variables, can capture some effects of the omitted variables. The results are not conclusive. The three additional variables have, as expected, negative and significant signs. The scale variable of HC loses part of its explanatory power, but has still a high p-value (0.92).

Point (2) is rather delicate. I do not find convincing the motivation given by HC (Note 13) to their choice of using yearly average rather than initial year observations for the constructed scale variable. If the motivation is to correct for error of measurement issues, they could have used yearly averages of the pre-sample period 1955–60 (or, in the case of limited availability of earlier data, averages of the first five years in the sample). I believe that right-hand side variables should be, as far as possible, initial period values, to minimize the issue of reciprocal causation. My suspicion is reinforced by the following observation. If we add to the list of regressors the (log of) initial absolute GDP, its explanatory power is almost null (a finding already known from previous literature, as acknowledged by the authors (Note 13). On the other hand, the explanatory power increases as we take more recent observations, and becomes a maximum when the log of the final year GDP is considered. In conclusion, it seems that the average variable used by HC is significant insofar that it is correlated with observations for recent years, which are precisely those for which the reverse causation criticism looks most severe.

REFERENCES

Barro, R (1991) 'Economic growth in a cross-section of countries', *Quarterly Journal of Economics* **106**, 407–43.

Mankiw, G. N., D. Romer and D. N. Weil (1992) 'A contribution to the empirics of economic growth', *Quarterly Journal of Economics* **107**, 407–37.

Rivera-Batiz, L. and P. Romer (1991) 'Economic integration and endogenous growth', *Quarterly Journal of Economics* **106**, 531–55.

Romer, P. M. (1986) 'Increasing returns and long-run growth', *Journal of Political Economy* **94**, 1002–37.

(1990) 'Endogenous technical change', *Journal of Political Economy* **98**, S71–102.

Saint-Paul, G. (1992) 'Technological choice, financial markets and economic development', *European Economic Review* **36**, 763–81.

Zilibotti, F. (1993) 'Endogenous growth and intermediation: an empirical analysis', London School of Economics, mimeo.

(1994) 'Endogenous growth and intermediation in an "Archipelago" economy', *Economic Journal* **104**, 462–73.

Part Four
Open economy macro and adjustment in the south

6 Analysing external adjustment in developing countries: a macroeconomic framework

CHRIS ALLEN, T.G. SRINIVASAN
and DAVID VINES

1 Introduction

In this paper we describe an approach to macroeconomic analysis for less-developed countries (LDCs). The paper presents the theoretical underpinnings of a series of regional models which a group of us have been building over a number of years, for the purpose of studying macroeonomic interactions between developed and developing countries. These models are for Latin America, Africa, Asian Newly Industrialized Economies and Other Asia. The paper also describes the most interesting features of the results which have been obtained from estimating these models on annual regional data.[1] It then presents some results of (stylized) simulations using them, which include the study of possible adjustment responses to external shocks.

Our method of presentation is deliberately intuitive. Our presentation is focused around a small analytical representation of the structure of the models, and the stability properties and comparative statics of this are presented. Econometric estimates are presented in the context of this analytical representation. The discussion is then used to illuminate two simulations of the models themselves in response to external shocks.

The paper proceeds as follows. In Section 2 we discuss possible approaches to LDC macroeconomics. In Section 3 we present our analytical representation of the models, and describe our empirical results for four regions. Section 4 describes the stability and comparative statics of the analytical version of the model and briefly discusses the theory of economic policy. Section 5 contains some illustrative simulations with the model and explores responses, including policy responses, to external shocks. Section 6 presents conclusions and describes plans for future work.

2   Approaches to LDC macroeconomics

2.1   Background

Our approaches to less-developed country macroeconomics attempts to synthesize three strands in the literature.

The first of these is the broadly eclectic modern approach to the macroeconomics of advanced countries, as described for example by Blinder (1988) and Gordon (1990), and implemented in, say, the OECD sectors of the IMF's Multimod model (IMF, 1990). This provides a starting point, against which features particular to less-developed countries can be compared. This tradition originated from Hicks' *IS–LM* formulation of Keynesian macroeconomics, but has gone very far beyond it. The following four features are of particular importance: (i) the interconnection of personal wealth with consumption decisions; (ii) the interconnection of capital accumulation with aggregate supply; (iii) the emergence of inflation as a result of divergences of demand from a fully specified natural rate of output which is endogenous as a result of capital accumulation and of movements in the real exchange rate; and (iv) the explicit modelling of the asset creation that emerges from the government budget deficit and from the current account of the balance of payments, together with the imposition of a solvency requirement which prevents these flows accumulating without limit.[2,3]

The second strand is the macroeconomics which has been practised by development economists. The history of development economics suggests that the appropriate way to come to the macroeconomics of developing countries (or regions) is not through *IS–LM*. Rather, the two central pieces of analytical apparatus have been the monetary approach to the balance of payments (popularized by the IMF, 1987) and the two-gap growth model (popularized by the World Bank, 1990). In the monetary approach to the balance of payments, the price level and the balance of payments are the two key endogenous variables, and they emerge jointly with the financial flows caused by the government budget deficit. In the two-gap model, the growth rate and the balance of payments are the two key endogenous variables, and emerge as a consequence of domestic and foreign savings gaps. These two models were synthesized in the late 1980s by Khan and Montiel (1989), and Khan et al. (1990), producing a very useful pedagogical analysis of 'Adjustment with Growth' in which all three – the price level, the balance of payments and the growth rate – are endogenous.[4] That work suggests that points (i) and (ii) above are particularly important for less-developed countries and, of course, that the evolution of wealth and capital must be treated as interdependent in any full description of macroeconomic processes.[5]

Third, the work of Bacha (1990), Taylor (1990, 1991), Ros (1991) and others has developed 'structuralist macroeconomics' into a spate of 'three-gap' models. These are 'gaps' for domestic savings, foreign savings and government savings: the analysis involves a consideration of how the economy adjusts to close these gaps. Such exercises emphasize, albeit in a slightly unconventional way, the importance of all of points (i) to (iv) above.

2.2   Our approach

What we have done can be viewed as a step towards integrating the insights of Khan *et al.* (1990) and Taylor *et al.* into mainstream macroeconomics.

We have taken the financial asset accumulation and the capital accumulation processes on which they focus, and put them at the core of our analysis. This means that, unlike the original *IS–LM* analysis, which holds financial assets constant, and abstracts altogether from capital accumulation, our model is explicitly dynamic from the beginning. Also, unlike the *IS–LM* system, interest rates are not endogenously determined within our LDC regions; rather they are driven by movements in world money market interest rates. The reason for this is our assumption that these economies operate a fixed nominal exchange rate regime.[6]

Our work has then gone on to graft the above synthesized approach to aggregate demand onto a fully explicit model of the supply side, along the lines of Bruno and Sachs (1985) and Jackman *et al.* (1991), which contains a non-accelerating inflation rate level of unemployment (NAIRU) that is affected by the real exchange rate and driven by capital accumulation.

The resulting model is one in which there is sluggish adjustment in the short run, with output determined by demand. In the long run, flexible prices and supply-constrained output are assumed. Both demand and supply are influenced by asset accumulation.

2.3   External shocks and adjustment policy in developing countries

Our work synthesizing these three strands of theoretical literature has a practical purpose. This is to produce a framework which can be used to investigate the consequences of external shocks and, following on from this, to understand how policies might be designed to cope with them. There is, of course, a wealth of literature on this subject: Corden (1993),

Khan and Montiel (1989), and Taylor (1990) provide helpful surveys from three contrasting points of view. Our framework stands out from this literature: by specifying a richer supply side, by allowing for wealth effects, and by fully investigating the stability of adjustment processes.

Outcomes for output, inflation and external balance are investigated 'open-loop' (i.e. without policy response). Time profiles of outcomes in both the short run and the long run are analysed, both analytically and using our estimated models. There is also a sketch of 'closed-loop' policy reaction in response to an external disturbances, using our estimated models. We find that, following a negative external shock and in the absence of policy response, there is a 'cumulative collapse' of output. In such a process, a reduction of exports leads to lower output, lower investment, a lower capital stock and so to output being lower still: a collapse of both demand and supply. We show that this is not actually dynamically unstable, a feature shared by our empirical models. But even in the absence of actual instability, this 'collapse multiplier', for want of a better term, is large.[7]

3   Model specification

Our models of Latin America, Africa and the NIEs and Other Asia[8] are all fully specified macroeconomic models, containing some forty equations, comparable in size to those for the G-7 countries in the UK global econometric model, GEM. They include a fully specified income–expenditure process (i.e., a demand side), a supply side, a foreign trade sector and balance-of-payments and government accounts. In line with the discussion above, amongst the distinctive features of the models are the presence of real balance effects on consumption, the determination through capital accumulation and the supply side of an endogenous 'natural rate' of output, the integration of the government budget deficit and foreign exchange reserves with the money supply process, and, where appropriate, the enforcement of a national external solvency constraint by means of a government fiscal rule. Our research has highlighted a number of structural differences between the regions, an understanding of which is helpful in interpreting their different responses to shocks.[9]

In presenting each part of the model we will first describe the equations estimated, then explain our analytical representation of these, and finally discuss noteworthy empirical results.

In what follows, all variables appear as deviations from an initial equilibrium. Prices appear in logs, but flow quantities (and stocks) are represented in absolute levels.[10]

3.1   Aggregate demand

In the empirical models there are separate equations for consumption, investment and export and import volumes; real net exports add to domestic demand to determine GDP.

The *consumption* function contains real income[11] (with an adjustment in the empirical model for changes in the terms of trade) and also a wealth effect driven by the accumulation of financial wealth. The latter is modelled as the accumulation of money, M2, as discussed below. *Investment* expenditure is determined by a stock adjustment process based on a neoclassical demand for capital function (see below). The desired capital stock is a function of output and the cost of capital. New investment is a lagged adjustment process to the desired capital stock. Because domestic interest rates follow world ones (see below) there is a strong negative effect of world interest rates on domestic investment. Gross investment includes an allowance for depreciation. Our treatment of *international trade* is quite conventional: export volumes depend on export markets and on relative export prices (export prices themselves depend on competitors' export prices and on domestic absorption prices); import volumes depend on domestic output and the real exchange rate.

In our analytical model we summarize the determinants of aggregate demand in a single equation (Equation (1)). The Keynesian output multiplier is for simplicity supposed to be instantaneous[12] and is denoted by κ_1. This incorporates the effects of income on consumption[13], asset effects are captured by the real asset term, a. Investment is explicitly entered as the rate of change of the capital stock[14], dk/dt and the term g is government spending. Net exports are captured by the competitiveness term, which is reduced by higher domestic prices, p, but raised by higher world prices of imports, p^*, and by a depreciation of the currency, which is represented by a *rise* in the exchange rate, e. Net exports are also an increasing function of world trade, z, and of relative world prices (competitors' export prices relative to world prices of imports, $q^* - p^*$).[15] The effect of output on imports, μy, is captured within the value of the multiplier, κ_1

$$y = \kappa_1 \left[z + \beta_1(e + p^* - p) + \beta_2 a + \dot{k} + g + \beta_3(q^* - p^*) \right] \qquad (1)$$

The most significant empirical differences between the models on the demand side appear in the trade-related equations. The world *income* elasticity of demand for NIE exports appears to be much higher than that for Latin American and African exports. (Some of this difference may be spurious, for reasons discussed in Muscatelli *et al.* (1990, 1992) and Krugman (1989), and elsewhere in the present volume.) The relevant *price* elasticities also appear to differ greatly between the regions: price elasticities of demand and supply for NIE exports appear to be much higher than those for Latin America, which, in turn, are higher than those for Africa. Nevertheless, for all these regions a real devaluation appears to lead to an improved trade balance, in that favourable volume effects outweigh any terms-of-trade loss; the relevant elasticity showing the effect on the trade balance of such an improvement in international competitiveness is 5 in the NIEs, as opposed to 2 in Latin America, and only 0.3 in Africa.

We have explored the overall properties of aggregate demand determination in the models when our estimated equations are brought together. Partial simulations were performed – with all prices held constant – of the response to an increase in government spending. The multiplier rises gradually to a value of between 1.3 and 1.6 for all regions.[16]

3.2   Aggregate supply

Our empirical implementation of the supply side consists of two equations: for prices and for the real wage.[17]

Prices are a mark-up on marginal costs, which are determined by wages, import prices, and the output–capital ratio.[18] This formulation can be derived from a production function showing the implied real wage which a profit-maximizing representative firm would pay at various levels of output, given the capital stock. It captures the 'wedge' effect on the mark-up caused by a rise in import prices. Admittedly it is unable to distinguish channels of influence coming through higher prices of intermediate inputs (e.g. oil) from effects coming from more expensive final goods imports (e.g. imported capital goods).[19] But – as we see below – the approach does capture the overall macroeconomic effects of higher import prices. This treatment also has the property that a rise in output, or a fall in capital, *ceteris paribus*, leads to an increase in the mark-up of prices over wages.[20] The equation for *wages* is formulated, a la Layard and Nickell (1992), in terms of a real wage target (i.e. for nominal wages relative to the CPI where the latter includes any effects of import prices) with an output term which is also affected by productivity growth.[21] Estimation of both the wage equation and the price equation allowed for lags in adjustment.

This approach implies a long-run equilibrium level of aggregate supply, corresponding to the natural rate of unemployment or NAIRU. As is familiar, this aggregate supply is a positive function of the capital stock[22] and a negative function of the real exchange rate (defined as the real domestic currency price of imports) – as a result of the wedge effect. In the estimated models there is the possibility of both sluggish adjustment of nominal wages (due to a non-clearing labour market) and sluggish adjustment of prices (due to menu costs, strategic interaction, etc).

In our analytical model we summarize this two-equation system by equation (2).

$$\dot{p} = \psi \left[e + p^* - p + \alpha_1 (\alpha_2 y - k) \right] \; , \; \alpha_2 > 1 \tag{2}$$

The term inside the square brackets can be interpreted as the aggregate supply equation, in which supply is a positive function of the capital stock and a negative function of the real exchange rate, $e + p^* - p$. Notice that a unit increase in capital will not cause an equiproportionate increase in output because of the existence of a labour constraint.[23] Equation (2), by setting ψ at less than infinity, explicitly allows for the economy to be off its supply curve as a result of sluggish price adjustment. But it implicitly assumes instant adaptation of wages, which is not very realistic but is assumed in our analytical model for tractability. As a result, those short-run 'Keynesian' or non-market-clearing features which we display below come from this product market rigidity, whilst those in the estimated models come from both labour and goods markets.

Our econometric modelling has uncovered profound differences in the supply curves of the economies of the various regions. In Latin America the supply curve is very steep (i.e. α is very large in Equation (2)). This appears to be the case for three reasons. First, this region appears to have the sharpest capital constraint, in the sense that diminishing returns to capital appear to set in more rapidly in this region as the demand for output rises relative to the capital stock.[24] Second, real wages appear to respond more sharply to output in Latin America than elsewhere. Third, the region is the most closed, so that changes in the 'wedge' between the price of imports and home produced goods can perform less of a function in facilitating an increase in output. By contrast, as we might expect, increases in demand call forth the greatest increase in supply for the NIE regions, i.e., the supply function for the NIEs is the flattest of all of the regions. This is because diminishing returns set in only slowly, as real labour costs per unit of output appear to be independent of output (due to induced productivity improvements) and because of the openness of these economies.

Our modelling has also shown that the degree of sluggishness of price and wage adjustment differs as between the three regions. In Africa, the Asian NIEs and other Asia, a considerable increase in output is enabled by an increase in the inflation rate ('surprise inflation'), and roughly half of this effect survives after three years. This corresponds to a small value of the coefficient ψ in equation (2). In the Latin American continent, with its inflationary experience, only an *increase in the rate of increase* of the inflation rate is sufficiently 'surprising' to provoke any increase in output. Also the effect is extremely small, and it is nearly all gone within a year.[25] In effect, for Latin America, ψ approximates to infinity.

We have simulated our supply-side systems empirically. Consider a permanent exogenous increase in output, with the capital stock fixed. Marginal costs rise and so prices increase. With real wage resistance, nominal wages rise along with prices. If the *nominal exchange rate* is fixed, domestic prices will rise relative to import prices, increasing the real exchange rate. We find the size of this effect accords closely with conventional numbers from OECD models for Africa and for other Asia: a 1 per cent increase in output requires an appreciation of the real exchange rate of approximately 3 per cent.[26] For Latin America the figure is an increase of 6 per cent, two-thirds of which occurs within two years. By contrast, for the Asian NIEs the increase is tiny: less than 0.2 per cent. These large differences occur for reasons which have been discussed above. If instead the *real exchange rate* is fixed, inflation must continually rise in order to depress real wages by the amount necessary to call forth the higher output, and here the differences between the models are even more marked. In Latin America the requirement is huge: a second difference in the inflation rate of *55 per cent per annum*. It is the huge size of this number, and the fact that the associated short-run adjustment dynamics of supply are mainly completed within a year, that leads us to neglect inflationary surprises by letting ψ go to infinity for Latin America in equation (2) in such an 'un-Keynesian' manner. For the Asian NIEs, by contrast, when this experiment is performed the price level rises by only 2 percentage points in *ten years*. The other economies lie in between.

3.3   *Investment and the evolution of capital*

As already discussed, investment generates a gradual adjustment of the capital stock to a level depending on the cost of capital. Domestic interest rates, r, are linked to foreign interest rates, r^*, through arbitrage, but that does not of itself tie down the cost of capital which will also depend on domestic inflation.[27] We therefore represent the investment function as

$$\dot{k} = \phi \left[y - k - \epsilon (r^* - \dot{p} + \dot{e}) \right] \tag{3}$$

We have explored empirically the influence of the capital stock adjustment process on aggregate demand determination, again within the context of fixed-price partial simulations (in which, *inter alia*, wealth effects on consumption are also suppressed). The result for Latin America is long cycles of multiplier–accelerator interaction with a periodicity of eleven years; for other regions these fluctuations are much more damped. The full multiplier converges to a long-run value of about 1.6 for Latin America.

3.4   The evolution of financial wealth

Domestic debt   Equation (4) represents the change in nominal debt of the government: the final term shows interest receipts on foreign reserves.[28] The empirical models include the necessary fully specified set of government accounts, whose principal effect is to make tax revenues and asset creation endogenous[29] for given tax rates.[30]

$$\dot{h} = -\tau y + g - r^* s \tag{4}$$

Reserves   Changes in reserves finance changes in the basic balance of the balance of payments. The capital account, including capital flight, is neglected. We also abstract from revaluations of reserves caused by exchange rate changes. Thus the change in the nominal value of reserves may be written as net exports plus debt interest, $r^* s$. Most of the determinants of net exports have already been identified in equation (1) as components of aggregate demand; from these we must subtract the effects of output on imports, μy.

$$\dot{s} = z + \beta_1(e + p^* - p) + \beta_3(q^* - p^*) - \mu y + r^* s \tag{5}$$

The empirical model includes a fully specified model of the balance-of-payments accounts[31]; interest and amortization payments on foreign debt are included as well as service transactions.

Money and wealth   The term showing the influence on consumption of the real stock of domestic assets is proxied, both here and in the empirical model, by the real money stock,[32] whose evolution we now discuss. The nominal money supply (M2 in the empirical model) is endogenous, and is dependent on the creation of base money. Base money in turn depends on domestic credit and foreign exchange reserves. Only a proportion of the government deficit, dh/dt, and of changes in reserves, ds/dt, are assumed to be monetized, the proportions being based on historical experience. We thus write the creation of nominal money as a function of the creation of nominal financial assets

$$\dot{m} = \eta \, (\dot{s} + \dot{h}) \tag{6}$$

The real money supply we write, in linearized form, as

$$a = m - \bar{a}p \tag{7}$$

4   The full model

4.1   The setting

We now consider how the model behaves with given policy settings. By 'given policy settings' we first mean fixed values for government spending, g, and tax rates, τ. Also the nominal exchange rate, e, is fixed, and as a result, by a standard small country assumption, so is the nominal interest rate, at the world level, r^*. In the corresponding 'open-loop' (i.e., uncontrolled) exercises with the empirical model the nominal exchange rate is pegged at baseline values against the US dollar, and nominal interest rates are fixed at the US rate of interest (there are no effects on interest rates from domestic capital markets). Taken together, these assumptions mean that, in such open-loop simulations, the inflation rate is under loose control; as a result of the fixed exchange rate peg it cannot wander very far from the world rate. But the trade balance is not, because nothing, in general, prevents exogenous fiscal policy settings from being inconsistent with such balance. As a result sustained trade deficits are possible, and these would cause an ever-increasing deficit on the balance of payments on current account as a result of mushrooming debt interest payments. And of course output is not under control: it is whatever emerges from the intersection of demand and supply.

The behaviour of the full model, in such a setting, is substantially different from that of a conventional macroeconomic model of an industrialized economy. The reasons for the difference include: the particular manner in which asset effects influence model behaviour; the fixity, rather than floating, of nominal exchange rates; and the exogeneity of nominal interest rates, and – for Latin America – the absence of even short-run effects of inflationary surprises on output.

We first analyse the stability of the evolution of the three dynamic state variables (nominal assets, the price level, and physical capital). We may call the short run the time period before any of them have moved significantly; the long run that period in which adjustment is complete. Such stability analysis is helpful for analysing the evolution of the empirical model, in which full adjustment to equilibrium requires upwards of fifteen years (a not unsurprising finding).[33]

4.2 Stability

We collect the equations of the system together to produce a set of four equations in four unknowns:[34] three dynamic equations for the evolution of prices, p, nominal financial assets, m, and capital, k, and a non-dynamic equation for the determination of output, y

$$\dot{p} = \psi[\alpha_1(\alpha_2 y - k) - p], \quad \alpha_2 > 1 \tag{8}$$

$$\dot{m} = \eta\,[-\beta_1 p - (\mu + \tau)y\,] \tag{9}$$

$$\dot{k} = \phi\,[\,y - k - \epsilon(r^* - \dot{p} + \dot{e})\,] \tag{10}$$

$$y = \kappa_1\,[-\beta_1 p + \beta_2(m - \bar{a}p) + \dot{k}\,] \tag{11}$$

We then substitute for output to obtain a set of three simultaneous differential equations showing the evolution of prices, real assets and capital. Straightforward manipulation reveals the following two necessary and sufficient stability conditions on asset-accumulation processes in the model

(i) $(1 - \phi\kappa_1) > 0$.

This requires that the conventional multiplier–accelerator interaction not be instantaneously explosive.

(ii) $1 - \phi\kappa_1 - \phi\kappa_1\psi\epsilon\alpha_1\alpha_2 > 0$.

This is equivalent to a condition that ϵ should not be too large (i.e. $\epsilon < \frac{1-\phi\kappa_1}{\phi\kappa_1\psi\alpha_1\alpha_2}$). Such a condition prevents the stimulus to investment given by inflation – in the presence of fixed nominal interest rates – from being so large that it causes aggregate demand to explode.

These conditions are important for understanding the simulation properties of the empirical models. Multiplier–accelerator interactions initially created such large cycles in some of the models,[35] as to lead us to consider very carefully the estimation of the investment function. The second condition is familiar from the work of Cagan on monetary instability, popularized by Friedman's critique concerning the 'instability of the price level with fixed nominal interest rates'. It has been resuscitated in the 'Walters critique' of potential instability within the exchange rate mechanism of the European monetary system. That problem is extendable to all fixed exchange rate arrangements; it is likely to be very important for our Latin American model where price adjustment appears to be so fast.

Notice that these conditions are what is necessary to prevent an increase in aggregate demand causing an infinitely large immediate expansion.

Given that they hold the process of price adjustment and the processes of asset accumulation are all stable.[36]

4.3   Comparative statics

We examine responses of the model to exogenous external disturbances and to exogenous changes in policy: an increase in government expenditure, g, an increase in world trade, z, a rise in world prices, p^* (which is exactly analogous to a devaluation), and an upward step in world interest rates, r^*.[37] We also consider an increase in import prices unaccompanied by a rise in export prices (which is equivalent to a rise in world prices accompanied by an equiproportionate worsening in the terms of trade). We look at the consequences for output, y, for prices, p, and for the trade balance, j (which equals the first three terms of equation (5)).

We now split time further. For Africa, the NIEs and Other Asia, we have found empirically – as noted above – that price adjustment is not instantaneous. After any shock we may thus usefully consider, as well as the short run and the long run, an artificial 'intermediate run' in which nominal assets and capital remain exogenous, but during which prices have fully adjusted, and at the end of which we are therefore on the supply curve shown in equation (2).[38] For Latin America, however, prices adjust so fast that this procedure is empirically irrelevant. Instead we treat this intermediate run as the short run for that region.

Short run (not relevant for Latin America)   The short-run comparative statics for Africa and the two Asian regions are shown in Table 6.1. They are evaluated on the assumption that the three state variables, the price level, the capital stock and the real stock of financial assets are all held constant.

The results can be illustrated in inflation–output space as in Figure 6.1. The aggregate supply part of the model (equation (2)) provides a supply curve which is upward sloping in terms of the inflation rate rather than the price level (marked SC):

$$\dot{p} = \psi\left[e + p^* - p + \alpha_1(\alpha_2\, y - \bar{k})\right] \tag{12}$$

A demand curve may be obtained by combining the investment equation with the aggregate demand equation. Note that this curve (marked DC) will have a perverse positive slope owing to the 'Cagan' effect of an increase in expected inflation in reducing the cost of capital. The slope of

Table 6.1 Short-run comparative statics (excepting Latin America)

Effect of	$\dot{p}$	j	$\dot{k}$	$\dot{a}$	y
g	$\psi\alpha_1\alpha_2\Lambda\kappa_1$	$-\mu\Lambda\kappa_1$	$\phi\Lambda\kappa_1 + \phi\epsilon\psi\alpha_1\alpha_2\Lambda\kappa_1$	$\eta - \Omega\Lambda\kappa_1$	$\Lambda\kappa_1$
z	$\psi\alpha_1\alpha_2\Lambda\kappa_1$	$1 - \mu\Lambda\kappa_1 > 0$	$\phi\Lambda\kappa_1 + \phi\epsilon\psi\alpha_1\alpha_2\Lambda\kappa_1$	$\eta - \Omega\Lambda\kappa_1$	$\Lambda\kappa_1$
p^*	$\psi + \psi\alpha_1\alpha_2\Lambda\kappa_1(\beta_1 + \phi\epsilon\psi)$	$\beta_1 - \mu\Lambda\kappa_1(\beta_1 + \phi\epsilon\psi) > 0$	$\beta_1(\phi\Lambda\kappa_1 + \phi\epsilon\psi\alpha_1\alpha_2\Lambda\kappa_1)$ $+ \Lambda\phi\epsilon\psi$	$\beta_1\eta - \Omega\Lambda\kappa_1(\beta_1 + \phi)$	$\Lambda\kappa_1(\beta_1 + \phi\epsilon\psi)$
r^*	$-\psi\alpha_1\alpha_2\Lambda\kappa_1\phi\epsilon$	$\mu\Lambda\kappa_1\phi\epsilon$	$-\phi\epsilon\Lambda$	$\Omega\Lambda\kappa_1\phi\epsilon$	$-\Lambda\kappa_1\phi\epsilon$

Note: where $\Lambda = [1 - \phi\kappa_1 - \kappa_1\phi\epsilon\psi\alpha_1\alpha_2]^{-1}$ and $\Omega = \eta(\mu + \tau) + \bar{\alpha}\psi\alpha_1\alpha_2$.

this curve must be steeper than the supply curve for the determination of aggregate demand and for inflation to be 'stable within the short run'.[39]

$$y=[1-\phi\kappa_1]^{-1}[z+\beta_1(e+p^*-p)+\beta_2\bar{a}+g-\phi\kappa-\epsilon(r^*-\dot{p})] \tag{13}$$

The comparative statics are shown in Table 6.1. The multiplier (Λ) is determined by two basic components. The first is the conventional multiplier–accelerator effect; the second, more unusual term is attributable to the 'Cagan effect' of an increase in expected inflation in reducing the cost of capital; however this latter effect cannot be too large or the model will be unstable 'within the short run'. Note that the condition that $\Lambda > 0$ is one of the stability conditions discussed above.

The impact effect of an increase in government spending is to increase output through the conventional multiplier and to push up inflation. The increase in government spending will definitely worsen the trade balance. It will however stimulate investment: the first term here is the direct accelerator effect of increased output on investment; the second term is as a result of the impact of increased inflation lowering the cost of capital. The initial impact of government spending on real asset accumulation is not strictly signed, but it seems highly likely that it will result in a net accumulation of real assets. The first term here is the direct effect of the increased budget deficit on asset creation; the second term contains both the effect from leakages (higher imports and taxes) and the impact of increased inflation in reducing the real value of assets.

An increase in world trade will have similar effects to those of an increase in domestic government spending in the short run. It can easily be shown that increased world trade will definitely improve the trade balance if it is also the case that a devaluation will improve it; that is, dj/dz is positive if dj/dp^* is positive.

An increase in the foreign price level (or a devaluation of the exchange rate) has both a direct effect through raising the domestic price level and an effect through increasing output. Output expands both through direct improved competitiveness and by the mechanism of pushing up expected inflation. We assume that the Marshall–Lerner conditions hold and therefore the net effect of higher foreign prices will be to improve the trade balance. Higher foreign prices will stimulate domestic capital spending and are likely to result in a higher real stock of financial assets.

An increase in the international interest rate will reduce domestic output and investment and push down inflation (there are no negative supply-side effects from a lower capital stock in this short-run analysis). The trade balance will definitely improve. The stock of real assets will also increase: this is because lower inflation and economic activity both point in that direction; any effects in the opposite direction which might

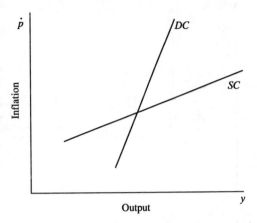

Figure 6.1   Short run (excepting Latin America)

be caused by additional interest payments abroad are not operative because of the way in which the government deficit is assumed to be financed.

Finally, the effect of a worsening of the terms of trade can be obtained by treating it as having the same effect as a rise in world prices and a reduction in world trade, z. All the positive effects of the former on output, inflation and the trade balance can be overturned if the latter effects are strong enough.

Intermediate run (in Latin America this is the short run)   The short-run comparative statics in the intermediate run after prices have adjusted (in Latin America this 'more or less immediately') are shown in Table 6.2. These are evaluated once again holding constant the capital stock and the nominal stock of financial assets, but now we allow full adjustment to take place in prices. This is equivalent to letting ψ be infinite in equation (2).

The situation can be illustrated in price–output space as in Figure 6.2. The supply curve is the long-run solution to the inflation equation (marked SS)

$$p = e + p^* + \alpha_1(\alpha_2 y - k) \tag{14}$$

The demand curve is again formed by substituting the investment equation into the demand equation (marked DD)

$$y = [1 - \phi\kappa_1]^{-1}[z + \beta_1(e + p^*) + \beta_2\bar{a} - (\beta_1 + \beta_2)p + g - \phi\bar{k} - \phi\epsilon r^*] \tag{15}$$

The multipliers now have three terms. The first is the conventional

Table 6.2 Intermediate-run comparative statics (short-run in Latin America)

Effect of	Effect on				
	y	$\dot{p}$	j	$\dot{k}$	$\dot{a}$
g	$\Gamma\kappa_1$	$\alpha_1\alpha_2\Gamma\kappa_1$	$-(\beta_1\alpha_1\alpha_2 + \mu)\Gamma\kappa_1$	$\phi\Gamma\kappa_1$	$\eta[1 - H\Gamma\kappa_1]$
z	$\Gamma\kappa_1$	$\alpha_1\alpha_2\Gamma\kappa_1$	$1-(\beta_1\alpha_1\alpha_2 + \mu)\Gamma\kappa_1$	$\phi\Gamma\kappa_1$	$\eta[1 - H\Gamma\kappa_1]$
p^*	$-\beta_2\Gamma\kappa_1$	$1 - \alpha_1\alpha_2\beta_2\Gamma\kappa_1 < 1$	$(\beta_1\alpha_1\alpha_2 + \mu)\beta_2\Gamma\kappa_1$	$-\phi\beta_2\Gamma\kappa_1$	$\eta H\beta_2\Gamma\kappa_1$
r^*	$-\phi_\epsilon\Gamma\kappa_1$	$-\alpha_1\alpha_2\phi_\epsilon\Gamma\kappa_1$	$(\beta_1\alpha_1\alpha_2 + \mu)\phi_\epsilon\Gamma\kappa_1$	$-\phi(\epsilon + \phi_\epsilon\Gamma\kappa_1)$	$\eta H\phi_\epsilon\Gamma\kappa_1$

Note: where $\Gamma = [1 - \phi\kappa_1 + \kappa_1\beta_1\alpha_1\alpha_2 + \kappa_1\beta_2\alpha_1\alpha_2]^{-1}$ and $H = \beta_1\alpha_1\alpha_2 + \mu + \tau$.

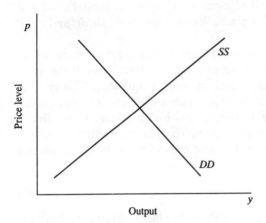

Figure 6.2   **Intermediate run (short run in Latin America)**

multiplier–accelerator term; the second is a term in competitiveness, which alters as the price level changes; the third is a term reflecting the real balance effects of an increase in the price level.

A rise in government spending increases output and prices as conventionally expected. The trade balance is worsened through lost competitiveness and higher domestic absorption. Investment is increased through the accelerator process. The effect of the government budget deficit is to increase the flow of nominal financial assets into the system. The impact of higher world trade is similar.

Increases in world prices have real effects – even although there is complete price flexibility – as a result of the erosion of asset values by the higher price level: output is reduced and prices rise by less than the international price level. The trade balance improves as a result of increased competitiveness and reduced absorption and nominal asset accumulation definitely *increases*.

An increase in world interest rates has a negative effect on output through a reduction in investment demand. Prices fall purely as a result of the demand effects (since the capital stock is constant in the short run). The trade balance improves and nominal financial asset accumulation definitely *increases*.

Finally, the effect of a worsening of the terms of trade can be obtained by treating it as having the same effect as a rise in world prices and a reduction in world trade, z. The negative effects on output of both of these events reinforce each other. Prices could fall if the demand effects outweighed the cost–push effects. The trade balance could go either way.

The long run   The long-run comparative statics are shown in Table 6.3. In the long run, we assume all adjustment in prices, the capital stock and real financial assets has taken place. We thus set dp/dt, dk/dt, and da/dt all equal to zero.

The results can be illustrated in capital stock–price space as in Figure 6.3. AS is the long-run aggregate supply curve, which is the result of the joint solution of the price and investment equations. This curve is upward sloping because of the labour supply constraint: a higher capital stock is associated with higher output and higher labour input: this is only forthcoming with higher real wages. That, in turn, requires a bigger import-price wedge, i.e. higher domestic prices (given the fixed nominal exchange rate). Its equation is

$$p = e + p^* + \alpha_1(\alpha_2 - 1)k - \alpha_1\alpha_2 er^* \tag{16}$$

AE represents the locus of asset equilibrium. This is solved from both the asset accumulation equation and the investment equation. It has a negative slope as higher prices result in loss of competitiveness and therefore require lower leakages, which will only happen if output and the capital stock are lower. The equation of AE is

$$p = e + p^* + \frac{z+g}{\beta_1} - \frac{\mu+\tau}{\beta_1}k \tag{17}$$

The actual level of assets is given by a third equation in prices and the capital stock (this is solved by inverting the output equation to solve for the stock of real assets)

$$a = \frac{1}{\kappa_1\beta_2}[k + \kappa_1\beta_1 p - \kappa_1(g+z) + \kappa_1\beta_1(e+p^*) + er^*] \tag{18}$$

The multipliers depend solely on the balance of various effects on financial asset leakages. The first two terms in the 'multiplier' Δ in Table 6.3 are the standard tax and import leakages. The third term, $\beta_1\alpha_1(\alpha_2 - 1) > 0$, represents the effect of the labour constraint in reducing competitiveness and hence exports.

A permanent increase in government expenditure or world trade works by injecting assets into the system.[40] The AE curve is raised and output and the capital stock are permanently higher. Prices are pushed up because of the labour constraint. An increase in government spending will worsen the trade balance, whilst an increase in world trade will definitely improve it. The effect of these shocks on the stock of real assets

Table 6.3 Long-run comparative statics

Effect of	Effect on				
	y	p	j	k	a
g	Δ	$\alpha_1(\alpha_2-1)\Delta$	$-(\alpha_1(\alpha_2-1)\beta_1+\mu)\Delta$	Δ	$\dfrac{\Pi\Delta}{\kappa_1\beta_2}$
z	Δ	$\alpha_1(\alpha_2-1)\Delta$	$\tau\Delta$	Δ	$\dfrac{\Pi\Delta}{\kappa_1\beta_2}$
p^*	0	1	0	0	0
r^*	$-\beta_1\alpha_1\epsilon\Delta$	$(\mu+\tau)\alpha_1\epsilon\Delta$	$-\tau\beta_1\alpha_1\epsilon\Delta$	$-(\epsilon+\beta_1\alpha_1\epsilon\Delta)$	$\dfrac{-\beta_1\alpha_1\epsilon\Pi\Delta}{\kappa_1\beta_2}$

Note: where $\Delta = [\mu+\tau+\beta_1\alpha_1(\alpha_2-1)]^{-1}$ and $\Pi = 1 - \kappa_1(\mu+\tau) > 0$.

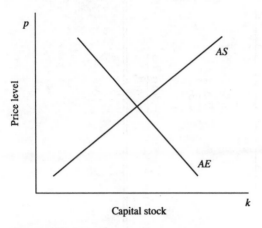

Figure 6.3   Long run

will depend on the size of induced leakages from the system: if Π is positive (as is most plausible from its definition in Table 6.3), then the stock of real assets will increase.

An increase in import prices will have no real effects on the economy in the long run; all of the short-run and intermediate-run effects discussed above disappear. Domestic prices will rise by exactly the extent of any rise in foreign prices.

An increase in world interest rates will move back both the AE and AS curves. Output will fall, though the capital stock will fall further. Thus on balance, prices will be increased because of supply-side factors. The trade balance will worsen, to balance the higher government deficit as a result of lower tax receipts. The stock of real financial assets will contract provided Π is positive.

Finally, the effect of a worsening of the terms of trade can be obtained by treating it as having the same effect as a rise in world prices and a reduction in world trade, z. Output falls and the trade balance worsens; whether the price level rises or falls depends upon whether the first or the second effect dominates. The negative effects on output of both of these events reinforce each other.

4.4   External adjustment policy using the model

The models can be used to discuss the appropriate policy responses to a negative external shock, caused, say, by a reduction in z.

One approach to external adjustment focuses on two targets (inflation and the trade balance) and two instruments (government expenditure and the exchange rate). This 'Swan-Salter' approach derives from Swan (1963) and Meade (1951); see also Corden (1988, 1993) and Khan and Montiel (1989). However, that approach is static and the present model is dynamic. Also, in the long run a depreciation of the exchange rate does not have any effect on the trade balance, but merely causes a one-for-one increase in the price level. Thus any correction of a balance-of-trade deficit will require a reduction in government absorption.

Specifically, a reduction in world trade of Δz, if it were in the long run to be completely counteracted, would inevitably require a reduction in government spending. The necessary reduction is $\Delta g^* = [(dj/dz)/(dj/dg)]\Delta z$. That would necessarily imply a fall in output of $(dy/dz)\Delta z + (dy/dg)\Delta g^*$; there is no way around that. And notice that this output loss is not a Keynesian problem; it is that which is necessary for a combination of current-account balance and *supply-side* equilibrium. Such an approach to policy could be coupled with a fixed nominal exchange rate in order to ensure approximate price stability.[41]

In order to allow for dynamics, in the face of an external deficit government expenditure can be adjusted according to the following sort of rule

$$\dot{g} = -\zeta \, (j - j^*) \tag{19}$$

Preliminary stability analysis (not reported here) shows that the addition of this adjustment rule adds an extra complication to the stability problems of the model. A too rapid speed of adjustment will set up a cyclical process which augments the oscillation coming from the capital stock adjustment process.

We have attempted such an approach to external adjustment on all of our empirical models, with one important amendment. We specified a feedback of government expenditure on the current account of the balance of payments, not just the trade balance, in order to avoid the need for the economy to borrow to pay the additional interest payments on any additional stock of debt accumulated during the adjustment process. With this amendment, we then set about designing a rule such as that shown in equation (19). One chooses the speed of adjustment (the analogue to the size of ζ) according to an implicit tradeoff between the output costs of very rapid adjustment, versus the long-lasting deficit which slow adjustment would imply. There are control-theory methods available for the empirical design of such rules. We used the rule-of-thumb version of these methods discussed in Weale *et al.* (1989, Chapter 11). Our feedback rule for all regions takes the form of a proportional-integral-derivative feedback of government spending, g, on the current-account balance[42], v, and is expressed in terms of deviations from the base (with both variables expressed as a proportion of GDP). The coefficients differ slightly as between regions. Those for Latin America are

$$\Delta g = -(0.3\Delta v + 0.45 v_{-1} + 0.8\Delta^2 v) \tag{20}$$

These coefficients give a relatively large and rapid response in government consumption to changes in reserves.

5   Simulations with the empirical models

The exercises just described in the previous section were performed empirically on our models. We briefly illustrate the results of a fiscal expansion (for Africa), a devaluation (for Other Asia), a *reduction* in world trade (for Latin America) and a worsening of the terms of trade (for the Asian NIEs). Figures 6.4–6.7 show differences from the base run for output (in absolute magnitude or percentages) and for prices (in percentages) in the top two pictures; in the bottom left-hand corner we display the changes in the current account (scaled as a percent of GDP) rather than in the trade balance, as would be required for precise comparison with what we have just described.[43] The dotted lines show outcomes when fiscal policy is adjusted to ensure external balance; the bottom right-hand corner shows the required movements in government expenditure (*GC*) and the outcomes for the current-account balance (*CBV*), both scaled as a per cent of GDP.

5.1   Fiscal expansion

We illustrate in Figure 6.4 the effects of a fiscal expansion in Africa of 1 per cent of 1972 GDP; namely $1.1b. This raises output (the multiplier is nearly 2) in the short term, prices rise and the current account worsens. The short-run multiplier is larger than the longer-run multiplier (this is true in all regions except the Asian NIEs). This happens for a number of reasons. In Africa, and in Latin America in particular, the multiplier-accelerator interactions are very strong. In all regions there are lags in the import equations which temporarily 'bottle up' at home any increase in aggregate demand.

In Africa, as particularly in Latin America, the development of output over time is cyclical (this is true of all regional models except Other Asia). In Africa (and in Latin America) these cycles are particularly

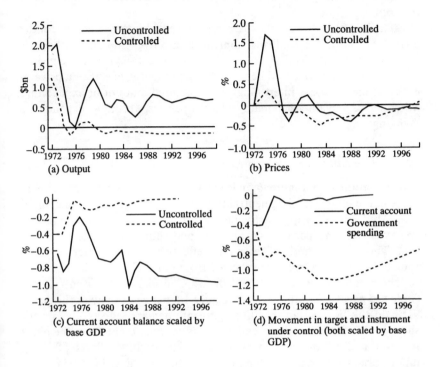

Figure 6.4   Fiscal expansion: Africa

pronounced and of much longer period than that of the multiplier–accelerator interaction on its own, because here there are further strong cyclical effects coming from the interaction of demand and supply. Over time, in all regions (and in Latin America especially) higher levels of demand raise prices which, with a lag, depresses net exports: a form of crowding out. However, over time, capital accumulation mitigates the price increase and dampens this effect. This effect is very clear in Africa.

Full long-run effects take many years to emerge: more than fifteen years here.[44] In the long run output converges towards a positive value, and the effect on the trade balance is negative as expected; the size of the multipliers is similar and somewhat below unity. This type of outcome is in line with open-economy versions of Blinder and Solow (1973); for example Branson (1976), in which a public-sector deficit is matched by a current-account deficit.[45] A surprising feature of the simulation is the small extent of the long-run increase in prices. This is because capital accumulation mitigates the price increase, and because exchange rates are fixed.

Notice that when the fiscal expansion is reversed in order to control the current account, the feedback control is effective, and the cutback is roughly 1 per cent of GDP as expected. This exercise gives some insight into how such control could be used to counteract the effects of a private-sector demand shock. Interestingly, the required amount of expenditure switching is small; the main effect operates through expenditure changing.

5.2   A devaluation, or foreign price increase

A devaluation (see Figure 6.5) leads to an equiproportionate rise in prices in the long run – i.e., neutrality holds – in all regions, as one might expect, but this takes approaching ten years.

We consider a 10 per cent devaluation and show the results for Other Asia. This has the kinds of temporary effects on output, prices and the trade balance which might be expected from our theoretical discussion of the short- and intermediate-run effects. Consider first output effects. These are negative: output falls by nearly 1.5 per cent. Only in the Asian NIEs do the 'Keynesian' positive aggregate demand effects – as in our 'short run' – dominate the negative effects – which come from the effect of lower real balances on demand or from negative effects of rising import prices on aggregate supply. Nevertheless, in Other Asia, since prices are so slow to respond, after negative real balance effects work themselves off, there is a period in which the positive effects of aggregate demand dominate. The trade balance effects are as one might expect, largely positive as a result of the transient competitiveness and real balance effects. The outcomes do not return to zero because of debt interest payments, which act as an 'integrator' of previous experience: they lead to a perpetual positive outcome since the short-run effects have been positive.

5.3   A slump in world trade

Figure 6.6 shows the effects for Latin America of a permanent reduction in world trade of 5 per cent. As expected, such a slump lowers output: the fall at its largest is approximately 5 per cent of 1972 GDP. Prices fall in the short term and the current account worsens. The short-run multiplier is smaller than the longer-run multiplier (this is true in all regions except the Asian NIEs). That is partly for reasons not evident from the pictures, since a reduction in

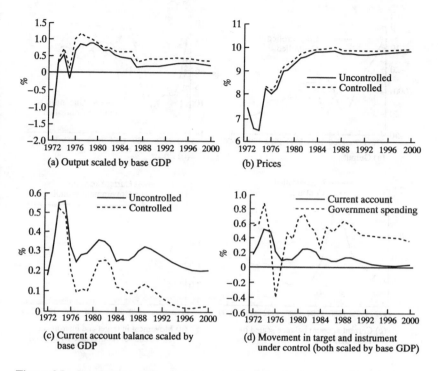

Figure 6.5 Devaluation: Other Asia

world trade of 5 per cent represents a shock of increasing absolute magnitude.[46] But it is also, in all regions except the Asian NIEs, because of the cumulative downward movement in output, and the rebound in prices, associated with the 'supply-side collapse' caused by capital decumulation. This is particularly strong (and quick) in Latin America.

In all regions except Other Asia the development of output over time is cyclical.[47] In Latin America these cycles are particularly pronounced, and with a long period, for reasons which we have already discussed. Over time, capital accumulation mitigates the price fall, dampening any recovery of export markets which might happen as a result of becoming more competitive.

Full long-run effects take many years to emerge: perhaps twenty.[48] In the long run output converges towards a negative value, and the effect on the trade balance is negative as expected. This type of outcome is again in line with Branson (1976), in which, in the absence of policy response, the current-account deficit is matched by a public-sector deficit.[49]

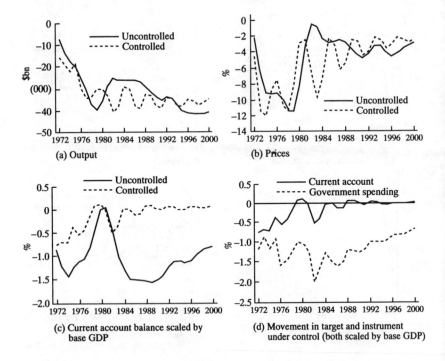

Figure 6.6   World trade slump: Latin America

When government spending is adjusted to ensure external balance the outcomes are as shown by the dotted lines in the figures. Fiscal contraction (expenditure changing) is necessary, which causes lower output and lower prices (expenditure switching). But the differences to output and prices are not great. This is essentially because output has fallen so much in the uncontrolled run – thereby reducing imports – that not much further adjustment is necessary. The volatile movements in fiscal policy suggest that the control rule discussed earlier in the text leaves something to be desired.

5.4   A worsening in the terms of trade

This is exactly equivalent to a combination of a slump in world trade and a rise in foreign prices (i.e., a slump in world trade and a rise in both import prices and competitors' export prices). The second component of this shock has been seen from our own devaluation simulation to have the kinds of temporary effects on output, prices and the trade balance

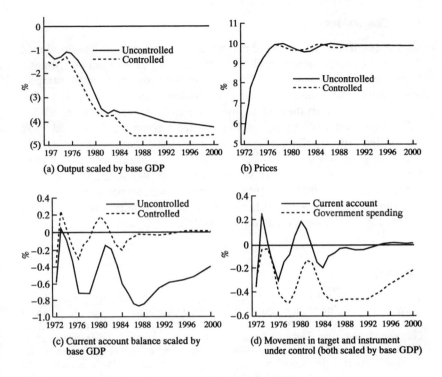

Figure 6.7   A worsening in the terms of trade: Asian NIEs

which might be expected from our theoretical discussion of the short-
and intermediate-run effects, but to lead eventually to a 10 per cent rise
in the price level. On this we can think of superimposing the effects of a
slump in world trade.

Consider first output effects. These are unambigously negative: GDP
falls, as shown in Figure 6.7, by between 1 and 4 per cent: any increased
competitiveness *vis-à-vis* imports is not large enough[50] to outweigh
negative demand effects arising both from the export side and from the
effect of rising prices lowering consumers' real wealth; there are also
negative effects of rising import prices on aggregate supply. The
(uncontrolled) trade balance effects are as one might expect, with the
transient cycle being due to the lags in the price rise and output downturn.

When government spending is adjusted to ensure external balance the
outcomes are as shown by the dotted lines in the figures. Again fiscal
contraction (expenditure changing) is necessary, which causes lower
output. Because of the special features of the supply side of NIEs,
expenditure switching is imperceptible.

6   Conclusions

This paper has given an initial exposition of our work on less-developed country macroeconomics, and on issues relating to external adjustment. It has aimed to show how the theory developed may be used to interpret and understand some illustrative simulations from our models. But connections between the existing literature and our own work are not yet fully drawn out, and our analyses are far from complete. These tasks will be carried out in the first part of a planned book entitled *Global Macroeconomics for the Third World* (Allen, Srinivasan and Vines, forthcoming). We have also yet to explore in detail the use of these models for the study of macroeonomic interactions between developed and developing countries, although some initial results can be found in Allen *et al.* (1992) and Allen and Vines (1993).

NOTES

This paper is part of a long-standing programme of work on North–South Macroeconomic Interactions initiated by David Currie and David Vines, which has also involved collaboration with Anton Muscatelli and Kul Luintel at Glasgow University. Early versions of parts of the present paper appeared in Allen *et al.* (1991, 1991). The financial support of the ESRC (grant no. R000232299) and the World Bank is gladly acknowledged. We are grateful to Warwick McKibbin, Anton Muscatelli, Martin Weale and Stephen Wright for helpful conversations on this work and to participants at the Conference and at seminars in Cambridge, Canberra, Geneva, Glasgow, and Oxford for useful comments.

1 Most of the description is for the first three regions; the last of the models is still at an exploratory stage.
2 There are two further components to this modern consensus macroeconomics: forward-looking behaviour, and the requirement that the economic structure be grounded to some extent in microeconomic maximizing behaviour. We have not proceeded that way, and because of this our treatment may be thought old fashioned. It would be desirable to extend our work in this direction. Our reasons for not doing so were practical. Partly we saw ourselves as producing models of the same kind as those in the national models of the UK global econometric model, which we are using as part of our study of North–South interactions, and which, when we set out on this work, contained forward-looking treatments only of floating exchange rates. But mainly it is because we have set ourselves a large task, and were aware that successfully estimating and simulating a number of forward-looking and intertemporal-maximizing regional models would make our task impossibly large, given the resources at our disposal. Our thought was better to have some results with a less ambitious model structure than no results with a more ambitious structure.
3 The way in which we impose the solvency constraint is also a limited one in

this paper. This is deliberate: we investigate the consequences if the nation as a whole is *not* externally constrained and then, as a separate activity, look at the effects of economic policy which would impose such a long-run external constraint. Our domestic private sector *is* constrained (even if only in the long run and even if not in a forward-looking way) as a result of asset effects on expenditures. As a consequence, if there is a national solvency constraint imposed by means of fiscal policy in the long run, then as a matter of accounting, the government itself must observe such a constraint in the long run.

4 To have two different, and potentially inconsistent, models of the balance of payments at the Fund and at the Bank across the road from each other in Washington was not really satisfactory; Mohsin Khan has told one of the authors that it was this insight that led to these papers.

5 See Khan and Knight (1985), Khan *et al.* (1990), Khan and Montiel (1989), and the critical review of the latter two papers by Vines (1990). Those papers, and that by Vines, include wealth effects on consumption and capital effects on supply; but they are static one-period models and so can only hint at the dynamic processes implied by the accumulation of wealth and capital.

6 We have sheltered behind the assumption of externally given interest rates to avoid studying the portfolio allocation process, something which we leave for further work. It has also often been argued that the existence of credit rationing makes it very difficult to model empirically, using published data, the endogenous determination of interest rates within less-developed countries.

7 This is a process which was much discussed in Latin America in the 1980s.

8 For full details see Srinivasan and Vines (1990, 1991a and b), and Allen (1991).

9 Implementing our ideas has required a considerable amount of empirical research. Our models of the NIEs, Africa, and Latin America have all been economically estimated using aggregate annual data for regions, constructed from country data supplied by the World Bank. There were enormous data gaps which needed to be filled. We were looking for data on components of GDP, wages and prices, current account variables, monetary sector variables and government accounts. Data series on these variables are readily available in the World Bank's World Tables published since 1984, but data aggregated into regional totals is not available from this source. Therefore we ventured into constructing our own data base for developing country regions, on the basis of country level data supplied specially to us by the International Economic Analysis and Projections Division of the World Bank. Such a task is a large and largely thankless one: this is the first time anywhere that such an effort has been made. Approximately eighty Fortran algorithms were written to scrutinize, clean, aggregate and prepare data for econometric analysis. Altogether seventy-six time series from 1961 to 1986 have been constructed. In the course of this work data deficiencies of three types have been remedied by suitable methods. First, missing observations in GDP components and in the money stock were interpolated, producing long time series from 1960 to 1986, suitable for our econometric work; for Brazil GDP components were not adding up to total GDP for some years and we corrected this. Second, pervasive gaps in government accounts were found which were filled by calibrating parameters from the available data. Third, capital stock data were not available and they had to be constructed by a perpetual inventory method

assuming reasonable depreciation rates. All of these procedures are described in Srinivasan (1991). National accounts data were assembled in the way just described for the longest period possible: for twenty-six years from 1961 to 1985; a simulation track into the future (up until 2000) has also been generated for all of the models. Many of the algorithms produced in the course of this work were installed at the World Bank in 1990 by one of the authors (T.G. Srinivasan). These algorithms mean that it will be possible to update the data series, thus making it possible to re-estimate the models in due course.

10 For simplicity, in the analytical model, the equilibrium capital to output ratio is taken as unity, an assumption not made in the empirical work.

11 Tax rates matter too, but these are exogenous in the present paper.

12 As noted above, this is not true of the empirical models.

13 We abstract from Laursen-Metzler/terms-of-trade-effect complications, although they are present in the estimated models.

14 We abstract here from depreciation, although it is considered in the empirical models.

15 This relative price is exogenous; changes in it cause changes in the terms of trade. But it is not the same as the terms of trade, which is $p - e - p^*$, and which is endogenous because p is endogenous. Note that for a given relative world price an increase in p^* will be associated with a rise in q^*, and so that the β_2 term captures export competitiveness as well as import competitiveness. The β_3 term captures changes in export competitiveness relative to import competitiveness.

16 These simulations were been performed with the capital stock adjustment process of equation (7) switched out, but allowing for the instantaneous effects of output on investment, and also without the effects of wealth accumulation on consumption. The effects of the evolution of the capital and wealth state variables are discussed below.

17 Except for Africa, for which a shortage of wage data meant that we had to estimate a reduced form.

18 For reasons of data availability the equation estimated is for the consumer expenditure deflator (*ced*). This can be thought of as subsuming an equation for domestic output prices, marked up on wage and import costs, into an equation for *ced* by taking a weighted average of domestic output prices and import prices.

19 Data limitations prevented the estimation of separate import equations.

20 In the estimation, which included the 1980s, which were heavily import-constrained in all regions except the NIEs, a term in the import–output ratio was included in the equation to proxy movements in the shadow price of imports. This term had been fixed out in simulations.

21 This equation, in effect, shows the real wage which would be required for the labour to be forthcoming to supply various levels of output.

22 Because a higher capital stock lowers prices, *ceteribus paribus*.

23 This formulation, with a unit coefficient on import prices and a larger coefficient on output than on capital, can be derived explicitly from the two equations for wages and prices described above, given diminishing returns in the application of capital to the fixed factor labour. See Srinivasan and Vines (1990).

24 The coefficient on the capital stock in the implicit production function for

Latin America is much higher than that in that in the NIEs. A 1 per cent change in the output–capital ratio therefore causes more serious diminishing returns – i.e, it raises marginal costs more – in Latin America as compared with the NIEs. This would be consistent with relative capital scarcity in Latin America.

25 See the following paragraph.

26 But the mean lags (the time taken for half the adjustment to be complete) are long, five years or more.

27 And on any crawl of the exchange rate.

28 Strictly, this equation should contain a term showing interest payments on domestic debt, h, and the empirical model does this. But that would introduce a term in h into the evolution equation for domestic debt, which we are keen to avoid for reasons of analytical tractability. Our implicit assumption in the analytical model, but not in our empirical models, is that there is some lump-sum instrument available to neutralize this effect.

29 In the empirical model government investment also partly follows private investment rather than being strictly exogenous.

30 This equation, and the two equations that follow, show the evolution of *nominal* assets as a function of real budgetary components, g and τy. This will only be true as a linear approximation if the budget is initially balanced and the price level does not change too much. Such an approximation is not necessary in the empirical model.

31 And does allow for the revaluation of foreign reserves.

32 No distinction is made between money and other financial assets created by the government; given the exogeneity of interest rates (changes in which might be expected to revalue long-dated non-monetary assets) and given our effective neglect of interest payments on such assets in equation (3), this does not matter. It might well be argued (see Blinder and Solow, 1973, and Tobin, 1982) that real capital should appear as part of the wealth influencing spending. We have not allowed for this, having failed to detect such an effect empirically. The reasons for this failure perhaps relate to the fact that the government owns much capital in Third World countries, and to the fact that valuation (and revaluation) of the capital stock is difficult in the absence of active equity markets.

33 See Weale *et al.* (1989).

34 For ease of exposition, we proceed in terms of deviations from an initial equilibrium and so set the exogenous variables z, g, e, p^* and r^* to zero.

35 Despite the fact that output in the model is supply-constrained, and *not* demand-determined in a Keynesian manner, even within a year or so.

36 Compare Allen *et al.* (1992).

37 A shift in the terms of trade has identical effects in the model to a combined change in z and r^*, a devaluation is the equivalent of a rise in p^*, and a cut in tax rates has the same effect as a rise in government expenditure: thus we do not report these changes explicitly. Empirically of course this is not quite true and the model captures this: the necessary separate simulations can be performed.

38 This procedure is used extensively in, for example, Turnovsky (1977).

39 We do not explicitly examine this dynamic process within the short run.

40 The experiment of an increase in government spending is to be thought of as

an exercise only, rather than some actual policy which could necessarily be maintained.

41 This begs three questions, none of which is there time to discuss here. The first is that it presupposes that inflation is under control at the world level, for it involves, in the words of Keynes (1930) the surrender of a national for an international monetary standard. Second, it would be inappropriate for an economy for which both domestic costs and prices were far out of line with world prices, in which a depreciation could influence the adjustment path. And third, it forgoes the opportunity for a once-for-all price increase which may be a necessary means of eliminating a monetary overhang as part of a process of curtailing domestic absorption so as to bring about external adjustment.

42 The current account, ν, is equal to the trade balance, j, plus interest payments, r^*s, which is exactly equal to ds/dt.

43 The reason for being interested in the current account is that, when analysing external adjustment below, we want the current account – including interest payments – to be controlled rather than just the trade balance. But we did not present analytical results for the current account in the previous section, precisely because the behaviour of interest payments makes this analytically much less transparent.

44 This is a well-known phenomenon (cf. Weale *et al.* 1989).

45 Of course, this could not be sustained indefinitely but is only a hypothetical experiment.

46 Notice that in this figure, output effects show absolute and not percentage changes in GDP.

47 This cyclical behaviour happens for a number of reasons. In Latin America, in particular, the multiplier–accelerator interactions are very strong. In all regions there are lags in the import equations (which may not be plausible) which 'bottle up' any reduction in aggregate demand temporarily at home. For Other Asia there is also the effect of a large short-run propensity to consume.

48 This is a well-known phenomenon (cf. Weale *et al.*, 1989).

49 Of course, this could not be sustained indefinitely but is a hypothetical experiment.

50 Competitiveness elasticities in imports alone are much less than unity.

REFERENCES

Allen, C. (1991) 'Simulations of an econometric model of Africa', London Business School, mimeo.

Allen, C., D.A. Currie, S. Hall, T.G. Srinivasan and D.A. Vines (1991) 'The simple macroeconomics of optimal debt default with an application to Latin America', Centre for Economic Forecasting, London Business School, mimeo.

Allen, C., D.A. Currie, T.G. Srinivasan and D.A. Vines (1992) 'Policy Interactions between OECD and Latin America in the 1980s', *Manchester School* **60**, 1–20.

Allen, C., T.G. Srinivasan and D. Vines (forthcoming) *Global Macroeconomics for the Third World*, draft manuscript in preparation.

Allen, C. and D. Vines (1993) 'Should Clinton cut the deficit, or is there a global paradox of thrift?' *The World Economy*, April.

Bacha, Edmar (1990) 'A three-gap model of foreign transfers and the GDP growth rate in developing countries', *Journal of Development Economics* 32, 279–96.

Blinder, A.S. (1988) 'The fall and rise of Keynesian economics', *Economic Record* 64, 278–94.

Blinder, A.S. and R.M. Solow (1973) 'Does fiscal policy matter?' *Journal of Public Economics* 2, 319–37.

Branson, W. (1976) 'The dual roles of the government budget and the balance of payments in the movement from short run to long run equilibrium', *Quarterly Journal of Economics* 90, 345–67.

Bryant, R., D. Currie, J. Frenkel, P. Masson and R. Portes (eds.) (1989) *Macroeconomic Policies in an Interdependent World*, Washington DC: International Monetary Fund.

Bruno, M. and J.D. Sachs (1985) *The Economics of Worldwide Stagflation*, Oxford: Basil Blackwell.

Corden, W.M. (1988) 'Macroeconomic adjustment in developing countries', Working Paper No. 88/13, Research Department, International Monetary Fund, Washington DC.

(1992) 'Exchange rate policies for developing countries', *Economic Journal Conference Supplement* 103, 198–207.

Gordon, R. (1990) 'What is new Keynesian economics?', *Journal of Economic Literature* 28, 1115–71.

International Monetary Fund (1987) 'Theoretical aspects of the design of fund supported adjustment programs', IMF Occasional Paper No. 55.

(1990) *Multimod II: A Multiregional Econometric Model*, Washington DC: International Monetary Fund.

Jackman, R., R. Layard, S. Nickell and S. Wadhwani (1991) *Unemployment*, Oxford: Oxford University Press.

Keynes, J.M. (1930) *A Treatise on Money*. Reprinted in the *Collected Works of John Maynard Keynes*, London: Macmillan (1971), vols. V and VI.

Khan, Mohsin S. and Malcolm D. Knight (1985) 'Fund supported adjustment programs and economic growth', IMF Occasional Paper No. 41.

Khan, Mohsin S. and Peter J. Montiel (1989) 'Growth orientated adjustment programs: a conceptual framework', *IMF Staff Papers* 36, 279–306.

Khan, Mohsin, S., Peter J. Montiel and Nadeem Hacque (1990) 'Adjustment with growth: relating the analytical approaches of the World Bank and the IMF', *Journal of Development Economics* 32, 155–79.

Krugman, P. (1989) 'Income elasticities and real exchange rates', *European Economic Review* 33, 1031–54.

Meade, J.E. (1951) *The Balance of Payments*, London: Oxford University Press.

Muscatelli, V.A. and D. Vines (1989) 'Macroeconomic interactions between the North and South', in R. Bryant, D. Currie, J. Frenkel, P. Masson and R. Portes (eds.), *Macroeconomic Policies in an Interdependent World*, Washington DC: International Monetary Fund.

Muscatelli, V.A., T.G. Srinivasan and D. Vines (1990) 'The empirical modelling of NIE exports: an evaluation of different approaches', CEPR Discussion Paper No. 426.

142   Chris Allen, T.G. Srinivasan and David Vines

(1992) 'Demand and supply factors in the determination of NIE exports: a simultaneous error-correction model for Hong Kong', *Economic Journal* **102**, 1467–77.

Ros, H. (1991) 'Foreign exchange and fiscal constraints on growth: a reconsideration of structuralist and macroeconomic approaches', Kellogg Institute for International Studies, University of Notre Dame, mimeo.

Srinivasan, T.G. (1991) 'Empirical macro models for developing countries: the case of Latin America', Ph.D. thesis, University of Glasgow.

Srinivasan, T.G. and D. Vines (1990) 'Simulations of an econometric model of Latin America', paper presented to a CEPR Workshop on North–South Macroeconomic Interactions, Rio de Janeiro.

(1991a) 'Simulations of an econometric model of Asian NIEs', University of Glasgow, mimeo.

(1991b) 'Simulations of an econometric model of Other Asia', University of Glasgow, mimeo.

Swan, T.W. (1963) 'Longer run problems of the balance of payments', in H.W. Arndt and W.M. Corden (eds.), *The Australian Economy, A Book of Readings*, Melbourne: Cheshire Press. Reprinted in R.E. Caves and H.G. Johnson (eds.), *Readings in International Economics*, London: Allen and Unwin, pp. 455–64 (1968).

Taylor. L. (1990) *Varieties of Stabilisation Experience*, Oxford: The Clarendon Press.

(1991) *Income Distribution, Inflation and Growth*, DEN Press.

Tobin, J. (1982) 'Money and finance in the macroeconomic process', *Journal of Money Credit and Banking* **14**, 171–204.

Turnovsky, S.J. (1977) *Macroeconomic Analysis and Stabilisation Policy*, Cambridge: Cambridge University Press.

Vines, D. (1990) 'Growth oriented adjustment programs: a reconsideration', CEPR Discussion Paper No. 406.

Weale, M.R., A. Blake, N. Christodoulakis, D. Vines and J.E. Meade (1989) *Macroeconomic Policy: Inflation, Wealth and the Exchange Rate*, London: Unwin Hyman.

World Bank (1990) 'The revised minimum standard model', Comparative Analysis and Projections Division, World Bank, mimeo.

7 Dynamic response to external shocks in Classical and Keynesian economies

KLAUS SCHMIDT-HEBBEL
and LUIS SERVEN

1 Introduction

A bewildering variety of macroeconomic tools is available to macro-economic policymakers and analysts. The model developed here forms part of a small but growing sub-family of macroeconomic frameworks which, while firmly based on microanalytic foundations, introduce critical real world features – such as short-run wage rigidities and liquidity constraints – which generate persistent deviations from the frictionless full-employment outcome of the unconstrained neoclassical paradigm. The dynamic general equilibrium model developed here nests as special cases the classical and neo-Keynesian benchmarks, and assumes rational expectation formation. Hence short-term equilibria depend on current and anticipated future trajectories of policy and external variables.

Forward-looking behaviour based on microanalytical foundations is a feature that this paper shares with an increasing number of recent models applied to open-economy issues such as oil shocks, interest rate changes or policy coordination in multicountry frameworks (Sachs, 1983; Giavazzi et al., 1982; Lipton and Sachs, 1983; Bruno and Sachs, 1985; McKibbin and Sachs, 1989; McKibbin and Sundberg, 1990; McKibbin and Wilcoxen, 1992). Nesting of classical and Keynesian benchmarks characterizes also the model by McKibbin and Sachs (1989), although they do not discuss its implications for the response of the economy to shocks. This paper extends previous work in four dimensions. First, it extends the analytical structure by incorporating simultaneously several realistic features that are relevant for most open economies: nominal wage rigidity, import content of capital goods, foreign holdings of domestic equity, public investment and monetary finance of budget deficits.[1] Second, it explores in some detail the short- and long-term consequences of liquidity constraints affecting private consumption and investment behaviour. Third, the paper compares the differential effects of external shocks in neoclassical and Keynesian benchmark economies, for both permanent/transitory and anticipated/unanticipated disturbances. Finally, the simulations are performed by solving the full non-linear model, in contrast with the conventional procedure that uses a linear approximation, whose accuracy can be highly unreliable when simulating 'large' shocks.

The plan of the paper is as follows. Section 2 summarizes the model structure. Section 3 describes the steady state and the stability properties of the economy. Section 4 presents simulation results for two favourable external shocks: a unilateral foreign transfer and a rise in the external terms of trade, brought about by a decline in the world price of an intermediate input (say an oil-price windfall in the case of an oil-importing economy). Section 5 closes the paper with some concluding remarks.

2   The model[2]

The economy produces one single good, that can be used for consumption and investment at home, or sold abroad (thus there is no distinction between production for domestic and export markets). It is an imperfect substitute for the foreign final good – which likewise can be used for consumption and investment – and its production requires the use of an imported intermediate input. The economy is small in its import markets, but faces a downward-sloping demand for its exports.

There are three basic agents in the model: the consolidated public sector, the domestic private sector and the external sector. The first lumps the non-financial and financial (central bank) public sector together, the second aggregates private firms and consumers, and the third adds foreign investors, creditors and trade partners. The private sector comprises one group of intertemporally optimizing agents with another of liquidity-constrained (or myopic) agents. Private firms take all production and investment decisions, own the economy's entire capital stock and benefit from a lump-sum public investment subsidy.

Domestic private agents hold four assets: money, domestic debt issued by the consolidated public sector, foreign assets, and equity claims on the domestic capital stock. Foreigners hold domestic equity but not domestic public debt. In turn, the public sector also holds foreign assets.[3] There are no restrictions on capital mobility and, in the absence of risk and uncertainty, all non-monetary assets are assumed to be perfect substitutes; hence their anticipated rates of return must be equalized at each point in time. In turn, imperfect substitutability between base money and other assets is reflected by a conventional transactions-based money demand.

Both goods and asset markets clear continuously. Equality between demand and supply of the domestic good determines the real exchange rate. Under a flexible nominal exchange rate regime, money market equilibrium then determines the nominal exchange rate. By contrast, the labour market may not clear instantaneously due to the existence of nominal and/or real wage rigidity.

The dynamics of the model arise from two basic sources: the accumulation of assets/liabilities, dictated by stock–flow consistency of the sectoral budget constraints, and the forward-looking behaviour of private agents. Expectations are formed rationally, which in this context of certainty amounts to perfect foresight. Thus, anticipated and realized values of the variables can differ only at the time of unexpected shocks or due to the arrival of new information about the future paths of exogenous variables.

Technology and preferences are kept as simple as possible, by assuming unit elasticities of substitution.[4] The production technology is summarized by a Cobb–Douglas production function for gross output, which combines value added (capital and labour) and intermediate imports. Harrod-neutral technical progress ensures the existence of steady-state growth, at a level given by the sum of the rates of technical progress and population growth, both of which are exogenous. In addition, a Cobb–Douglas investment technology is used to combine domestic and foreign goods into capital goods, whose accumulation is subject to quadratic adjustment costs. This allows separation between the intertemporal aggregate investment decision and its intratemporal allocation to domestic goods and imports (see Gavin, 1991; Serven, 1991; or Hayashi and Inoue, 1991). Consumers' preferences also display unit inter- and intratemporal substitution elasticities, likewise allowing two-stage budgeting in consumption decisions.

Behavioural rules combine explicitly two benchmark specifications: the neoclassical case of unconstrained, intertemporally optimizing firms and consumers, along with full wage flexibility (ensuring continuous full employment), and the Keynesian case of liquidity-constrained firms and households, along with wage inflexibility.

Firms' use of variable inputs (labour and imported intermediates) is determined by the standard marginal productivity conditions. In turn, investment decisions are different for constrained and unconstrained firms. The latter derive their investment plans from market value maximization; following the standard theory of investment under convex adjustment costs (Lucas, 1967; Treadway, 1969), their investment is linked to Tobin's marginal q (Tobin, 1969), i.e., the present value of the additional profits associated with the marginal unit of capital relative to its installation cost (Hayashi, 1982).[5] By contrast, liquidity-constrained firms gear their investment expenditure to their current profits. Aggregate investment is then a weighted average of investment by constrained and unconstrained firms.

Consumption by unconstrained consumers is derived from standard maximization of intertemporal utility over an infinite horizon, subject to the intertemporal budget constraint (e.g., Ramsey, 1928). Solving the maximization problem yields the standard result that consumption is equal to the subjective discount rate (net of effective labour growth) times total (human and non-human) wealth. Unconstrained consumers are of course Ricardian, as they internalize the government's intertemporal budget constraint by anticipating the entire stream of current and future tax payments; since they face the same discount rate as the government,[6] they are indifferent between tax, debt, or money financing of the public deficit (Barro, 1974). By contrast, some labour-income earners are liquidity-constrained and cannot borrow against their human wealth; hence they consume their current net labour income.[7] Total private consumption demand is an aggregate of consumption by unconstrained and constrained consumers.

Real or nominal wage rigidity may prevent continuous full employment of the labour force. In such case, employment is determined by labour demand, as conventionally assumed, and wages follow an indexation rule linking nominal wage growth to current and lagged consumer price inflation and also to current labour market conditions.

Finally, the public sector is assumed to determine its policy exogenously; hence public consumption and investment expenditures follow pre-determined trajectories. To finance its activity, the public sector can choose among taxes (which fall exclusively on labour income), money, domestic debt or external borrowing (or any combination of them).

3   Steady state, model solution and parameterization

3.1   The steady state

The long-run equilibrium of the model is characterized by constant output in real per-capita terms (so that long-run growth equals the growth rate of the effective labour force), constant per-capita real asset stocks, constant relative prices, and constant real wages with full employment. Thus, the government's budget must be balanced, and the current-account deficit must equal the exogenously given flow of foreign investment, which in turn is just sufficient to keep foreign equity holdings (in real per-capita terms) unchanged.

Since the per-capita real money stock is constant, long-run inflation equals the rate of expansion of per-capita nominal balances. In turn, with a constant real exchange rate, domestic and foreign real interest rates are equalized by uncovered interest parity, and nominal exchange depreciation is determined by the difference between domestic and (exogenously given) foreign inflation. Hence, across steady states changes in the rate of money growth are fully reflected in the inflation rate (and thus in the nominal interest rate) and in the rate of nominal depreciation.

By combining the model's equations, the steady-state equilibrium can be reduced to two independent relations in the real exchange rate and real wealth: a goods-market equilibrium condition and a zero private wealth accumulation condition (in real per-capita terms). Together they imply a constant stock of per-capita net foreign assets. Goods-market equilibrium defines an inverse long-run relationship between real wealth and the real exchange rate: higher wealth raises private consumption demand and requires a real exchange rate appreciation for the domestic goods market to clear.

In turn, real wealth accumulation can cease only when per-capita consumption equals the per-capita return on wealth. This poses the well-known requirement that, for a steady state to exist, the rate of time preference must equal the exogenously given world interest rate.[8] But then the zero-wealth accumulation condition provides no information whatsoever on the steady-state *level* of wealth: with the return on wealth being entirely consumed, *any* wealth stock is self-replicating. In other words, we are left only with the goods market equilibrium condition to determine both long-run wealth and the real exchange rate – an obviously impossible task.

This means that the steady-state wealth stock must be found from the economy's initial conditions and from its history of wealth accumulation or decumulation along the adjustment path. Hence the steady-state values of wealth and the real exchange rate (and therefore all other variables related to them) depend not only on the long-run values of the exogenous variables, but also on the particular trajectory followed by the economy. In other words, the model exhibits hysteresis. As noted by Giavazzi and Wyplosz (1984), this follows from the assumption of forward-looking consumption behaviour derived from intertemporal optimization by infinitely lived households with a constant rate of time preference and facing perfect capital markets.

An important implication of the model's hysteresis property is that transitory disturbances have long-run effects. For the case of fiscal policy, this has been recently highlighted by Turnovsky and Sen (1991).[9] But in our framework even transitory monetary disturbances can have permanent real effects: if some consumers are liquidity-constrained (or myopic), a transitory increase in inflationary taxation matched by a reduction in direct taxes will raise disposable income and consumption, leading to reduced wealth accumulation and eventually causing a fall in long-run wealth and a permanent real depreciation.[10]

The fact that production requires the use of imported inputs (inter-mediates and capital goods) has important consequences for the economy's long-run properties: across steady states, real output (and also the capital stock and the real wage) is inversely related to the real exchange rate. The reason is that a real depreciation raises the real cost of imported inputs and therefore reduces the profitability of production.

3.2   Dynamics and stability

The model's dynamics combine predetermined variables (i.e., asset stocks) subject to initial conditions, and 'jumping' variables (i.e., Tobin's q, the real exchange rate, real money balances, human wealth, the present value of the investment subsidy, and the present value of the cost of holding money). For the dynamic system not to explode, these non-predetermined variables have to satisfy certain terminal (transversality) conditions. Solving the model basically amounts to finding initial values for the non-predetermined variables such that, following a shock, the model will converge to a new stationary equilibrium. The necessary and sufficient conditions for the existence and uniqueness of such initial values are known for the case of linear models,[11] but not for non-linear systems such as the one at hand.[12] While a formal proof of stability cannot be provided, numerically the model was always found to converge to the new long-run equilibrium under reasonable parameter values.

The requirement that the predetermined variables satisfy initial conditions, while the jumping variables must satisfy terminal conditions, poses a two-point boundary-value problem, for whose numerical solution several techniques exist. Two leading examples are the 'multiple shooting' method proposed by Lipton et al. (1982), and the 'extended path' algorithm of Fair and Taylor (1983). For the simulations below, we combine both techniques as follows. First, we solve the model over an arbitrarily chosen time horizon using multiple shooting. To prevent the solution from being distorted by the choice of too short a time horizon (which would force the model to reach the terminal conditions too early), we then extend the horizon and recompute the solution path until the resulting changes in the solution trajectory of the endogenous variables fall below a certain tolerance,[13] at which time the process stops. In practice, the length of the simulation horizon required for this procedure to converge is strongly affected by two parameters governing the speed of adjustment of the system: the elasticity of real wages to employment (i.e., the slope of the expectations-augmented Phillips curve), and the magnitude of adjustment costs associated with investment.

3.3   Parameterization

Within the general structure spelt out above, three economies will be considered: (i) a neoclassical (NC) benchmark with full employment and no liquidity constraints, (ii) an economy with liquidity constraints but with full employment (LCFE), and (iii) a Keynesian benchmark combining liquidity constraints and unemployment (LCUN). In the latter two economies, 50 per cent of the households and enterprises face liquidity constraints; in addition, in the Keynesian benchmark nominal wages are fully indexed to the average of current and lagged consumer price inflation (recall that wages are fully flexible in the first two economies).

The remaining parameter values are representative of open, developing economies. For a full description of the parameters and exogenous variables, as well as their initial values for all three economies, see Schmidt-Hebbel and Serven (1992). Numerical values for most coefficients in the structural equations were borrowed from empirical estimates (Serven and Solimano, 1991; Elbadawi and Schmidt-Hebbel, 1991; Haque et al., 1990) and preceding simulation models (McKibbin and Sachs, 1989; Giavazzi et al. (1992) for various countries, complemented by estimates deemed to be representative for open economies.

Scale parameter values were chosen so that real output equals unity at the initial steady state. Hence the values of all variables reported below can be interpreted as relative to initial output. Recall also that initial (and final) steady-state output growth is determined exclusively by the rate of growth of the labour force in efficiency units, which was set at 3 per cent.

Finally, to close the model it is necessary to specify how the public and private sectors finance their activity – i.e., which two endogenous variables are determined residually by their budget constraints. For the simulations discussed below, the adjusting variable for the public sector is total taxes, and for the private sector the residual budgetary variable is foreign asset holdings.[14]

4   Simulation results

To explore the impact of external disturbances, we simulate the dynamic adjustment to a favourable foreign transfer shock (an external grant to the public sector) and a favourable terms-of-trade shock (a decline in the price of the intermediate import used in production, say oil). In a companion paper (Schmidt-Hebbel and Serven, 1993) we have explored the model's response to fiscal and monetary policy shocks.

The first-round magnitude of both shocks is common, equivalent to a 4 per cent gain of initial steady-state output. In the case of the foreign transfer shock, we consider three alternatives: a permanent unanticipated (P) disturbance (hitting the economy in period 1 and lasting forever), a transitory unanticipated (TU) shock (hitting during periods 1–4), and a transitory anticipated (TA) shock (hitting during periods 2–5). In the case of the oil-price windfall, only a permanent (P) shock will be considered.

To discuss the simulations below, we start from an initial steady-state equilibrium (represented by period 0), and distinguish between the impact effects (in period 1) and the transition toward the new steady-state equilibrium (from period 2 to terminal period T, which is in the range of 60–80 periods). The discussion will follow the figures depicting the dynamic paths of the main endogenous variables. For the foreign transfer simulations, each figure is divided into an upper panel, which reports the dynamic trajectories under the three types of shocks (P, TU and TA) for the NC case, and a lower panel which combines the three shock types with two remaining economies: LCFE and LCUN. For the oil price windfall simulations (which are limited to a permanent shock), each panel represents a different variable, depicting three dynamic trajectories – i.e., one for each benchmark economy.

4.1   A foreign transfer shock

With taxes being the adjusting variable in the public-sector budget, a foreign transfer to the public sector is fully passed on to the private sector through a tax reduction. Private disposable income and wealth rise accordingly, leading to increased consumption. Thus, on impact higher private consumption causes both a real exchange rate appreciation and an increase in output. Over time, output increases further due to capital accumulation, which responds gradually to the decline in the real cost of imported capital goods triggered off by the appreciation, and causes a gradual depreciation of the real exchange rate.

The dynamic trajectories of the main endogenous variables in response to a 4 per cent of output transfer from the rest of the world to the public sector are shown in Figures 7.1–7.6, for different model categories and types of shocks.[15] Consider first the neoclassical economy (*NC*), positively affected by a permanent shock. Ricardian consumers internalize the government's intertemporal budget constraint and anticipate not only current but also future tax cuts and higher output; thus, their consumption increases sharply in period 1, by over 4 percentage points of output (Figure 7.1). In the long run, consumption increases by 9.7 per cent.[16]

The consumption-based increase in aggregate demand causes a contemporaneous output expansion (Figure 7.2) and a real appreciation (Figure 7.3).[17] Higher production in period 1 is made possible by importing more intermediate goods in response to the appreciated real exchange rate, and hence by shifting the input mix away from value added. In subsequent periods the real exchange rate depreciates as a result of aggregate supply shifts due to higher capital. Therefore the real exchange rate initially overshoots its new long-run level – a result of the existence of adjustment costs to investment. In the new steady state, the real exchange rate exhibits a 7.4 per cent appreciation relative to the initial long-run equilibrium, while output has risen by 2.8 per cent.

With the adjustment path characterized by a gradual real exchange rate depreciation, the domestic real interest rate slightly exceeds its foreign counterpart throughout the transition. Nevertheless, the fall in the real cost of capital goods is sufficient to promote an investment expansion despite the higher real interest rate; thus investment rises initially by some 1.5 percentage points of output (Figure 7.4). Subsequent additions to the capital stock drive down the profitability of new projects and hence investment levels off towards its new long-run value; the latter exceeds the initial value (relative to output) due to the higher capital-intensity of production, which requires higher replacement investment.

An important result refers to the current-account adjustment. In the long-run equilibrium, the current-account deficit is unchanged – equal to the exogenous flow of direct foreign investment. But along the transition path, the current account *deteriorates*: the reason is that Ricardian consumers immediately raise consumption in anticipation of future output gains, causing an increase in the current-account deficit by about 0.5 per cent of output in period 1 (Figure 7.5). The increased deficit is gradually reversed in subsequent periods as the anticipated output gains materialize.[18]

Finally, the initial increase in aggregate demand and subsequent rise in the capital stock stimulate labour demand. However, since wage flexibility ensures full employment, higher labour demand is entirely reflected in a real wage increase; the new long-run real wage exceeds its initial level by 2.8 per cent.

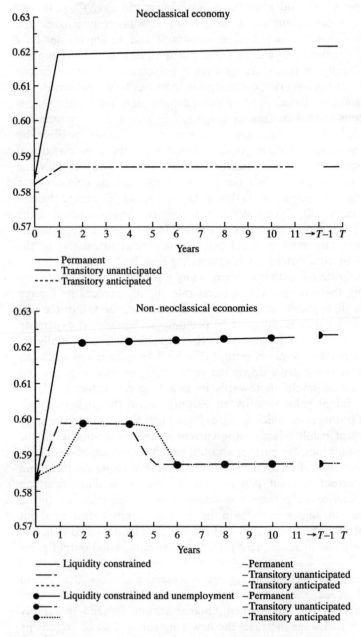

Figure 7.1   Foreign transfer shock: private consumption/output

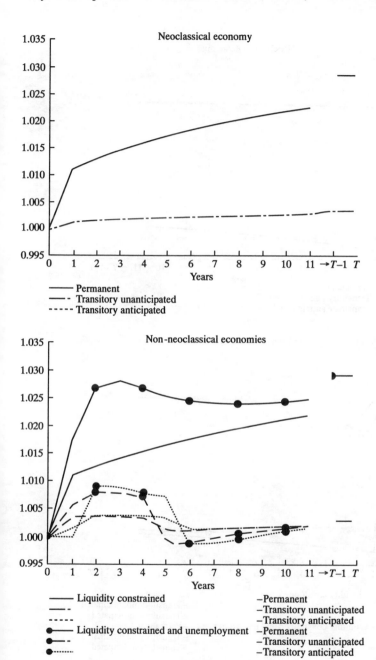

Figure 7.2   **Foreign transfer shock: output**

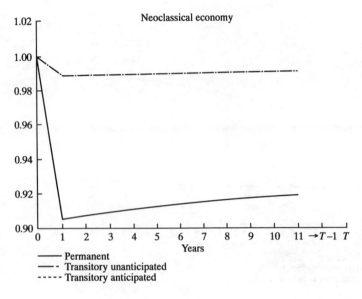

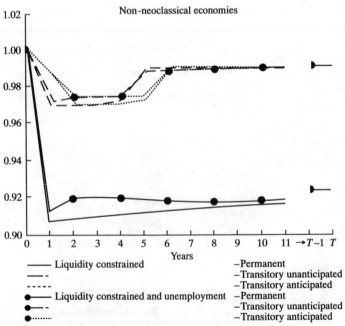

Figure 7.3   Foreign transfer shock: real exchange rate

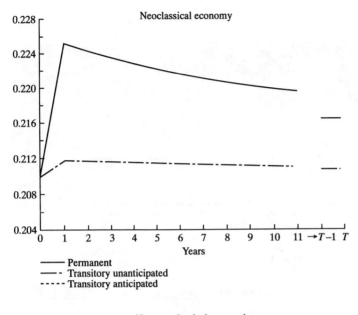

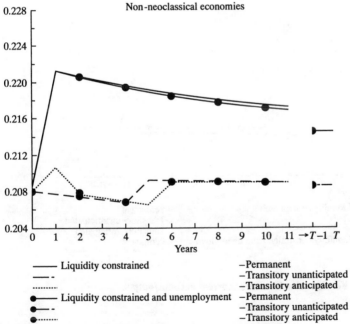

Figure 7.4   Foreign transfer shock: private investment/output

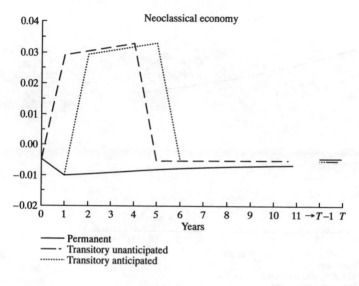

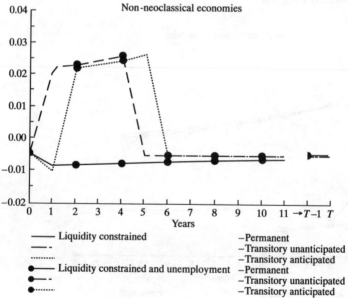

Figure 7.5   Foreign transfer shock: current account/output

It is worth underscoring that all these dynamic effects arise because of the *import content of production*. If capital goods had no import content, and if no imported materials were required for production, adjustment to the transfer shock would simply entail an instantaneous rise in private wealth and consumption, along with a real appreciation, without any change in real output, the capital stock, or the current account.

Consider next the case of a temporary unanticipated (*TU*) foreign transfer in this neoclassical economy, lasting from periods 1 to 4. As Figures 7.1–7.6 show, the qualitative effects on most variables are very similar to the case of a permanent shock. However, a temporary decrease in taxes raises permanent income by only a small amount, hence consumption increases by only a little. Consequently, all the effects described above occur with diminished force. The only qualitative difference is that now the current account shows a significant surplus while the shock lasts – a surplus of approximately 4 per cent of output as compared to deficit under the permanent shock – as consumers accumulate wealth to smooth out their consumption over the entire future horizon (see the dashed line in the top panel of Figure 7.5).

Consider now the case of a temporary anticipated (*TA*) shock, which takes place during periods 2 to 5. The effects are nearly identical to the unanticipated temporary shock. Consumption rises already in period 1 in anticipation of future lower taxes.[19] The current account goes initially into deficit, followed by four periods of surplus while the transfer lasts.

Next we focus on a full-employment economy with liquidity-constrained consumers and firms (*LCFE*). Aggregate consumption and investment respond only in part to forward-looking variables (wealth and Tobin's q), while now they are also sensitive to contemporaneous flow variables (consumer disposable income and operational profits).

For the permanent shock the dynamic paths of the endogenous variables in the *LCFE* economy are similar to the neoclassical case. By contrast, richer dynamics are observed under temporary shocks. Because temporary tax cuts relax the liquidity constraints of some consumers, aggregate consumption is boosted far beyond the smooth consumption levels of the *NC* economy during the four periods of shocks (cf. upper and bottom panels, Figure 7.1). Thus the *LCFE* economy exhibits a more pronounced cycle. Output expansion and real exchange rate appreciation are stronger than under the comparable temporary shocks in the *NC* economy, following U or inverted-U patterns during the four periods (bottom panels, Figures 7.2 and 7.2).

These real exchange rate fluctuations are reflected in a cycle in the real interest rate. Under a *TU* shock, the real exchange rate appreciates initially and then depreciates gradually for three periods (2 to 4); in period 5 it depreciates abruptly – due to the decline in consumption by liquidity-constrained agents (see Figure 7.3). Therefore, the real interest rate must rise sharply in period 4, in anticipation of the strong real exchange rate depreciation. By contrast, under a *TA* shock – which arrives in period 2 – the real exchange rate is expected to appreciate in period 2 and to depreciate abruptly in period 6. Hence the real interest rate must fall in period 1 and rise sharply in period 5. Under both types of shocks, the rise in the real interest rate after the arrival of the shock causes an aggregate investment slump until the fiscal expansion is reversed (Figure 7.4).

Finally, notice also that the transitory current-account surplus is lower than in the *NC* economy (Figure 7.5). The reason is that consumption is now higher due to the four-period relaxation of liquidity constraints.

The third and last economy to consider is the Keynesian benchmark, which combines liquidity constraints with wage rigidity and unemployment (*LCUN*). The new long-run values of all endogenous variables are similar to those attained in the previous full-employment economy (*LCFE*). The difference lies in the adjustment path: now real wages do not rise as much in response to higher labour demand, allowing a transitory increase in employment above the full-employment level. Lagged wage indexation introduces a strong cyclical pattern in output and employment, which is absent in the full-employment economies.

In the case of a *P* shock, consumption rises more than in the *LCFE* case, a result of the anticipation by unconstrained consumers of higher employment and production during the adjustment period. However, as a ratio to (also higher) output, consumption remains practically unaltered from the previous economy. Output follows an oscillatory path, first rising to a temporary peak in period 3, then declining to reach a trough in period 8, and finally converging towards its long-run value (which exceeds the levels achieved by the full-employment economies). The output dynamics are a result of slowly increasing capital and the cyclical pattern of employment. The latter exhibits a peak of 2.3 per cent overemployment in period 2 (as real wages decline in that period due to lagged indexation), after which it starts an asymptotic convergence back to full employment (Figure 7.6). The real exchange rate mimics the dynamics of output after period 1.

Higher operating profits from higher output contribute to raise investment by constrained firms and hence aggregate investment, above the levels attained in the *LCFE* economy. However, as a ratio to output, it remains roughly at the same level as in the *LCFE* economy.

Concerning the simulation results for temporary shocks in a Keynesian (*LCUN*) economy, the main point to be emphasized is related to the

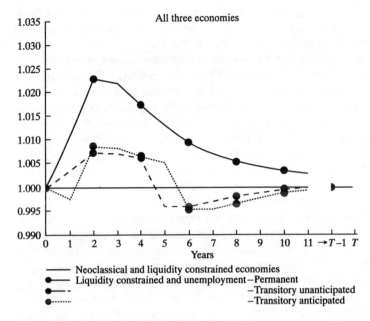

Figure 7.6 Foreign transfer shock: employment

cyclical behaviour of output. Aggregate demand, and hence output, rise much more during the four periods of foreign transfers, and then decline to lower levels than in the preceding full-employment economies. We conclude that, like liquidity constraints under temporary transfer shocks, wage rigidity intensifies the amplitude of the adjustment cycle to both temporary and permanent transfer shocks.

4.2 A permanent oil-price windfall

We analyse now the dynamic response to a permanent decline in the price of intermediate imports. This can be interpreted as an oil price fall in an oil-importing economy. The shock has been normalized again to a first-round gain (or direct effect) of 4 per cent of output, reflecting a 40 per cent drop in the international price of intermediate imports, whose output share equals 10 per cent initially. Figures 7.7–7.9 report the dynamic trajectories of the main macroeconomic variables in response to a permanent oil price windfall, for each of the three economies.

While the first-round magnitude is similar to that of the foreign transfer analysed above, a lower oil price entails a production substitution effect in addition to the transfer's income effect. That is, even before considering second-round income and substitution effects stemming from induced real exchange rate changes, the oil price fall encourages the substitution of capital and labour by cheaper oil.

Again consider first the *NC* economy (represented by continuous lines in Figures 7.7–7.9). Consumption (Figure 7.7) exhibits a dynamic pattern which is qualitatively similar to that in response to a transfer shock: a strong first-period increase and subsequently a gradual convergence to higher long-run levels. Wealth rises by a similar amount to that under the transfer shock. But private consumption increases by much less (long-run consumption as a share of output is now 58.7 per cent instead of 62.1 per cent before), due to a strong *increase* in the private consumption deflator, caused in turn by the real exchange rate depreciation.

Output grows much more than under the foreign transfer shock. The impact effect on output is now 5.4 per cent (as compared to 1.1 per cent before), and long-run output is 6.8 per cent higher (as compared to 2.8 per cent under the transfer shock). This significantly higher output level reflects the massive incentive to change the input mix away from value added and towards intermediate imports, in response to the lower international price of the latter. The strong supply expansion causes a 3.5 per cent initial real exchange rate *depreciation* (Figure 7.8), which stands in contrast to the initial *appreciation* under a foreign transfer shock. In the long run the real exchange rate depreciates by 5.4 per cent, while it had appreciated by 7.4 per cent under the transfer shock. Long-run intermediate imports grow now by a massive 69 per cent, a result of a positive substitution effect (a significantly lower international oil price slightly dampened by the moderate real exchange rate depreciation) and a positive scale effect; by comparison, they rose only 11 per cent under the transfer shock, resulting from a more modest scale effect and a substitution effect stemming only from the real exchange rate appreciation. The significant substitution effects – in both cases – reflect the high (unitary) elasticity of substitution between imports and value added, embodied by the Cobb–Douglas production technology.

Investment reflects the conflicting effects of the anticipated output rise, which boosts profitability, and the real depreciation, which makes capital goods more expensive due to their import content. Hence aggregate investment rises in period 1 by only a moderate amount (Figure 7.8). The long-run capital–output ratio is now 2.94, lower than in the initial steady state, as a result of the real exchange rate depreciation; by contrast, under the foreign transfer shock it had risen to 3.09, helped by the real exchange rate appreciation. Therefore the new long-run investment ratio to output must be lower after the oil-price windfall.

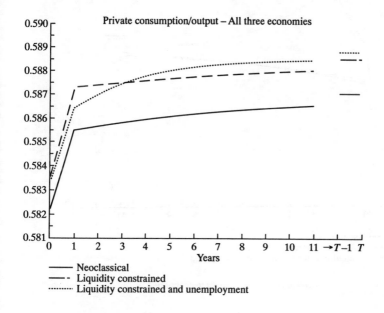

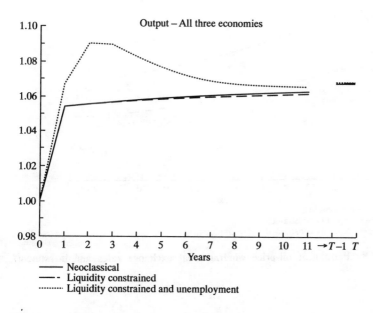

Figure 7.7   Permanent oil-price windfall: private consumption/output and output

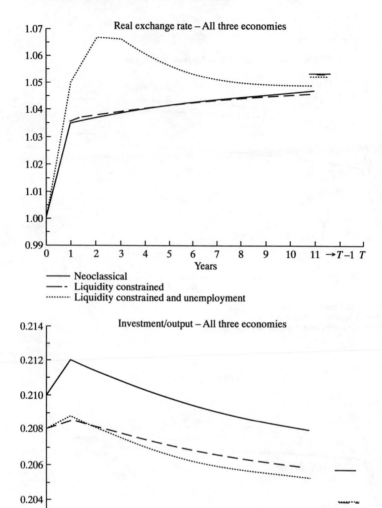

Figure 7.8   **Permanent oil-price windfall: real exchange rates and investment/ output**

The current account again replicates the interesting result that a favourable external shock causes a transitory *deficit* (Figure 7.9), due to the combination of investment adjustment costs (which delay the capacity expansion) and forward-looking consumers (who anticipate higher future income levels and therefore raise their current spending). Finally, with full employment holding continuously, real wages are boosted by the higher output levels. The long-run real wage increases in the same proportion as output (6.8 per cent), exceeding significantly the 2.8 per cent rise observed under the foreign transfer shock.

The full-employment economy with liquidity constraints (the *LCFE* case, depicted by dashed lines in Figures 7.7–7.9) displays a pattern very similar to that of the fully neoclassical case. The chief difference is that liquidity-constrained consumers do not initially adjust their consumption in anticipation of future output gains. As a result, the current-account deficit is now smaller, allowing for additional asset accumulation, which in the long run leads to higher wealth and sustains an increased consumption–output ratio.

The Keynesian benchmark *LCUN* (represented by the dotted lines in Figures 7.7–7.9) yields richer dynamics, due to the more pronounced change in output made possible by transitory overemployment. While consumption rises further than in the *LCFE* economy, as a share of (higher) output it follows a path which is very similar to the previous one. The short-term real exchange rate depreciation exceeds significantly the levels reached under the full-employment economies, due to the additional output expansion made possible by sluggish real wage adjustment. Real output reaches a peak in period 2, with a level which is 9.0 per cent higher than in the initial steady state, and also exceeds significantly the 5.6 per cent increase in the full-employment economies. Subsequent catch-up of real wages reduces output (which reaches a local minimum of 1.066 in period 10) until convergence to its new long-run equilibrium of 1.069. The real exchange rate mimics the cyclical pattern of output; in turn, investment as a share of output shows similar behaviour as in the *LCFE* economy.

Finally, consider the dynamic pattern of employment under a permanent external transfer. The real wage, determined by backward nominal indexation, reaches a trough in period 2, reflecting the price deflation of the initial period. Afterwards it catches up fast to converge towards its higher long-run value. Employment reflects this real wage pattern, reaching an all-time high of 5.4 per cent overemployment in period 2, subsequently returning asymptotically to full employment. Average overemployment is 3.8 per cent during periods 1 to 5, exceeding significantly the corresponding average of 1.7 per cent in the Keynesian

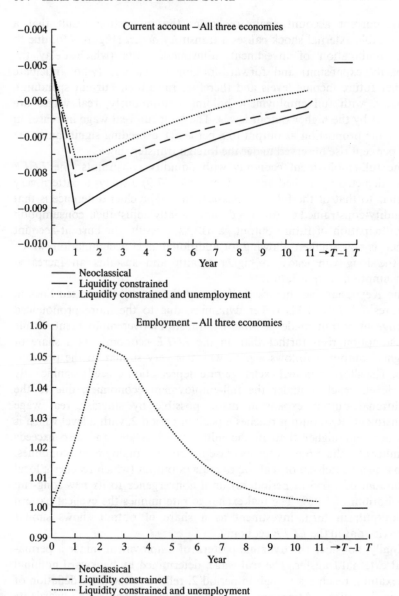

Figure 7.9　Permanent oil-price windfall: current account/output and employment

economy affected by a permanent transfer shock. Thus, like in the case of the transfer shock, wage rigidity intensifies substantially the amplitude of the cyclical response to an oil-price shock.

In concluding, the main difference between the oil-price windfall and the permanent transfer is that the former involves both a favourable supply shock – which boosts production directly and depreciates the real exchange rate – and a real income gain, while a foreign transfer implies only an income effect which boosts aggregate demand and appreciates the real exchange rate – with an indirect induced effect on supply. Apart from the real exchange rate, most other variables behave in a qualitatively similar fashion under both shocks, although the quantitative response is significantly more intense under the oil-price windfall.

5   Concluding remarks

This paper has developed a dynamic macroeconomic general equilibrium model encompassing three economies: a neoclassical case with frictionless, instantaneous clearing in goods, assets and labour markets, a full-employment economy with groups of liquidity-constrained consumers and investors, and a Keynesian benchmark with liquidity-constrained agents and wage rigidity giving rise to temporary deviations from full employment.

The model has been applied to simulate the impact, transitional and steady-state effects of permanent, temporary unanticipated and temporary anticipated external shocks. Two shocks have been considered: a rise in foreign transfers and a fall in the international price of intermediate imports.

The simulations demonstrate the usefulness of a consistent framework based on first principles for tracing out and understanding the macroeconomic response to disturbances. The numerical exercises illustrate three main points. First, due to the import content of production in the model, both permanent *and* transitory external shocks lead to long-run changes in productive capacity and real output, as well as in the other endogenous variables. Second, when favourable permanent shocks lead to higher steady-state capital and output (as is the case in the simulations above), their short-run effect is to cause a current-account *deterioration*. The reason is that consumption by unconstrained consumers immediately rises in response not only to current, but also to anticipated future real income gains, and the latter accrue only gradually, due to the existence of investment adjustment costs. This is in sharp contrast with the effect of favourable transitory shocks, which unambiguously *improve* the current account while they last. Third, market imperfections have important consequences for the dynamic response of the economy to exogenous disturbances. In contrast with the smooth, monotonic adjustment pattern displayed by the neoclassical benchmark economy in the simulations above, liquidity constraints or wage rigidity tend to amplify the cyclical response to external shocks. This suggests that market imperfections could be a major factor behind the complex dynamic adjustment patterns observed in actual economies.

Appendix   The model

This appendix describes the structure of the model, preceded by notation and definition of variables. All prices are defined relative to the price of the domestic good or to the foreign price level. All lower case variables other than prices and interest rates are defined in real terms (relative to the domestic or foreign price level, as applicable) and scaled to the labour force in efficiency units.[20] The model is written in continuous time. Dots over variables denote right-hand time derivatives.

Notation and definition of variables

1   Labour and employment

pg	Labour force growth rate
tg	Harrod-neutral technical progress rate
$g = pg + tg$	Growth rate of labour force in efficiency units
l	Employment (relative to labour force in efficiency units)

2   Incomes, transfers and capital flows

Domestic

d	Dividends paid
op	Operational profits
td	Taxes
yd	Private disposable income
$prem$	Profit remittances abroad

External (all exogenous):

$ftrg$	Foreign transfers to the public sector
$ftrp$	Foreign transfers to the private sector
yf	Foreign income
dfi	Direct foreign investment

3   Stocks

Domestic

a	Non-human wealth of the private sector
bg	Domestic debt of the public sector
fe	Stock of domestic equity (shares in domestic firms) held by foreigners

hb	Domestic base money
hu	Human wealth of the private sector
k	Physical capital
$pvig$	Present value of government investment subsidy
$pvihb$	Present value of cost of holding money
External	
fbg	Foreign assets held by the public sector
fbp	Foreign assets held by the private sector

4   Goods flows

y	Gross output of final goods
cp	Private aggregate consumption
cmp	Private imported goods consumption
cnp	Private national goods consumption
cng	Public national goods consumption
inv	Gross domestic investment
in	Private national goods investment
im	Private imported goods investment
ig	Public investment subsidy
iac	Investment adjustment costs
x	Exports
mr	Intermediate imports

5   Various rates

Domestic rates

i	Nominal interest rate on public debt
r	Real interest rate on public debt
nmg	Rate of growth of the nominal money stock

External Rates (all exogenous)

if	Nominal interest rate on foreign assets/liabilities
rf	Real interest rate on foreign assets/liabilities

6   Goods prices

Domestic (all relative to the price of the domestic final good):

pc	Private aggregate consumption deflator
pi	Aggregate investment deflator

External (all relative to the price of the foreign final good and exogenously given):

$pcmp$	Private imported goods consumption deflator
pim	Imported goods investment deflator
pmr	Intermediate imports deflator
px	Deflator of export-competing goods

7   Other prices

Domestic prices

q	Real equity price (Tobin's q) in units of domestic output

v Real wage per effective labour unit
W Nominal wage per labour unit
PC Nominal private consumption deflator
Real exchange rate
$e = (EP^*)/P$ Real exchange rate
E Nominal exchange rate
P Nominal price of the domestic good
P^* Nominal price of the foreign final good

Model structure

Budget constraints

Public-sector budget constraint

$$[td + e\,ftrg - cng - pi\,ig] - (r - g)bg + (g + \dot{P}/P)hb$$
$$+ e(rf - g)fbg = e\,\dot{fbg} - \dot{bg} - \dot{hb} \qquad (1)$$

External-sector budget constraint (balance of payments)

$$\left[\frac{x}{e} - pcmp\,cmp - pim\,im - pmr\,mr + ftrg + ftrp\right] + (rf - g)[fbp + fbg]$$
$$- \frac{prem}{e} = (\dot{fbp} + \dot{fbg}) - dfi \qquad (2)$$

Private-sector budget constraint

$$[y - pi\,inv - pi\,iac - e\,pmr\,mr + e\,ftrp - td + pi\,ig - pc\,cp] - (g + \dot{P}/P)hb$$
$$+ (r - g)bg - prem + (rf - g)\,e\,fbp = \dot{hb} + \dot{bg} - e\,dfi + e\,\dot{fbp} \qquad (3)$$

Market equilibrium conditions

Goods market

$$y = cnp + cng + in + pi\,iac + x \qquad (4)$$

Money market

$$hb = \phi_1 y^{\phi_2} exp(\phi_3 i) \qquad (5)$$

where ϕ_1, $\phi_2 \geq 0$, $\phi_3 \leq 0$.

Bond market

$$r = rf + \frac{\dot{e}}{e} \qquad (6)$$

Equity market

$$\dot{q} = r\,q - \frac{d}{k} \qquad (7)$$

Standard Fisher equation

$$i = r + \frac{\dot{P}}{P} \tag{8}$$

Labour market

The nominal wage equation in discrete time form

$$W = exp(tg)l^\omega \left(\frac{PC}{PC_{-1}}\right)^\theta \left(\frac{PC_{-1}}{PC_{-2}}\right)^{1-\theta} W_{-1} \tag{9}$$

where $\omega \geq 0$, $0 \leq \theta \leq 1$.
The relation between the nominal wage and the real (product) wage per effective labour unit

$$\frac{W}{P} = exp(tg\ t)\ v \tag{10}$$

where t is the time index.

Firms

Production function

$$y = \alpha_0 l^{\alpha_1}\ k^{\alpha_2}\ mr^{(1-\alpha_1-\alpha_2)} \tag{11}$$

where $\alpha_0 \geq 0$, $0 \leq \alpha_1$, $\alpha_2 \leq 1$.
Investment adjustment costs

$$iac = \mu \left[\frac{(inv - (g+\delta)k)^2}{k}\right] \tag{12}$$

where $\mu > 0$.
The evolution of the capital/effective labour ratio

$$\dot{k} = inv - (g+\delta)k \tag{13}$$

Marginal productivity condition for labour

$$l = \alpha_1 v^{-1}\ y \tag{14}$$

Marginal productivity condition for imported inputs

$$mr = (1 - \alpha_1 - \alpha_2)(e\ pmr)^{-1}\ y \tag{15}$$

Investment demand

$$inv = \beta_1 \left[\frac{k}{2\mu}\left[\frac{q}{pi} - \frac{pvig}{pik} - 1\right] + (g+\delta)k\right] + (1 - \beta_1)\left[\beta_2 \frac{op}{pi} + ig\right] \tag{16}$$

where β_1 is the share of non-constrained firms and β_2 is the marginal propensity of liquidity-constrained firms to invest out of operational profits; $0 \leq \beta_1$, $\beta_2 \leq 1$. The present value of the public investment subsidy

$$pvig = (r - g)\, pvig - pi\, ig \tag{17}$$

Aggregate operational profits

$$op = y - vl - e\, pmr\, mr \tag{18}$$

Dividends

$$d = op - pi\, inv - pi\, iac + pi\, ig + q(\dot{k} + gk) \tag{19}$$

Share of domestic goods in aggregate investment

$$in = \gamma\, pi\, inv \tag{20}$$

Share of imported goods in aggregate investment

$$im = (1 - \gamma)\left[\frac{pi}{e\, pim}\right] inv \tag{21}$$

where $0 \leq \gamma \leq 1$.
The aggregate investment deflator

$$pi = (e\, pim)^{(1-\gamma)} \tag{22}$$

Consumers

Private-sector non-human wealth

$$a = hb + bg + e\, fbp + q(k - fe) - pvihb \tag{23}$$

The path of money holding costs

$$p\dot{v}ihb = (r - g)\, pvihb - i\, hb \tag{24}$$

The path of human wealth

$$\dot{hu} = (r - g)hu + [td - vl - e\, ftrp] \tag{25}$$

Total private consumption demand

$$cp = \lambda_1\left[(\lambda_2 - g)\frac{a + hu}{pc}\right] + (1 - \lambda_1)\left[\frac{yd}{pc} + (\lambda_2 - g)\frac{a}{pc}\right] \tag{26}$$

where $0 \leq \lambda_1 \leq 1$ is the share of unconstrained consumers, and λ_2 is the subjective discount rate.

Disposable income

$$yd = v\ l + e\ ftrp - td \tag{27}$$

Share of domestic goods in aggregate private consumption

$$cnp = \eta\ pc\ cp \tag{28}$$

Share of imported goods in aggregate private consumption

$$cmp = (1 - \eta)\left[\frac{pc}{e\ pcmp}\right] cp \tag{20}$$

where $0 \le \eta \le 1$.
The aggregate private consumption deflator

$$pc = (e\ pcmp)^{(1-\eta)} \tag{30}$$

The accumulation of per-capita real balances

$$\dot{hb} = [nmg - (\dot{P}/P) - g]hb \tag{31}$$

where nmg is endogenous under money-financing of the public deficit, and exogenous otherwise.

Foreigners

Foreign demand for the domestically produced good

$$x = \rho_1 (e\ px)^{\rho_2}\ yf^{\rho_3} \tag{32}$$

where $\rho_1,\ \rho_2,\ \rho_3 \ge 0$.
Path of foreigners' equity holdings

$$\dot{fe} = \frac{e\ dfi}{q} - g\ fe \tag{33}$$

Profit repatriation

$$prem = \frac{fe}{k} d \tag{34}$$

NOTES

We are indebted to Warwick McKibbin and Steven Symansky for stimulating discussions of model solution and simulation techniques, and to David Currie and Warwick McKibbin for their very valuable comments. We also thank Leonardo

Auernheimer, Michael Ellis and participants at the XIth Latin American Meetings of the Econometric Society, the World Bank Macroeconomics Seminar, and the Oxford North–South Conference for useful comments. Very efficient research assistance by Paul Bergin and Gylfi Zoega is gratefully acknowledged.

1 Three of these features (wage rigidity, import content of capital goods and foreign holdings of domestic equity) are considered in different forms by previous models, in particular McKibbin and Sachs (1989). Explicit inclusion of public investment and monetary finance of budget deficits are novel features of this framework.

2 The model's variables and equations are listed in the appendix to this paper. For a more complete description of the model, see Schmidt-Hebbel and Serven (1992).

3 Foreign assets held by the domestic private and public sectors are net assets (equal to gross foreign reserves plus other gross foreign assets less gross foreign liabilities) and therefore can have either sign.

4 However, the model can be easily extended to allow a less restrictive formulation of substitution possibilities in consumption, production and investment.

5 The general reasons that cause marginal and average q (which represents just the market value of existing capital) to diverge are spelt out in Hayashi (1982). In our framework they differ due to the lump-sum investment subsidy that firms receive from the government. Marginal q equals average q minus the present value of the subsidy per unit of capital. Hence the subsidy has no effect whatsoever on the investment decisions of unconstrained firms, due to its lump-sum nature. It does affect, however, investment by liquidity-constrained firms.

6 The assumption of equal discount rates is crucial for Ricardian equivalence to hold. Higher private-sector discount rates, whether due to finite lifetimes (reflected by a given probability of death, as in Blanchard, 1985) or to a risk premium on consumers' debt relative to the borrowing cost of the government (e.g., McKibbin and Sachs, 1989) would cause Ricardian equivalence to break down.

7 For discussion and empirical analyses of the implications of liquidity constraints for consumer behaviour – as well as for Ricardian equivalence – see Hayashi (1985), Hubbard and Judd (1986), Bernheim (1987), Leiderman and Blejer (1988), Seater (1993) and Easterly et al. (1994).

8 Recall that, because of perfect asset substitutability, the per-capita real return on wealth is just equal to the real interest rate (net of effective labour force growth) times the wealth stock. In turn, steady-state consumption equals the rate of time preference (also net of effective labour force growth) times the wealth stock.

9 Turnovsky and Sen (1991) use a non-monetary model with intertemporally optimizing consumers in which transitory fiscal disturbances have long-run effects. Their result depends critically on the endogeneity of labour supply in their framework, which makes long-run employment endogenous. In our case, the dependence of the long-run capital stock on the real exchange rate ensures that transitory fiscal shocks have permanent effects despite the constancy of full employment across steady states. This issue is investigated analytically in Serven (1993).

10 Without liquidity constraints, the experiment would just amount to a change in the composition of taxation between the inflation tax and direct taxes, without any effect on wealth, consumption, or any other real variable.

11 See Blanchard and Kahn (1980) and Buiter (1984).

12 In principle, we could linearize the system around a steady state to determine analytically the conditions under which the transition matrix possesses the saddle-point property. Given the large dimensionality of our system, however, this would be an intractable task.

13 We used a very strict convergence criterion, requiring that the maximum relative change between solutions in any variable at any time period not exceed one-thousandth of 1 per cent. This typically required a horizon between sixty and eighty periods for convergence. For the actual simulations, the model was made discrete.

14 Recall that Walras' law ensures that one of the three sectoral budget constraints (of the public, private and foreign sectors) holds identically when markets clear. Hence we do not need to specify a third residual variable.

15 Note that in Figures 7.1–7.9 different schedules often overlap. For instance, the schedules for temporary unanticipated and temporary anticipated shocks are virtually the same in the upper panels of Figures 7.1, 7.2 and 7.3. The schedules for any given shock coincide for the liquidity-constrained and liquidity-constrained with unemployment economies in the lower panels of Figures 7.1 and 7.5. Finally, the employment schedule coincides exactly for the neoclassical and liquidity-constrained economies in the bottom panel of Figure 7.9.

16 Long-run consumption rises more than real wealth. The reason is the decline in the private consumption deflator, prompted by the real exchange rate appreciation.

17 In Figure 7.3, an appreciation is represented by a decline in the value of e, in accordance with the model's definition of the real exchange rate.

18 This result, however, depends on our choice of parameter values. In general, the change in the current account is given by two main factors. First, the degree of intertemporal substitutability in consumption: the lower substitutability, the stronger the consumption-smoothing effect described in the text and the more likely a current-account deterioration. Second, the magnitude of adjustment costs to investment: the higher adjustment costs, the smaller the investment rise, and the more likely a current-account improvement. The analytical details are provided in Serven (1993).

19 The rise is slightly smaller than under TU because the temporary tax reduction must be discounted one additional period.

20 Labour force in efficiency units is equal to the actual labour force augmented by Harrod-neutral technical progress.

REFERENCES

Barro, R. (1974) 'Are government bonds net wealth?' *Journal of Political Economy* **82**, 1095–117.

Bernheim, B. (1987) 'Ricardian equivalence: an evaluation of theory and evidence', in S. Fischer (ed.), *NBER Macroeconomics Annual*, Cambridge MA: MIT Press, pp. 263–304.

Blanchard, O. (1985) 'Debt, deficits, and finite horizons', *Journal of Political Economy* **93**, 223–47.
Blanchard, O. and C. Kahn (1980) 'The solution of linear difference models under rational expectations', *Econometrica* **48**, 1305–11.
Bruno, M. and J. Sachs (1985) *Economics of World-Wide Stagflation*, Cambridge MA: Harvard University Press.
Buiter, W. (1984) 'Saddlepoint problems in continuous time rational expectations models: a general method and some macroeconomic examples', *Econometrica* **52**, 665–80.
Easterly, W., C. Rodriguez and K. Schmidt-Hebbel (1994) *Public Sector Deficits and Macroeconomic Performance in Developing Countries*, Oxford University Press.
Elbadawi, I. and K. Schmidt-Hebbel (1991) 'Macroeconomic structure and policy in Zimbabwe', PRE Working Paper No. 771, The World Bank, September.
Fair, R. and J. Taylor (1983) 'Solution and maximum likelihood estimation of dynamic nonlinear rational expectations models', *Econometrica* **51**, 1169–85.
Gavin, M. (1991) 'Economic policy, exchange rates and investment in a Keynesian economy', manuscript, Columbia University.
Giavazzi, F., M. Odekon and C. Wyplosz (1992) 'Simulating an oil shock with sticky prices', *European Economic Review* **18**, 11–39.
Giavazzi, F. and C. Wyplosz (1984) 'The real exchange rate, the current account, and the speed of adjustment', in C. Bilson and R. Marston (eds.), *Exchange Rates: Theory and Policy*, Chicago: Chicago University Press.
Haque, Nadeem V., Kajal Lahiri and Peter J. Montiel (1990) 'A macroeconometric model for developing countries', *IMF Staff Papers* **37**, 537–59.
Hayashi, F. (1982) 'Tobin's marginal *q* and average *q*: a neoclassical interpretation', *Econometrica* **50**, 215–24.
(1985) 'Tests for liquidity constraints: a critical survey', NBER Working Paper No. 1720.
Hayashi, F. and T. Inoue (1991) 'The relation between firm growth and *q* with multiple capital goods: theory and evidence from panel data on Japanese firms', *Econometrica* **59**, 731–53.
Hubbard, G. and K. Judd (1986) 'Liquidity Constraints, Fiscal Policy and Consumption', *Brookings Papers on Economic Activity*, 1–59.
Leiderman, L. and M. Blejer (1988) 'Modelling and testing Ricardian Equivalence', *IMF Staff Papers* **35**, 1–35.
Lipton, D., J. Poterba, J. Sachs and L. Summers (1982) 'Multiple shooting in rational expectations models', *Econometrica* **50**, 1329–33.
Lipton, D. and J. Sachs (1983) 'Accumulation and growth in a two-country model', *Journal of International Economics* **15**, 135–59.
Lucas, R.E. (1967) 'Adjustment costs and the theory of supply', *Journal of Political Economy* **75**, 321–34.
McKibbin, W.J. and J. Sachs (1989) 'The McKibbin–Sachs global model: theory and specification', NBER Working Paper No. 3100.
McKibbin, W.J. and M.W. Sundberg (1990) 'Macroeconomic linkages between the OECD and the Asia-Pacific region', Brookings Discussion Papers in International Economics No. 80.
McKibbin, W.J. and P.J. Wilcoxen (1992) 'G-CUBED: a dynamic multi-sector equilibrium model of the global economy (qualifying the costs of curbing

CO_2 emissions)', Brookings Discussion Papers in International Economics No. 98.

Ramsey, F. (1928) 'A mathematical theory of saving', *Economic Journal* **38**, 543–59.

Sachs, J. (1983) 'Energy and growth under flexible exchange rates: a simulation study', in J.S. Bhandari and B.H. Putnam (eds.), *Economic Interdependence and Flexible Exchange Rates*, Cambridge MA: MIT Press.

Schmidt-Hebbel, K. and L. Serven (1992) 'Dynamic response to foreign transfers and terms-of-trade shocks in open economies', Policy Research Working Paper Series No. 1061, The World Bank, December.

(1993) 'Dynamic effects of fiscal and monetary policy in classical and Keynesian economies', Manuscript, The World Bank.

Seater, J. (1993) 'Ricardian equivalence', *Journal of Economic Literature* **31**, 142–90.

Serven, L. (1991) 'Anticipated real exchange rate changes and the dynamics of investment', paper presented at the 1991 Latin American meeting of the Econometric Society, Uruguay, August.

(1993) 'Capital goods imports, the real exchange rate, and the current account', manuscript, The World Bank.

Serven, L. and A. Solimano (1991) 'An empirical macroeconomic model for policy design: the case of Chile', PRE Working Paper No. 709, The World Bank, June.

Tobin, J. (1969) 'A general equilibrium approach to monetary theory', *Journal of Money, Credit and Banking* **1**, 15–29.

Treadway, A. (1969) 'On rational entrepreneurial behaviour and the demand for investment', *Review of Economic Studies* **36**, 227–39.

Turnovsky, S. and P. Sen (1991) 'Fiscal policy, capital accumulation, and debt in an open economy', *Oxford Economic Papers* **43**, 1–24.

Discussion

DAVID CURRIE

In this paper, Schmidt-Hebbel and Serven illustrate the simulation properties of a calibrated rational expectations macromodel, that by appropriate choice of parameter values can variously exhibit both neoclassical and non-neoclassical properties. That sounds a fairly standard diet, but the authors provide some interesting variations that appeal to the palate, incorporating sluggishness of wage adjustment and liquidity influences on consumers and firms, constraining consumer spending and investment and thereby reducing the effective degree of forward-lookingness. Their careful choice of issues coupled with the care with which they set up and analyse their model yields unexpected rewards.

Two results are of particular interest. First, perhaps not surprisingly, they find that the version of the model that incorporates liquidity constraints and wage stickiness gives rise to greater variability of output than the neoclassical version. Second, a favourable oil-price windfall can generate an immediate balance-of-payments deficit. This arises because of forward-looking consumption behaviour coupled with adjustment costs in investment. Consumers spend now against higher future income resulting from a lower oil price (the economy is assumed to be an oil importer); while production expands only slowly because of the lags in installing new capacity. The result is a short-run payments deficit.

My comments on the paper comprise a set of points about features of the model, its relevance to the analysis of North–South macroeconomic interactions, and possible directions for future work.

A key question is how far we should regard this model as being of a developing, rather than developed, economy. Now that is not to suggest that different principles drive Southern economies as compared with Northern ones: I do not hold that view, as my collaborative modelling work with David Vines demonstrates. But the model may need adaptation to reflect the following particular features of Southern economies:

(a) The parameterization of the model may need to vary to reflect different features of a Southern economy; for example, the levels of asset holdings (government debt, foreign debt, level of money holdings) which vary with the extent of economic development. In particular, the level of external indebtedness may be rather critical when considering the economy's response to external shocks.

(b) Financial constraints on consumers and investment, though not an exclusively Southern phenomenon, may be more important in Southern economies, particularly those (which are most common) that have non-liberalized, repressed financial systems.

(c) Southern economies, not just the highly indebted countries, may well have a much lower capacity to borrow overseas. An external constraint of this kind will have important consequences for adjustment to shocks, particularly external ones. For this reason, I am a little concerned at the fact that in Schmidt-Hebbel and Serven's model foreign asset holdings are the residual in the private-sector budget constraint. This may well misspecify the ability of the private sector in a typical Southern economy to borrow overseas. A related point is that liquidity constraints in the model are independent of the level of foreign borrowing.

(d) Institutional and political constraints in Southern economies may well influence the type of policy regime that is relevant. All the simulations reported in the paper assume that taxes adjust to balance the public-sector deficit. But it is often hard for governments in Southern economies (and in a number of Northern ones) to levy taxes, especially when the economy is hit by an adverse shock that depresses living standards and tax revenues simultaneously. For this reason, it would be of considerable interest to use the model to examine other financing regimes, notably money financing.

Given these areas for potential difference between Southern and Northern economies, it would be of interest to examine how sensitive the model's behaviour is to variations in these key model assumptions. Does the model exhibit larger fluctuations in response to shocks with a 'Southern' set of parameter values and policy settings than with a 'Northern' set? If there are significant differences, it would also be of interest to hook up two such economies, one with Northern and the other with Southern features. With symmetric countries, global fluctuations are driven by aggregate shocks, not by their distribution across countries. But with parameter and policy asymmetries of the type that I am suggesting, global developments will be influenced by the differences in structure and the distribution of shocks between North and South. This might mean, for example, that a Northern fiscal stimulus that takes the form of transfers to the South may well have a different, possibly larger, impact than transfers within the North.

A feature of the model simulations is that the differences between neoclassical and non-neoclassical versions are not as large as one might have expected, particularly when the differences are scaled by the size of the shock. (In examining the simulation charts, it is important to notice that the vertical axis is often truncated: in terms of deviations from base, the simulation differences are usually rather small.) This is, of course, a fairly common experience: forward-looking rational expectations models are often hard to move around, because forward-looking behaviour can often smooth out fluctuations. Relaxing the informational assumptions assumed in computing the rational expectations solution can be one way of modifying this, though my experience is that again the differences are not large.

A more radical route is to abandon the assumption of rational expectations in favour of bounded rationality and learning. Although I am a regular user of rational expectations models, I have always been rather sceptical about them, because of the extreme informational assumptions that they make: complete knowledge of the model and considerable knowledge of the exogenous processes driving the model. But structural change and model uncertainty mean that the rational expectations solution is inappropriate: since far distant events are much more uncertain than closer events, the backward recursion implicit in the rational expectations solution is inappropriate. I am not sure that Southern economies are more subject to structural change than Northern ones, though it is possible, but for both it is important. It is for that reason that we at London Business School use bounded rationality and learning, implemented through a Kalman filter procedure, in both our UK model and in GEM, our international model. A learning approach seems of equal relevance for Southern economies, and may well generate very different simulation results in the model of Schmidt-Hebbel and Serven, in both its neoclassical and non-neoclassical versions.

Part Five
Global scenarios

8 Macroeconomic effects on developing countries of shocks in the OECD: evidence from multicountry models

RALPH C. BRYANT and
WARWICK J. McKIBBIN

1 Introduction

Economists and policy makers possess only a rudimentary understanding of macroeconomic interactions between the OECD industrial countries and the non-OECD developing countries in the global economy. The lack of understanding, in particular of reliable empirical estimates, is attributable primarily to the intrinsic complexity of the required analysis. Suppose, for example, that analysts wish to study the process by which a shock emanating from the OECD countries (hereafter 'OECD') works through the global economy to produce final outcomes in the developing countries ('non-OECD'). They must consider all of the following stages: (i) the first-round effects within the OECD itself; (ii) the initial transmission of influences to non-OECD countries; (iii) the subsequent impacts on non-OECD regions and adjustments within those regions; (iv) feedback effects to the OECD, with subsequent adjustments there; and (v) further rounds of feedbacks, in both directions, among OECD and non-OECD countries. In practice these various stages blur into each other. In principle, only a systemic model of the global economy can capture adequately the general-equilibrium interactions.

Economists working on North–South macroeconomic interactions have met several times in recent years to consolidate existing knowledge and to discuss research plans for extending it. For one of these meetings, a conference held in Korea in May 1991, a variety of groups operating empirical multicountry models prepared a set of commonly specified simulations exploring how, within the models, various types of standardized shocks influence the global economy.[1] In this paper, we make use of the simulation data prepared in 1991. Our focus is on understanding how shocks originating in the OECD may have impacts in non-OECD economies.

Only a few of the existing multicountry models have an explicit

181

sub-model or sub-models for non-OECD regions. Most models either ignore these regions or treat them as a passive 'rest of world' sector. Because the manner of treatment of non-OECD regions in the existing models is so diverse, at this stage of our knowledge it is not feasible to try to standardize the generation and reporting of simulation results for the developing countries. It has been feasible, however, to go some way towards standardizing simulation results for the OECD economies. Given the constraints of the available simulation data, we summarize here some key impacts of the standard shocks within the OECD and then use this information to develop some insight into how these shocks are likely to influence non-OECD countries.[2]

The paper is structured as follows. In Sections 2 and 3, we present a selective overview of the available simulation data, focusing on the consequences of standardized shocks to monetary and fiscal policies, first for the United States alone and then for similar policies undertaken symmetrically throughout the OECD. In Section 4 we present a simplified accounting framework for beginning to examine the linkages between OECD and non-OECD economies. The framework serves to identify those OECD variables that are most important in the transmission of shocks to developing countries. In Section 5, we use the simulation data of Section 3 and the framework of Section 4 to highlight the likely implications of these shocks for non-OECD economies in the aggregate. We conclude in Section 6 with a summary of main points and some comments on the implications of this study for future research on the linkages between the OECD and non-OECD economies.

2   Background to the comparative simulations

The simulation results presented at the May 1991 conference were prepared in accordance with a set of guidelines circulated to the modelling groups after initial consultations. We indicate here those features of the guidelines essential for an understanding of the simulations discussed below.

2.1   Participating models

Invitations to participate in the 1991 Seoul conference were extended to a variety of modelling groups, with an emphasis on groups that had a research interest in the macroeconomic interactions between industrial and developing countries. Nine groups were able to participate. Simulations for seven of the models are used in this paper. In alphabetical order, these seven models are (with a three-letter mnemonic in parentheses used for short reference:)[3]

GEM (GEM): a version of the Global Economic Model resulting from a collaboration between the London Business School and the National Institute for Economic and Social Research in London. Chris Allen and David Currie prepared the simulations for this conference.[4]

INTERMOD (INA or INC): a policy simulation model originally developed by a Canadian team under the direction of John Helliwell (following the IMF effort to construct MULTIMOD), sponsored by the Canadian Department of Finance and subsequently supported also by the Bank of Canada. The model can be run with adaptive expectations (INA) or forward-looking model-consistent expectations (INC); both types of simulations are included in the results here. Mary MacGregor, Krishna Pendakur, Shane Williamson and other colleagues at the Department of Finance prepared the simulations for the 1991 conference.

LIVERPOOL (LVE or LIV): the model developed by Patrick Minford and several associates at the University of Liverpool. Michael Beenstock, now at the Hebrew University in Jerusalem, has recently been collaborating with the Liverpool group on modelling developing countries. The Liverpool model can be run with European countries' exchange rates constrained as in the European Monetary System (LVE) or freely fluctuating against each other (LIV); in this paper we have used the results only for the former version (LVE). Minford and E. Nowell prepared the OECD region simulations for the 1991 conference. Beenstock prepared the results for non-OECD regions.

MSG (MSG): a policy simulation model originally developed by Warwick McKibbin and Jeffrey Sachs at Harvard University, now revised and maintained by McKibbin at the Brookings Institution.

MULTIMOD (MUL): an updated version of the policy simulation model developed in the Research Department of the International Monetary Fund. The research team has included Paul Masson, Richard Haas, Steven Symansky, Michael Dooley and Guy Meredith, as well as other IMF staff. Steven Symansky prepared the simulations for the 1991 conference.

OECD INTERLINK (OEC): the Interlink model system, constructed and maintained by the Economics and Statistics Department of the

OECD. Pete Richardson oversees the model team at the OECD and prepared the simulations for the 1991 conference.

TAYLOR (TAY): an augmented version of the policy simulation multi-country model developed originally by John Taylor and associates at Stanford University. Recent modifications in the model and the simulations generated for the 1991 conference are due to Andrew Levin of the University of California, San Diego.

Among these models, GEM and TAY have quarterly frequencies; OEC is a semi-annual model; INA/INC, LVE/LIV, MSG and MUL have annual frequencies.

The INA and OEC models treat expectations adaptively. INC, LVE/LIV, MSG, MUL and TAY enforce model-consistent expectations. For these simulations, the GEM model's use of rational expectations is limited to exchange rates only.

2.2   Supplementary assumptions about fiscal and monetary policies

When modelling groups prepare simulations, they inevitably make assumptions within the context of their models about the stance of fiscal and monetary policies, for both the short and the long runs. Differences across models in the assumptions can lead to significant differences in simulation results. For the simulations here, an effort was made to attain more standardization across models in terms of the rules for 'unchanged' fiscal and monetary policies. For similar reasons, efforts were also made to define the intertemporal aspects of fiscal shocks more precisely.[5]

'Unchanged monetary policy' was defined as maintaining the stock of nominal money balances unchanged along a baseline path. The guidelines did not try to specify which definition of money should be chosen, but instead asked the modelling groups to select the definition of a monetary aggregate that, for their model, seemed most natural to treat as exogenous.[6] For 'unchanged fiscal policy', modelling groups were asked to implement two different intertemporal fiscal 'closure rules'. For the simulations discussed in this paper, the level of real government expenditures on goods and services was to be kept unchanged along its baseline path and the total fiscal deficit was to be allowed to deviate from baseline in the first several years of the simulation, but then subsequently return back to the baseline path by the fifth year of the simulation (thereafter remaining unchanged from its baseline path). Changes in personal income taxes were to be used to enforce the stipulated path of the fiscal deficit (and the associated path for government debt).

This assumption about the intertemporal behaviour of fiscal policy, labelled 'rule 2' in the simulation guidelines, does not necessarily correspond to the most likely behaviour of governments in the real world. A typical set of assumptions used by models with backward-looking expectations has been to specify that real government expenditures and tax rates are kept unchanged along baseline paths. Models with forward-looking, model-consistent expectations, however, typically cannot reach a convergent solution without more explicitly making some type of assumption that enforces the intertemporal budget constraint facing the government. The assumption used here has the advantage of imposing somewhat more standardization of fiscal assumptions that was characteristic of past model-comparison exercises.[7]

2.3   Specification of the standard shocks

The guidelines requested simulation results for 7 patterns of shocks, each identified by a letter (A through G). When combined with the two alternative fiscal rules, a total of twelve simulations were run for the 1991 conference.

The shocks were of three general types: contractionary changes in monetary policy, contractionary changes in fiscal policy and an increase in oil prices. The monetary policy actions assumed here have consequences somewhat analogous to those resulting from a private-sector increase in the demand for money. The fiscal actions have consequences qualitatively similar to an autonomous decline in private-sector spending.

In this paper, we make use of four of the twelve simulations. The detailed specifications for these four are as follows:

A2 *US monetary contraction*. A permanent 5 per cent decrease in the nominal money supply in the United States – that is, the simulation path for the US Money stock, 'exogenous definition', is set 5 per cent below baseline path throughout the simulation – with all other countries keeping monetary policy unchanged and every country (the United States and all others) following fiscal rule 2.

B2 *OECD-wide monetary contraction*. Every OECD country simultaneously implements a permanent 5 per cent decrease in its nominal money supply, with all governments following rule 2 for their fiscal policies.

D2 *US fiscal contraction, with debt-GDP ratio permanently changed*. The US government implements a permanent 1 per cent of baseline real GDP decrease in US government real spending on goods and services (size of reduction in real government spending equal to 1 per cent of baseline real GDP).[8] In the initial year of the simulation, the change in spending was to be financed by retiring debt relative to baseline (the total fiscal deficit decreasing relative to baseline by a substantial fraction of the 1 per cent of real GDP change in expenditures). In subsequent years, the simulated stock of nominal government debt was to adjust smoothly such that by the tenth year of the simulation it was below baseline by an amount equal to 10 per cent of baseline nominal GDP in year 10. From the tenth year onwards, the ratio of the simulated stock of debt to simulated nominal GDP was to remain at the value of the ratio attained in year 10. All residual adjustment in the US government's accounts was to be made via changes in personal income taxes. All countries including the United States were to keep monetary policies unchanged. Countries other than the United States were to follow fiscal rule 2.

F *OECD-wide fiscal contraction, with debt–GDP ratios changing permanently.* Every OECD country simultaneously implements a permanent 1 per cent of baseline real GDP decrease in real government spending, with each OECD country having the same type of pattern for fiscal deficits (reduced below baseline for the first ten years of the simulation) and scaled-by-GDP levels of debt (fall to a new sustained lower level) as assumed for the United States in the D2 simulation. Each country's monetary policy remains unchanged from baseline.

Modelling groups were asked to start their simulations in 1990 and to generate results for eleven years, ending in the year 2000. Quarterly models were to start the shocks in the first quarter of 1990.

2.4   Figures summarizing the simulation results

As background for the comparison of simulation results shown in the next section, we entered the data for the various models in comparably structured worksheets, tried to eliminate possible inaccuracies or inconsistencies in the data and then prepared derivative tables. We also calculated statistics for the mean, standard deviation, maximum value, minimum value and range of the reported results. These derived data are used in the figures for this paper.[9]

Model groups were asked to report country/region results for, at a minimum, the United States, Japan and Germany. A preference was expressed for individual-country data for other OECD countries, or aggregations of the smaller OECD countries. Model groups were also asked to report data for an aggregate-OECD total, using weights for the individual country/regions appropriate for their model. Some model groups – OEC, MUL, INA/INC and MSG – did supply us with data for an aggregate-OECD total. In the cases of TAY and LVE/LIV, where the underlying data for all of the G7 countries were reported to us, we constructed an aggregate-G7 total by weighting the individual country results by real GDPs in 1990. GEM reported an aggregate-G7 total to us, but only for the variables real GDP and the GDP deflator; moreover, the GEM aggregate G7 results exclude the United Kingdom. Individual country data for GEM were available only for the United States, Germany and Japan, so it was not possible to construct aggregate-G7 data for GEM.

It is convenient for interpretive purposes to be able to describe the OECD in three large pieces – the United States, Japan and 'Other' – that add to the total OECD. Where feasible given the underlying data reported to us, therefore, we calculated figures for a non-US, non-Japan, 'Other-Industrial' remainder of the OECD (using 1990 real GDP weights to weight the individual country results). These calculations are not strictly comparable across the models.[10]

The comparison of simulation results in the subsequent charts show a path for the average across models as well as paths for the individual models. When it is possible to calculate an average for all eight of the models GEM, INC, INA, LVE, OEC, MSG, MUL and TAY, this average is plotted with a heavy solid line. For averages including only a subset of these models, the averages are plotted with a heavy dashed line.[11] These cross-model averages can sometimes be misleading. Calculations of the averages, because of the small number of participating models, are very sensitive to a figure from a single model that deviates by a large amount from the other models.

Simulation paths for each individual model are always shown with the same symbol and curve type. For example, the OEC INTERLINK model is always shown with a dashed curve and an open-diamond symbol. Models making use of model-consistent expectations are shown with solid lines. Models with adaptive, backward-looking expectations are shown with dashed lines.

The series plotted for each model and for the average of reporting models always refer to deviations of the shock simulation from the baseline simulation. The types of deviations from baseline differ. For most variables, including outputs, prices and exchange rates, the values reported are per cent deviations from baseline. Interest rates, however, are measured as level deviations from baseline in percentage points; variables such as the ratios of budget deficits or current accounts to nominal GDP are measured as level deviations of the ratio from the baseline ratio in percentage points.

Omissions and non-comparabilities in the simulation results are the main cause of gaps or problems apparent in the figures.

3   Consequence within the OECD of standardized shocks

We turn now to the simulation results themselves, first to the monetary shocks and then subsequently to the fiscal shocks. We focus only on variables of importance for North–South macroeconomic interactions and emphasize broad tendencies that hold across most or all of the models. The charts reveal fascinating, and often unexplained, differences among the models. Limited space precludes a discussion of these differences in this overview.

When discussing the simulation results, we use – as a benchmark for intuition – the theoretical Mundell–Fleming model (hereafter M–F) with sticky wages, floating exchange rates and a high degree of capital mobility. Not all the participating empirical models are adequately characterized as complicated M–F models. Yet the M–F theoretical framework does provide some intuition as to what to expect and then helps us understand why the results from some models differ from this paradigm.

US monetary contraction (shock A2). The theoretical M–F model predicts that a home–country monetary contraction will cause, at least initially, a rise in home interest rates, an appreciation of the home currency and declines in both home output and the home price level. The empirical results for shock A2 accord with these theoretical presumptions, but with large variations across the models in the magnitude of effects.

US real GDP falls below baseline by an average of $1\frac{1}{4}$ to $1\frac{1}{2}$ per cent of the first one or two years and then begins moving back towards baseline, in accordance with the presumption in many theoretical models of long-run neutrality of money (Figure 8.1).

The timing of the reversal is quite different across models, and in some models output rises above baseline in the medium run. The US price level, indexed by the GDP deflator, falls quickly in some models and sluggishly in others (Figure 8.2); in most models prices fall continuously over the simulation period.

The range of first-year increases in the US short interest rate (Figure 8.3 runs from 1 per cent to $5\frac{1}{2}$ per cent, with an average somewhat less than 3 per cent. The effects fall away fairly quickly by the second and third years, even turning negative for some models.

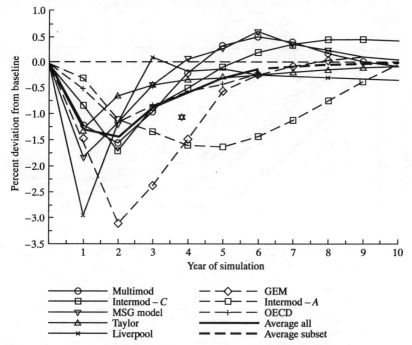

Figure 8.1   US real GDP under shock A2, permanent 5% US monetary contraction

The amount of dollar appreciation varies more widely across the models (Figure 8.4). About half the models exhibit some mild over-shooting in the first year, with the dollar initially dropping below (appreciating more than) the value attained in the longer run. Long-run 'neutrality of money' would entail a dollar appreciation of roughly 5 per cent, though some models have long-run appreciations of rather different amounts.[12]

Theoretical models yield ambiguous predictions about the direction in which a home country's current account will move following a monetary contraction. Lower home output tends to reduce imports and the income-absorption effects thus work to improve the trade and current balances. Expenditure-switching effects associated with the appreciation of the home currency, however, tend to worsen the trade and current balances. The empirical results for the ratio of the US current account to nominal GDP for US monetary contraction are shown in Figure 8.5; with the exception of MSG, the models show the income-absorption effects dominating the expenditure-switching effects in the first year, with a widely varying pattern of net effects across the models after the first year. On average across the models, the current-account effects are small.

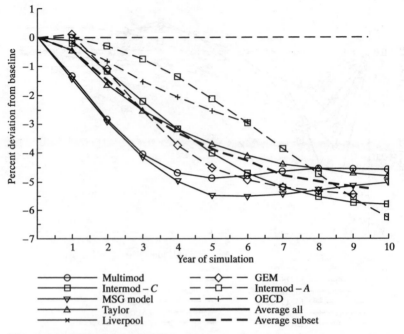

Figure 8.2   US price level (GDP deflator) under shock A2, permanent 5% US monetary contraction

The spillover effects of a US monetary contraction on output and prices in OECD countries outside the United States are ambiguous in theoretical models, even in direction. Not surprisingly, the empirical simulations prepared for this conference, as for earlier model comparisons, show mixed results. For most, but not all, of the models the effects are relatively small. Output in Japan and output in the non-US non-Japan 'Other Industrial' region, according to a majority of the models, rises modestly above baseline for the first several years (Figures 8.6 and 8.7). This 'negative transmission' to foreign output is the property observed in Mundell–Fleming theoretical models with very high capital mobility, sticky wages and static exchange rate expectations. As can be seen in Figures 8.6 and 8.7, however, some models are exceptions to the negative-transmission outcome, and in any case there exist significant differences in the time pattern of effects across models.

Some sense of how the weighted average of the OECD region as a whole behaves under the influence of the US monetary contraction can be gleaned from Figure 8.8, which plots aggregate real GDP for all OECD countries, and Figure 8.9, which plots the OECD-wide average

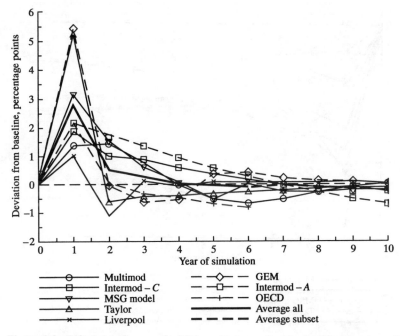

Figure 8.3   US short-term nominal interest rates under shock A2, permanent 5% US monetary contraction

short-term nominal interest rate. Averaged across the models, OECD output falls relative to baseline by roughly $\frac{1}{2}$ of 1 per cent in the first two years, and then gradually moves back towards baseline. Short-term interest rates rise by an average of roughly $\frac{3}{4}$ of a percentage point in the first year, then fall back towards baseline already in the second year.

OECD-wide monetary contraction (shock B2). As expected, short nominal interest rates at the onset of a simultaneous monetary contraction by all OECD countries tend to rise sharply in all regions. The size and time pattern of the rise in the United States (Figure 8.10) is qualitatively similar to that observed for the US monetary contraction alone (compare Figure 8.3). The increases in short rates in Japan (not shown) and in other industrial countries (not shown) are on average modestly less than for the United States. With each model, the structure of financial sectors across countries appears to be quite similar, at least to judge by a similar time patterns for any given model.

Simulated paths for the US dollar per Yen exchange rate are shown in

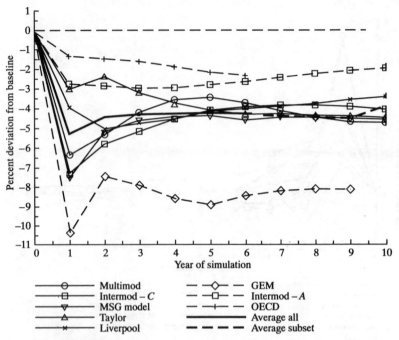

Figure 8.4   US$/Yen exchange rate ($ appreciation −) under shock A2, permanent 5% US monetary contraction

Figure 8.11. Most, but not all, of the models exhibit the theoretically presumed result that exchange rates among the major countries change by relatively small amounts when a monetary contraction occurs simultaneously in all OECD countries.

The qualitative patterns followed by outputs and price levels after an OECD-wide monetary contraction are similar to the pattern observed for the US monetary contraction alone. Given the limited transmission of home-country monetary-policy actions to outputs and prices abroad, the fall in output in the United States (Figure 8.12) is of roughly the same magnitude as for shock A2 (compare Figure 8.1). Output relative to baseline in Japan (Figure 8.13) and in the remainder of the OECD (Figure 8.14) falls in the first year by some $1\frac{1}{4}$ to $1\frac{1}{2}$ per cent on average, then moves gradually back towards baseline in subsequent years. Price levels fall in the United States (Figure 8.15), in Japan (not shown), and in the remainder of the OECD (not shown) in qualitatively similar patterns, with similar variations across models as those observed for the US monetary contraction alone.

The weighted-average responses of output and the short-term nominal

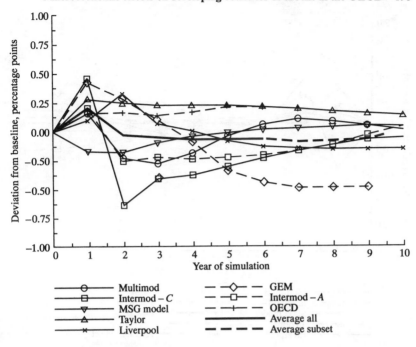

Figure 8.5   Ratio of US current account to nominal GDP under shock A2, permanent 5% US monetary contraction

interest rate for the entire OECD region are plotted in Figures 8.16 and 17. The first-year fall in output averaged across models is some 1.3 per cent. The first-year increase in short interest rates is some $2\frac{1}{2}$ percentage points, while the first-year rise in long rates (not shown) is roughly $\frac{3}{4}$ of a percentage point. These OECD-region magnitudes for the simultaneous monetary contraction in shock B2 are roughly $2\frac{1}{4}$ times the size of the OECD-region effects from the US monetary contraction in shock A2. In the very rough sense, this comparison of the results for shocks B2 and A2 is consistent with the United States being some 45 per cent of the OECD region as a whole (real GDP weights) and monetary-policy actions having only small cross-border effects.

US fiscal contraction, with debt–GDP ratio permanently changed (shock D2). The model groups implemented this fiscal simulation in qualitatively similar ways, as can be seen from the paths for the debt–GDP ratio in Figure 8.18. Differences in quantitative terms, however, turn out to be significant and interesting, as can be seen in Figure 8.19, showing the ratio of the government's budget deficit to nominal GDP.

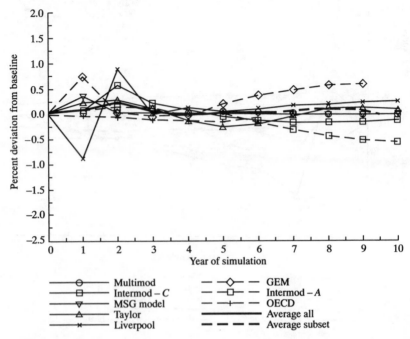

Figure 8.6　Japanese real GDP under shock A2, permanent 5% US monetary contraction

The divergence among the models in paths for the deficit–GDP ratios when the debt–GDP assumptions were relatively similar can be traced to the significant differences across models in growth rates of potential output and in real rates of interest.

Consider the effect on the ratio of debt to GDP over time of a dollar of deficit reduction in the initial simulation year. Each year after the initial cut in the deficit, the size of the reduction in debt will tend to grow at the rate of interest on government debt. Offsetting this effect on future debt is the effect of a growing economy on the ratio of this debt to GDP. If the real growth rate of the economy is larger than the real interest rate, then the reduction in the ratio of debt to GDP due to the deficit reduction in year 1 will be gradually smaller over time. To maintain a given cut in the ratio of debt to GDP would then require additional budget surpluses (reductions in future deficits). In contrast, for a model with the real interest rate greater than the real growth rate, the effective size of the initial debt reduction will tend to grow ever larger in the future (without any changes in taxes). The initial dollar decrease in the deficit would then need to be offset in future periods by higher primary deficits.

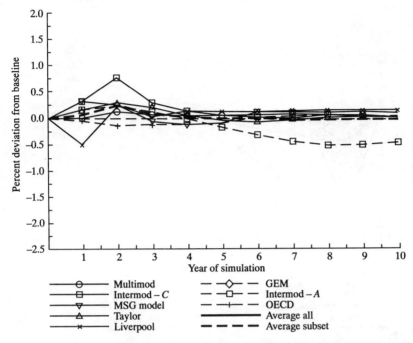

─────⊖───── Multimod   ─ ─◇─ ─ GEM
─────⊟───── Intermod – C   ─ ─□─ ─ Intermod – A
─────▽───── MSG model   ─ ─+─ ─ OECD
─────△───── Taylor   ─────── Average all
─────✕───── Liverpool   ─ ─ ─ ─ Average subset

Figure 8.7   Real GDP of other industrial countries under shock A2, permanent 5% US monetary contraction

The possibilities can be divided into three classes. If the real interest rate is greater than the potential growth rate (as, for example, in the MSG model), a permanently smaller ratio of debt to GDP with a permanently lower government spending would ultimately require a higher primary fiscal deficit over time as taxes fall to offset the falling servicing costs. If the real interest rate is approximately equal to the real growth rate (as it appears to be in the LVE model), a dollar of deficit reduction leads to a dollar of debt to GDP reduction forever. Debt can be permanently changed in models with this rough equality between the real interest rate and the real growth rate, but there cannot be a permanent change in the fiscal balance. The third possibility, which seems to be the situation for many (all?) of the remaining participating models, is that the growth rate is higher than the real interest rate; under these conditions, a permanent fall in the ratio of debt to GDP can be achieved by a permanent fall in the primary budget deficit.

Now consider the consequences of these paths of deficits, debt and government spending on other key macroeconomic variables. US real GDP initially falls relative to baseline by amounts that on average are

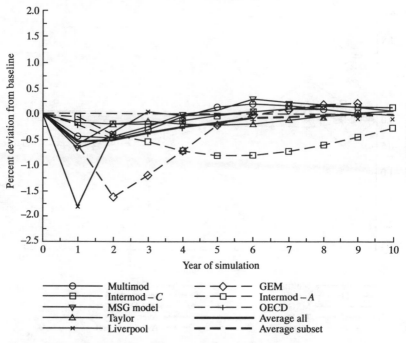

Figure 8.8   Real GDP of total OECD under shock A2, permanent 5% US monetary contraction

close to the size of the decrease in government spending (Figure 8.20); but the size of the initial fall varies widely across these models. After the first year for all models except OEC, and after the second year for OEC, the simulations exhibit 'crowding-in' behaviour; the negative income effects of the government spending reduction begin to be offset by increases in other spending on domestic output induced by lower interest rates (Figure 8.22) and by a depreciation of the dollar in exchange markets (Figure 8.23). The amount and timing of these offsetting effects on output differ considerably across the models, just as the size and timing of the interest rate and exchange rate effects themselves differ greatly. For a majority of the models, output has returned most or all of the way to baseline by the fourth year. Downward effects on the price level as measured by the GDP deflator tend to cumulate over the simulation period (Figure 8.21), with the level reaching 1 per cent or more below baseline by the fourth year (GEM being a notable exception).

The direction of movement of the exchange value of a country's currency after a fiscal action is ambiguous across a range of theoretical

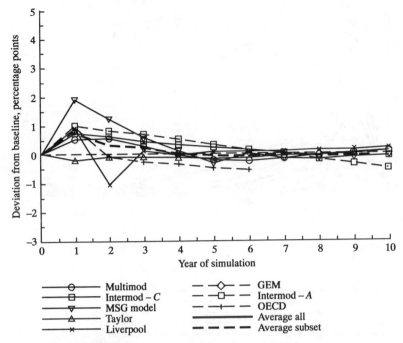

Figure 8.9 OECD average short-term nominal interest rate under shock A2, permanent 5% US monetary contraction

models. It depends on, among other things, the degree of substitutability between assets denominated in the home currency and in foreign currencies. In simplified expositions of the theory, the direction of movement of the exchange rate depends on the relative slopes of the '*BP*' and '*LM*' curves (representing, respectively, equilibrium in the external sector and the money market). The greater the degree of substitutability between home currency and foreign currency assets, the flatter will be the slope of the *BP* curve. A flatter (steeper) slope for the *BP* curve than for the *LM* curve implies that a contractionary fiscal action will depreciate (appreciate) the home currency.[13]

The ambiguity in theoretical models is not prominently evident in these simulations for a US fiscal contraction (Figure 8.23). In the multicountry empirical models represented here, with two exceptions, the home currency depreciates in the initial years following a fiscal contraction. These models tend to embody either perfect or near-perfect substitutability of assets denominated in different currencies (relatively flat *BP* curves). Exchange rates are determined for the most part in asset-market equations, for example via interest-parity conditions. Hence nominal

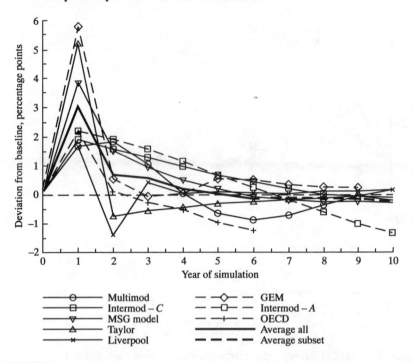

Figure 8.10 US short-term nominal interest rate under shock B2, permanent OECD-wide 5% monetary contraction

exchange rates move in response to changes in nominal interest rate differentials, expected inflation differentials, current and expected relative price levels (and, in a few cases, factors that may influence equilibrium real exchange rates in the long run, such as the wealth of national residents and the stocks of governments' debts).

Under the 1 per cent US fiscal contraction and the debt–GDP assumptions specified for the shock, the average increase in the US dollar price of foreign currencies relative to baseline is some 2 to 3 per cent, with a suggestion for a majority of the models that the size of the initial depreciation is slightly reversed after the first year. Wide variation exists, however, across the models. As observed in earlier model comparisons, a weaker domestic economy and a tendency for the dollar to depreciate causes an improvement in the US current account (absolutely, and relative to nominal GDP – see Figure 8.24). For this variable too, however, substantial differences exist across the models.

Cross-border transmission of the US fiscal contraction to foreign output is 'positive' (foreign output moves in the same direction as US

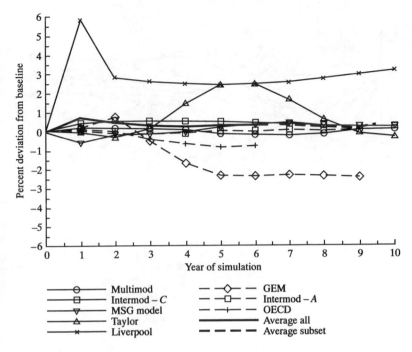

Figure 8.11   US$/Yen exchange rate ($ appreciation –) under shock B2, permanent 5% OECD-wide monetary contraction

output) for most models in the first two years, as shown in Figures 8.25 and 8.26. Even for the first two years, however, the models differ considerably; differences become even more marked for subsequent years. The initial effects on foreign GDP are about one-fifth to one-quarter as large as the effects in the United States (scaling both as a percentage of own-country GDP).

The models agree that a US fiscal contraction lowers foreign price levels relative to baseline (not shown). Most models have the amounts of the reduction growing over time up to about the fifth or sixth year. Interest rates in Japan and in the Other-Industrial region fall unambiguously in all the models, but typically by a fraction of the fall observed in the United States.

The weighted-average outcomes for the OECD region as a whole are suggested by Figures 8.27 and 8.28. The first-year fall in output averaged across models is roughly $\frac{1}{2}$ percent, with a range from about $\frac{1}{5}$ per cent to $\frac{4}{5}$ per cent. Output averaged across the models is back fairly close to

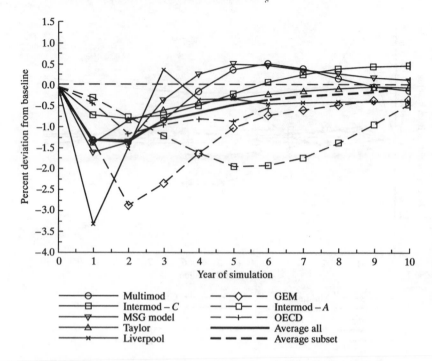

Figure 8.12   US real GDP under shock B2, permanent 5% OECD-wide monetary contraction

baseline by the fourth year of the simulation. The model-average fall in long-term nominal interest rates is some $\frac{1}{3}$ to $\frac{1}{2}$ of a percentage point (with a large standard deviation).

OECD-wide fiscal contraction, with debt–GDP ratios changing permanently (shock F). The final set of simulations we discuss here is an OECD-wide analogue of the US fiscal contraction in shock D2. Shock F assumes that each OECD country simultaneously implements a reduction in real government expenditures equivalent to 1 per cent of real GDP, while permitting a gradually increasing but (after ten years) permanent reduction of 10 percentage points in the ratio of nominal government debt to nominal GDP.[14]

Output effects of the simultaneous fiscal contraction are shown for the United States in Figure 8.29, for Japan in Figure 8.30), and for the Other-Industrial remainder of the OECD in Figure 8.31. As expected from the tendency for fiscal actions to be transmitted positively across national borders (at least initially), the Shock-F fall in output in the United

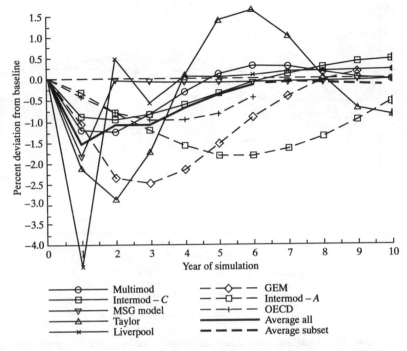

Figure 8.13   Japanese real GDP under shock B2, permanent 5% OECD-wide monetary contraction

States is larger than for the Shock-D2 fiscal contraction in the United States alone (compare Figures 8.20 and 8.29, noting that the vertical scales in the charts are different). Interestingly, the crowding-in effects also seem to work somewhat faster and more strongly in several of the models.

The general time pattern for outputs in Japan and Other-Industrial is analogous to that in the United States: a sharp initial fall, with movement back towards baseline thereafter. Notable differences exist across the models; to mention only a single example, the LVE model has output in Japan and Other-Industrial remaining depressed throughout the simulation period, while US real GDP is sharply and persistently boosted from the second year on.

Price levels show similar movements in all three OECD regions, but there are striking differences across the models. A similarly wide degree of across-model diversity occurs with nominal interest rates. Interest rates fall initially in all regions (with the exception of Japan and Other-Industrial in one model), but the sizes of the decline and the subsequent changes (further decline, persistence or reversal) differ substantially.

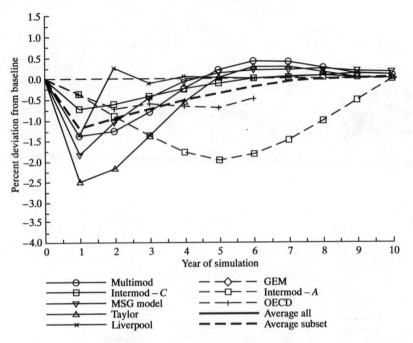

Figure 8.14   Real GDP of other industrial countries under shock B2, permanent 5% OECD-wide monetary contraction

What happens to key exchange rates when all the OECD countries simultaneously implement a fiscal contraction with debt–GDP ratios declining permanently? The reporting models argue that the US dollar will appreciate against the Yen (Figure 8.32); most models predict only a slight appreciation, but one model (LVE) simulates a very large appreciation. Changes in the US dollar per Deutschmark exchange rate are also slight in most models (Figure 8.33), but the TAY model simulates a dollar depreciation and the LVE model again simulates a large dollar appreciation.

As for the early shocks, we include two charts showing the weighted-average effects for the entire OECD region. OECD-wide output (Figure 8.34) falls by somewhat more than 1.1 per cent in the first year judging by the model-average calculation, slightly larger than the OECD-wide decline in real government expenditures of 1 per cent. The range of first-year multipliers, however, runs all the way from −0.5 to −2.2 per cent. By the fifth year of the simulation, model-average OECD output is back at baseline and moving above it. Without the sluggishly reversing results for the INA model, which pull the model

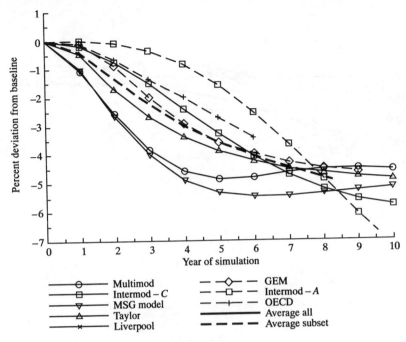

Figure 8.15 US price level (GDP deflator) under shock B2, permanent 5% OECD-wide monetary contraction

average down considerably, output would be back near baseline sometime during the fourth year.

Averaged across OECD countries, nominal interest rates are well below baseline for all the models – with, as customary, long rates moving by a fraction of the fall in short rates. Long-term rates are plotted in Figure 8.35. The sizes of interest rate reductions vary greatly across the models.

4   An accounting framework for describing the linkages between the OECD and non-OECD economies

To facilitate the analysis of the impacts on non-OECD economies of shocks originating outside those economies, it can be helpful to think in terms of a simple accounting framework. This framework is motivated by asking whether shocks transmitted to the non-OECD economies are on balance harmful or helpful.

Appraising the welfare effects of shocks on the non-OECD could proceed by considering each non-OECD country separately. For some

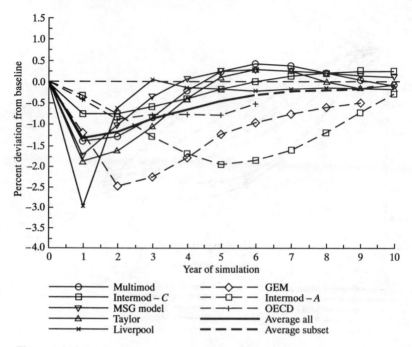

Figure 8.16   Real GDP of total OECD under shock B2, permanent 5% OECD-wide monetary contraction

purposes, such disaggregation would be essential. From an aggregate perspective, however, some rough-and-ready insight can be obtained by turning to a concept from trade theory, the notion of *compensating variation*.[15]

Consider an initial set of paths for the volumes of exports and imports, export and import prices, exchange rates, interest rates and the external debts of the non-OECD region. Then consider what happens when an externally originating shock hits one or more of these variables. It is revealing to ask how large an income transfer to the non-OECD would be required to allow the non-OECD in the aggregate to be able to purchase the same bundle of imported goods it was purchasing prior to the shock. This income transfer, the compensating variation, is a rough measure of what would be required to keep the non-OECD region as well off as before the shock.

For analytical purposes, compartmentalize the global economy into three regions: two regions within the OECD (so that we can focus on both symmetric and asymmetric shocks within the OECD) and an aggregate non-OECD region. We label these regions here with the

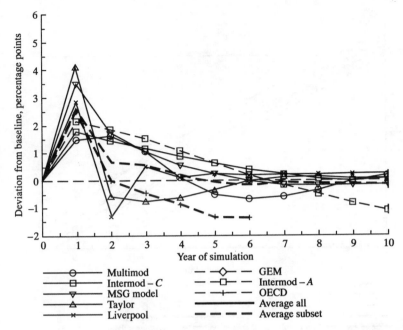

Figure 8.17   OECD average short-term nominal interest rate under shock B2, permanent 5% OECD-wide monetary contraction

superscripts U (for the United States), R (for the rest of the OECD, hereafter referred to with the acronym ROECD), and N (the non-OECD economies).

The balance-of-payments identity in a given period for the current account of the non-OECD, defined in real terms and measured in terms of real US goods, may be written as follows

$$CA^N \equiv \Lambda^N X - M - r^U D_U - R^R \Lambda^R D_R \tag{1}$$

The real imports of the non-OECD from the other two regions are

$$M \equiv M_U + \Lambda^R M_R \tag{2}$$

and the non-OECD regions's real exports to the rest of the world are

$$X \equiv X_U + X_R \tag{3}$$

The variables in the identities are defined as:

CA^N = the non-OECD region's current account, defined in terms of real US Goods;

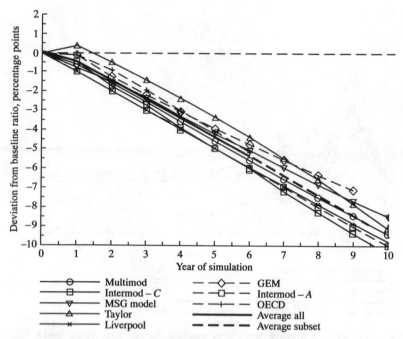

Figure 8.18   Ratio of US government debt to nominal GDP under shock D2, US fiscal contraction by 1% of real GDP, with debt–GDP ratio permanently changed

Λ^N = the real exchange rate of the non-OECD region relative to the United States (i.e., the price of non-OECD goods relative to the price of US goods);

Λ^R = the real exchange rate of the ROECD region relative to the United States (i.e., the price of ROECD goods relative to the price of US goods);

X_U = the exports from the non-OECD to the United States, measured in units of non-OECD goods;

X_R = exports from the non-OECD to the ROECD, in units of non-OECD goods;

X = the total exports from the non-OECD region, in units of non-OECD goods;

M_U = imports by the non-OECD from the United States, measured in units of US goods;

M_R = imports by the non-OECD from the ROECD in units of ROECD goods;

M = the total imports of the non-OECD, measured in units of US goods.

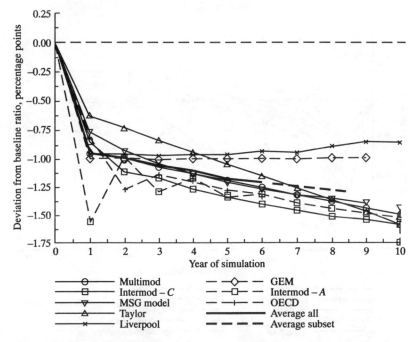

Figure 8.19   Ratio of US budget deficit to nominal GDP under shock D2, US fiscal contraction by 1% of real GDP, with debt–GDP ratio permanently changed

r^U = the real interest rate prevailing in the United States;

r^R = the average real interest rate prevailing within the ROECD;

D_U = real external debt of the non-OECD region denominated in $US; and

D_R = real external debt of the non-OECD region denominated in currency units of the ROECD.

Given the preceding identities and definitions, one can calculate an expression for the compensating variation by totally differentiating equation (1). For the exposition here, we assume for simplicity that the non-OECD is constrained to maintain a given stock of external debt in the face of external shocks (because OECD creditors are unwilling to extend further credit). Hence the current account is assumed not to be able to change in the light of this fixed borrowing constraint, and the terms dD_U and dD_R drop out of the total differentiation of equation (1).[16] Under this assumption, the transfer required to enable the non-OECD region to consume the pre-shock physical quantities of M_U and M_R, labelled here as dT, is

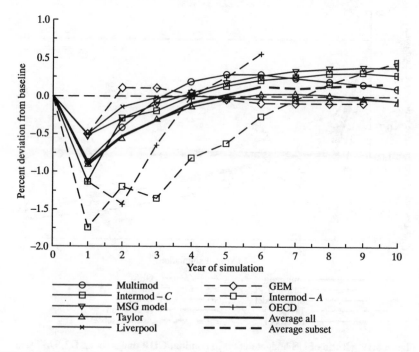

Figure 8.20 US real GDP under shock D2, US fiscal contraction by 1% of real GDP, with debt–GDP ratio permanently changed

$$dT = -\Lambda^N dX - Xd\Lambda^N + M_R d\Lambda^R + D_U dr^U$$
$$+ D_R \Lambda^R dr^R + D_R r^R d\Lambda^R \tag{4}$$

This expression, with an algebraic manipulation of several of the terms, can be rearranged as follows

$$dT = -\Lambda^N X(d\Lambda^N/\Lambda^N) + M(d\Lambda^N/\Lambda^N) - M(d\Lambda^N/\Lambda^N)$$
$$+ M_R d\Lambda^R - \Lambda^N dX + D_U dr^U + D_R \Lambda^R dr^R + D^R r^R d\Lambda^R \tag{5}$$

By defining λ^i as the proportionate change in real exchange rate of region i

$$\lambda^i = d\Lambda^i/\Lambda^i, i = N, R \tag{6}$$

and defining $TB^N = (\Lambda^N)X - M$, we can rewrite equation (5) as

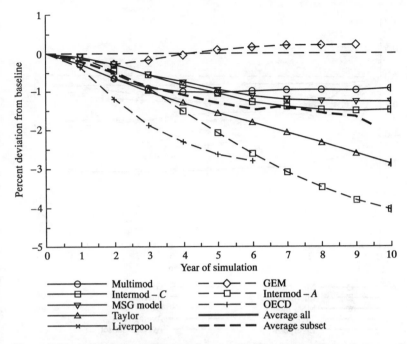

Figure 8.21   US price level (GDP deflator) under shock D2, US fiscal contraction by 1% of real GDP, with debt–GDP ratio permanently changes

$$dT = - \lambda^N TB^N - M\lambda^N + \Lambda^R M_R \lambda^R - \Lambda^N dX + D_U dr^U$$
$$+ D_R \Lambda^R dr^R + D_R r^R d\Lambda^R \tag{7}$$

We can also use the following transformation for the third term on the right-hand side of equation (7)

$$\Lambda^R M_R \lambda^R = \Lambda^R M_R \lambda^R \left(\frac{M_U + \Lambda^R M_R}{M_U + \Lambda^R M_R} \right) = \lambda^R \left(\frac{\Lambda^R M_R}{M_U + \Lambda^R M_R} \right) M \tag{8}$$

We can now define λ^M as the proportional change in import prices in the non-OECD region relative to US prices

$$\lambda^M = \lambda^R \left(\frac{\Lambda^R M_R}{M_U + \Lambda^R M_R} \right) \tag{9}$$

Equation (8) can then be rewritten

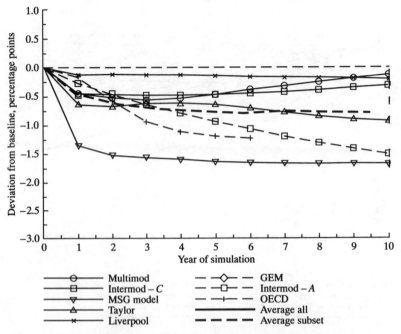

Figure 8.22 US long-term nominal interest rate under shock D2, US fiscal contraction by 1% of real GDP, with debt–GDP ratio permanently changed

$$\Lambda^R M_R \lambda^R = \lambda^M M \tag{10}$$

We can now rewrite equation (7) as

$$
\begin{aligned}
dT =& - TB^N(\lambda^N) - M(\lambda^N - \lambda^M) - \Lambda^N X_U(dX_U/X_U) \\
& - \Lambda^N X_R(dX_R/X_R) + D_U dr^U + D_R \Lambda^R dr^R + D_R \Lambda^R r^R(\lambda^R)
\end{aligned}
\tag{11}
$$

Note that $(\lambda^N - \lambda^M)$ is the terms of trade of the non-OECD economies.
Equation (11) reveals that the compensating-variation transfer can be interpreted as having four components. First, when real export prices in terms of US goods increase (λ^N rises), the required transfer is reduced if the country is running a trade surplus ($TB > 0$); however, the required transfer increases if the country is running a trade deficit. Second, when external shocks cause the terms of trade to deteriorate (real export prices fall more or rise less than real import prices, so that $(\lambda^N - \lambda^M) < 0$), the required transfer rises ('welfare' judged by this compensating-variation index is lower) by the percentage change in the terms of trade multiplied

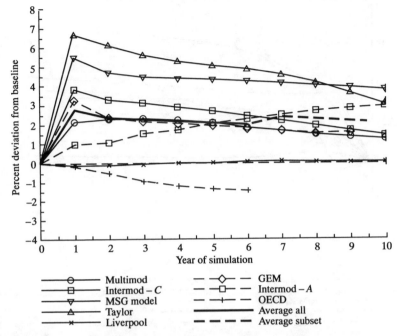

Figure 8.23   US$/Yen exchange rate ($ appreciation –) under shock D2, US fiscal contraction by 1% of real GDP, with debt–GDP ratio permanently changed

by the initial level of total real imports. Third, when real exports rise to either region ($dX_U > 0$ and/or $dX_R > 0$), the required real transfer is of course reduced. Finally, as shown by the last set of terms (second line of equation (11)), when the non-OECD region is a net debtor ($D_U > 0$ and/ or $D_R > 0$), the required transfer is raised (welfare is lowered) by increases in real interest rates within the OECD multiplied by the levels of initial debt.

The preceding framework identifies the main channels of transmission of shocks from the OECD to non-OECD economies. This transmission depends on three broad categories of channel: changes in the terms of trade, changes in real exports, and changes in real interest rates.[17] It is also important to stress that both US and ROECD variables enter in the above expression and therefore the transmission of shocks to the non-OECD region depends on the transmission to countries within the OECD itself. For a shock that has asymmetric consequences within the OECD, it will of course be important whether the United States or the ROECD region is the major market for the non-OECD economies' exports. Similarly, if US interest rates rise and ROECD interest rates fall

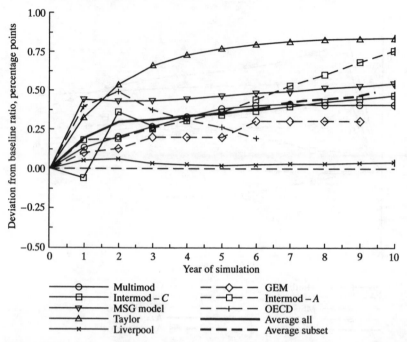

Figure 8.24   Ratio of US current account to nominal GDP under shock D2, US fiscal-contraction by 1% of real GDP, with debt–GDP ratio permanently changed

(or vice versa), then it can matter in what currency the debt is denominated and at what interest rates the debt is serviced.

Even in principle, the preceding framework accounts for only a part of the transmission process. Each of the price terms outlined above is a relative price, in other words a combination of changes in foreign prices, changes in exchange rates, and changes in domestic prices. The ultimate impact on non-OECD economies, therefore, will depend on the exchange rate regimes prevailing in the world economy; on the degree of mobility of private capital (which is ignored in the stylized presentation in equation (11)); on the adjustment of prices and wages within the non-OECD region; and on the reactions of OECD and non-OECD policy-makers, either automatic through some policy rule or due to discretionary changes in policy.

5   Consequences of shocks for non-OECD economies

In the analysis of this section, we use the Section 3 results for the within-OECD consequences of policy shocks and the accounting framework of

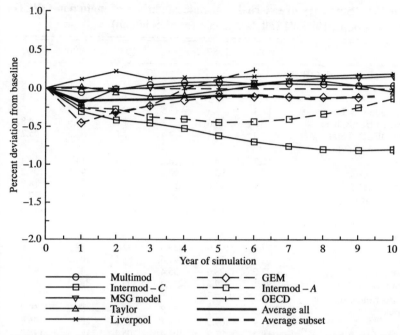

Figure 8.25   Japanese real GDP under shock D2, US fiscal contraction by 1% of real GDP, with debt–GDP ratio permanently changed

Section 4 to derive approximations of the overall impacts on the non-OECD economies of policy changes in the OECD. This approach provides estimates of the magnitude of the various macroeconomic channels through which the OECD affects non-OECD regions. It also provides useful guidance about the channels of North–South macroeconomic interactions that need to be incorporated into explicit empirical models.

As a point of reference and baseline for our calculations, Table 8.1 summarizes the external economic conditions for four main non-OECD regions: Africa, Asia (excluding Japan, Australia and New Zealand), the Middle East and non-OECD Europe, and the non-OECD Western Hemisphere. The table also shows aggregated data for the non-OECD as a whole (the consolidation of the four main regions). The variables reported in the table, with data for the years 1986–91, correspond to the key variables in equation (11) above: the region's trade balance with OECD countries, regional exports to the United States, regional exports to the ROECD, total imports of the region from the OECD, the region's net external debt (presumed to be overwhelmingly *vis-à-vis* OECD countries), and interest payments on the region's external debt.

Table 8.1   Summary of external economic conditions of main non-OECD regional groups, 1985–91 (all data in current $US billion)

	1986	1987	1988	1989	1990	1991
Trade balance with OECD						
Africa	−3.7	−0.3	−6.5	−3.0	0.6	1.5
Asia	−0.5	13.3	1.6	−1.1	−10.5	−23.1
Middle East & Europe	−17.3	−6.3	−13.5	0.1	−1.5	−18.7
Western Hemisphere	9.5	9.6	8.8	11.6	13.9	−4.8
Non-OECD, Total	−12.0	16.3	−9.4	7.6	2.5	−45.2
Exports to the US						
Africa	7.3	9.3	10.2	13.2	14.5	13.4
Asia	63.8	80.2	90.4	97.9	99.6	105.2
Middle East & Europe	10.1	13.6	14.3	18.7	22.4	18.7
Western Hemisphere	33.0	39.1	39.8	43.1	49.7	57.6
Non-OECD, Total	114.2	142.2	154.7	172.9	186.2	194.9
Exports to ROECD						
Africa	29.5	34.1	34.1	36.2	46.8	47.9
Asia	77.6	103.0	129.3	142.5	159.1	178.0
Middle East & Europe	62.0	73.8	73.6	86.5	103.5	110.8
Western Hemisphere	27.0	28.6	35.4	38.3	42.9	45.5
Non-OECD, Total	196.1	239.5	272.4	303.5	352.3	382.2
Imports from OECD						
Africa	40.5	43.7	50.8	52.4	60.7	59.8
Asia	141.9	169.9	218.1	241.5	269.2	306.3
Middle East & Europe	89.4	93.7	101.4	105.1	127.4	148.2
Western Hemisphere	50.5	58.1	66.4	69.8	78.7	107.9
Non-OECD, Total	322.3	365.4	436.7	468.8	536.0	622.2
External Debt						
Africa	158.9	182.2	188.3	195.4	207.4	207.2
Asia	186.7	174.1	179.3	176.6	188.1	196.7
Middle East & Europe	156.1	169.5	192.0	198.1	205.1	220.4
Western Hemisphere	348.3	380.8	378.6	376.8	376.3	377.8
Non-OECD, Total	850.0	906.6	938.2	946.9	976.9	1,002.1
Interest payments						
Africa	24.0	22.4	24.3	24.1	23.5	25.9
Asia	18.9	16.4	15.5	15.2	14.8	15.8
Middle East & Europe	18.2	19.4	19.1	20.1	18.1	20.4
Western Hemisphere	115.6	88.8	98.7	72.9	58.9	79.7
Non-OECD, Total	176.7	147.0	157.6	132.3	115.3	141.8

Sources: Total imports from the OECD: International Monetary Fund, *Direction of Trade Statistics Yearbook*, 1992, pp. 14, 20, 26, 32, 38. 44. Exports to the United States: International Monetary Fund, *Direction of Trade Statistics Yearbook*, 1992, pp. 14, 20, 26, 32, 38, 44. Exports to the ROECD: International Monetary Fund, *Direction of Trade Statistics Yearbook*, 1992, pp. 14, 20, 26, 32, 38, 44. External Debt: International Monetary Fund, *World Economic Outlook*, October 1992, Tables A43 and A46, pp. 151–8. (Reserve Holdings (Table A43) are subtracted from Total Debt (Table A46).) Although reserve holdings are netted against gross external debt, data for the claims of the private sectors in non-OECD countries on OECD countries are not readily available or are less reliable. It was therefore not possible to calculate 'net external debt' in the fullest sense of the 'net' concept. For details of the individual-nation composition of regions, see one of the IMF publications listed above, or the IMF *International Financial Statistics*.

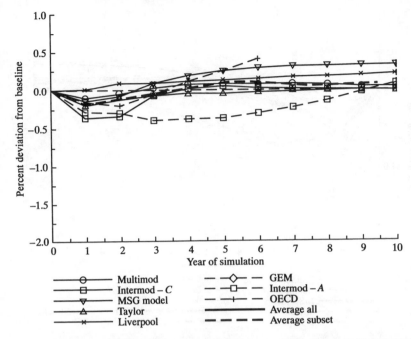

Figure 8.26   Real GDP of other industrial countries under shock D2, US fiscal contraction by 1% of real GDP, with debt–GDP ratio permanently changed

Substantial amounts of trade occur between OECD and non-OECD economies. Table 8.1 shows, for example, that imports from OECD economies into all non-OECD regions were $US 536 billion in 1990. Non-OECD exports to OECD economies in 1990 were the same order of magnitude, $186 billion going to the United States and $352 billion to ROECD countries. Trade flows between the OECD and the four non-OECD regions were often fairly well balanced, though exceptions occur for some regions in some years (for example, 1991). The summary data for trade flows in Table 8.1 also reveal asymmetries that have important consequences. The Asia region and the Western Hemisphere region rely relatively more on exporting to the United States than do the other two non-OECD regions. Africa and the Middle East plus Europe have the opposite bias, relying relatively more on exporting to the ROECD.

The baseline data in Table 8.1 and Section 3's simulation results can be used to calculate Section 4's compensating-variation measure of the transfer to non-OECD economies (the transfer required to allow those economies, following a change in OECD policies, to consume the same bundle of goods as along the baseline). To proceed, however, it is

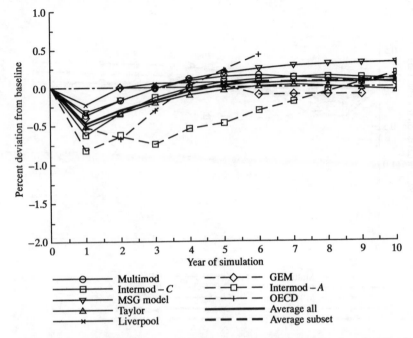

Figure 8.27   Real GDP of total OECD under shock D2, US fiscal contraction by 1% of real GDP, with debt–GDP ratio permanently changed

necessary to introduce several additional assumptions. In particular, we need to make explicit working assumptions about the demand for non-OECD goods in the OECD regions. This information is not available directly from the simulation results (and of course differs across the models).

Accordingly, we first make the conventional assumptions that the US demand for non-OECD exports is a positive function of US income and a negative function of the price of non-OECD goods relative to US goods. Similarly, we assume that the ROECD demand for non-OECD exports is a positive function of ROECD income and a negative function of the price of non-OECD goods relative to ROECD goods. These demand functions for non-OECD exports may be expressed as

$$dX^U/X^U = \beta_1(dY^U/Y^U) - \beta_2\lambda^N \tag{12}$$

$$dX^R/X^R = \beta_3(dY^R/Y^R) - \beta_4(\lambda^N - \lambda^R) \tag{13}$$

where the coefficients β_1 and β_3 are income elasticities and β_2 and β_4 are price elasticities. For the supply of non-OECD goods, we assume that the

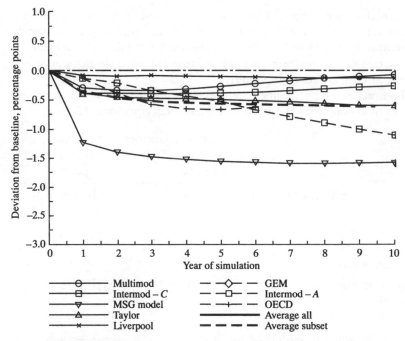

Figure 8.28   OECD average long-term nominal interest rate under shock D2, US fiscal contraction by 1% of real GDP, with debt–GDP ratio permanently changed

total supply of non-OECD exports is a function of the price of those exports relative to the price of a bundle of OECD imports into the non-OECD region. This assumption may be written as

$$dX/X = \delta(\lambda^N - \lambda^M) \qquad (14)$$

where δ is the supply-price elasticity, where total non-OECD exports are by assumption divided into exports to the two OECD regions according to

$$dX/X = \alpha_1(dX_U/X_U) + (1 - \alpha_1)(dX_R/X_R) \qquad (15)$$

and where the coefficient $\alpha_1 = X_U/X$ is assumed proportional to the existing pattern of trade.

When incorporating the preceding equations in our accounting framework, what numerical assumptions should be made about the parameters in the above functions? As discussed in other papers in this volume issues about the appropriate price and income elasticities for exports from non-OECD regions are far from settled. Our strategy here is to make alternative assumptions about the income and price elasticities for non-OECD exports so that we can see how sensitive our results are to alternative assumptions. This procedure provides some insight into the quantitative importance of this debate for the transmission of shocks between the North and South. To minimize the number of combinations of parameter assumptions, we assume that the price elasticity of supply for non-OECD exports, δ, is unity.[18]

To bracket the possibilities, we present results based on four combinations of assumptions about the β parameters in equations (12)–(15)

		Income elasticities for non-OECD exports	Price elasticities for non-OECD exports
(a)	benchmark case of unitary elasticities	$\beta_1 = \beta_3 = 1$	$\beta_2 = \beta_4 = 1$
(b)	benchmark income elasticities but high price elasticities	$\beta_1 = \beta_3 = 1$	$\beta_2 = \beta_4 = 5$
(c)	benchmark price elasticities but high income elasticities	$\beta_1 = \beta_3 = 3$	$\beta_2 = \beta_4 = 1$
(d)	high values for both price and income elasticities	$\beta_1 = \beta_3 = 3$	$\beta_2 = \beta_4 = 5$

With the preceding information – alternative assumptions about price and income elasticities for non-OECD exports, the baseline data in Table 8.1, and the simulation results summarized in Section 3 – we now calculate the implied measures of the compensating variation transfer in equation (11) for the non-OECD region as a whole. We perform the calculations for each of the years 1986 through 1991, for each of the four shocks studied in Section 3. Each shock is assumed to begin in 1986.[19]

The results of the calculations are summarized in Tables 8.2–8.5. Each table has a standard format. Data are reported for three years: the initial two years (1986 and 1987) showing the size of the effects in the short run, and the final year (1991) showing the size of the effects in the medium term. For each of the reported years, four columns of data are presented, labelled (a), (b), (c) and (d). These four columns correspond to the alternative assumptions about price and income elasticities for non-OECD exports, as outlined above. The first row in each of the tables, dT, reports the net size of the compensating-variation transfer (the left-hand side of equation (11)). The seven subsequent rows report the seven individual components of the right-hand side of equation (11). All figures in the table are in billions of current US dollars.[20]

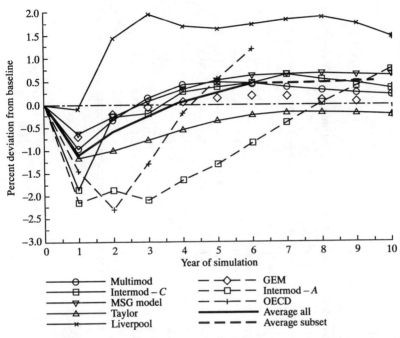

Figure 8.29   US real GDP under shock F, OECD-wide fiscal contraction by 1% of real GDP, with debt–GDP ratios permanently changed

As an example, consider the results in Table 8.2 for a US monetary contraction of the size studied in shock A2 in Section 3. The column labelled (a) under the year 1986 contains the calculations for the assumption of unity price and income elasticities. For a monetary contraction in the United States, the non-OECD countries would need to be given a net positive transfer of $16.1 billion to allow them to consume the same bundle of goods as before the shock. The policy change in the United States, in other words, on balance has negative welfare consequences for the non-OECD economies in the initial year. By reading down the (a) column for 1986, one can discern the contribution of each of the seven components to the $16.1 billion figure; for example, the dominant contribution comes from the negative effects of the rise in US interest rates on interest payments on debt to the United States $(D_U dr^U)$. By comparing the (a), (b), (c) and (d) columns for 1986, one can see how the calculations were influenced by the alternative assumptions about price and income elasticities; for example, higher price elasticities by themselves reduce the size of the implied welfare loss to $13.7 billion (and substantially alter the pattern of exports to the two

Table 8.2 US monetary contraction; compensating-variation transfer and its components, all non-OECD economies combined (US\$ billion)

	1986				1987				1991			
	(a)	(b)	(c)	(d)	(a)	(b)	(c)	(d)	(a)	(b)	(c)	(d)
dT (net transfer)	16.1	13.7	18.9	14.6	2.2	-0.4	5.2	0.6	-4.7	-6.0	-3.9	-5.8
$-TB^N(\lambda^N)$	-0.5	-0.4	-0.5	-0.5	0.5	0.5	0.6	0.5	-1.4	-1.3	-1.4	-1.4
$-M(\lambda^N - \lambda^M)$	-0.5	-1.8	0.9	-1.3	-0.4	-1.6	1.1	-1.2	-0.6	-1.4	-0.2	-1.2
$-A^N X_U(dX_U/X_U)$	-3.1	-19.2	-0.6	-17.0	-2.6	-19.0	1.0	-15.8	-5.7	-28.8	-5.3	-28.4
$-A^N X_R(dX_R/X_R)$	2.6	17.5	1.5	15.8	2.2	17.3	0.1	14.6	5.1	27.5	5.1	27.2
$+D_U dr^U$	19.0	19.0	19.0	19.0	3.6	3.6	3.6	3.6	-0.7	-0.7	-0.7	-0.7
$+D_R A^R dr^R$	0.5	0.5	0.5	0.5	0.2	0.2	0.2	0.2	-0.1	-0.1	-0.1	-0.1
$+D_R A^R r^R(\lambda^R)$	-1.9	-1.9	-1.9	-1.9	-1.3	-1.3	-1.3	-1.3	-1.3	-1.3	-1.3	-1.3

Table 8.3 OECD-wide monetary contraction: compensating-variation transfer and its components, all non-OECD economies combined (US$ billion)

	1986				1987				1991			
	(a)	(b)	(c)	(d)	(a)	(b)	(c)	(d)	(a)	(b)	(c)	(d)
dT (net transfer)	29.4	26.7	37.8	29.5	9.7	6.4	18.2	9.3	-3.8	-5.7	-0.8	-4.7
$-TB^N(\lambda^N)$	-0.1	0.0	-0.2	-0.1	0.2	0.2	0.4	0.2	-1.3	-1.2	-1.4	-1.2
$-M(\lambda^N-\lambda^M)$	2.2	0.8	6.5	2.2	1.7	0.2	5.8	1.5	0.1	-1.0	1.7	-0.5
$-\Lambda^N X_U(dX_U/X_U)$	0.8	0.7	2.3	1.2	-0.1	-4.9	2.2	-3.7	-4.8	-25.2	-3.8	-24.5
$-\Lambda^N X_R(dX_R/X_R)$	1.3	0.0	4.0	1.0	1.9	5.1	3.9	5.3	4.8	24.3	5.3	24.1
$+D_U dr^U$	20.7	20.7	20.7	20.7	4.9	4.9	4.9	4.9	-1.1	-1.1	-1.1	-1.1
$+D_R\Lambda^R dr^R$	4.5	4.5	4.5	4.5	1.3	1.3	1.3	1.3	-0.4	-0.4	-0.4	-0.4
$+D_R\Lambda^R r(\lambda^R)$	0.0	0.0	0.0	0.0	-0.3	-0.3	-0.3	-0.3	-1.1	-1.1	-1.1	-1.1

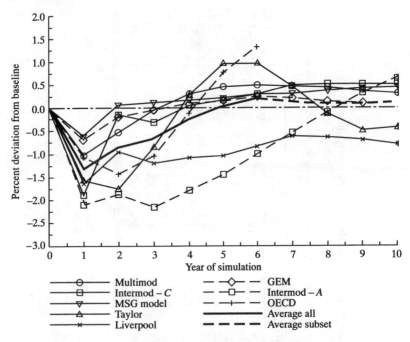

Figure 8.30   Japanese real GDP under shock F, OECD-wide fiscal contraction by 1% of real GDP, with debt–GDP ratios permanently changed

OECD regions in offsetting directions) whereas higher income elasticities alone increase the implied welfare loss to $18.9 billion.

Examination of Table 8.2 and the corresponding Table 8.3 for an OECD-wide monetary contraction leads to several points of general interest. First, a monetary contraction in the North, either in the United States alone or throughout the OECD economies, on the whole has negative consequences for non-OECD economies in the short run; the effects become mildly positive, however, by the medium term (compare the columns for 1986 and 1991). Second, the largest effects on the economic welfare of developing countries may stem from changes in Northern interest rates on the cost of servicing their external debt. Third, alternative assumptions about price and income elasticities of non-OECD exports do not seem to have substantial effects on the overall size of the compensating-variation transfer in the short run or medium run. Fourth, the contribution of the terms-of-trade effect can change sign depending on the assumption about elasticities (but the overall effect of this is small). Finally, alternative assumptions about price elasticities can have large effects on the regional composition of non-OECD exports (US

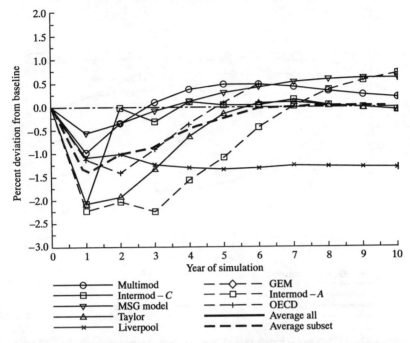

Figure 8.31   **Real GDP of other industrial countries under shock F, OECD-wide fiscal contraction of 1% of real GDP, with debt–GDP ratios permanently changed**

versus ROECD) but the sum of these effects tend to be offsetting, leaving the contribution of the change in total exports to the size of the transfer fairly small.

More generally, the higher the price elasticities for non-OECD exports, the smaller are the adverse consequences for non-OECD economies of monetary-policy contractions in the OECD (compare the (a) and (b) columns in Tables 8.2 and 8.3) On the other hand, the higher are the income elasticities of demand for non-OECD exports in the United States and the ROECD, the larger are the adverse consequences for non-OECD economies (compare the (a) and the (c) columns).

Several other points of interest emerge when one compares the US-only shock in Table 8.2 with the OECD-wide shock in Table 8.3. The terms-of-trade component of the compensating-variation transfer – refer to the rows labelled $-M(\lambda^N - \lambda^M)$ – moves adversely for the OECD-wide shock, causing non-OECD welfare to worsen (other things equal). But this terms-of-trade component moves in the other direction, tending to improve non-OECD welfare, for the US-only shock.[21] This differing behaviour of the terms-of-trade component is driven by the change in the

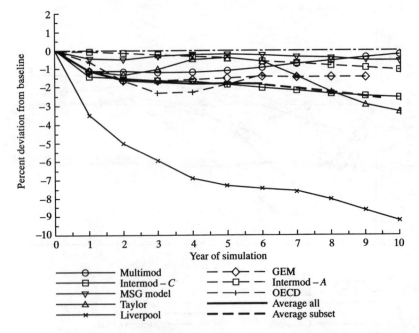

Figure 8.32   US$/Yen exchange rate ($ appreciation –) under shock F, OECD-wide fiscal contraction by 1% of real GDP, with debt–GDP ratios permanently changed

real exchange rate between the United States and the ROECD; the US dollar is little changed against ROECD currencies when all OECD countries together undertake monetary contraction, but appreciates in real terms when the United States acts on its own. The change in the real exchange rate between the two OECD regions is also indirectly responsible for the result that the contributions of non-OECD exports to the two OECD regions diverge in sign (see equation (13), in which λ^R plays an important role in the relative-price term).

Now consider the calculations for, respectively, a US fiscal contraction alone and an OECD-wide fiscal contraction (Tables 8.4 and 8.5). In contrast to monetary contractions in the North, the impacts of Northern fiscal contractions tend to have positive effects on the welfare of non-OECD economies. This fact can be seen in the negative figures for dT in Table 8.4 and in the (substantially larger) negative figures in Table 8.5

The net positive effect on non-OECD welfare occurs in important part because of lower interest rates in the United States and the ROECD, which in turn translate into a lower debt burden in the non-OECD economies.[22] Previous scholarly analyses of North–South macroeconomic

Table 8.4 US fiscal contraction: compensating-variation transfer and its components, all non-OECD economies combined (US$ billion)

	1986				1987				1991			
	(a)	(b)	(c)	(d)	(a)	(b)	(c)	(d)	(a)	(b)	(c)	(d)
dT (net transfer)	−1.6	−1.7	1.2	−0.8	−2.7	−2.6	−0.5	−1.9	−6.2	−5.6	−6.7	−5.8
$-TB^N(\lambda^N)$	0.2	0.2	0.2	0.2	−0.2	−0.2	−0.2	−0.2	0.5	0.4	0.5	0.4
$-M(\lambda^N - \lambda^M)$	1.3	1.3	2.8	1.7	1.1	1.1	2.1	1.5	0.1	0.4	−0.2	0.3
$-A^N X_U(dX_U/X_U)$	3.0	10.9	4.6	12.1	2.7	10.6	3.8	11.4	1.7	9.0	1.4	8.8
$-A^N X_R(dX_R/X_R)$	−1.7	−9.6	−1.9	−10.4	−1.6	−9.5	−1.6	−9.9	−1.6	−8.7	−1.6	−8.5
$+D_U dt^U$	−5.0	−5.0	−5.0	−5.0	−4.6	−4.6	−4.6	−4.6	−6.3	−6.3	−6.3	−6.3
$+D_R A^R dr^R$	−0.4	−0.4	−0.4	−0.4	−0.7	−0.7	−0.7	−0.7	−0.9	−0.9	−0.9	−0.9
$+D_R A^R r^R(\lambda^R)$	1.0	1.0	1.0	1.0	0.6	0.6	0.6	0.6	0.4	0.4	0.4	0.4

Table 8.5 OECD-wide fiscal contraction: compensating-variation transfer and its components, all non-OECD economies combined (US$ billion)

	1986				1987				1991			
	(a)	(b)	(c)	(d)	(a)	(b)	(c)	(d)	(a)	(b)	(c)	(d)
dT (net transfer)	−5.1	−8.2	2.9	−5.5	−10.0	−12.9	−3.8	−10.9	−20.9	−21.2	−23.3	−22.0
$-TB^N(\lambda^N)$	−0.2	−0.1	−0.4	−0.2	0.3	0.3	0.5	0.3	−1.3	−1.3	−1.2	−1.3
$-M(\lambda^N - \lambda^M)$	1.8	0.2	6.0	1.6	0.9	−0.5	3.9	0.5	−1.5	−1.6	−2.8	−2.1
$-\Lambda^N X_U(dX_U/X_U)$	−0.6	−5.2	0.5	−5.1	−2.1	−11.4	−1.6	−11.6	−6.6	−29.4	−8.1	−30.5
$-\Lambda^N X_R(dX_R/X_R)$	2.3	5.3	5.2	6.6	3.1	10.8	5.6	12.1	5.3	27.9	5.5	28.6
$+D_U dr^U$	−6.3	−6.3	−6.3	−6.3	−8.8	−8.8	−8.8	−8.8	−12.4	−12.4	−12.4	−12.4
$+D_R \Lambda^R dr^R$	−1.6	−1.6	−1.6	−1.6	−2.6	−2.6	−2.6	−2.6	−3.0	−3.0	−3.0	−3.0
$+D^R \Lambda^R_r(\lambda^R)$	−0.5	−0.5	−0.5	−0.5	−0.7	−0.7	−0.7	−0.7	−1.2	−1.2	−1.2	−1.2

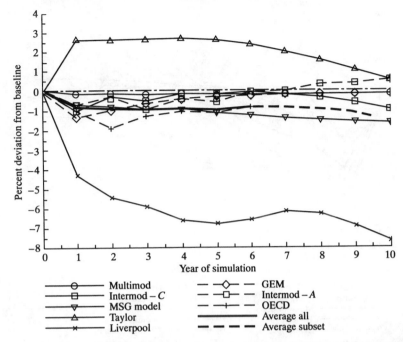

Figure 8.33   US$/DM exchange rate ($ appreciation –) under shock F, OECD-wide fiscal contraction by 1% of real GDP, with debt–GDP ratios permanently changed

interactions have observed that the interest rate and the trade consequences for developing economies of fiscal-policy actions in the North
tend to move in opposite directions. Fiscal expansions in OECD countries
tend to expand OECD aggregate demand, which has favourable welfare
consequences for developing countries by raising their exports, but also
tend to drive up OECD interest rates, which has detrimental welfare
consequences for developing countries by increasing the costs of servicing
their external debt. Conversely, fiscal contraction in the OECD lowers
non-OECD exports but also reduces debt-service payments.[23] It is plainly
an empirical issue of major consequence which of the two opposing effects
on non-OECD welfare is larger in size. In the illustrative calculations for
the OECD fiscal contractions in Tables 8.4 and 8.5, the favourable effects
of lower OECD interest rates (summarized in the last three components in
the compensating-variation calculation) tend to dominate the unfavourable consequences for non-OECD trade flows of the initial falls in OECD
aggregate demand (incorporated in the first four components).

Note also in Tables 8.4 and 8.5 that the welfare gains to non-OECD

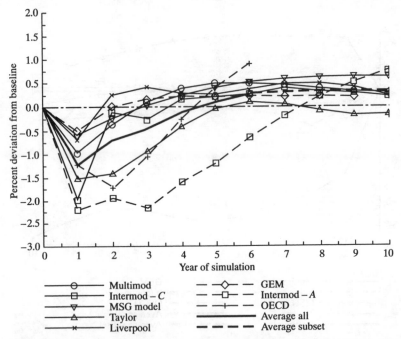

Figure 8.34   Real GDP of total OECD under shock F, OECD-wide fiscal contraction by 1% of real GDP, with debt–GDP ratios permanently changed

economies from Northern fiscal contractions grow larger over time. This effect is in marked contrast to the consequences of monetary-policy changes, for which the initial effects are unfavourable but are then subsequently reversed with the passage of time. Tables 8.4 and 8.5 report only one exception to the generalization that fiscal contractions in the OECD have net welfare-improving consequences for non-OECD economies. Not surprisingly, this exception occurs in the case where the income elasticities of demand for non-OECD exports are very high but price elasticities are only unitary (case c). Even for this case of high income elasticities, however, the unfavourable consequences for non-OECD welfare are reversed after the initial year.

6   Conclusions

We have demonstrated in this paper how it is possible to use model-based simulations of the within-OECD effects of policy shocks in conjunction with a simplified accounting framework for the balance-of-payments accounts of non-OECD regions to derive estimates of the

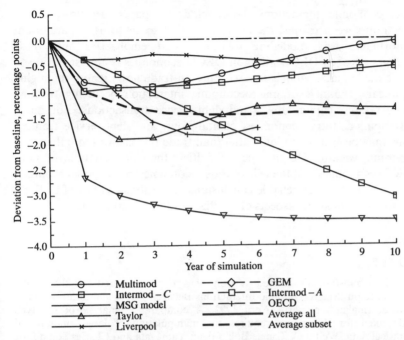

Figure 8.35 OECD average long-term nominal interest rate under shock F, OECD-wide fiscal contraction by 1% of real GDP, with debt–GDP ratios permanently changed

welfare consequences of the shocks for the non-OECD regions. In the absence of explicit model-based calculations of the consequences for non-OECD regions, estimates obtained with our procedures can provide useful empirical insights.

The simplified framework illustrated here is valid only for obtaining estimates that are rough orders of magnitude. Our approach is an interim procedure, not a preferred method of analysis. For one thing, any extended application of our approach should adapt the accounting framework so as explicitly to include changes in the current-account balance and the outstanding stock of external debt (an adaptation easily made, as noted earlier). But more fundamentally, our approach is an analytical short cut that in the long run is bound to be inferior to careful explicit modelling of non-OECD countries or regions and inclusion of such models as integral components in a global, general-equilibrium modelling system.[24]

The illustrative calculations presented here do have, we believe, several implications for the appropriate modelling of North–South macroeconomic interactions. To conclude the paper, because of space constraints we stress just the implication that seems to us of paramount importance. Any modelling treatment that emphasizes only trade linkages between OECD and non-OECD economies is almost certain to prove inadequate. Models focused only on trade flows ignore the highly significant channels of macroeconomic interaction occurring through interest rates, capital flows, and debt-service transactions. For many developing-country economies, capital flows and debt-service transactions may be even more influential than trade transactions in influencing economic welfare. Despite the difficulties, therefore, analysts of non-OECD economies and the role of those economies in the global economy cannot hope to reach reliable conclusions in the absence of careful efforts to model the financial aspects of North–South interdependence.

NOTES

This is a substantially revised version of a paper prepared for the CEPR conference on 'Macroeconomic Interactions Between North and South', held in Oxford, England, on 23–4 April 1993. A comparative analysis of the type undertaken for this paper requires the manipulation of large amounts of empirical data. We thank Tomas Bok, Glenn Yamagata and Charles Soludo for their assistance in compiling and manipulating the data. The modelling groups themselves devoted considerable resources to the preparation of the simulations and to discussions with the compilers at Brookings. The wider circle of analysts who benefit from the comparative analysis should be particularly grateful to the modelling groups, without whose thoughtful participation the analysis would be impossible. The views expressed in this paper are those of the authors and should not be interpreted as the views of any of the above-mentioned individuals or the modelling groups, nor those of the staff or trustees of the Brookings Institution.

1 The initial conference in the series of meetings, held in Sussex, England, resulted in a conference volume, Currie and Vines (1988). A subsequent workshop was held in Brazil in October 1990. The Korean conference, on 'Global Interdependence: Theories and Models of the Linkages Between OECD and Non-OECD Economies', was held in Seoul, Korea on 27–8 May 1991; it was jointly sponsored by the OECD, the Korea Development Institute, the Brookings Institution, and the Centre for Economic Policy Research.

2 In another paper we hope to write, we will provide more detail about the transmission of the standardized shocks within the OECD region itself. In that paper we will also discuss some of the issues involved in trying to standardize simulation data across a heterogeneous group of macroeconomic models.

3 Readers not familiar with the models can find references to them in Bryant et al. (1988); Bryant et al. (1989); and Bryant et al. (1993). The two models not used in this paper are the world econometric model of the Japanese Economic Planning Agency (EPA) and the Project LINK aggregation of many

    individual country models (LNK); these model groups were not able to provide results for the particular simulations discussed below.

4 A few features of the GEM simulations reported here, for example for exchange rates, appear to differ somewhat from the counterpart features of other simulations prepared with slightly different variants of the GEM model. (The National Institute for Economic and Social Research and the London Business School, although developing the GEM model jointly, sometimes work with alternative versions of the model for different research purposes.)

5 These efforts to standardize were only partially successful.

6 For modelling groups accustomed to using a short-term interest rate as the instrument of monetary policy, the guidelines required the modelling groups to change their model so as to make the money stock explicitly exogenous, or alternatively to add a reaction function to the model that endogenously varies the short-term interest rate so as to keep the money stock very close to its baseline path.

7 A more complete analysis and comparison of alternative intertemporal fiscal rules will be the basis for another paper we hope to complete in coming months. The issue of appropriate specification of fiscal intertemporal closure rules is a major unresolved problem that needs more attention in future research with macroeconometric models.

8 For this shock – and also F – the amount of the shock to real government expenditures, *measured in constant local-currency units*, was to increase gradually through the simulation period (to keep the amount of the shock continuously at 1 per cent of baseline GDP).

9 The figures of the annual models are the raw data supplied to us by the modelling groups. The entries for GEM and TAY are annual averages of the quarterly figures supplied to us. The OEC entries are annual averages of the underlying semi-annual data reported to us.

10 The 1990 real GDP weights, as for the 1990 total-OECD weights mentioned in the preceding paragraph, were taken from the OECD's *Main Economic Indicators*. For the models that have all OECD countries represented in the model (either individually or consolidated in a sub-region) – namely, OEC, MUL, INA/INC and MSG – the Other-Industrial aggregate does comprise all *OECD* countries other than the United States and Japan. For the TAY and LVE/LIV models, however, this aggregate pertains only to the *G7* countries other than the United States and Japan. (Calculations for an Other-Industrial aggregate were not possible for the GEM simulations).

11 Data for GEM are not available for the tenth simulation year, and for some variables are not available at all. Data for OEC are available only for the first six years of the ten-year simulation period. Data are also unavailable for GDP deflators for LVE.

12 The OEC results pertain to only a 2 per cent rather than 5 per cent monetary contraction (one of the most serious non-comparabilities in the simulations), which distorts the cross-model averages.

13 In the textbook theoretical framework, the exchange rate responds to interest rates (via capital flows) and to income/absorption (via the effects through imports on the trade balance). A fiscal contraction tends to lower the home interest rate (putting pressure on the home currency to depreciate) and to reduce home income (putting pressure on the currency to appreciate by improving the trade balance). The flatter the *BP* curve relative to the *LM*

curve, the more the interest rate effects on the exchange rate dominate the effects working through income and the trade balance. In more complex theoretical models, the home currency's exchange value may follow a complex dynamic pattern – for example, depreciating temporarily after a fiscal contraction but then eventually appreciating to an inflation-adjusted value significantly above its original level.

14 Implementations of this OECD-wide fiscal shock by the model groups tended to differ in an analogous manner to the differences discussed above in connection with the D2 US fiscal contraction. Debt–GDP ratios for the OECD countries were changed over time in a broadly comparable manner (analogous to the movements shown in Figure 8.18). But noteworthy differences across the models are apparent when one examines the ratios of budget deficits to nominal GDP (again analogous to the diversity apparent in Figure 8.19). Such cross-model differences in the implementation of fiscal shocks are an important obstacle to appropriate interpretation of cross-model differences in other macroeconomic variables.

15 See Sachs and McKibbin (1985) for a related used of the concept.

16 This simplifying assumption is probably appropriate, at least approximately, for some highly indebted countries, for example in Latin America and Africa. For other non-OECD countries, on the other hand, the assumption is not appropriate, for example many Asian countries and even some Latin American countries that have regained access to the international capital markets. The accounting framework can obviously be developed without the simplifying assumption that the non-OECD current account remains unchanged.

17 If capital flows and debt stocks can change, there is of course a fourth type of channel.

18 It can be shown that with price elasticities for demand equal to unity, the value of this supply-price elasticity is irrelevant for calculations of the compensating-variation transfer.

19 To economize on space, we report the calculations only for the non-OECD region as a whole. The procedures we follow can of course be applied to the four disaggregated non-OECD regions shown in Table 8.1 (or to individual developing countries).

20 The magnitudes defined in equations (1)–(11) are measured in terms of real US goods. For the calculations in Tables 8.2–8.5, we have in effect multiplied all the terms in equation (11) by a US price index, converting them to nominal magnitudes. Hence the magnitudes in Tables 8.2–8.5 are measured in billions of current US dollars.

21 The case in which the income elasticities for non-OECD exports are very high – see column (c) – is an exception.

22 All of the individual regions defined in Table 8.1, as well as the non-OECD as a whole, are probably net debtors *vis-à-vis* the OECD region. (Data for the external assets of private sectors in non-OECD countries are unavailable or unreliable, so these data could not be incorporated in Table 8.1).

23 See, for example, Masson and Helliwell (1990) and Allen *et al.* (1992). Bryant's comments on the Hughes Hallett paper in Currie and Vines (1988) also flags the issue.

24 Examples of exploratory research to model non-OECD regions as components of a world macroeconomic system include efforts with the MSG model

(McKibbin and Sachs, 1991; McKibbin and Sundberg, 1992, 1995); with the MULTIMOD model (Masson *et al.*, 1990; Symansky, 1991; Bayoumi *et al.*, 1995); with the INTERMOD model (Helliwell *et al.*, 1990; Meredith, 1989); with the University of Glasgow/GEM modelling project (Allen *et al.*, 1992; Allen *et al.*, 1995); and with the World Bank/GEM modelling project (Petersen *et al.*, 1991; Petersen and Srinivasan, 1995). Participants in Project LINK have for many years sought to incorporate models of developing countries in the LINK system (see Hickman, 1991, for an overview and references).

REFERENCES

Allen, Chris, David Currie, T. G. Srinivasan and David Vines (1992) 'Policy interactions between the OECD countries and Latin America in the 1980s', *The Manchester School* **60** Supplement, 1–20.

Allen, Chris, T. G. Srinivasan and David Vines (1995) 'Analysing external adjustment in developing countries: a macroeconomic framework', chapter 6 in this volume.

Bayoumi, Tamim, Daniel Hewitt and Steven Symansky (1995) 'MULTIMOD simulations of the effects on developing countries of decreasing military spending', Chapter 10 in this volume.

Bryant, Ralph C., John F. Helliwell and Peter Hooper (1989) 'Domestic and cross-border consequences of US macroeconomic policies', in Bryant, Currie *et al.* (eds.), *Macroeconomic Policies in an Interdependent World*, Washington DC: International Monetary Fund, Brookings Institution, Centre for Economic Policy Research. Unabridged version available as Brookings Discussion Paper in International Economics No. 68 Washington DC: Brookings Institution, January 1989.

Bryant, Ralph C., Dale W. Henderson, Gerald Holtham, Peter Hooper and Steven A. Symansky (eds.) (1988) *Empirical Macroeconomics for Interdependent Economies*, Washington, DC: Brookings Institution.

Bryant, Ralph C., Peter Hooper and Catherine L. Mann (eds.) (1993) *Evaluating Policy Regimes: New Research in Empirical Macroeconomics*, Washington DC: Brookings Institution.

Currie, David A. and David Vines (1988) *Macroeconomic Interactions between North and South*, Cambridge: Cambridge University Press.

Helliwell, John F. and Paul R. Masson (1990) 'The effects of industrial country fiscal policies on developing countries in the 1980s,' *Revista di Politica Economica* **80**, 195–231.

Helliwell, John F., Guy Meredith, Philip Bagnoli and Yves Durand (1990) 'INTERMOD 1.1: A G-7 Version of the IMF's MULTIMOD', *Economic Modelling* **7**, 3–62.

Hickman, Bert G. (1991) 'Project LINK and Multi-country Modelling', in Ronald G. Bodkin, Lawrence R. Klein, and Kanta Marwah (eds.), *A History of Macroeconometric Model-Building*, Edward Elgar Publishing Company.

Masson, Paul R., Steven Symansky and Guy Meredith (1990) 'MULTIMOD Mark II: A Revised and Extended Model', IMF Occasional Paper No. 71, Washington DC.

McKibbin, Warwick J. and Jeffrey D. Sachs (1991) *Global Linkages: Macro-*

economic Interdependence and Cooperation in the World Economy, Washington DC: The Brookings Institution.

McKibbin, Warwick J. and Mark Sundberg (1992) 'The implications for the Asia-Pacific Region of coordination of macroeconomic policies in the OECD', *Journal of Policy Modeling* 15, 13–48.

(1995) 'Macroeconomic linkages between the OECD and the Asia-Pacific region', chapter 9 in this volume.

Meredith, Guy (1989) 'Model specification and simulation properties', Working Paper No. 89–7, Ottawa: Working Group on International Macroeconomics, Department of Finance.

Petersen, C. E., K. N. Pedersen, E. J. Riordan, R. A. Lynn and T. Bradley (1991) 'BANK-GEM: a World Bank global economic model', paper presented at the Project LINK Conference, Moscow, 23–7 September, 1991.

Petersen, C. E. and T. G. Srinivasan (1995) 'Effects of a rise in G-7 real interest rates on developing countries', chapter 11 in this volume.

Sachs, Jeffrey D. and Warwick J. McKibbin (1985) 'Macroeconomic policies in the OECD and LDC external adjustment', Brookings Discussion Paper in International Economics No. 25.

Symansky, Steven (1991) 'Closure rules and a new developing country region for MULTIMOD,' paper presented at the conference on 'Global Interdependence: Theories and Models of the Linkages Between OECD and Non-OECD Economies', held in Seoul, South Korea, 27–8 May 1991.

9 Macroeconomic linkages between the OECD and the Asia-Pacific region

WARWICK J. McKIBBIN and
MARK W. SUNDBERG

1 Introduction

In this paper we present an extended version of the Asia-Pacific McKibbin–Sachs Global Model (called APMSG hereafter) originally developed in Sundberg (1991).[1] The APMSG is designed for analysis of linkages between industrial countries and developing country regions, and therefore represents a significant extension to the earlier MSG and MSG2 models of Sachs and McKibbin (1985) and McKibbin and Sachs (1992),[2] which incorporated only the external accounts of developing country blocs. We use this model to explore the impacts on the Asia-Pacific region of the recently announced US fiscal consolidation and a Japanese fiscal expansion. We also consider the transmission of a monetary expansion in Japan and the United States to the Asia-Pacific region.

We model two groups of countries within the Pacific region.[3] Apart from Japan, which is already in the MSG2 model, we model a group we call Asian NIES consisting of Korea, Taiwan, Singapore and Hong Kong (hereafter called ANIES), and a group consisting of four members of the ASEAN group of countries: Indonesia, Malaysia, Philippines and Thailand (hereafter called ASEAN4). Each Asian region has three traded goods sectors and one non-traded sector. In addition to the sectoral disaggregation, the internal macroeconomic structure of these two Asia-Pacific regions differ significantly from the typical country model in the MSG2 model. For these economies we follow the theoretical under-pinnings of the first MSG work (Sachs and McKibbin, 1985; McKibbin and Sachs, 1988). This was basically a Mundell–Fleming–Dornbusch model with Keynesian macrofoundations, rather than the more rigorous microfoundations used in the MSG2 work of McKibbin and Sachs (1991). In selecting specifications for the APMSG model, we face the trade-off between theoretical rigor and empirical regularities by focusing

235

on the key empirical relationships in the region, while sacrificing theoretical rigor at times. The developing country blocs which have been added are based on richer trade and sectoral specifications while using a less sophisticated approach to handling the intertemporal aspects of agents' behaviour.

The model solves for a full global intertemporal equilibrium where forward-looking agents are assumed to have perfect foresight. Both the developing and developed regions carefully observe the key stock–flow relationships in the world economy. Fiscal deficits and current-account deficits accumulate into public debt and changes in the net foreign asset position, and physical investment accumulates into capital stocks.

The main features of the APMSG model are summarized in Section 2. In Section 3 we discuss the structure of the Asian regional blocs. A summary of the key features of the industrial country blocs is outlined in Section 4. We also highlight the changes made to the subsectors representing the industrial countries that were required to accommodate the multisectoral approach taken in the developing regions. Model calibration, data issues and the solution technique are briefly described in Section 5. In Section 6, we examine the impact of shocks in the OECD and how they are transmitted to the Asia-Pacific regions. We first consider the impacts of a gradual deficit reduction programme in the United States similar in magnitude to the programme announced by the Clinton Administration. We contrast this with a programme which is implemented without phasing in the spending cuts and tax increases. We also consider a Japanese fiscal expansion and a monetary expansion in both the United States and Japan. A final overview and directions for future work are presented in Section 7.

2   General features of the APMSG model

The intermediate size of the model, along with the moderate disaggregation of commodities, has required grouping countries into regional blocs that clearly reflect its Pacific orientation and limit its applicability to other developing regions.[4] We have compressed the disaggregated models for Germany, the rest of the EMS and the rest of the OECD regions from the MSG2 model described in McKibbin and Sachs (1991) into one Rest of the OECD region (hereafter called ROECD).[5] There are seven world regions in the model comprising three developed country blocs (the US, Japan and the ROECD), and three developing country groups (the ANIES, the ASEAN4 region and OPEC). In addition, there is a rest of world bloc which serves to ensure full accounting consistency for the key stock–flow relationships in the global economy.

The two developing country regions in the Pacific are based on an input–output framework with three traded and one non-traded sectors. Exports are demand-determined and prices are fully endogenous to ensure market clearing. The industrial economies, however, are single-commodity economies with domestic consumption, investment and production activities that require imported inputs from the other industrial blocs and from the developing countries. The choice of bloc structures reflects emphasis here on developing countries, in particular on trade flows between industrial and developing country blocs.

Computable General Equilibrium (CGE) modelling techniques have long been used for country-specific models.[6] These are multisectoral models, based on a national social accounting matrix, and generally treating exchange rates, international prices and interest rates, and external demand exogenously. Another application of CGE modelling, often used to study policy coordination issues, has typically focused on multiregional models with little or no commodity disaggregation and with fully endogenous prices and intertemporally optimizing agents. The APMSG model occupies an intermediate position which provides some commodity disaggregation, designed specifically to capture sectoral end-use characteristics of import demands, and is multiregional with full-price endogeneity. This is similar in some respects to recent work by Whalley (1985), and Masson et al. (1988).[7]

The behavioural structure of the developed country blocs in the model is characterized by:

(i)   efficient asset markets in which asset prices are determined assuming rational expectations, risk-neutrality, and intertemporal arbitrage conditions;

(ii)   a mix of intertemporally profit-maximizing firms, in which capital stocks adjust according to a 'Tobin's q' model of investment, and liquidity-constrained firms;

(iii)   a mix of intertemporally optimizing consumers and liquidity-constrained consumers;

(iv)   different wage–price dynamics in the US (nominal rigidities), Japan (market clearing with a one-period lag) and the ROECD (more real wage rigidity).

In the developing country regions, however, expectations are assumed to be static and agents are constrained in their ability to substitute intertemporally. This is not based on empirical evidence but rather on the observation that the institutional environment allowing agents to act on their expectations (futures markets, forward exchange markets, instantaneous market information, etc.) is often lacking or poorly developed in developing countries. While the argument could be made that agents are 'as rational' and markets act in fundamentally similar ways in developing countries, particularly in asset markets, there is typically a greater degree of market failure and a less well-developed institutional base in developing countries, factors which make this assumption less tenable.[8]

3   Structure of the developing country blocs

Both the ANIES and the ASEAN4 blocs have similar structural features, although differences in their endowments, trade patterns and financial flows to other regions result in different patterns of response to external shocks. For convenience we focus here on describing the structure of the ANIES bloc, while separately addressing the ASEAN4 countries only where important differences arise.

In modelling exercises of this nature there is always some sacrifice of detail for the sake of generalization, and elaboration where it proves essential to the issues at hand. Our purpose here is to better understand macroeconomic linkages between major world regions and the transmission of monetary and fiscal policies through the Pacific region. The model reflects this through the greater care given to international trade and financial relations, while domestic labour and financial markets, for example, lack sufficient disaggregation to undertake detailed domestic policy analysis.

The basic framework for the Asian blocs is a highly aggregated social accounting matrix (SAM) that provides a map of annual flows between sectors, factors of production, and institutions.[9] This captures interindustry flows at a given moment in time, and is discussed in greater detail below. Demand sources correspond to the standard national accounting presentation, comprising private consumer demand, investment demand, government and foreign demand. The framework has been kept as simple as possible while retaining many of the essential features of the regional economies. Equation (1) shows the basic income accounting identity

$$YP = \sum_{i=1}^{4} (V^i P_v^i) = CP_c + GP_g + IP_I + (XP_x - MP_m) \qquad (1)$$

where the capital letters refer to real (constant price) values, P is the GDP deflator, and P_i is the respective i sector price index. Specification of each of these aggregates and a description of the supply side of the economy is provided in detail below.

3.1   Production and investment

The domestic economy of the bloc is divided into four productive sectors comprising light manufacturing (X), heavy manufacturing (M), agriculture and mining (R) and services (S). These labels are somewhat artificial, however, and from the standpoint of trade classification used in our data (summarized below) may be better thought of as consumer manufactures, capital goods, primary commodities plus industrial intermediates and non-tradables (principally government and services output), respectively. Outputs from the first three of these sectors are traded.

The basis for aggregate supply in the economy is the representative firm in each sector, which is assumed to be perfectly competitive with zero profits. Production is described using a nested, two-input constant elasticity of substitution (CES) production function comprised of a value-added input bundle and intermediate inputs

$$Q^i = [\beta_{1i}(V^i)^{\rho_{1i}} + (1 - \beta_{1i})(N^i)^{\rho_{1i}}]^{(\frac{1}{\rho_{1i}})} \tag{2}$$

$$\beta_{1i} = \frac{1}{1 + (\frac{V^i}{N^i})^{-\frac{1}{\sigma_i}}(\frac{P^i_n}{P^i_v})} \tag{3}$$

where Q^i is gross output of sector i, V^i is value added in sector i, and N^i is the bundle of intermediate inputs in i. Time subscripts are left off, but it should be understood that $t = 1$, unless otherwise indicated. Here, β_{1i} is the CES share parameter for the top level, and is a function of relative input shares, the elasticity of substitution parameter σ_i, and of relative nominal prices.[10] Both the value-added input bundle and intermediate bundles are themselves nested CES functions. The former is produced with inputs of capital (K) and labour (L) and the latter with inputs from each of the other sectors (X,M,R,S) as well as imported inputs from the OECD countries (IM) and oil imported from OPEC (E).

$$V^i = [\beta_{2i}(K^i)^{\rho_{2i}} + (1 - \beta_{2i})(L^i)^{\rho_{2i}}]^{(\frac{1}{\rho_{2i}})} \tag{4}$$

$$N^i = [\beta_{3i}(X^i)^{\rho_{3i}} + \beta_{4i}(M^i)^{\rho_{3i}} + \beta_{5i}(R^i)^{\rho_{3i}} + \beta_{6i}(S^i)^{\rho_{3i}} + \beta_{7i}(IM^i)^{\rho_{3i}}$$
$$+ (1 - \beta_{3i} - \beta_{4i} - \beta_{5i} - \beta_{6i} - \beta_{7i})(E^i)^{\rho_{3i}}]^{(\frac{1}{\rho_{3i}})} \tag{5}$$

This specification allows for separate elasticity parameters between the value-added components, $\sigma_2 = 1/(1 - \rho_2)$, and the Allen elasticities between inputs to the intermediate bundle, $\sigma_3 = 1/(1 - \rho_3)$.[11] The imported input, IM_i, is itself a composite bundle of imports from other regions, discussed in greater depth below. Oil (E) is also imported and comes principally from the OPEC bloc.[12] The β CES share parameters are similar to that shown in (2).

Solution of the firm's profit-maximization problem yields the standard first-order conditions with marginal revenue products equalized across all inputs to production.[13] All prices are determined endogenously, ensuring that supply is equal to demand in each period and inventories are assumed constant or zero. Gross national product is equal to the sum of value added in the four sectors.

$$Y = \sum_{i=1}^{4} \left(\frac{V^i \, P_v^i}{P} \right) \tag{6}$$

where P is the GNP price deflator.

Investment demand is determined by the firm's intertemporal maximization problem which depends on the expected returns to capital in each industry. The maximization problem is simply

$$Max \sum_{\tau=t}^{\infty} (1 + \beta_\tau)^{-1} (P_\tau^i Q_\tau^i - W_\tau^i L_\tau^i - Pn_\tau^i N_\tau^i - P_{I\tau}^i I_\tau^i)/P_\tau^i \tag{7}$$

where $(1 + \beta_\tau)^{-1}$ is the period τ discount factor; $(1 + r_v) = \prod_{s=t}^{v}(1 + r_s)$, where r_s is the period s short-term real interest rate. Solution of this yields the familiar derived demand for current inputs of labour and intermediates such that demand equates the marginal product of each input to that input's marginal cost.

The intertemporal features of investment demand are included in a simple static expectations version of Tobin's 'marginal q'

$$q_{it} = \frac{MPK_{it} \, P_{it}}{P_{It}^i \, (r_t + \delta)} \tag{8}$$

where $MPK_{it} = \dfrac{\partial Q_{it}}{\partial V_{it}} \dfrac{\partial V_{it}}{\partial K_{it}}$.

Static expectations imply that the short-term real interest rate is expected to remain at its current level indefinitely and is not adjusted for capital gains or investment. Thus investment demand adjusts to the value of q each period. This can lead to sharp adjustments in investment, which may be unrealistic in a situation where low interest rates may not be expected to endure, or where forms may be liquidity-constrained. In developing countries, however, it is often the case that domestic firms are liquidity-constrained with limited access to capital markets. We have modified the investment demand function to include a term for the current cash-flow return to capital of the firm.

$$I_i = \alpha_i \left[\frac{(q_i - 1)}{\phi_o} \right] K_i + \gamma^i \frac{(P^i Q^i - L^i W - Pn^i N^i)}{PI} \tag{9}$$

The first term represents the portion of investment driven by Tobin's q, that is by firms that have full access to capital at the market rate of interest. The second term represents the cash-flow constraint on investment. Time subscripts have been left off for convenience. Note that α_i and γ_i are not constrained to sum to one. The choice of parameter values is not, however, straightforward. There is no information on the share of investment by firms that are constrained in capital markets, nor of firms using the conceptual basis of Tobin's q for investment decisions. Instead we have looked at the sensitivity of investment to the α and γ parameters, and chosen values that appear 'plausible' given past values of investment and interest rates.[14]

The capital stock in a given period is a function of the current period level of physical investment and the inherited capital stock net of depreciation

$$K^i_{t+1} = J^i_t + K^i_t (1 - \delta - \xi) \quad \text{for all } i, i = X, M, R, S \tag{10}$$

where J^i is the level of investment in sector i net of adjustment costs, δ is the rate of capital depreciation, assumed to be equal across all sectors, and ξ is the rate of population growth plus the rate of technical progress.[15] Gross investment (I_i) differs from investment net of adjustment costs (J_i). A rising marginal cost of investment, due to the standard formulation of installation costs, is a linear function of the rate of investment

$$PI\, I^i = \left[1 + \left(\frac{\phi_o}{2} \right) \left(\frac{J^i}{K^i} \right) \right] P_j\, J^i \tag{11}$$

Investment is treated as a composite good produced from both imported and domestic inputs using a Cobb–Douglas technology (constant value shares). It is assumed to be the same composite across all industries

$$I = (I_x)^{\kappa_1} (I_m)^{\kappa_2} (I_s)^{\kappa_3} (I_{im})^{(1-\kappa_1-\kappa_2-\kappa_3)} \tag{12}$$

and

$$I_{im} = (I_{us})^{\kappa_4} (I_{japan})^{\kappa_5} (I_{roecd})^{(1-\kappa_4-\kappa_5)} \tag{13}$$

where I is gross investment, inclusive of adjustment costs.

3.2   Household consumption and savings behaviour

Private consumption demand by households and private savings behaviour are of course jointly determined. For the purpose of macroeconomic modelling it suffices to specify either savings or consumption behaviour, leaving both to sum to total disposable income. Households exhaust disposable income between these two activities, and are not able to borrow abroad to supplement domestic incomes. Here we chose to specify savings behaviour and leave consumption to be determined residually from disposable income. This approach was chosen because there is in general a richer macroeconomic literature on savings behaviour in developing countries than on consumption behaviour.

The specification here follows closely on Fry (1988) whose cross-country work on savings behaviour in Asian developing countries is among the most recent and complete available. Some modifications have been necessary in keeping with the structure of the APMSG model. The share of savings out of disposable income is a function of four arguments: the lagged ratio of savings to real disposable income, real income growth, the terms-of-trade component of income growth and the real rate of interest

$$\frac{S_t}{Yd_t} = \alpha\left(\frac{S_{t-1}}{Yd_{t-1}}\right) + \beta\frac{(Y_t - Y_{t-1})}{Y_{t-1}} + \lambda\left(ToT_t - ToT_{t-1}\right) + \delta(i_t - \pi_t) \tag{14}$$

where Yd = disposable income, Y = total income, ToT is the terms of trade and $(i_t - \pi_t)$ is the nominal domestic interest rate minus domestic inflation.

Most empirical work on savings behaviour in developing countries has used savings as a share of current GNP and regressed this on income growth, the real interest rate and demographic factors. Fry (1988) finds that for a sample of fourteen Asian countries for the period from 1961 to 1983 the real income growth rate, income growth attributable to terms-of-trade changes, the real interest rate and lagged savings are significant and affect the savings rate positively, while the dependency ratio (population aged under fifteen plus those over sixty-five, divided by the population aged fifteen to sixty-four) affects savings negatively.[16]

The positive coefficient on income growth is in keeping with the observation of a positive correlation between real per-capita income levels and the national savings rate as shown by Collins (1989). In addition, Collins (1988) reveals that savings behaviour in Korea has been highly cyclical in nature, and is driven primarily by the growth rate of the economy, possibly due to the transitory nature of cyclical income shocks.

One source of cyclical income shocks is from terms-of-trade changes, a variable which Fry adds to account for income gains that real GNP growth fails to capture. The positive sign could be explained if this is viewed as a transitory income increase and there is consumption-smoothing behaviour. An alternative explanation could be that terms-of-trade shocks induce income variability, which directly affects agricultural incomes of many poorer families. The rise in savings may be seen as a 'high frequency' savings response by poor households, as described in Deaton (1989).

The influence of real interest rates on savings in developing countries has been tested by many authors with mixed results. Several studies in the 1970s and 1980s concluded that there is a significant positive relationship, whereas Giovannini (1983, 1985) has challenged this result on the grounds of misspecification, finding no statistically significant relationship between them. In Fry's (1988) study, written partly in response to Giovannini's criticisms, the data set was extended to cover more countries and a longer time period. The consensus that appears to have emerged is that there is a statistically significant relationship between them, but the elasticity is very weak, on the order of 0.1 per cent to 0.2 per cent increase in savings for a 1 per cent rise in the real interest rate (see Fry, 1988; Balassa, 1989; Nam, 1989, on Korea and the Philippines).

The dependency rate (defined above) has also been found to be an important determinant of savings differentials across countries and across time (see Collins, 1989; Fry, 1988; Mason, 1987; Webb and Zia, 1989). We have left this out of the savings equation since movements in the dependency ratio happen very gradually, whereas we are mainly interested in the short and medium run.[17] Furthermore, there is some evidence from Korea that the age–savings profile is flattening out; and savings are becoming independent of age (Collins, 1989, p. 23). This is less likely, however, to be true of the ASEAN countries.

The counterpart of savings is private consumption, included here simply as total disposable income less private domestic savings. Note that present discounted human and financial wealth are not arguments of consumption demand, largely because of how we have handled savings specification, although this is treated differently in the OECD countries (see below).

$$C_t \equiv Y_t - T_t - S_t \equiv Yd_t - S_t \tag{15}$$

where T_t is total taxes collected by the central government in period t and C_t is current private consumption. This provides the total level of consumption. We then assume that given this total consumption, consumers allocate their spending between the alternative consumption goods based on total expenditure and relative prices as if they were maximizing a utility function which consisted of multilevel CES nesting of each good similar to that used in the production functions (1), (2) and (3) above. Total consumption is allocated between domestic (C^d) and imported (C^m) final goods. Each of these are nested composites, the first comprising inputs from all four domestic sectors, and the latter comprising imports from all foreign sources, excluding OPEC. All goods are normal, homothetic of degree zero in prices, and the utility function is concave, yielding diminishing marginal utility.

3.3   The balance of payments and government accounts

Exports of the Asian NIEs have increased rapidly in recent years, while imports have in general not increased commensurately. Korea and Taiwan account for nearly the entire regional surplus. Successive large trade surpluses have resulted in accumulation of enormous foreign exchange reserves in Taiwan, while Korea has been able to significantly reduce its stock of outstanding debt. Both countries have also maintained relatively closed capital accounts and have retained control over their exchange rates as an instrument of government policy. Neither Singapore nor Hong Kong has chosen to follow this path, both for historical reasons and due to the extremely open nature of their economies which are founded on the principle of laissez-faire trading practices.

Balance of payments adjustment is patterned after the Korean and Taiwanese experience because of the important role these two countries now play in Pacific current-account imbalances and the relative size of their economies. Together, Korea and Taiwan account for 80 per cent of Asian NIE output. Although this comes at some cost to capturing the diversity of the region, it is the closest approximation to the regional paradigm and makes application and interpretation of the model much more transparent. The capital accounts are therefore modelled as being closed and money supply is determined endogenously (see below). Conceptually, this is similar to the Dornbusch (1973) model of current-account adjustment.

Consumption, investment and intermediate inputs to production all include an imported component. Imports are obtained from all of the other country blocs, while the share of each world source varies according to the importance of that country in supplying the given inputs. Imported capital goods for investment, for example, are principally from the US and Japan, with a smaller share coming from Europe and none supplied by the rest of world developing country bloc. Imported intermediate inputs, on the other hand, are mainly from the ASEAN4 bloc, the US and the rest-of-world bloc, with Japan supplying a smaller share.

Foreign import demand is discussed in detail below. Each of the three industrial blocs, as well as the ASEAN4 bloc, imports part of the output of the three tradables sectors. The ROW and OPEC blocs import only light industrial goods. This is a simplification that has little impact on the overall trade mix.

External capital accounts have been consolidated under the public sector to further simplify analysis. Only the government is assumed to have access to international capital markets. This is fairly representative of experience in Taiwan, where until recently all foreign exchange was compulsorily surrendered to the authorities, and in Korea.

Government consumption is set exogenously as a constant proportion of total national income, and the government is assumed to run a balanced budget in every time period. While this is not strictly appropriate for the Asian NIEs, they have maintained nearly balanced budgets which have not resulted in large cumulative deficits, unlike many other developing countries. This implies that taxes adjust each period to cover current government outlays, with an additional term to finance net service flows on the outstanding public debt. Since the Asian NIEs are net creditors, this is a positive flow which reduces the annual tax rate on household income

$$G_t = \alpha^g (Y_t) + i_t^i (B_t) \tag{16}$$

where α^g is the exogenous government expenditure share of GDP, and B_t is net consolidated external liabilities (assets) of the government.

The government consumes domestic services, and is responsible for servicing the national net external debt. Apart from the lump-sum tax revenues the government receives out of labour and capital income, the government also receives interest payments on the stock of net foreign assets of the central bank. Greater detail in the specification of government revenues could be added, but is not important to the current applications of the model.[18]

Consolidation of the central bank and government accounts results in treatment of external debt as net of reserve holdings. In each period the level of real government spending on domestic output is exogenously fixed as a percentage of real national income so that gross expenditure varies only with changes in the level of debt service obligations. National debt is further divided between fixed and floating-rate debt. Only the portion of debt with floating rates will be affected by interest rate shocks from abroad. All government spending is on the output of the services (non-traded) sector, government expenditure on imports and the output of other sectors is indirect, intermediate demands of the service sector. Rewriting (16) we have

$$G_t = \alpha^g (Y_t) + i_t^i (B_t - R_t) = \alpha^g (Y_t) + i_t^i (D_t) = T_t \qquad (17)$$

The share of government expenditure in GDP, α^g, is exogenous. B_t is net consolidated external liabilities (assets) of the government, R_t is net foreign assets of the central bank and D_t is the total net asset position of the region.[19]

$$BC_t^g = T_t - \alpha^g (Y_t) - i_t^i (D_t) = 0 \qquad (18)$$

With zero capital mobility and a fixed exchange rate, the level of the nominal money supply becomes endogenous and the government freely converts all foreign exchange requirements for current-account transactions at the fixed exchange rate. We turn next to these financial variables and price determination.

3.4   Money demand, exchange rates and domestic prices

Demand for nominal money balances is a function of the domestic nominal interest rate, real national output, and the domestic price level according to a standard Goldfeld-type money demand equation

$$\frac{M_t}{P_t} = (Y_t)^\eta (1 + i_t)^{-\nu} \qquad (19)$$

where η and ν equal the income and interest elasticity of money demand, respectively.

This leads to a natural adjustment mechanism. As the domestic money supply is increased domestic interest rates fall, which in turn stimulates domestic demand and gradually reduces the external surplus.

Specification of prices in the model is determined largely by the functional form chosen for demand specification. For example, the price of the investment good, which is a Cobb–Douglas composite, is simply a weighted average of its constituent parts.

$$P_i = \theta_x P_x + \theta_m P_m + \theta_r P_r + \theta_s P_s + \theta_{im} P_{im}^i + \theta_e P_e \sum_{i=1}^{5} \theta_i = 1 \qquad (20)$$

where θ_j is the base period share of the jth component in the investment good and P_{im}^i is the price of the imported component in investment, itself a price index weighted by the price of exports from each foreign supplier. P_e here is the price of petroleum from OPEC.

Wage specification, however, has been separately estimated, as discussed in detail in Sundberg (1991). Drawing on regression analysis for the Asian NIE bloc, wage adjustment is determined through four terms; excess labour demand, contemporaneous and lagged domestic price inflation, and movements in the current period's terms of trade. This is shown in equation (21).

$$w_t = w_{t-1} + \alpha (p_t - p_{t-1}) + (1 - \alpha)(p_{t-1} - p_{t-2})$$
$$+ \beta (Ld_t - Ls_t) + \gamma (px_t - pm_t) \qquad (21)$$

where nominal wages (w_t), the consumer price index along with export and import prices (p, px, pm), as well as labour supply and demand (ls, ld), are all expressed in logs. The α parameter therefore represents a current and lagged 'indexation' parameter[20] $(\alpha = 0.73)$, while β $(= 0.22)$ and γ $(= 0.3)$ represent the responsiveness to domestic unemployment and the external terms of trade, respectively. Wages are assumed to be equalized across all industries. Ideally one would want to distinguish between the labour markets in each sector and allow for different wage-setting mechanisms, for example, in the agricultural and urban manufacturing sectors. In the ASEAN4 members of the region, with sizeable agricultural sectors, some form of the Harris–Todaro specification may be more appropriate, with a wedge between the urban, manufacturing and the agricultural labour markets. That exercise may be left for later versions of the model. For the ANIES, however, labour markets are generally considered to be efficient. Hong Kong and Singapore have relatively flexibly and homogeneous labour markets, with under 2 per cent of the workforce employed in the primary sector. Korea and Taiwan have more substantial primary employment, but are considered to be well past the labour surplus stage.[21]

The terms-of-trade term is an especially important transmission mechanism to the Asian NIEs because they are among the most open economies in the world. Trade as a share of GDP (exports plus imports) in 1987 ranged from 67 per cent in Korea to 277 per cent in Singapore, and averaged 114 per cent for the four countries. This compares with the average in low-income developing countries of 24 per cent, in middle-income countries 45 per cent, and 28 per cent in the developed market economies. This causes greater 'vulnerability' to price shocks in the world economy. As world relative prices change the response of domestic firms is affected through the price paid and received for the products, as well as through endogenous price changes in domestic factor markets. During the 1970s all four countries weathered sharp swings in their terms of trade, particularly following the OPEC I and OPEC II oil price shocks. Korean net barter terms of trade suffered a fall of 32 per cent between 1973 and 1974 and fell again by 22 per cent after the 1979 shock. Taiwanese experience was of similar magnitude, with the terms of trade falling by 17 per cent after the first shock and by 11 per cent after OPEC II.

The other two terms in the wage equation, on inflation and unemployment, are the principal features of the standard Phillips curve relationship. In the face of external disturbances or domestic policies which affect the domestic price level, such as the oil price shocks of the 1970s or expansionary monetary policies, nominal wages only partially adjust, with the consequence that real wages are relatively flexible in the ANIES. The coefficient on unemployment captures the neoclassical market adjustment mechanism. As the labour supply constraint is relaxed or tightened nominal wages fall or rise, which in turn feeds back to the domestic price level.

For the ASEAN4 bloc Sundberg (1990) was unable to obtain sufficient data to estimate the regional Phillips curve in this manner. A modified specification similar to that of the Asian NIEs has been adopted based on secondary evidence on labour markets in the region. Labour markets vary across the four ASEAN economies, and any specification necessarily involves some approximation between them. Regional shares of labour in manufacturing and unionization rates are much higher in the Philippines and Malaysia, for example. We might expect that wages there are more responsive to nominal price shocks than in Thailand and Indonesia. None of the four has very active labour unions, and institutional arrangements for social security, fringe benefits or unemployment compensation are almost entirely absent.[22] Unlike the Asian NIEs, it is hard to argue that these countries are past the 'Lewis stage of labour surplus'. Evidence from Indonesia, with nearly two-thirds of the regional workforce, suggests that real wages have been fairly stagnant in agriculture and the unskilled urban sector over most of the 1970s and early 1980s (World Bank, 1985). Pitt (1981) argues, however, that labour markets in Indonesia are responsive to price signals and wages are flexible. This description of the ASEAN4 labour markets appears not dissimilar from those pertaining in the Asian NIEs during the 1960s. Due to a lack of sufficient data for separate estimation, however, we have chosen to use the same wage adjustment specification as that of the ANIES.

Other prices that are used in the CES functional forms, such as the product price coming from value added and intermediate bundles, are derived from the dual to the relevant CES function. In the above mentioned example we have

$$P_i = [\beta_{2i}^{\sigma_{2i}} P_v^{(1-\sigma_{2i})} + (1 - \beta_{2i})^{\sigma_{2i}} P_n^{(1-\sigma_{2i})}]^{(\frac{1}{1-\sigma_{2i}})} \tag{22}$$

where β and σ are the share and substitution elasticity parameters discussed above.

Price adjustment is of course critical to the stabilizing properties of general equilibrium models, since through prices supply is ensured to match demand. This is true of domestic product prices in the goods markets, and also of the domestic interest rates in equilibrating domestic money demand and the credit market. The domestic nominal interest rate is determined by the total demand and supply of credit in domestic market, and is not directly linked to external financial markets. A current-account surplus which increases the money supply will reduce the domestic interest rate while increases in income or the price level (lower real money balances) increase interest rates. The relationship of the interest rate to domestic money supply can be seen by inverting the money demand equation and obtaining i_t as a function of the money stock, income level, and current price level. After taking logs on both sides this yields

$$i_t = \frac{1}{v} (p_t + q_t^{-\eta} - m_t) \tag{23}$$

The real interest rate is of course the nominal rate less the current period's level of consumer price inflation, which is assumed to be part of any agent's current information set, and is one determinant of their investment and savings decisions.

Under a closed capital account and endogenous money supply regime, the exchange rate is retained as an instrument of government policy control. None of the regional currencies is freely floating, and most have maintained an undisclosed basket with a heavy weight on the dollar. The weights selected here are 0.65 against the US dollar, 0.25 against the Japanese yen and 0.10 against the European currency unit (for the ASEAN4 region we assume 0.75, 0.15 and 0.10 respectively).

4   Structural features of the industrial country blocs

4.1   Features of domestic supply and demand

Structural aspects of the industrial countries in the model draw on the earlier work of McKibbin (1986) and McKibbin and Sachs (1991). However, the addition of fully articulated developing country blocs to the MSG framework has required several modifications, particularly in the treatment of trade relations. The principal differences between the developing regions and the industrialized blocs is the more sophisticated intertemporal aspects of agents' behaviour and markets in the industrialized blocs. Since the industrial country blocs share similar specifications, we will provide a sketch of only the US equations.[23] The US is both the largest single bloc in the model and the most important destination country for regional exports.

Three general differences from the developing country blocs deserve some special attention. First, consumers maximize intertemporal utility according to both their current and expected future stream of income.

$$MAX \int_t^\infty [U(C_s)] \, e^{-(\theta-n)s} ds \tag{24}$$

where n is the exogenous rate of population growth plus labour-augmenting technical progress (i.e., potential growth) and θ is the subjective rate of discount.

Current consumption is determined by the present discounted value of total financial and human wealth, where human wealth is defined as the discounted value of the entire stream of future, real, after-tax labour income. Financial wealth includes real money balances, government bonds held by the public, net foreign assets, equity wealth, and domestic oil reserves. Aggregate consumption is therefore based on the well-known life-cycle model and is a linear function of total real wealth. To capture the effects of liquidity constraints it is also assumed that a portion of total consumption depends on current disposable income.

Second, firms select intermediate inputs to production, labour, and current investment through maximizing intertemporal net-of-tax profits. The assumption of rational expectations implies that the firm has expectations of the future path of prices, interest rates, etc. with subjective certainty. Inputs to production are hired up to the point where their marginal products equal their prices. A 'Tobin's q' model of investment, similar to that used in the developing blocs, with the difference that agents are perfectly rational and anticipate the future path of interest rates and output. Thus, anticipated future events affect current investment. Again total investment is then specified as a weighted average of the investment of forward-looking firms and investment of firms that invest out of retained earnings.

Third, financial markets are integrated across all OECD country regions and exchange rates are perfectly flexible. The expected returns to assets are equalized across regions using an interest arbitrage condition of the form

$$i_t^i = i_t^j + \frac{({_tE_{jt+1}^i} - E_{jt}^i)}{E_{jt}^i} \tag{25}$$

where i_t^i is the nominal interest rate at time t and ${_tE_{jt+1}^i}$ is the expectation at time t of the nominal exchange rate between country i and country j in the next period. Interest rate differentials therefore reflect agents' expectations of the forward exchange rate. The exchange rate similarly reflects future expectations but in addition is modified to allow for lagged exchange rate passthrough to import prices, as has been pointed out in several recent papers.[24]

$$z_t^i = z_{t-1}^i + \beta^i (e_t^i - e_{t-1}^i) + (1 - \beta^i)(e_{t-1}^i - e_{t-2}^i) \tag{26}$$

where z_t^i is the log of the exchange rate entering into import pricing and demand equations, while e_t^i is the log of the actual nominal exchange rate.

An additional point of relevance to policy simulations is that government expenditures are exogenous while tax revenues are endogenous. Any resulting deficit (surplus) is financed by issuing (retiring) bonds, held by the public, that yield the domestic rate of interest. The intertemporal budget constraint on government expenditure imposes the requirement that total revenues equal total expenditure in present discounted value terms.

4.2   Import demand in the industrial countries

Demand for developing country imports by the US is a major change in the specification of the US model from that in McKibbin and Sachs (1991).

The model distinguishes between three products categories exported by developing countries. This categorization was selected to map directly to the demand structure in the industrial country blocs for intermediate, consumer and investment goods imports. These three functional divisions are not normally used for classifying international trade flows.

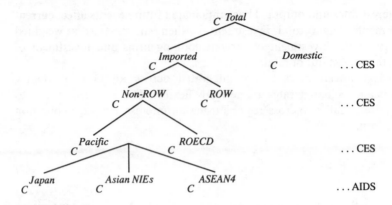

Figure 9.1   The structure of US consumer demand

The US, however, does provide an end-use import classification, which has been applied here to separate imports into their respective categories.[25] Demand for primary goods and industrial intermediates is the firm's demand for intermediate inputs arising from the firm's optimization problem, consumer goods demand (including consumer durables) is through utility maximization, and capital goods demand is derived from the firm's intertemporal investment decision.

Each of these import categories is handled in a different manner. Imports of consumer goods, the largest category of trade in the Pacific region, uses a combination of CES and AIDS (Almost Ideal Demand System) specifications as illustrated in Figure 9.1. At the top level, consumption is divided between domestic goods and imports according to a nested CES function. Domestic goods are not distinguished by sector in the industrial blocs. The import bundle is again divided between two bundles representing Pacific and ROECD imports, and rest of world imports, again using a CES specification. The last CES bundling is between ROECD imports and the Pacific bundle, of which the latter is specified using the AIDS approach of Deaton and Muellbauer (1980). Investment demand for imports is set in an analogous manner, however imports of capital goods from the ROW bloc was left out because it represents a minuscule amount of their total trade flows. Again, an AIDS specification was used for the Pacific region countries.

Imports of primary goods and raw materials are handled differently due to the more homogeneous and integrated characteristics of their markets. Only exports of the developing country blocs are explicitly modelled, though OECD country trade in these products is acknowledged to be the largest component of world trade. The absence of OECD trade is partly made up for by treatment of price determination in the model which aims to account for the important role of the US and the dollar exchange rate in primary product price determination. The relationship between the dollar exchange rate and the terms of trade for primary exporters has been explored by several authors. The stylized fact is that the terms of trade for primary exporters deteriorates as the dollar appreciates.[26] This is taken into account in the model in two steps; first, by specifying the ROW price of primary exports as a function of world output and prices, inversely related to the US real exchange rate, and, second, by using a high degree of substitution between suppliers so that there is little deviation from the world price, and this is never persistent. The log price of ROW exports, p^{row}, is given by

$$p^{row} = \sum_i \theta_i (p_i - e_i) + \phi (\sum_i X_i^w) \qquad (27)$$

where θ_i is the share of country i in ROW exports, p_i is country i's export price, e_i the nominal exchange rate, and X_i^w is the real value of ROW's exports to country i. The first term serves to maintain the price of ROW against a basket of world prices weighted by their import share while the last term is the upward slope to the supply curve. Allowing for a high elasticity of substitution in the model forces the prices charged by other exporters towards the ROW export price. In the extreme, with perfect substitution, primary export prices $(p_i^r + e_i - e_w)$ are forced to be equal across all suppliers, i.e., purchasing power parity is maintained in all periods.

Oil prices are handled in a similar manner, maintaining the real price against a basket of trading partner prices, and with a upward-sloping supply term. Oil is also exported by Southeast Asia to the US, Japan, ROECD and Asian NIE blocs, specified using constant value shares.

5   Calibration, data and simulation of the model

5.1   Calibration and data

A combination of standard techniques is used to calibrate the model. The first issue is to select a base period around which to linearize the model. This provides the initial period variable values that serve in turn as the basis for calibrating many of the parameter values (such as export shares or the CES β coefficients). Other parameters are derived econometrically, such as the AIDS trade demand elasticities and wage adjustment equations discussed in Sundberg (1991), or by using common values found in the econometrics literature.

Three product categories are exported by developing countries; (1) primary goods (agriculture and mining), (2) consumer manufactures and manufactured industrial intermediates and (3) capital goods. Demand for imported primary goods and industrial intermediates is derived from the firm's optimization problem in the importing country, demand for imported consumer goods from utility maximization, and demand for capital goods is derived from the firm's intertemporal investment decision. Oil exports from the ASEAN4 countries are handled separately from these categories and are priced according to the OPEC oil price. Disaggregation of goods to match these commodity characteristics was done following the US Bureau of the Census end-user classification system. A mapping was then made to the SITC classification (at the two-digit level) as reported by the United Nations.

Import demand of the US from Pacific exporters has been estimated to obtain price and income elasticities using a modified Almost Ideal Demand System (AIDS) specification, following Deaton and Muellbauer (1980). Demand elasticities for the other OECD blocs are taken from other studies, principally Whalley (1985).

The model has been initialized around 1987. Trade flows reproduce the actual levels and direction of trade between regions in that year. For example, the pattern of trade between Japan, the US and the Asian NIEs reflects the prevalence of imported capital goods and industrial intermediates by the ANIES and exports of consumer manufactures to the US market. The ASEAN4 countries similarly export mainly raw materials to Japan and light manufactured goods to the US. Table 9.1 shows the 1987 trade matrix used to initialize the model. These aggregate trade flows are disaggregated into the corresponding sectoral outputs and demand categories mentioned above. The 1986 exports and imports of the Asian NIEs are shown in Table 9.2.

The Asian NIE imports are disaggregated into fuels 4 per cent (from OPEC), other raw materials 6.8 per cent (from ASEAN4 and ROW), machinery and transport equipment 30.4 per cent, and other manufactured goods 58.5 per cent. Out of total imports 6.3 per cent are of consumer goods, 9.8 per cent are of investment goods (used in production of investment goods), and 84 per cent are intermediate manufactured and raw inputs to production. This last category is very sizeable since it includes amongst other things imported components into assembly industries.

For the developing country blocs the basic framework for initialization is national input–output matrices. These are not uniformly available for the base year and required some updating to reflect changes in the structure of the economy as far as possible.[27]

Table 9.1   1987 regional trade matrix (in current US$ millions)

Importer:	US	Japan	ROECD	ASEAN4	ANIES	OPEC	ROW
Exporter:							
US	*	22,631	107,017	5,319	18,743	10,877	23,464
Japan	66,684	*	35,356	8,231	31,370	11,253	21,698
ROECD	145,238	21,228	*	7,496	18,347	37,062	113,680
ASEAN4	9,230	12,462	8,097	*	8,280	1,100	2,900
ANIES	49,279	13,530	19,821	8,534	*	4,588	17,600
OPEC	14,610	25,830	23,467	2,300	7,457	*	5,275
ROW	37,861	14,628	106,138	4,000	20,939	9,413	*

Table 9.2   Structure of Asian NIE exports, 1986 (per cent)

Exports to	United States	Japan	ROECD
Exports			
Food & intermediates	2.3	33.6	29.1
Light manufactures	56.7	41.9	42.3
Capital goods	41.0	24.5	28.6

A simplified version of the input–output table used for initializing the Asian NIE bloc in the model is shown in Table 9.3. The coefficients reported represent an average of those reported in the individual country tables, weighted by share of regional GNP. Table 9.3 reports the coefficient values normalized to regional GDP in the base year, 1987. Total value added accruing to labour, for example, is the sum of the labour factor input coefficients reported for the four industries, or 42.9 per cent of value added. Summing across the total expenditure row indicates that total intermediate inputs are equal to 92 per cent of GDP and that the capital goods industry (heavy manufactures) is the most intermediate input-intensive sector.

Values for the OECD macroaggregates (consumption, foreign assets, etc.) rely on actual data as far as possible. The more difficult and controversial task of selecting parameter values relies, however, on a mixture of procedures. Three approaches have been used in the current model. The parameter values used in the model are available from the authors on request. First, to the extent possible actual data and empirical estimates of the relevant parameters has been used. Trade share parameters, for example, are easily obtained from the base-year trade data. Furthermore, econometric estimates for some of the trade elasticities, wage adjustment specifications, and exchange rate pegging

Table 9.3 Interindustry accounting matrix for the Asian NIEs bloc (as per cent of regional GDP)

RECEIPTS	ACTIVITIES				Consumpt	Gov't	Inv'ment	Exports	Final imports	Total receipts
	Light M	Heavy M	Primary	Non-traded						
COMMODITIES										
Light manu.	10.4	6.1	3.4	8.3	55.0	12.0	25.7	34.0	−11.1	26.7
Heavy manu.	4.2	5.3	0.0	3.6	4.0	0.0	2.7	20.1	−6.6	48.5
Primary	4.6	0.0	2.5	0.0	2.1	0.0	18.0	4.8	−1.1	36.9
Non-traded	5.7	5.2	1.3	15.4	15.2	0.0	0.0	9.1	−3.4	27.8
					33.7	12.0	5.0	0.0	0.0	78.4
Tot dom inputs	25.0	16.6	7.2	27.4						
Imported inputs	3.5	7.5	0.0	4.6						
(OPEC)	0.3	0.3		0.9						
(other)	3.2	7.2		3.7						
Total intermediates	28.5	24.1	7.2	32.0						
FACTORS										
Labour	8.0	4.4	8.1	22.4						
Capital	12.0	8.4	12.7	24.0						
VALUE ADDED	20.0	12.8	20.8	46.4						
TOTAL EXPEND.	48.5	36.9	28.0	78.4						

rules has also been used. In a highly aggregated model, however, this is often difficult or impossible.

Second, in some cases the steady-state properties of the model place requirements on parameter selection. For example the steady-state growth rate of the model is selected at 3 per cent and the real interest rate is set at 5 per cent in the steady state for all regions. The rate of time preference is also set equal to the real interest rate, and is equal across all regions since any deviation of these parameters would lead to a solution in which one region would come to dominate the world economy in the steady state.

Third, the use of the CES or Cobb–Douglas specification in much of the model implies a unique relationship between many of the parameters in the model. For example, given the price elasticity of demand for one of the goods in a given CES demand equation the elasticity of substitution is uniquely determined, as well as the share or β coefficient values. Hence, given an estimate of one of these, the rest of the relevant parameters can be calculated. The assumptions in the model about substitutability in production and consumption are based on secondary empirical estimates of these elasticities where possible. There is an extensive literature on trade price and income elasticities upon which to draw. Few studies exist, however, on input substitution elasticities in production at the aggregate level needed here and this has required selecting values within the range found in empirical studies.[28]

In standard CGE modelling exercises the data are adjusted in order to reproduce an initial point of equilibrium. In dynamic, forward-looking CGE models, such as the APMSG model, the equivalent procedure is to begin from the steady-state solution of the model. This is clearly not in keeping with the exercise here, to recreate the economic relationships at a given moment in time and then examine the impact of undertaking different policy actions. The values of the macro aggregates used in the model are clearly inconsistent with the steady-state solution of the model. For example, outstanding debt stocks and trade flows in 1987 are not consistent with the steady state. Therefore, one aspect of the mixture of procedures used here is application some steady-state values at the initial equilibrium, for example all prices, exchange rates, and Tobin's q's are initialized at unity, while others are disequilibrium values, such as current-account data. The starting point of the model can be interpreted as a point along the stable manifold as the economy is adjusting to the steady state. Further details can be found in McKibbin and Sundberg (1990).

We solve for the full rational expectations equilibrium of the global economy using a technique called the MSG technique. See McKibbin and Sachs (1991) for further details.

6   Transmission of shocks in the OECD to the Pacific Basin

The aim of this section is to consider the transmission of changes in monetary and fiscal policies in the OECD to the two Asian regions. In early 1993, a number of significant changes in the policy mix in the United States and Japan have been announced. This presents us with an opportunity to undertake a multiplier analysis with a policy relevant frame of reference. We will first consider a fiscal contraction in the United States which is the same order of magnitude as the Clinton programme after full implementation, but with the cuts in spending and increases in taxes implemented fully when announced in 1993. We will then consider a policy which is close to that announced by the Clinton Administration, in which the cuts in spending and increases in taxes are gradually phased in. It is also likely that this contraction of fiscal policy will be accompanied by a relaxation of monetary policy. To illustrate the implications of this, we next consider a permanent increase in US money supply of 1 per cent.

In addition to the fiscal contraction in the United States there has been a substantial fiscal expansion announced in Japan. We consider the transmission of this policy to the Asia-Pacific Region. The policy considered is actually smaller than that which has been announced but this can be scaled appropriately to get closer to the likely magnitude of impacts.

Finally we consider a monetary expansion in Japan.

6.1   A US fiscal contraction

In this section we consider the implication for the two Asia-Pacific regions of a fiscal contraction in the United States. This is intended to give some insight into the likely implications of the recent deficit reduction policy announced by the Clinton Administration. The details of the actual deficit reduction programme, as outlined in recent announcements of the Clinton Administration, are not presented in this paper. A detailed analysis concentrating on modelling the specific aspects of the programme can be found in McKibbin and Bagnoli (1993).[29] Indeed, that paper shows that the composition of the deficit reduction programme between cuts in spending, increases in taxes (income, company and energy) and changes in the composition of spending from current to capital spending by the government is important. This paper abstracts from the details of the programme and explores the implications of cuts in government spending which permanently reduce the budget deficit. To understand the crucial role of expectations, we first present the results for a reduction in the US fiscal deficit that occurs in 1993 and is maintained permanently. This is then followed by results for an announced gradual reduction in the deficit which has the same ultimate outcome but is phased in gradually of several years. Specifically, it is a reduction of zero in 1993, 0.4 per cent of GDP in 1994, 0.8 per cent of GDP in 1995, 1.2 per cent of GDP in 1996, and 1.6 per cent of GDP from 1996 for ever.

These two simulation assume that other economies maintain a 'no policy change' policy. This involves holding the stock of money fixed as well as government spending relative to GDP. As already mentioned, there is likely to be a policy response in Japan and Europe, as a result of the change in US policy. We therefore are not projecting the most likely scenario for the world economy, but the impacts of the US policy taking all other foreign reactions as given by our assumptions.

6.1.1   Permanent reduction in US fiscal expenditures

In specifying policy simulations in the MSG2 model we need to be careful to specify how the policy is implemented. A US fiscal contraction, for example, is assumed to be a permanent reduction in the level of US government expenditure of 1.6 per cent of GDP. The revenue saved by this cut in spending is assumed to be used to permanently cut the US fiscal deficit and therefore reduces the expected future path of US government debt.

The results of policy simulations for the US, Japan and ROECD are familiar from other studies with the MSG2 model. Figure 9.2 presents some key variables for the five main regions. This figure contains results for output, employment, inflation, current account, interest rates and exchange rates relative to the US dollar. The results are deviations from baseline as a result of the shock. A full set of results are contained in an Appendix which is available from the authors upon request.

These results show that a US fiscal contraction leads to a fall in demand in the US, which lowers US real interest rates. This leads to an outflow of capital which causes the US dollar to depreciate relative to other floating currencies (by close to 10 per cent against the yen). The lower interest rate and weaker currency crowd-in private expenditures, especially investment and net exports for the US. Over time there is complete crowding-in of the spending cuts. The permanent increase in US saving raises the capital stock and permanently lowers real interest rates. Foreign industrial economies face a small short-term contraction in output due to the reduced demand for their goods. By the end of the first year, lower world interest rates tend to crowd-in their own domestic

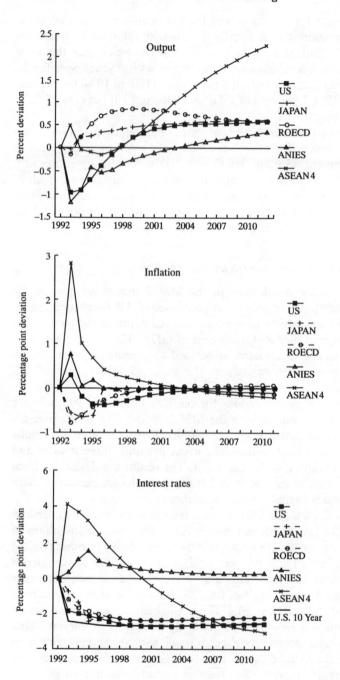

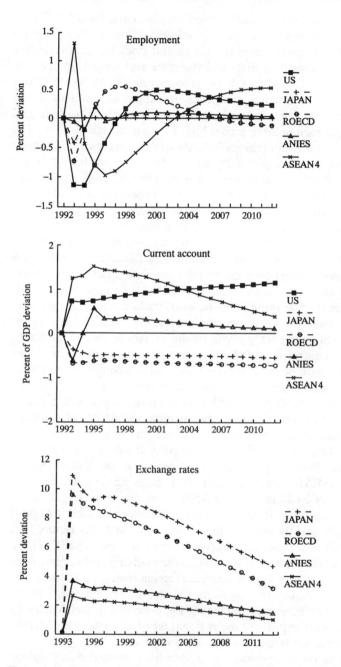

Figure 9.2   Permanent 1.6% of GDP reduction in US government spending

expenditure. The result is a positive effect on Japan and the other OECD countries after two years. The positive effects of raising US saving are permanent. This not only raises the US capital stock but also raises the global stock of physical capital, and therefore real output, in the new long-run equilibrium. Note that the growth rate of the world is not permanently affected because it depends on exogenous population and productivity growth rates. In the long run, the level of real output, and hence income, at each point in time is higher than in the baseline.

The results for the Asian regions indicate striking structural differences between the two developing country blocs.[30] In the case of the ANIES, a permanent US fiscal contraction results in slow growth from the demand contraction, whereas the ASEAN4 countries experience a small rise in output. The sharp contrast arises because of differences between the regions in their commodity composition of trade, the direction of trade, their exchange rate pegging rules, and characteristics of regional debt.

In the ANIES, exports to the United States fall due to weaker US growth and lower import demand, which more than offset the expansion in import demand from Japan or the ROECD. At the same time there is a slight deterioration in the ANIES terms of trade since import prices in local currency rise (the yen appreciates against the dollar) relative to the export prices. Slow export growth results in falling foreign exchange reserves and a contraction of the domestic money supply. In turn this serves to raise domestic interest rates which further contracts the region through a decline in investment relative to baseline.

In sharp contrast to this, the ASEAN4 countries experience a rise in growth, due to four principal differences. First, the ASEAN4 countries are more reliant than the ANIES countries on trade with industrial regions other than the United States, especially Japan. These regions do not experience the strong demand contraction of the United States. Second, the ASEAN4 currency unit depreciates against the yen and ROECD currency by more than the ANIES unit due to the larger weight placed on the US dollar in the basket of currencies to which it pegs. It also depreciates slightly against the ANIES unit, and this results in a rising share of the US market relative to Japan and the ANIES. Third, the ASEAN4 countries are net debtors and the fall in world interest rates improves their current account, increases foreign reserves and leads to a gradual domestic monetary expansion. Finally, dollar commodity prices rise as the dollar depreciates (including the price of oil, which rises by close to 4 per cent) improving the regional terms of trade. The ANIES, however, experience a terms-of-trade deterioration.

The changes in the composition of exports from the two Asian regions follows from the shift in world demand. Exports by both groups to Japan

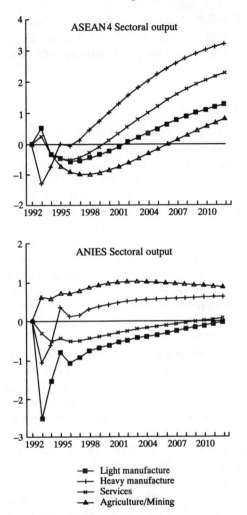

Figure 9.3 Sectoral output under permanent 1.6% of GDP reduction in US government spending

and ROECD rise while exports to the US fall. The ANIES region suffers particularly from weak demand in the US for final consumption goods, which is not as helpful as for the ASEAN4 economies. There is a much smaller fall in demand for intermediate goods in the US, showing up in both Asian regions.

Figure 9.3 illustrates the impact of the policy on sectoral production in the two Asian regions. In the ANIES region, light manufacturing is most severely impacted because of a fall in consumer demand in the US economy. In contrast, heavy manufacturing recovers quickly because of the ultimate increase in global demand for capital goods resulting from lower long-term real interest rates.

6.1.2   Gradual deficit reduction

Figure 9.4 contains results for a credible gradual sustained reduction in government expenditures as a long-run deficit reduction policy. We assume a path for spending cuts announced in 1993 and implemented from 1994. The announced path for government spending is 0.4 per cent of GDP in 1994, 0.8 per cent of GDP in 1995, 1.2 per cent of GDP in 1996 and 1.6 per cent of GDP in 1997 and thereafter. The medium-term reduction in government spending is therefore 1.6 per cent of GDP relative to baseline.

In these results it is assumed that there is no reaction by the Federal Reserve. In McKibbin and Bagnoli (1993) we show that adjustment by the Fed can be successful in partially dampening the short-run demand contraction. The first point to note from looking at Figure 9.4 is that a policy of cutting the budget deficit through future spending cuts can actually stimulate US demand in 1993 (the first year of the policy). This occurs because the cuts are announced in 1993, but the actual reduction in spending does not reduce demand in the economy until 1995. Three factors explain this outcome: a fall in long-term real interest rates (shown at the bottom left panel of Figure 9.4) stimulates private investment; a realization of lower future tax burdens stimulates private consumption; and a depreciation of the US dollar in anticipation of lower future interest rates stimulated net exports. Over time, as the cuts are implemented, there is a contraction in aggregate demand which cannot be offset by the reactions of the private sector alone.

During the process of adjustment to a lower fiscal deficit, short-run demand in the United States is first stimulated. There is then a medium-term slowdown and finally, towards the end of the decade, an eventual rise in GDP relative to baseline. This latter effect is the outcome of absorbing resources into the private sector, that were dislocated by the cuts in government spending. The implication that a credible deficit reduction package can be used for a mild short-run stimulus and long-run deficit reduction with resulting permanent increases in real GDP depends crucially on the credibility of the package in the first two years.

Figure 9.4 also shows that the impact on other industrialized countries is now quite different. In these results there is no short-term decline in foreign GDP, in contrast to the deficit reduction programme that was fully implemented in 1993. The lowering of global real interest rates before the spending cuts take place is sufficient to prevent demand from falling by large amounts in these economies.

In the ASEAN4 economies there is also a slight stimulus to output, however, this is smaller than it was under the first simulation. The key difference is due to the lack of capital mobility which in other open economies drives down domestic real interest rates. In both the ANIES and ASEAN4 economies this positive aspect of the adjustment process is absent. In fact interest rates rise in both regions.

6.2   A permanent US monetary expansion

The results for a permanent rise in US money balances of 1 per cent are contained in Figure 9.5. Again the results for the industrial countries follow closely those described in McKibbin and Sachs (1991) for the MSG2 model. US output rises because of the short-run rigidity of nominal wages. The rise in money reduces nominal and real interest rates, which stimulates private demand. The trade balance changes by very little, because the rise in imports due to stronger demand is offset by a depreciation of the exchange rate, which stimulates exports and partly reduces the demand for imports. The exchange rate change follows from the outflow of capital in response to the fall in interest rates. The other industrial economies experience slight declines in output because of the rise in the relative price of their goods.

We again find opposite effects on output in the ANIES and ASEAN4 regions. Output falls in ANIES region partly for the same reason as in the non-US industrial regions. The relative price of ANIES goods rises in the US market.

In contrast the ASEAN4 economies experience a stimulus to output. With a higher weight on the US dollar in the basket to which they peg, the relative price of ASEAN4 goods falls in foreign markets, especially in Japan. This stimulates the demand for ASEAN4 products.

6.3   Japanese fiscal expansion

Results for a Japanese fiscal expansion of 1 per cent of Japanese GDP, are contained in Figure 9.6. This is negatively transmitted to the other industrialized regions through the rise in world interest rates.

The results for the two Asian regions again diverge. The ANIES now lose initially from the Japanese fiscal expansion, whereas they gained substantially from the US fiscal change. This result can be traced to the AIDS demand nesting in the model. The large appreciation of the yen

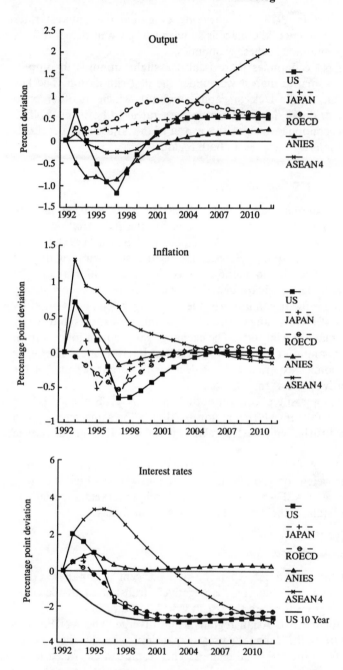

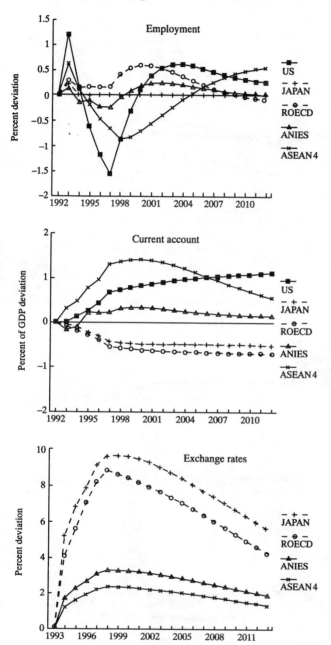

Figure 9.4 Gradual, permanent 1.6% of GDP reduction in US government spending

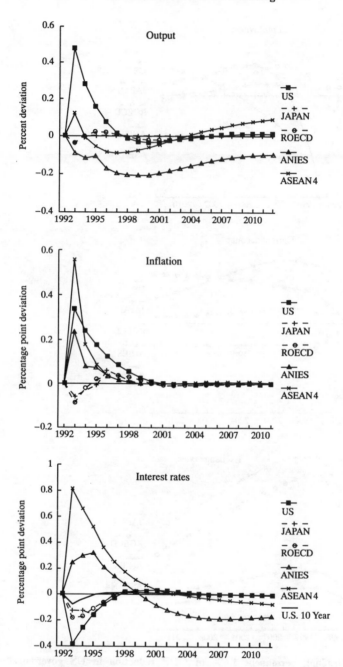

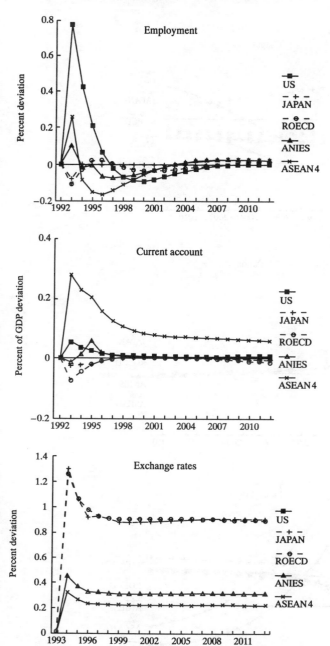

Figure 9.5   Permanent 1% increase in US money balances

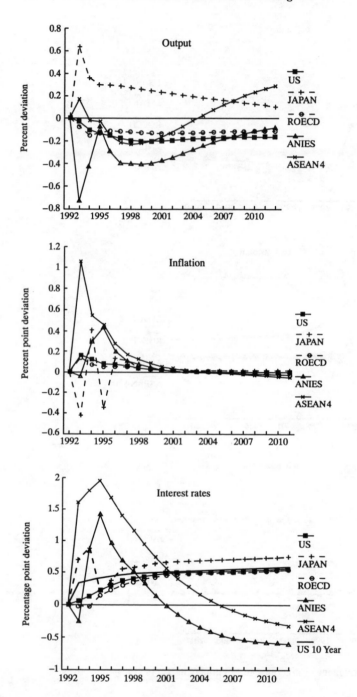

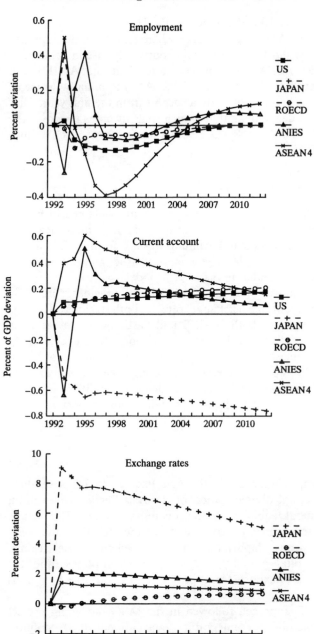

Figure 9.6 Permanent 1% of GDP increase in Japanese government spending

drives up the price of all Pacific goods in the US market. Demand for these goods falls. The ANIES gain market share relative to the Japanese over time, but in the short run lose total exports. The rise in demand in Japan benefits the ASEAN4 countries more than the ANIES and therefore the overall trade balance of the ANIES initially worsens, whereas the ASEAN4 countries enjoy a surplus from the first year. That part of the Japanese demand stimulus which spills overseas improves the trade positions of the US and ROECD blocs, but mainly spills over into the OPEC and ROW economies.

6.4   Japanese monetary expansion

The results for a Japanese monetary expansion are contained in Figure 9.7. The flexibility of the Japanese labour market shows quite clearly in these results. The initial demand stimulus results from a fall in real wages, which is offset in 1994. There is very little spillover into the industrial regions, as is familiar in the MSG2 model.

There is more spillover into the Asian Pacific regions, primarily because of the fixity of the exchange rate in both regions. There is some real depreciation of both ANIES and ASEAN4 exchange rates relative to the US dollar, which stimulates exports to the US. There is also a small domestic monetary expansion in each region as a result of a build up in reserves reflecting the exchange rate adjustment. Both effects tend to raise demand in 1993 in these regions, especially in the ANIES, which gains some export share to the US market.

7   Conclusions

We have presented, in some detail, the Asia-Pacific MSG model which has substantial sectoral disaggregation of the Asia-Pacific region in an intertemporal general equilibrium multi-country model. The results indicate that the transmission of policies from the OECD to the Asia-Pacific region depends importantly on the exchange rate regime, assumptions of capital mobility, wage-setting assumptions, and the sectoral composition of exports from the developing countries in various OECD markets.

The dynamic CGE approach followed in the MSG modelling project illustrates the potential for integrating conventional CGE country models and the standard macroeconometric models in a theoretically appealing global framework.[31] Future work will extend the regional disaggregation to other developing countries, while integrating this with the work already undertaken on industrial country disaggregation, especially within Europe.

We have also cast the simulations in the context of current policy shifts in major economies. It is shown that the policy of a gradually implemented (but credible) deficit reduction programme of the type announced by the Clinton Administration dampens the negative impact of spending cuts in the US and other industrialized economies with open capital markets. The beneficial effects of lower long-term real interest rates are transmitted quickly to these countries. In contrast, regions such as the ANIES and ASEAN4 regions, which we assume have capital controls, do not immediately feel the benefit of lower real interest rates that accompany a gradual deficit-cutting programme in the United States. In contrast, these regions experience a more sustained negative shock from a gradually phased-in US deficit-reduction programme. In addition, the ASEAN4 region is much less affected by the US programme than the high-income ANIES region. This is due to a number of favourable factors including: the greater reliance of ASEAN4 economies on trade with Japan, compared with the ANIES economies that rely more on trade in final consumption goods with the United States; the benefits from a reduction in the debt burden of the ASEAN4 countries, resulting from falls in world interest rates; and due to a greater weight placed on a depreciating dollar in the basket to which the ASEAN4 countries peg, which results in increased competitiveness in third markets relative to the ANIES economies that are assumed to place a smaller weight on the US dollar in the basket to which they peg.

In the medium to long term, the US deficit-reduction programme and higher US saving rate, raises output in all economies as a result of lower real interest rates and a permanently higher global capital stock.

As mentioned in the introduction to this paper, a crucial aspect of the US policy for the Asia-Pacific region will be the response of Japan. We show above that there is also a crucial asymmetry in the response of the ASEAN4 and ANIES regions to a Japanese fiscal shock. This asymmetry acts to reinforce the effects of the US fiscal shock. In particular we find that the ASEAN4 region benefits far more than the ANIES region from a Japanese fiscal expansion. This is primarily due to the reliance of the ANIES on the US market and the dependence of ASEAN4 on the Japanese market. In addition the assumption that the ANIES region places greater weight on pegging to the yen than the ASEAN4 region, implies that the ANIES lose market share in the US economy as the yen appreciates following a Japanese fiscal expansion.

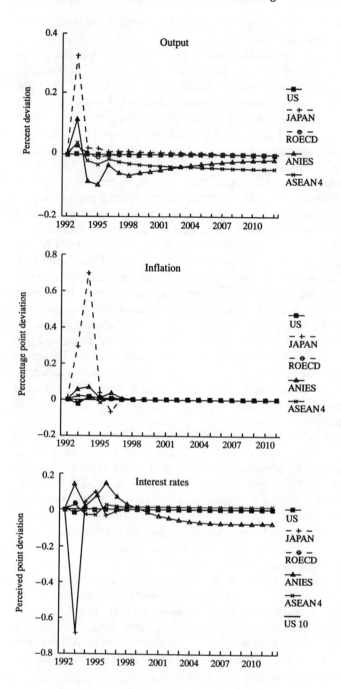

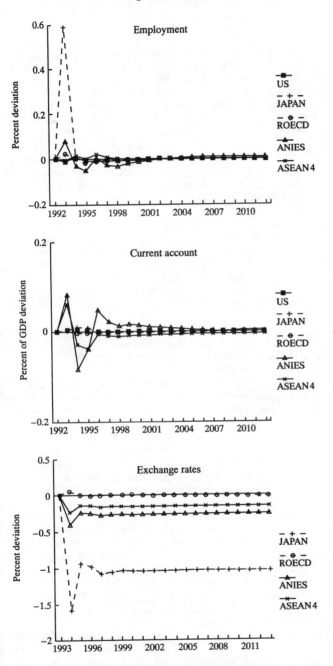

Figure 9.7   Permanent 1% increase in Japanese money balances

NOTES

Mark Sundberg is at the World Bank. This paper revises and extends earlier papers presented at the OECD Conference on Macroeconomic Linkages and International Adjustment, held in Tokyo, as well as a paper presented at the Brookings/CEPR conference in Oxford. We thank participants at those conferences for helpful comments. In addition we thank Barry Bosworth, Ralph Bryant, H. Don, T.G. Srinivasan and David Vines for helpful comments on various drafts. The research reported reflects work in progress under Brookings Network programme for encouraging Empirical Research in International Macroeconomics (NERIM), which is supported in part by the Ford Foundation and the John D. and Catherine T. MacArthur Foundation. The views expressed are those of the authors and should not be attributed to the World Bank or the trustees, officers, or staff members of the Brookings Institution.

1 The major difference between the model used in this paper and the earlier work of Sundberg (1991) is the treatment of the industrial country blocs, which now coincide with the latest MSG2 model presented in McKibbin and Sachs (1991). The reader is referred to Sundberg (1991) for a more detailed derivation of the Asia-Pacific bloc and details on estimation results. See also McKibbin and Sundberg (1993) for an application of the model to the issue of coordination of macroeconomic policies in the industrial economies.

2 For alternative approaches that also explicitly model the internal structure of developing countries see Allen *et al.* (1994) and Masson *et al.* (1988).

3 For an overview of the key features of the region see Balassa (1981), Bradford and Branson (1987) and OECD (1988).

4 In an earlier version Latin America and the Caribbean were separately disaggregated as one region, making the model more useful for addressing policy issues affecting the highly indebted countries, but less useful for understanding trade dynamics in the Pacific region.

5 ROECD consists of all OECD countries except US and Japan.

6 See Brooke *et al.* (1988) for a description of the GAMs technology, and see Dervis *et al.* (1982) and Dixon *et al.* (1982) for analytical discussions of country general equilibrium modelling techniques and applications.

7 An alternative approach has recently been developed in the G-CUBED model by McKibbin and Wilcoxen (1992) which has full integration of the macroeconomic and sectoral linkages. See McKibbin (1993) for an overview of the integration of this approach into a macroeconomic framework.

8 Ideally one would want to specify the market behaviour in the absence of intervention or market failure, as we assume in the developed regions, and then introduce the relevant areas of intervention. In practice this is very difficult in a general equilibrium model because of the absence of information and the complexity of the task.

9 See Dervis *et al.* (1982) for a thorough discussion of the use of social accounting matrices in CGE modelling.

10 Note that when ρ_i is equal to zero, the CES function is Cobb–Douglas, with unitary elasticity of substitution. As ρ_i approaches infinity the functional form approaches Leontief, with zero substitution, and as ρ_i approaches unity, it approximates the case of perfect substitution between inputs.

11 Little use is actually made of this capability at this stage, unfortunately, since separate estimation of each of these elasticities has not been possible. In the absence of estimates we employ the Cobb–Douglas assumption of unitary elasticities.

12 The ASEAN4 bloc is also an exporter of oil, most of which is sold to Japan and the US. Domestic production and consumption of oil is handled somewhat differently in this case, with an exogenously specified value share of production being used in the domestic economy.

13 That is, $dQ_j/dN_{ij} = P_i/P_j$ for all inputs N_i to sector j.

14 We use $\alpha = 0.1$ and $\gamma = 0.1$ in the model, which is close to the values used by Boone et al. (1989) for Korea.

15 The growth rate of population adjusted by the rate of labour-augmenting technical progress is included here to maintain measurement in real per efficiency unit levels. In the steady-state investment must be sufficient to hold the per efficiency unit level of capital constant.

16 The exact equation Fry reports is $Sn/Y_t = 0.375(\hat{Y}) + 0.188(T\hat{o}T) + 0.041(Rr) - 2.498(DEP) + 0.664(Sn/Y_{t-1})$, with t-statistics of 7.2, 4.4, 3.2, -5.3, and 18.1 respectively, and an $\bar{R}^2$ statistic of 0.91. Sn is gross national savings, Y is real income, $\hat{Y}$ is the growth of real income, $T\hat{o}T$ is the income growth attributable to terms of trade changes, Rr is the 12-month deposit rate minus expected inflation (proxied by a distributed lag of past inflation), and DEP is the dependency ratio.

17 Webb and Zia (1989) examine the effects of dependency ratio changes on household savings for six developing countries, among them Korea. They project no change in the savings rate through the year 2000 and then an increase of around 3 per cent in the Korean savings ratio by the year 2010. Our projection period is over a much shorter range, however. Nam (1989), on the other hand, finds that the dependency ratio is not significant at all for Korean savings after accounting for income level, income growth, interest rates, and lagged savings.

18 Trade taxes, for example, represent under 5 per cent of revenues for the Asian NIEs and under 10 per cent for the ASEAN4 countries, and have been steadily declining in importance during the 1980s.

19 Seigniorage revenues are not explicitly included and are assumed to be netted out from taxes, maintaining budgetary balance. While straightforward to include, this has not been an important revenue source for these countries.

20 This should not be confused with institutionalized indexation to the CPI, which is relatively uncommon in the region.

21 Lindauer (1984) and Bai (1982) both put the transition from the Lewis-type labour surplus stage around 1975/76 in Korea, based on accelerated real wage trends and a sharp reduction in wage dispersion around the middle of the decade. Kuo et al. (1981) put the 'turning point' in Taiwan at 1968, and identify this by the rise in the real wage in line with rising labour productivity.

22 See World Bank (1958) for recent evidence on labour relations and wage structure in Indonesia.

23 A full description of the industrial countries in the model is provided in McKibbin and Sachs (1991). Any substantive differences between their presentation and the APMSG are discussed here.

24 See for example Krugman and Baldwin (1987) or Catherine Mann (1987) for a discussion of import price passthrough and US current-account adjustment.

25 Disaggregation of goods to match these commodity characteristics was done following the US Bureau of the Census end-user classification system. Although only the US trade flows are classified by this system, a rough concordance mapping these to the SITC classification system was used (at the two-digit level) in order to reorganize the United Nations data.

26 Van Wijnbergen (1985), for example, suggests an explanation for the persistent stylized fact that the terms of trade for primary commodity exporters tends to be inversely related to the strength of the US dollar appreciation on shifting demand between the US and 'Euran' (Europe and Japan) markets. The dollar's appreciation causes commodity prices to fall in terms of the dollar and rise relative to the Euran currencies, while US demand rises for given commodity prices. All else equal, the smaller the US share in world demand for the commodity, the larger the US share in the primary exporters' total imports, and the lower the US demand elasticity, the greater will be the decline in the primary exporters' terms of trade.

27 The Institute for Developing Economies publishes the only consistent set of input-output tables available for all the eight countries covered in the two Pacific regions. These vary somewhat in their years (all are from 1980 or more recent), industrial definitions and number of industries. Since both regions are aggregated into four industrial groups, this is not too important. National accounts data were used to update the value-added cells and final demand columns of the matrix, but only limited data were available to update any of the interindustry accounts.

28 Khan and Goldstein (1985) and Stern et al. (1976) provide excellent surveys of the literature on income and price elasticities in international trade, and a range of the empirical estimates. Behrman (1982) has also conducted an exhaustive survey of elasticities of substitution between capital and labour in production, across many industries, countries and periods. Studies of the substitution elasticity between total intermediate inputs and factor inputs have not to our knowledge been done. For these parameters we have assumed unitary elasticities when empirical estimates are unavailable.

29 The reader should note that the analysis in McKibbin and Bagnoli (1993) uses a more recent version of the MSG2 model than the analysis in the current paper. Some properties of the model may have changed slightly between the two versions.

30 The transmission of macroeconomic shocks in the Asian region is described in greater detail in Sundberg (1991) and in Krause and Sundberg (1990).

31 See McKibbin (1992) for a detailed exposition.

REFERENCES

Allen C., T.G. Srinivasan and D. Vines (1994) 'Analysing external adjustment in developing countries: a macroeconomic framework', Chapter 6 in this volume.

Bai, M.K. (1982) 'The Korean labor market in transition', mimeo, Korea Development Institute.

Balassa, Bela (1981) The Newly Industrializing Countries in the World Economy, New York: Pergamon Press.

(1989) 'The effects of interest rates on savings in developing countries', World Bank Working Paper No. 56, Washington DC.

Behrman, Jere (1982) 'Country and sectoral variations in manufacturing elasticities of substitution between labor and capital', in Anne Krueger (ed.), *Trade and Employment in Developing Countries, Vol. II: Factor Supply and Substitution*, University of Chicago Press and NBER.

Boone P., Lee, J-W and J. Sachs (1989) 'Structural adjustment and international linkages in the Korean economy', Harvard University, mimeo.

Bradford, Colin and William Branson (eds.), (1987) *Trade and Structural Change in the Pacific Area*, National Bureau of Economic Research, University of Chicago Press.

Brooke, Anthony, David Kendrick and Alexander Meeraus (1988) *GAMS, A User's Guide*, International Bank for Reconstruction and Development, California: The Scientific Press.

Collins, Susan M. (1988) 'Savings and growth experiences of Korea and Japan', paper prepared for the NBER-TCER conferences on Savings: Its Determinants and Macroeconomic Implications, Tokyo, Japan.

(1989) 'Savings behavior in ten developing countries', paper prepared for the NBER conference on Savings, Hawaii.

Deaton, Angus (1989) 'Saving in developing countries: theory and review', paper prepared for the World Bank conference on Economic Development, Washington DC.

Deaton, Angus and John Muellbauer (1980) 'An almost ideal demand system', *American Economic Review* **70**, 312–26.

Dervis, K., J. de Melo and S. Robinson (1982) *General Equilibrium Models for Development Policy*, Cambridge: Cambridge University Press.

Dixon P.B., B.R. Parmenter, J. Sutton and D. Vincent (1982) *ORANI: A Multisectoral Model of the Australian Economy*, Amsterdam: North-Holland.

Dornbusch R. (1973) 'Money, devaluation, and nontraded goods', *American Economic Review* **63**, 871–80.

Fry, Maxwell J. (1988) *Money, Interest, and Banking in Economic Development*, Baltimore Md.: Johns Hopkins University Press.

Giovannini, Alberto (1983) 'The interest elasticity of savings in developing countries: the existing evidence', *World Development* **11**, 601–7.

(1985) 'Saving and the real interest rate in LDCs', *Journal of Development Economics* **18**, 197–217.

Khan, Mohsin and Morris Goldstein (1985) 'Income and price effects in foreign trade', *The Handbook of International Economics*, Amsterdam: North-Holland.

Krause, Lawrence and Mark Sundberg (1990) 'Inter-relationship between the world and Pacific economic performance', paper prepared for the 18th Pacific Trade and Development Conference, Kuala Lumpur.

Krugman, P. and R. Baldwin (1987) 'The persistence of the US trade deficit,' *Brookings Papers in Economic Activity*, 1–43.

Kuo, Shirley, Gustav Ranis and John Fei (1981) *Taiwan's Success Story: Rapid Growth with Improved Distribution in the Republic of China, 1952–79*, Boulder, Colorado: Westview Press.

Lindauer, David (1984) 'Labor market behavior in the Republic of Korea', World Bank Staff Working Papers No. 641.

Mann, Catherine (1987) 'After the fall: the declining dollar and import prices', Federal Reserve Board of Governors, Washington DC, mimeo.

Mason, Andrew (1987) 'National savings rates and population growth: a new model and new evidence', in D.G. Johnson and R. Lee (eds.), *Population Growth and Economic Development: Issues and Evidence*, Madison: University of Wisconsin Press.

Masson P., S. Symansky, R. Hass and M. Dooley (1988) 'Multimod – a multiregion econometric model', Part II, *IMF Staff Studies for the World Economic Outlook*, New York.

McKibbin, W.J. (1986) 'The international coordination of macroeconomic policies', Ph.D. Dissertation, Harvard University.

—— (1992) 'The new European economy and its economic implications for the world economy', *Economic and Financial Modelling*.

—— (1993) 'Integrating macroeconomic and computable general equilibrium models', Brookings Discussion Paper in International Economics No. 100, presented at ESRC and CEPR Conference on 'The future of macroeconomic modelling in the UK'.

McKibbin W.J. and P. Bagnoli (1993) 'A quantitative evaluation of the Clinton budget and some alternative options', Brookings Discussion Paper in International Economics, Brookings Institution.

McKibbin W.J. and J. Sachs (1988) 'Co-ordination of monetary and fiscal policies in the industrial economies', in J. Frenkel (ed), *International Aspects of Fiscal Policies*, University of Chicago Press, pp. 73–113.

—— (1991) *Global Linkages: Macroeconomic Interdependence and Cooperation in the World Economy*, Brookings Institution.

McKibbin W.J. and M. Sundberg (1990) 'Macroeconomic linkages between the OECD and the Asian Pacific Region', Brookings Discussion Paper in International Economics No. 80.

—— (1993) 'The implications for the Asian Pacific Region of macroeconomic policy coordination in the OECD', *Journal of Policy Modeling* 15, 13–48.

McKibbin W.J. and P. Wilcoxen (1992) 'G-cubed: a dynamic multi-sector general equilibrium growth model of the global economy (quantifying the costs of curbing CO_2 emissions)', Brookings Discussion Paper in International Economics No. 97, Brookings Institution. Prepared for the US Environmental Protection Agency.

Nam, Sang-Woo (1989) 'What determines national savings: a case study of Korea and the Philippines', World Bank Policy Planning and Research Working Paper, WPS 205, Washington DC.

OECD (1988) *The Newly Industrialising Countries: Challenge and Opportunity for OECD Industries*, Organization for Economic Cooperation and Development, Paris.

Pitt, Mark (1981) 'Alternative trade strategies and employment in Indonesia', in Anne Krueger et al. (eds.), *Trade and Employment in Developing Countries*, vol. I, Chicago University Press for the National Bureau of Economic Research.

Sachs, J. and W.J. McKibbin (1985) 'Macroeconomic policies in the OECD and LDC external adjustment', National Bureau of Economic Research Working Paper No. 1534; Background Paper for 1985 *World Development Report*, World Bank.

Stern, R.M. *et al.* (1976) *Price Elasticities in International Trade: An Annotated Bibliography*, London: Macmillan for the Trade Policy Research Centre.

Sundberg, M. (1991) 'Transmission of macroeconomic disturbances within the Pacific Basin', Unpublished Ph.D. Dissertation, Harvard University.

Van Wijnbergen, S. (1985) 'Interdependence revisited: a developing countries perspective on macroeconomic management and trade policy in the industrial world', *Economic Policy* 1 (1), 81–137.

Webb, Steven and Heidi Zia (1989) 'The effect of demographic changes on saving for life-cycle motives in developing countries', World Bank Policy, Planning and Research Working Paper, WPS 229, Washington DC.

Whalley, John (1985) *Trade Liberalization Among Major World Trading Areas*, Cambridge MA: MIT Press.

World Bank (1985) *Indonesia: Wages and Employment*, World Bank Country Study, Washington DC.

10 MULTIMOD simulations of the effects on developing countries of decreasing military spending

TAMIM BAYOUMI, DANIEL HEWITT
and STEVEN SYMANSKY

1 Introduction

The world has witnessed a precipitous fall in worldwide military spending over the last few years.[1] One of the most striking features of this reduction is its universality. Military spending has fallen in rich countries and in poor countries, in the Western democracies and in Eastern Europe and the USSR, in oil-exporting countries and oil-importing countries. Furthermore, it seems reasonable to believe that these trends will continue into the future. In short, military spending cuts are a very general phenomenon, in part reflecting the 'peace dividend' from the end of the cold war.

Despite the generality of the fall in military spending, most of the analytic work on the macroeconomic effects of such cuts has focused on the implications of military spending cuts for the rich industrial countries.[2] The impact on developing countries of reducing military spending has received only modest attention. Indeed, some skepticism has been expressed as to the size of the peace dividend for the very poorest countries in the world, since, in general, military expenditures among the lower income nations are modest in relation to the size of their economies. Since the potential for releasing resources through cutbacks in military spending is likely to be small, so, it is argued, will be the gains. However, low-income developing countries comprise a very diverse group of countries, with very different levels of military spending. Furthermore, some of the indirect benefits of the peace dividend, such as lower world interest rates that result from lower government spending, may well be particularly important for these countries.

There are relatively few analytic studies of the impact of cutting military spending on developing countries. One exception is an earlier paper by some of the same authors as this one, namely Bayoumi, Hewitt and Schiff (1993) (hereafter BHS) who used the MULTIMOD macroeconomic model developed at the IMF to examine the impact on the world economy of a universal cut in military spending of 20 per cent. They found that worldwide cuts in military spending had a strong impact on developing countries. As a ratio of output, the long-term economic gains for net debtor developing countries in aggregate were found to be double those of industrial countries, even though the military spending cuts among developing and industrial countries were similar (again as a proportion of output). This more favourable impact largely reflects the fact that developing countries face an external finance constraint. Cuts in military spending allow non-military imports to grow, permitting higher private consumption and productive investment. This suggests that the potential gain for developing countries from reducing military expenditures could be relatively large.[3]

While suggestive, the BHS results pertaining to developing countries suffer from a number of limitations. They are for net debtor developing countries in the aggregate and are obtained in a relatively crude manner. The purpose of this paper is to investigate the economic impact of reducing military spending on developing countries in more detail. To this end, a new variant of MULTIMOD was developed in which aggregate developing countries are divided into four geographic regions. In addition, the determination of the various components of aggregate demand was reformulated to more closely resemble the typical industrial country, with private consumption and investment being made to depend on forward-looking measures of wealth. This allows us to investigate the domestic impact of changes in military spending in a more sophisticated manner. These changes amount to a complete remodelling of the developing country sector of the MULTIMOD model.

The main findings are that a permanent 20 per cent worldwide military spending cut raises private consumption and investment after ten years by 0.8 per cent and 2.1 per cent, respectively, a somewhat lower estimate than that in BHS. Larger private sector gains are associated with bigger cuts in military spending (which free up more resources for civilian use), with bigger cuts in military imports (which allow higher levels of non-military imports), and with close bilateral trade links with the US (whose demand for imports from developing countries rises the most). Among the different regions, Africa, despite having lower military spending than some other regions, gains the most in relation to output.

2   Trade in military spending, military imports and military exports

Between 1985 and 1990, the world has witnessed a 20 per cent drop in military spending in proportion to GDP, falling from 5.6 per cent to 4.3

Table 10.1 Military expenditure, arms exports and arms imports, 1987–9 average

	(In per cent of GDP)			(In billion US dollars)			(In per cent of country's total)	
	Military expenditures	Arms exports	Arms imports	Military expenditures	Arms exports	Arms imports	Arms exports	Arms imports
Developing countries	4.46	0.15	1.10	134.77	4.50	32.82	0.64	4.78
Oil exporters (1)	10.29	0.02	3.23	36.30	0.07	11.45	0.06	11.51
Africa (2)	3.42	0.02	1.42	11.43	0.06	4.72	0.09	7.52
Western Hemisphere (3)	1.89	0.31	0.39	16.04	2.59	3.27	2.44	3.53
Other developing	4.20	0.10	0.96	49.27	1.14	11.12	0.30	2.34
Asian (4)	3.61	0.02	0.55	33.47	0.22	5.03	0.11	2.30
Other (5)	6.44	0.37	2.50	15.81	0.92	6.09	0.53	2.37
NIES (6)	4.74	0.04	0.59	15.17	0.13	1.77	0.09	1.27
Industrial countries (7)	3.68	0.17	0.07	503.00	22.70	8.10	1.18	0.42
of which								
United States	6.07	0.28	0.04	296.10	13.40	2.10	4.29	0.57
Japan	1.00	0.00	0.04	26.80	0.10	1.20	0.04	0.52
Germany	2.96	0.11	0.07	34.30	1.30	0.90	0.41	0.29
Eastern Europe & USSR (8)	14.35	1.31	0.22	269.00	24.30	3.90	9.80	1.60

Notes: (1) Iran, Kuwait, Libya, Oman, Qater, Saudi Arabia and the UAE.
(2) Algeria, Angola, Benin, Botswana, Burkina Faso, Burundi, Cameroon, Central African Republic, Chad, Comoros, Congo, Cote d'Ivoire, Ethiopia, Gabon, Gambia, Ghana, Guinea-Bissau, Kenya, Liberia, Madagascar, Malawi, Mali, Mauritania, Mauritius, Morocco, Mozambique, Niger, Nigeria, Rwanda, Senegal, Sierra Leone, Somalia, South Africa, Sudan, Swaziland, Tanzania, Togo, Tunisia, Uganda, Zaire, Zambia and Zimbabwe.
(3) Argentina, Belize, Bolivia, Brazil, Chile, Colombia, Costa Rica, Dominican Republic, Ecuador, El Salvador, Guatemala, Guyana, Haiti, Honduras, Jamaica, Mexico, Nicaragua, Panama, Paraguay, Peru, Suriname, Trinidad and Tobago, Uruguay and Venezuela.
(4) Afghanistan, Bangladesh, Bhutan, Brunei, Cambodia, People's Republic of China, Fiji, French Polynesia, Guam, India, Indonesia, Lao, Malaysia, Myanmar, Nepal, Pakistan, Papua New Guinea, Philippines, Sri Lanka, Thailand, Tonga and VietNam.
(5) Cyprus, Turkey, Yugoslavia, Egypt, Iraq, Israel, Jordan, Lebanon, Syrian Arab Rep., Yemen Arab Republic, and Yemen, P.D. Rep.
(6) Korea, Singapore, Hong Kong and Taiwan.
(7) United States, Canada, Australia, Japan, New Zealand, Austria, Belgium, Denmark, Finland, France, Germany, Greece, Iceland, Ireland, Italy, Netherlands, Norway, Portugal, Spain, Sweden, Switzerland and United Kingdom.
(8) Bulgaria, Czechoslovakia, German Democratic Republic, Hungary, Poland, Romania, USSR and Yugoslavia.
Sources: ACDA, SIPRI, *IFS*, Steinberg (1992).

per cent of world GDP (see Hewitt, 1993, for full details).[4] The change has been widespread; more than half of the countries lowered expenditure significantly relative to GDP, and only a small fraction increased expenditures significantly.

Industrialized countries spent 3.7 per cent of GDP on the military during 1987–9, the base years for the simulation analysis herein (see Table 10.1). This was over 55 per cent of total world military spending. Military expenditures in Eastern Europe and the USSR were 14.4 per cent of GDP and about 30 per cent of world military expenditures. Developing countries as a group spent 4.5 per cent of GDP on the military, about 15 per cent of world military expenditures.

The drop in trade of military goods has been even steeper than the drop in military expenditures, on the order of 50 per cent. According to US government estimates, arms imports and exports for the world as a whole averaged over $50 billion during 1987–9. Military trade makes up about 2 per cent of total trade, while military spending makes up nearer 4 per cent of total spending. In short, military spending is relatively domestically orientated. The two major blocs, industrial countries and Eastern Europe, each accounted for about 45 per cent of total military exports and the remaining 10 per cent of military exports originated in the developing countries. In contrast, nearly three-fourths of arms exports were sent to developing countries. For the industrialized countries, arms exports only accounted for 1.2 per cent of their total exports. Military exports of Eastern Europe and the USSR were 9.8 per cent of total exports during 1987–98. Arms exports were only 0.6 per cent of the exports of developing countries.

Deliveries of military goods to developing countries fell from $36.2 billion in 1985 (1991 constant prices) to $18.4 billion in 1991, Grimmett (1992). The peak year was 1987, with deliveries to developing countries estimated at $41.3 billion. A more forward view is provided by arms transfers agreements, which by necessity precede deliveries. These peaked in 1985 at $63.6 billion (1991 constant prices) and fell to $24.6 billion in 1991. Thus the value of traded military exports to developing countries is less than 40 per cent of the level reached in the mid 1980s. It is likely that the major decrease in trade in military goods that has taken place in the last few years will continue.

Developing countries spent an estimated US$135 billion on the military during 1987–9 and imported about $33 billion worth of military goods (about 5 per cent of total imports). Military expenditures of the *oil-exporting* countries were considerably higher than the average, over 10 per cent of GDP and arms imports were 11.5 per cent of their total imports. *Western Hemisphere* countries' military spending was considerably below average at 1.9 per cent of GDP, with arms imports 3.5 per cent of total imports. This is the only region among developing countries where arms exports were significant, at 2.4 per cent of total exports. Military expenditures in *Africa* averaged 3.4 per cent of GDP; arms imports, however, were well-above average at 7.5 per cent of total imports. Military expenditures among *other developing countries* stood at 4.2 per cent of GDP, with arms imports of 2.3 per cent of total imports. Military spending in the newly industrialized economies (NIEs) was 4.7 per cent of GDP and arms imports were 1.3 per cent of their total imports.

3   The simulation model

The simulations were done using a variant of MULTIMOD, a multi-region econometric model developed at the IMF to analyse the economic interactions among industrial and developing countries.[5] The main linkages among the regions are through trade, exchange rates and interest rates. Imports of the industrial and capital-exporting developing countries are functions of relative prices and aggregate demand, while imports by other developing countries depend upon the amount of available foreign exchange. Short-term interest rates depend on monetary policy through the money demand equations, while long-term interest rates are a moving average of current and expected future short-term rates. Nominal exchange rates are determined by relative interest rates.

In the existing version of MULTIMOD, domestic aggregate demand in developing countries was modelled in a relatively simple manner. Non-oil-developing countries are assumed to face a constraint on borrowing from abroad. This constraint depends upon their ability to service loans in the future, becoming less severe as interest rates decline or exports increase. Behavioural equations determine the level of exports[6] and total consumption (the sum of government consumption and private consumption). The level of imports and of investment are then calculated as residuals given the behavioural equations for external finance and for internal supply of goods, respectively. The oil- and capital-exporting countries (hereafter simply oil exporters)[7] have a similar underlying domestic framework. As the residual supplier of oil, exports are given by the balance of demand and supply in the oil market, and imports reflect the difference between absorption and the aggregate supply of goods for the home market. In both developing country regions output is assumed to equal underlying supply, which in turn depended upon factors such as export performance.

While useful in many respects, the standard developing country model has certain disadvantages for the types of simulations being considered in this paper. Since output is always equal to underlying supply it is difficult to model the impact of a reduction in government consumption.[8] In addition, as discussed above, government spending on the military varies widely across developing countries, with big differences across geographic regions. In the variant of MULTIMOD which was developed for the simulations presented here, aggregate demand in non-oil-developing countries is modelled in a manner similar to that used in industrial countries. In addition, the non-oil-developing countries are divided into four geographic regions: Western Hemisphere, Africa, and newly industrializing economies (NIEs), and other non-oil-developing countries.[9] The model for oil-exporting countries was left largely unchanged due to data limitations.

The NIEs were modelled in exactly the same manner as the other industrial country groups; in particular, it is assumed that they faced no constraint on external finance. For the other three groups, it is assumed that they do face an external finance constraint, determined in the same manner as the non-oil-developing countries; constraint in the standard MULTIMOD model, but imports are no longer residually determined. Data on the components of aggregate demand, namely private consumption, investment, government consumption, exports and imports in US dollars were collected from the World Bank and IMF. Imports were sub-divided between oil and manufactured goods and exports were sub-divided between oil, non-oil commodities and manufacturing (the regions' imports of non-oil commodities from other developing countries were subtracted from their total commodity exports). As all of the variables are measured in dollars, there is no estimate of the domestic inflation rate. Rather, the domestic price level measures the real exchange rate against the dollar.

Equations were estimated for private consumption, investment and exports and imports of manufactures along the lines of those used for the industrial countries. As in the main MULTIMOD model, trade in oil and non-oil commodities is a function of conditions in their respective markets. Government consumption is exogenous, and it was assumed that there is no domestic bond market, so that all changes in government spending which are not financed externally require an equal change in taxation. Formally, the model assumes that all of these revenues come from conventional taxes which feed through into the future wealth and hence consumption and investment.[10]

Since none of the elements of aggregate demand are determined residually, it is necessary to have mechanisms which ensure that the external finance constraint is satisfied and that output returns to under-lying supply potential The external finance constraint is satisfied through changes in the domestic price level in dollars. This can be interpreted as saying that the country has a freely floating exchange rate, with the market rate being determined by the external financing constraint rather than the international asset arbitrage assumed for industrial countries.[11] For this system to be stable devaluations/appreciations in the exchange rate must improve/worsen the current account of all times, and hence the Marshall–Lerner conditions must be satisfied in both the short run and the long run. This was achieved by boosting the estimates of the short-run price elasticities, as discussed below.

Finally, it is necessary to ensure that actual output, as determined by aggregate demand, returns to the underlying level of aggregate supply. This is accomplished by an equation which raises the real interest rate if output is above capacity, and lowers it if output is below capacity. Since there is no internal bond market, this real interest rate is best regarded as the shadow price of domestic capital, which can vary from the international real interest rate because the region is finance-constrained. The real interest rate feeds into the underlying wealth variables which affect consumption and investment, and hence change aggregate demand in the appropriate manner.

Two considerations guided the estimation. First, except for the influence of the finance constraint, developing countries should behave in a similar manner to industrial countries, and in particular consumption and investment should be forward looking. Second, in order to highlight the different behaviour across developing countries caused by external factors, such as differences in the size of military spending and geographic trade patterns, all of the coefficients in the estimated equations were constrained to be equal across regions.

The consumption and capital stock equations are

$$\Delta ln(C/C_{-1}) = \alpha_i + 0.061 ln(W/C_{-1}) + 0.153(YD/C)\Delta ln(YD)$$
$$+ 0.306(IT/C)\Delta ln(IT) \tag{1}$$

$$\Delta ln(K/K_{-1}) = \beta_i + 0.472 ln(WK/K_{-1}) + 0.034 ln(WK_{-1}/K_{-2})$$
$$+ 0.253(IT/K)ln(IT) \tag{2}$$

where C is private consumption, W is wealth, IT is total imports, YD is disposable income, K is the capital stock and WK is the market value of the capital stock, all in real terms. The wealth variables were calculated from the national accounts data by projecting into the future and using the appropriate forward-looking formulae to calculate the current level of wealth.

The first term in the consumption function is an error correction mechanism which ensures that in the long run consumption moves in line with wealth. The coefficient is smaller than in the industrial countries, indicating a slower rate of adjustment to changes in wealth. The next two terms represent the short-term impact of liquidity constraints on consumption. The first, which is relatively standard, relates changes in consumption to changes in disposable income. The second reflects the fact that, because external finance is assumed to be constrained, the shadow of price of imports is larger than that for domestically produced goods and hence imports will have a direct impact on consumption. Because the terms are multiplied by the ratio of the variable to consumption, they can be interpreted as the marginal propensity to consume. Hence, for the aggregate of all developing countries around 15 per cent of all changes in disposable income flow into consumption in the short run, while 30 per cent of changes in imports do. Real interest rates were also included in the estimation, but were dropped because they were incorrectly signed and insignificant.[12] All of the coefficients were freely estimated.[13]

In the capital stock equation, the first two terms are error correction mechanisms which ensure that investment reacts to deviations between the (forward-looking) market value of the capital stock and the actual level of the capital stock. The coefficients are constrained to be the same as in the industrial countries. The final term, which relates the capital stock to imports, is a liquidity constraint effect. The coefficient implies that some 25 per cent of imports feed into the capital stock.

The equations for imports and exports of manufactures are

$$\Delta ln(XM) = \lambda_i + 1.67\Delta ln(FA) - 0.70\ \Delta REER$$
$$- 0.50 ln(XM_{-1}/FA_{-1}) - 0.24\ REER_{-1} \qquad (3)$$

$$\Delta ln(IM) = \delta_i + 2.25\Delta ln(A) = 0.76\Delta ln(PIM/PGNP)$$
$$- 0.22 ln(IM_{-1}/A_{-1}) - 0.19 ln(PIM_{-1}/PGNP_{-1}) \qquad (4)$$

where XM is real exports of manufactures, FA is real foreign trade-weighted absorption, $REER$ is the log of the real exchange rate in foreign markets, IM is real imports of manufactures, $(PIM/PGNP)$ is the ratio of the price of imported goods prices to domestic goods prices (both in dollars), and A is real domestic absorption.

Both equations have the same functional form. The first two terms represent the short-term elasticities with respect to real output and the real exchange rate, respectively. The short-run activity elasticities are both noticeably greater than 1, while the price elasticities are around 0.7. The third terms are error correction mechanisms, which ensure a long-run activity elasticity of unity. The final term shows the level effect of the real exchange rate on trade; the long-run elasticity can be calculated by dividing the estimated coefficient on the level of the real exchange rate by the coefficient on the error correction mechanism. This implies a coefficient of around 0.8 for both exports and imports.

All of the coefficients were freely estimated except those on the change in the real exchange rate, which were both set equal to double the freely estimated value. This ensured that the Marshall–Lerner conditions were satisfied, which was required for stability of the model.[14] In both equations, the effect of doubling the short-term elasticity on the exchange rate was to make it relatively close to the estimated long-run elasticity.

The result is a version of MULTIMOD in which developing countries are modelled in a forward-looking manner, with consumption, investment and financing reacting to anticipated changes in economic welfare. It is the interaction between the external financing constraint and the forward-looking nature of consumption and investment which generates most of the simulation results.

4   Main case simulation

The policy change which is simulated is one in which all countries simultaneously carry out a 20 per cent reduction in military *expenditures* relative to their average values in 1987–9, phased in gradually over five years in equal increments. This translates into a fall in government consumption after five years of 0.7 per cent of GDP for industrial countries and 0.6 per cent of GDP for developing countries. Each nation is assumed to also lower its military *exports* and military *imports*, based on the information on military trade discussed earlier. These cuts are also phased in over five years, so the simulation can be thought of as representing a gradual reduction in all types of military spending. It was assumed that governments adjust taxes (or government transfers, which are equivalent to negative taxes in the model) in order to keep the fiscal deficit unchanged, while the residuals on the trade equations were changed so that the *ex ante* effects on trade corresponded to the data on military trade. The monetary authorities in most industrial countries are assumed to follow a target path for the money supply; however France, Italy, the United Kingdom and the smaller industrial countries are assumed to keep their exchange rates pegged to the Deutschmark.

Two further changes, specific to the non-oil-developing countries, were made. First, the residuals on the investment and consumption equations were adjusted so that the direct 'shadow price' effect of the fall in military imports was eliminated, because the fall in imports is associated with a reduction in government spending, not that of the private sector. Second, part of the fall in imports was offset by a reduction in assistance from industrial to developing countries, since some military imports are paid for by loans or grants. The financing of developing country military imports is a very murky area, and hence it is difficult to be very precise about the ratios involved. Furthermore, the level of external assistance associated with arms imports has almost certainly fallen significantly over the last few years due to the end of the cold war. Since these simulations measure the effects of future cuts in military spending, it was assumed that 40 per cent of the decline in military imports were associated with a decline in assistance from the exporting country, with half coming in the form of loans and half in the form of grants.[15]

The simulation results are shown in Table 10.2. for developing countries in general, the fall in military spending induces an immediate rise in private consumption of 0.1 per cent and investment of 0.4 per cent. This is brought about by a number of factors. Lower government spending on the military lowers income and investment taxes. In addition, lower government spending tends to lower the domestic real interest rate, which improves investment prospects and increases household wealth. Finally, lower world interest rates in the medium term also tends to reduce interest payments on foreign debt and loosen the external finance constraint, which further stimulates private consumption and investment.

The response of investment and private consumption is actually larger than the cut in government spending in the first year for developing countries, and both absorption and real GDP rise slightly. This reflects the fact that the cuts in military spending are phased in over several years. Since consumers and investors are forward looking, they anticipate the beneficial effects of future cuts in spending and raise consumption immediately.[16] Private consumption and investment continue to rise over the medium term, approximately offsetting the cuts in military spending over the first five years. Output and absorption both rise in the longer run, as the rise in investment translates into higher potential output.

For developing countries as a whole, real exports and real imports both rise in the short run, reflecting the replacement of military spending by relatively more import-intensive consumption and investment both at home and abroad. The military spending cuts put pressure on the external finance constraint, and result in a depreciation of the real exchange rate. As a result, while trade volumes rise, real exports rise by more than real imports over the medium term. In the long run lower world interest rates ease the external constraint, allowing the real exchange rate to appreciate, imports to increase, and absorption to rise by more than output.

In order to understand these results it is useful to consider the nature of the shock. In doing this, it is best to distinguish between the effects of *domestic* military spending cuts and of *foreign* military spending cuts. Unlike a standard government spending reduction, in which the trade impact of the fall in government consumption is determined endogenously, the *ex ante* impact of the *domestic* spending cuts on trade is imposed exogenously. Since military spending generally has a relative lower import propensity than other forms of spending, the exogenous fall in imports is relatively small.[17] As a result, the private consumption and investment which are crowded in by these cuts has a much higher import content. The net effect is to put pressure on the external balance, which leads to a depreciation in the real exchange rate. Hence the *domestic* spending cuts tend to hurt the external constraint.

By contrast, the *foreign* military cuts tend to help the external constraint through exactly the same mechanism. Demand for developing country exports by the industrial countries is raised as private consumption and investment is crowded in by cuts in military spending. In addition, the lower world interest rate caused by worldwide cuts in military spending raises wealth and reduces interest repayments on debt. Hence *foreign* cuts in military spending help the external accounts, leading to an appreciation in the real exchange rate, higher real imports and absorption, and lower real exports. Since the simulation involves cuts in both domestic and foreign military spending, the overall effect on the external position is ambiguous. It depends upon the relative importance of the domestic and foreign cuts.

The results for individual developing country regions illustrate these opposing forces at work. The *Western Hemisphere* region experiences the smallest cut in military spending, and hence a relative small negative shock to its external position from domestic spending cuts. At the same time, its trade is dominated by the United States, which implements the largest cut in military spending among the industrial countries, and hence experiences the largest increase in demand for exports. The *ex ante* improvement in the external position of the region translates into an appreciation of the real exchange rate and higher real imports, consumption, investment and absorption. The exchange rate appreciation lowers real exports, which in turn causes a small short-term fall in output. The beneficial effects of lower interest rates on the external constraint can be seen in the substantial appreciation of the exchange rate between the fifth and tenth years of the simulation.

The cuts in military spending in *Africa* are larger than those in the western hemisphere, but smaller than in the other developing country regions. The negative effect of these domestic military cuts on the

Table 10.2 Simulation results: main case (in per cent deviation from baseline)

	Government consumption	Private consumption	Private investment	Total absorption	GDP	Real exchange rate	Exports	Imports
Developing countries								
Year 1	−1.1	0.1	0.4	0.0	0.0	−0.1	0.1	0.1
Year 5	−5.5	0.5	1.7	0.0	0.0	−0.3	0.5	0.2
Year 10	−5.5	0.8	2.1	0.3	0.2	0.4	0.3	0.8
Western Hemisphere								
Year 1	−0.7	0.1	0.5	0.1	−0.0	0.3	−0.2	0.4
Year 5	−3.4	0.5	1.7	0.3	0.1	0.2	−0.2	0.6
Year 10	−3.4	0.7	1.9	0.5	0.3	1.0	−0.3	1.3
Africa								
Year 1	−0.8	0.1	0.6	0.0	0.0	0.0	0.0	0.1
Year 5	−4.2	0.6	2.1	0.1	0.2	−0.1	0.4	0.2
Year 10	−4.2	0.9	2.4	0.4	0.3	0.7	0.2	0.8
Other developing countries								
Year 1	−1.4	0.1	0.3	0.0	0.0	−0.3	0.2	−0.1
Year 5	−7.1	0.5	1.6	−0.1	0.1	−0.7	0.8	0.0
Year 10	−7.1	0.9	2.2	0.2	0.2	0.0	0.6	0.5
Industrialized countries								
Year 1	−0.7	0.0	0.5	0.0	0.0	−0.1	0.1	0.2
Year 5	−3.9	0.8	1.6	0.1	0.0	−0.1	0.7	0.8
Year 10	−3.9	1.0	1.8	0.3	0.3	−0.2	0.6	0.6
United States								
Year 1	−1.3	0.0	0.4	−0.2	0.0	−1.0	0.5	−0.5
Year 5	−7.1	0.9	1.7	−0.3	0.0	−1.4	1.3	−0.8
Year 10	−7.1	1.2	2.0	−0.1	0.3	−1.6	1.5	−0.9

Japan								
Year 1	-0.2	0.1	0.5	0.1	0.0	1.3	-0.3	1.0
Year 5	-1.3	0.5	1.1	0.4	0.1	1.9	-0.3	2.0
Year 10	-1.3	0.6	1.3	0.5	0.2	1.9	-0.5	1.7
Newly industrialized economies								
Year 1	-2.0	0.0	0.2	-0.1	-0.1	0.1	0.1	0.1
Year 5	-9.8	0.7	1.2	-0.1	0.0	0.1	0.8	0.6
Year 10	-9.8	0.8	1.4	0.0	0.1	0.3	0.7	0.5

Only developing countries cut their military spending

Developing countries								
Year 1	-1.1	0.1	0.3	0.0	0.1	-0.4	0.2	-0.2
Year 5	-5.5	0.3	1.1	-0.3	-0.1	-0.6	0.2	-0.6
Year 10	-5.5	0.5	1.4	0.0	0.1	-0.6	0.3	-0.6
Western hemisphere								
Year 1	-1.1	0.0	0.2	0.0	0.0	-0.5	0.1	-0.3
Year 5	-5.5	0.1	0.7	-0.2	-0.1	-0.6	-0.2	-0.8
Year 10	-5.5	0.3	0.9	0.0	0.1	-0.7	-0.1	-0.8
Africa								
Year 1	-0.8	0.1	0.5	0.0	0.1	-0.4	0.2	-0.2
Year 5	-4.2	0.4	1.3	-0.2	-0.1	-0.2	0.1	-0.5
Year 10	-4.2	0.6	1.7	0.0	0.2	-0.3	0.2	-0.5
Other developing countries								
Year 1	-1.4	0.1	0.4	0.0	0.1	-0.4	0.4	-0.2
Year 5	-7.1	0.3	1.2	-0.3	-0.1	-0.7	0.4	-0.4
Year 10	-7.1	0.6	1.7	-0.1	0.2	-0.9	0.6	-0.4

external constraint, however is reduced by the relatively high import content of military spending in this region (Table 10.1). However, trade is heavily orientated towards Europe, an area of the world whose military spending as a ratio to output is lower than the United States, and hence the boost to exports from cuts in foreign military spending is smaller than for the Western hemisphere region. Overall, there is a small depreciation of the real exchange rate and real exports rise by slightly more than imports. As in the other regions, the benefits of the fall in interest rates are reflected in a long-term appreciation of the real exchange rate.

Despite implementing larger cuts in military spending, the increases in consumption and investment in the *other developing countries region* are slightly smaller than those in the African region. Output is deflected abroad as pressures on their external balance cause a depreciation in their exchange rate and a deterioration in real net trade. As well as the size of their domestic spending cuts, the exchange rate depreciation reflects the regional pattern of trade. Unlike the other two developing country regions, who export and import to different areas of the world in roughly equal proportions, other developing countries are net importers from Japan and net exporters to the United States. As discussed below, the military spending cuts in the industrial countries lead to an depreciation in the real exchange rate in those countries with large amounts of military spending as a proportion of GDP, principally the United States, and an appreciation in the real exchange rates of those countries with small levels of military spending, most notably Japan. This results in a loss in the terms of trade of other developing countries, which increases pressure on the external constraint, and leads to a diversion of domestic output into exports.

The differential impact of domestic and foreign military spending cuts is further illustrated in the bottom part of Table 10.2, which reports the results of a simulation in which only the finance-constrained developing country regions (Western Hemisphere, Africa and Other Developing Countries) cut their military spending. These three developing country regions experience a depreciation in their currency that is larger than that in the main case, reflecting the negative impact of domestic military spending cuts on the external constraint. Higher investment means that real GDP rises in the long run, however much of this higher output goes into exports and the rise in domestic absorption is smaller than the rise in GDP for every region.

The results from the main case simulation for the *industrial countries* are similar to those reported in BHS, and hence we will summarize them relatively briefly. Industrial countries as a whole experience little change in output in the short run, as the fall in government consumption is largely offset by rises in investment, consumption, and net trade.[18] In the long run private consumption and investment rise by 1.0 per cent and 1.8 per cent, respectively, with the countries that implement the largest cuts having the largest longer-term gains in consumption and investment (as well as the largest short-term losses in output). The long-run differences in performance are smaller than the differences in military spending, reflecting a positive international externality coming from lower world real interest rates and higher world trade. This externality is transmitted through changes in the international terms of trade, with those countries that implement the largest cuts in their military budgets experiencing a depreciation in their real exchange rate, and those countries with the smallest cuts experiencing an appreciation.

The *newly industrialized economies*, which were not analysed in BHS, have military spending of 4.7 per cent of GDP, somewhere between the polar extremes of the United States (6.1 per cent) and Japan (1.0 per cent). Their responses also generally fall part way between those of the extremes. Both exports and imports rise, illustrating the beneficial effect of lower military spending on trade as a whole. One interesting feature of these results, not reported in Table 10.2, is that their current account does considerably worse than might be expected. Like the other developing countries region, their trade involves net imports from Japan and net exports to the United States, so they experience a negative terms-of-trade shock. They also have a particularly low import content of military expenditures. However, since they do not face a constraint on external finance, but can borrow from abroad, the shock is partly reflected in a deterioration of the current account.

Comparing the overall results for industrial countries with those for developing countries, the most striking characteristic is their similarity. Developing countries do rather better on imports and investment, and slightly worse on output and consumption; however, these differences are not striking. Since the main difference between industrial and developing countries is the imposition of an external finance constraint on the latter, this would appear to indicate that this constraint is not particularly important for the overall results. Indeed, the movements in the real exchange rate across different developing country regions are actually smaller than those across industrial countries, implying smaller changes in their real net export position. While the United States, which has the highest ratio of military spending amongst the industrial countries, experiences a fall in its real exchange rate of over 1 per cent and an improvement in its current account, the other developing countries region, which has the highest ratio of military spending in developing countries, experiences a smaller fall in its real exchange rate and a largely unchanged current account.

As discussed in detail in BHS, GDP is not a good measure of the economic benefits from cutting military spending since it includes military spending. The appropriate measure for the *economic* benefits from cutting military spending is the rise in non-military consumption over time. The cost from cutting military spending comes from any decrease in security produced by lower military spending, however this is difficult to measure, particularly for the type of coordinated military spending considered in these simulations. For these reasons we focus on the economic benefits from military spending cuts, while acknowledging that these benefits should be weighed against any impact on national security. Accordingly, we will consider long-run changes in consumption and investment in some detail; these economic welfare gains are discussed in more detail in a companion paper (Bayoumi, Hewitt and Symansky, 1993).

Private consumption in developing countries (excluding NIEs) rises by 0.8 per cent after ten years and private investment by 2.1 per cent, which adds up to around $40 billion per annum in 1993 prices (Table 10.2). These percentage increases are similar to those experienced by industrial countries, although developing countries gain somewhat more on investment and less on consumption (for industrial countries, private consumption rises by 1.0 per cent and private investment by 1.8 per cent). It should be stressed that these are permanent rises in consumption and investment, and hence the benefits cumulate year by year. These developing country gains are, however, significantly lower than the results reported in BHS, where the large response of investment leads to a long-run rise in potential output of over 1 per cent, as opposed to 0.2 per cent in this simulation.

Within the developing countries, Africa is the region whose consumption and investment rise by the largest percentage despite the fact that it has a lower ratio of military spending to output than the other developing countries region. This reflects both the relatively high propensity to import military goods in Africa and the negative terms-of-trade shock experienced by the other developing countries region. The gains in the Western Hemisphere region are slightly smaller than in the other regions, however, since their military spending cuts are also smaller as a ratio of GDP, their gain per dollar of military spending is the highest.

5   Variations on the main case

To this point the analysis has focused on the main case scenario. This section reports the outcomes from three variants of the main case, which are used to test the sensitivity of the results to variations in some of the underlying assumptions. The first variant alters the financing assumption for arms imports to developing countries. The next scenario looks at how the phasing of the military spending cuts affects the results. The final scenario assumes that part of the reduction in military spending comprises productive investment, and hence cuts in military spending have a direct negative impact on the capital stock and hence on underlying output.

The results from these alternative scenarios are summarized in Table 10.3 and given in more detail in Table 10.4. In the first variant it is assumed that 80 per cent of the cuts in military trade are associated with cuts in grants and loans, rather than the 40 per cent assumed in the main case (in both cases half the aid is assumed to be grants and the other half loans). Cutting aid by a larger amount tightens the external constraint faced by developing countries, and hence reduces the benefits from any given cut in military spending. For developing countries as a whole absorption and investment are both slightly lower than in the main case, with these reductions being concentrated in the African and the other developing countries region (military trade in the western hemisphere region is approximately balanced, and hence this region is largely unaffected by changes in assumptions about military aid).[19]

The second variant shows the results when the full 20 per cent military spending cuts occur immediately, rather than being phased in steadily over five years. This allows some estimate of the importance of the assumption that the spending cuts are phased in over time. This simulation produces significantly larger short-term falls in real absorption (and output) than is the case in the main case scenario. This is most striking in the case of the United States, which implements the largest cuts in both absolute terms and as a ratio to GDP, and where absorption falls by 0.9 per cent in the first year, compared to a decline of 0.2 per cent in the main case.

However, these negative effects are relatively short lived, and GDP recovers rapidly, as can be seen in the more detailed results in Table 10.4. The speedy recovery reflects the response of investment and private consumption. Larger short-term reductions in military spending free more resources for the private sector, and both private consumption and investment rise by more than in the main-case scenario. These benefits continue into the medium term, and both absorption and investment are considerably higher than in the main case after five years, particularly in the developing country regions. The results after ten years indicate very little long-term impact from changing the speed of the military spending cuts. As might be expected, the differences in behaviour are particularly

Table 10.3 Simulation results: main case and variants (in per cent deviation from baseline)

	Government consumption	Main case		More military aid		Faster cuts		Part investment	
		Absorption	Investment	Absorption	Investment	Absorption	Investment	Absorption	Investment
Developing countries									
Year 1	−1.1	0.0	0.4	0.0	0.4	−0.3	0.9	0.0	0.3
Year 5	−5.5	0.0	1.7	0.0	1.6	0.4	2.3	0.0	1.1
Year 10	−5.5	0.3	2.1	0.3	2.0	0.4	2.0	0.2	1.4
Western Hemisphere									
Year 1	−0.7	0.1	0.5	0.1	0.5	−0.1	1.0	0.1	0.4
Year 5	−3.4	0.3	1.7	0.3	1.7	0.6	2.3	0.2	1.3
Year 10	−3.4	0.5	1.9	0.5	1.9	0.5	1.8	0.4	1.3
Africa									
Year 1	−0.8	0.0	0.6	0.0	0.5	0.3	1.2	0.1	0.5
Year 5	−4.2	0.1	2.1	0.0	1.8	0.5	2.9	0.1	1.4
Year 10	−4.2	0.4	2.4	0.3	2.1	0.5	2.4	0.5	1.6
Other developing countries									
Year 1	−1.4	0.0	0.3	−0.1	0.3	−0.5	2.8	0.0	0.2
Year 5	−7.1	−0.1	1.6	−0.2	1.5	0.2	2.2	−0.1	1.0
Year 10	−7.1	0.2	2.2	0.1	2.0	0.3	2.1	0.1	1.4
Industrialized countries									
Year 1	−0.7	0.0	0.5	0.0	0.5	−0.4	0.9	0.1	0.9
Year 5	−3.9	0.1	1.6	0.1	1.6	0.3	1.9	0.0	1.0
Year 10	−3.9	0.3	1.8	0.3	1.8	0.3	1.8	0.2	1.2
United States									
Year 1	−1.3	−0.2	0.4	−0.2	0.5	−0.9	1.1	−0.1	0.3
Year 5	−7.1	−0.3	1.7	−0.3	1.7	0.0	2.2	−0.3	0.7
Year 10	−7.1	−0.1	2.0	0.0	2.0	0.0	2.1	−0.1	0.7

Japan									
Year 1	−0.2	0.1	0.5	0.1	0.5	0.0	0.7	0.1	0.4
Year 5	−1.3	0.4	1.1	0.4	1.2	0.4	1.2	0.3	0.9
Year 10	−1.3	0.5	1.3	0.5	1.3	0.5	1.4	0.3	0.9
Newly industrialized economies									
Year 1	−2.0	−0.1	0.2	−0.1	0.2	−0.6	0.5	−0.1	0.1
Year 5	−9.8	−0.1	1.2	−0.1	1.2	0.1	1.4	−0.1	0.8
Year 10	−9.8	0.0	1.4	0.0	1.4	0.0	1.5	−0.1	0.8

Table 10.4 Simulation results: main case and variants (changes in billion 1993 US dollars)

	1993	1994	1995	1996	1997	1998	1999	2000	2001	2002	2003
Developing countries											
Main case											
Government spending	−4.2	−8.8	−13.5	−18.4	−23.6	−24.2	−24.9	−25.5	−26.1	−26.8	−27.2
GDP	0.6	0.6	1.5	2.4	3.7	6.9	8.1	8.4	8.6	9.7	11.9
Consumption	1.7	3.5	5.9	8.7	11.9	15.2	17.7	19.4	20.7	21.8	23.0
Investment	2.8	4.9	7.2	9.7	13.0	15.8	17.4	17.9	17.8	17.9	18.6
More military aid											
GDP	0.6	0.7	1.9	3.0	4.3	7.2	8.1	8.1	8.1	9.1	11.0
Consumption	1.5	3.2	5.4	8.1	11.2	14.3	16.7	18.3	19.4	20.4	21.6
Investment	2.5	4.4	6.5	8.9	12.0	14.7	16.1	16.5	16.4	16.4	17.0
Faster cuts											
GDP	−5.1	7.2	9.3	8.6	7.1	6.0	6.9	9.1	12.1	14.7	16.7
Consumption	4.6	10.5	15.0	18.0	19.3	19.8	20.2	21.0	22.3	24.1	26.0
Investment	6.3	14.4	17.5	18.5	17.4	15.8	14.8	14.8	15.9	17.4	19.0
Part investment											
GDP	−0.5	0.4	0.5	2.9	3.6	6.4	6.5	5.3	4.7	5.1	6.9
Consumption	1.8	3.5	4.2	6.9	10.1	13.6	16.4	18.0	18.8	19.2	19.8
Investment	2.1	4.0	3.9	6.1	8.3	11.3	12.9	12.9	12.3	11.7	11.8
Western Hemisphere											
Main case											
Government spending	−0.7	−1.5	−2.4	−3.2	−4.1	−4.2	−4.3	−4.5	−4.6	−4.7	−4.7
GDP	−0.1	0.1	0.6	1.1	1.5	2.1	2.3	2.4	2.7	3.2	3.9
Consumption	0.6	1.1	1.6	2.4	3.3	4.3	5.1	5.6	5.9	6.1	6.4
Investment	0.9	1.4	2.0	2.7	3.6	4.4	4.8	4.8	4.7	4.6	4.7

More military aid											
GDP	0.0	0.2	0.6	1.1	1.5	2.1	2.3	2.4	2.7	3.2	3.9
Consumption	0.6	1.0	1.6	2.4	3.3	4.3	5.1	5.6	5.8	6.1	6.4
Investment	0.9	1.4	2.0	2.7	3.6	4.4	4.8	4.8	4.7	4.6	4.7
Faster cuts											
GDP	−0.3	2.5	2.6	2.1	1.6	1.6	2.1	3.0	3.9	4.6	5.2
Consumption	1.2	3.0	4.4	5.3	5.6	5.7	5.7	5.8	6.2	6.7	7.2
Investment	1.8	4.2	5.2	5.4	4.9	4.3	3.8	3.7	3.9	4.3	4.7
Part investment											
GDP	−0.5	−0.2	0.3	1.2	1.6	2.1	2.0	1.7	1.7	2.1	2.7
Consumption	0.7	1.1	1.1	1.8	2.7	3.8	4.6	5.0	5.2	5.3	5.4
Investment	0.7	1.3	1.3	1.9	2.6	3.4	3.9	3.8	3.5	3.2	3.1
Africa											
Main case											
Government spending	−0.6	−1.2	−1.9	−2.6	−3.3	−3.5	−3.5	−3.6	−3.7	−3.8	−3.8
GDP	0.1	0.2	0.4	0.6	0.8	1.3	1.4	1.4	1.4	1.6	2.0
Consumption	0.3	0.6	1.0	1.4	1.9	2.4	2.7	3.0	3.1	3.2	3.4
Investment	0.5	0.8	1.2	1.6	2.1	2.5	2.7	2.8	2.8	2.8	2.9
More military aid											
GDP	0.1	0.2	0.5	0.7	1.0	1.3	1.4	1.3	1.3	1.4	1.7
Consumption	0.2	0.5	0.8	1.2	1.7	2.1	2.4	2.6	2.7	2.8	3.0
Investment	0.4	0.7	1.0	1.3	1.8	2.2	2.3	2.4	2.4	2.4	2.5
Faster cuts											
GDP	−0.4	1.6	1.8	1.5	1.1	0.9	1.0	1.3	1.8	2.3	2.7
Consumption	0.8	1.7	2.4	2.8	2.9	2.9	2.9	3.0	3.2	3.5	3.0
Investment	1.1	2.4	2.9	3.0	2.8	2.5	2.3	2.3	2.5	2.8	3.1
Part investment											
GDP	0.0	0.2	0.2	0.6	0.8	1.2	1.2	1.0	0.9	0.9	1.2
Consumption	0.3	0.6	0.7	1.1	1.6	2.1	2.6	2.8	2.9	2.9	2.9
Investment	0.4	0.7	0.6	1.0	1.3	1.8	2.0	2.0	2.0	1.9	1.9

Table 10.4 (*Contd.*)

	1993	1994	1995	1996	1997	1998	1999	2000	2001	2002	2003
Other developing countries											
Main case											
Government spending	−2.8	−6.1	−9.3	−12.6	−16.2	−16.6	−17.1	−17.4	−17.8	−18.3	−18.7
GDP	0.6	0.3	0.5	0.8	1.4	3.5	4.4	4.5	4.5	4.9	6.0
Consumption	0.8	1.9	3.2	4.8	6.7	8.5	9.9	10.9	11.7	12.4	13.2
Investment	1.4	2.6	4.0	5.5	7.4	9.0	9.9	10.3	10.3	10.5	10.9
More military aid											
GDP	0.6	0.4	0.8	1.1	1.9	3.7	4.4	4.4	4.2	4.5	5.4
Consumption	0.7	1.7	2.9	4.4	6.2	7.9	9.2	10.2	10.9	11.5	12.2
Investment	1.2	2.3	3.6	4.9	6.7	8.2	9.0	9.3	9.3	9.5	9.9
Faster cuts											
GDP	−4.4	3.2	4.8	5.0	4.3	3.5	3.7	4.8	6.3	7.7	8.8
Consumption	2.6	5.8	8.2	9.9	10.7	11.2	11.6	12.1	13.0	14.0	15.1
Investment	3.4	7.8	9.5	10.2	9.8	9.1	8.7	8.8	9.4	10.3	11.2
Part investment											
GDP	0.0	0.4	0.0	1.2	1.2	3.1	3.3	2.6	2.1	2.1	3.0
Consumption	0.8	1.8	2.4	4.0	5.8	7.7	9.2	10.2	10.7	11.1	11.5
Investment	0.9	2.0	2.0	3.2	4.3	6.1	7.0	7.1	6.9	6.6	6.8
Industrial countries											
Main case											
Government spending	−26.5	−54.3	−83.7	−114.6	−146.6	−150.0	−154.2	−157.7	−161.4	−165.3	−169.7
GDP	−6.2	6.4	6.7	8.3	9.2	34.8	51.3	58.5	59.4	58.6	59.6
Consumption	3.7	27.8	48.6	70.0	90.8	109.1	122.9	131.9	137.1	140.6	143.9
Investment	17.2	34.8	44.5	55.9	67.7	76.6	80.8	81.3	80.3	80.3	82.6

More military aid												
GDP	-6.3	6.7	7.1	8.8	9.6	35.6	52.3	59.4	60.3	59.5	60.5
Consumption	3.8	28.2	49.4	71.0	92.2	110.6	124.6	133.6	138.8	142.3	145.6
Investment	17.6	35.6	45.5	57.1	69.1	78.0	82.2	82.6	81.6	81.6	83.9
Faster cuts												
GDP	-83.9	-14.7	27.9	52.8	60.0	57.5	51.9	49.6	52.7	59.9	68.9
Consumption	18.4	57.2	86.4	107.6	119.9	126.9	130.6	134.0	138.3	143.8	149.6
Investment	32.4	67.6	80.6	84.3	81.7	76.2	72.3	72.4	76.2	81.9	88.1
Part investment												
GDP	17.3	37.6	6.4	-1.2	-7.3	19.1	43.0	53.7	54.5	50.9	47.4
Consumption	8.1	29.8	38.8	54.9	72.3	90.3	106.4	117.0	122.9	126.2	128.5
Investment	30.0	52.5	38.5	40.5	41.5	49.5	56.6	57.2	54.6	51.7	50.6
United States												
Main case												
Government spending	-15.3	-31.5	-48.7	-66.8	-85.6	-87.7	-89.8	-92.0	-94.3	-96.5	-98.8
GDP	-3.1	2.2	-0.5	-2.2	-3.4	9.6	18.0	21.5	21.9	21.7	22.5
Consumption	0.7	12.4	21.9	31.8	41.8	50.4	57.0	61.3	63.8	65.4	67.0
Investment	4.2	8.4	11.2	15.2	19.7	23.4	25.4	25.9	25.9	26.2	27.3
More military aid												
GDP	-3.1	2.3	-0.4	-2.1	-3.2	9.9	18.3	21.8	22.2	21.9	22.8
Consumption	0.7	12.6	22.3	32.2	42.3	51.0	57.7	62.0	64.4	66.0	67.6
Investment	4.3	8.6	11.5	15.5	20.1	23.8	25.8	26.3	26.2	26.5	27.7
Faster cuts												
GDP	-48.0	-9.3	11.3	22.2	24.4	21.4	18.2	17.7	20.1	24.3	28.7
Consumption	8.3	28.8	43.1	53.0	58.2	60.5	61.6	63.0	65.0	67.7	70.5
Investment	10.7	22.1	26.3	27.2	25.8	23.7	22.6	23.0	24.8	27.2	29.6
Part investment												
GDP	-0.5	4.3	-2.4	-5.3	-7.2	5.2	12.7	14.3	12.2	9.5	8.3
Consumption	1.3	11.7	19.4	28.7	38.5	47.0	53.2	56.5	57.7	57.9	58.2
Investment	2.9	5.4	5.1	6.2	7.8	11.4	12.6	12.0	10.6	9.6	9.7

Table 10.4 *(Contd.)*

	1993	1994	1995	1996	1997	1998	1999	2000	2001	2002	2003
Japan											
Main case											
Government spending	−1.7	−3.4	−5.1	−6.8	−8.5	−8.5	−8.5	−9.4	−9.4	−9.4	−10.3
GDP	−0.4	3.5	4.4	5.1	5.3	7.2	8.5	9.2	9.9	10.6	11.5
Consumption	1.2	4.6	7.2	9.6	11.7	13.6	15.0	16.0	16.8	17.5	18.3
Investment	4.5	8.7	10.2	11.5	12.6	13.3	13.7	13.8	14.0	14.4	15.0
More military aid											
GDP	−0.4	3.6	4.5	5.2	5.5	7.3	8.6	9.4	10.1	10.8	11.8
Consumption	1.2	4.7	7.3	9.8	12.0	13.8	15.3	16.3	17.1	17.8	18.6
Investment	4.6	8.9	10.4	11.7	12.9	13.6	14.0	14.1	14.3	14.6	15.3
Faster cuts											
GDP	−4.5	3.1	6.5	8.0	7.9	7.9	8.1	9.0	10.5	12.0	13.1
Consumption	2.5	7.0	10.1	12.2	13.4	14.3	15.1	16.1	17.3	18.4	19.3
Investment	6.2	12.4	14.0	14.1	13.6	12.9	12.9	13.4	14.4	15.3	16.0
Part investment											
GDP	0.3	3.4	3.1	3.5	3.9	5.9	7.1	7.4	7.5	7.7	8.3
Consumption	1.0	3.7	5.7	7.9	9.9	11.6	12.8	13.5	13.9	14.3	14.8
Investment	3.4	6.6	7.5	8.6	9.7	10.5	10.5	10.1	9.8	9.8	10.2
Newly industrializing countries											
Main case											
Government spending	−1.0	−2.0	−3.1	−4.2	−5.4	−5.6	−5.7	−5.8	−5.9	−6.2	−6.3
GDP	−0.4	−0.3	0.0	0.1	0.1	0.8	1.1	1.1	1.0	0.8	0.8
Consumption	0.0	0.6	1.1	1.7	2.2	2.6	2.8	2.9	2.9	2.8	2.9
Investment	0.4	1.1	1.5	2.1	2.7	3.1	3.2	3.2	3.1	3.1	3.2

More military aid											
GDP	-0.3	-0.3	0.0	0.1	0.1	0.8	1.2	1.1	1.0	0.8	0.9
Consumption	0.0	0.6	1.1	1.7	2.2	2.6	2.9	2.9	2.9	2.9	2.9
Investment	0.5	1.1	1.6	2.1	2.7	3.1	3.3	3.2	3.1	3.2	3.3
Faster cuts											
GDP	-3.0	-0.9	0.7	1.6	1.5	1.0	0.6	0.5	0.7	1.0	1.4
Consumption	0.5	1.5	2.2	2.6	2.7	2.7	2.6	2.6	2.7	2.9	3.1
Investment	1.1	2.4	3.0	3.2	3.0	2.8	2.7	2.8	3.1	3.4	3.6
Part investment											
GDP	-0.1	0.2	-0.2	-0.2	-0.2	0.6	1.1	1.1	0.8	0.5	0.3
Consumption	0.0	0.5	1.0	1.5	2.0	2.5	2.8	2.8	2.7	2.6	2.6
Investment	0.3	0.6	0.8	1.3	1.8	2.3	2.4	2.2	1.9	1.8	1.8

important in those regions where the military spending cuts are the largest, such as Africa, other developing countries, the United States and the NIEs.

In the final simulation, part of the spending cut on military goods is in the form of a decline in productive investment. It is now well established both theoretically and empirically that certain types of government expenditures promote productivity. A question that has been hotly debated is the extent to which military activities enhance productivity. The question raised here is the extent to which the military provides a direct effect on productive investment.[20] This simulation assumes that one-fifth of the reduction in military spending in the industrial countries constitutes a cut in productive investment, together with one-tenth of the cuts in developing countries. The remaining spending cuts were assumed to be from government consumption.

The main effect of the simulation is to reduce the long-run gains from cutting military spending, as part of the increase in civilian investment brought about by lower taxes and interest rates is offset by lower government investment. While the short-run output declines are similar to the main case, the long-run gains to consumption and investment are only about three-quarters of the value in the main case (Table 10.4). Hence, while the short-term impact of the spending cuts is similar, the long-term benefits are lower. A similar effect occurs in the industrial countries.

6   Conclusions

This paper reports the results of a number of simulations using MULTIMOD, a macroeconomic model, to investigate the impact on developing countries of lowering military expenditures in the world economy. Such a model makes it possible to investigate the implications of a complicated set of assumptions whose interactions are too complex to be traced theoretically. As with any set of simulations, the results reflect the structure and parameter values in the model. There are many factors, particularly of a microeconomic type, that have not been considered in the relatively simple approach pursued in this paper. Despite these caveats, the results provide several insights into the economic effects of military expenditures in both the short and long run.

The timing of the gains from cutting military spending accrues approximately as the cuts occur. In the short run, there is an immediate boost to the civilian economy, and these gains accelerate over time as the level of military spending is decreased further. In the long run, cutting military spending by 20 per cent worldwide could produce a permanent increase in private consumption and investment in developing countries of 0.8 per cent and 2.1 per cent, respectively. The overall gain to private consumption and investment after ten years is estimated at $40 billion in 1993 prices. Since this is a permanent increase, these benefits cumulate steadily over time.

The gains across different developing country regions are affected by a number of factors. Larger gains are associated with bigger cuts in military spending, bigger cuts in military imports, and close bilateral trade links with the US. On the other hand, triangular patterns of trade in which countries import from Japan and export to the United States are associated with lower benefits, due to an unfavourable terms-of-trade effect. Overall, the developing country region of the world which benefits the most from military spending cuts is Africa.

The long-run gains are relatively unaffected by the financing assumptions or the timing of the military spending cuts, although the latter does have an impact on the size of the short-term losses to output. However, when 10 per cent of developing country and 20 per cent of industrial country cuts in military spending were assumed to represent a fall in productive investment, the estimated long-run gains fell by around a quarter. While about two-thirds of the long-run gains for developing countries comes from domestic cuts in military spending, cuts in industrial countries also produce significant economic gains. As a result, the distribution of the economic benefits across countries is considerably more even than the distribution of the cuts. Developing countries have much to gain from military spending cuts in all parts of the world.

NOTES

Bayoumi and Symansky are in the Research department of the IMF, while Hewitt is in the Fiscal Affairs department. The views are those of the authors, and do not necessarily represent the views of the IMF. A companion paper by the same authors, 'The impact of worldwide military spending cuts on developing countries: simulation results,' provides additional description of the results reported in this paper.

1 Hewitt (1993) estimates that the ratio of military spending to output fell by one-fifth between 1985 and 1990.

2 Atesoglu and Mueller (1990), Thomas *et al.* (1991), Lowenstein and Peach (1992) and CBO (1992) all focus on the impact of domestic cuts in military spending on the US economy. McKibbin and Thurman (1992) and Mayoumi *et al.* (1993) focus on the impact of cutting military spending on industrial countries more generally.

3 Leontief and Dutchin (1983) study the long-term consequences of reducing worldwide military expenditures and note that the poorest nations benefit proportionally more from cuts in military spending. Cunningham and Ruffing

(1992) find that worldwide cuts in military spending can lead to modest increases in growth in developing countries if they are used to increase capital formation.

4 The data on military expenditures used in this study is based on Stockholm International Peace Research Institute (SIPRI) estimates, which are generally believed to be the most accurate available. Trade data were taken from the US Arms Control and Disarmament Agency (ACDA), which is widely regarded as the best available source for these data. SIPRI does not provide estimates for the USSR and China; estimates in Steinberg (1992) and ACDA were used instead.

5 See Masson et al. (1990) for a detailed description of the model.

6 A conventional equation was estimated for exports of manufactures. Exports of primary commodities and oil were determined by the behavioural equations for imports of these goods by industrial countries.

7 Comprising Iran, Kuwait, Libya, Oman, Qatar, Saudi Arabia and the USE.

8 See Bayoumi, Hewitt and Symansky (1993) for further discussion.

9 Definitions were taken from the World Economic Outlook, so Egypt and Libya are not included in the African region, but rather are part of the other developing country region (which essentially consists of the Middle East and South East Asia other than the NIEs). The NIEs are Korea, Singapore, Hong Kong and Taiwan, Province of China.

10 Since there is no estimate of the domestic inflation rate, it is possible to think of some of this 'taxation' as coming from the inflation tax.

11 For those countries which use controls on the trade in goods and services rather than the exchange rate to solve balance-of-payment difficulties, this can be interpreted as movements in the shadow price of traded goods.

12 In simulations, the coefficient on a real interest rate term was set equal to that in the industrial countries.

13 One surprising feature of the results is the relatively small coefficient on the change in disposable income, implying that consumers in developing countries were not very liquidity-constrained. Further investigation indicated that this largely reflected the addition of the liquidity constraint on imports. When this term was eliminated, the coefficient on the change in disposable income became very similar to that found for the industrial countries. Since the coefficient on the error correction mechanism is smaller, this would imply a larger role for disposable income compared to wealth in the developing country equation.

14 One justification for increasing the short-term exchange rate elasticities is that developing countries often resort to direct controls on the traded goods sector to solve balance-of-payments problems in the short term, rather than allowing the exchange rate to change, which could tend to an underestimation of the actual elasticity.

15 The results from a simulation in which 80 per cent of military imports are associated with assistance from the exporting country, a proportion that is probably more in line with the state of affairs prior to the collapse of the Soviet Union, is reported as a variant of the main case.

16 If the entire cut in military spending occurs immediately, as is done in a variant discussed in Section 5, output falls in the short run.

17 This effect is exacerbated by the elimination of the negative impact of the reduction in imports on consumption and investment.

18 As with the developing countries, the short-run output decline is significantly larger in the scenario in which the military spending cuts are implemented immediately, rather than being phased in gradually.

19 There is almost no effect on industrial countries since assets are assumed to be perfect substitutes between these countries, which means that changes in aid have little impact on their behaviour.

20 This could come from military-related research that has civilian applications, training given to demobilized military personnel, or possibly from infrastructure constructed by the military that is used by civilian producers. The scope for these is obviously more limited in the developing countries, which import more of their military equipment.

REFERENCES

Atesoglu, H. Somnez, and Michael Mueller (1990) 'Defence spending and economic growth', *Defence Economics* **2**, 19–27.

Bayoumi, Tamim, Daniel Hewitt and Jerald Schiff (1993) 'Economic consequences of lower military spending: some simulation results', IMF Working Paper No. WP/93/17, March.

Bayoumi, Tamim, Daniel Hewitt and Steven Symansky (1993) 'The impact of worldwide spending cuts on developing countries: simulation results', IMF Working Paper No. WP/93/86, November.

Congressional Budget Office (1992) *The Economic Effects of Reduced Defense Spending*.

Cunningham, Simon and Kenneth G. Ruffing (1992) 'Some macroeconomic aspects of reductions in military expenditures', paper presented at the United Nations University Conference on 'Arms Reduction and Economic Development in the Post Cold War Era'. Tokyo.

Grimmett, Richard F. (1992) 'Conventional arms transfers to the third world, 1984–1991', Congressional Research Service.

Hewitt, Daniel (1993) 'Military expenditures 1972–90: the reasons behind the post-1985 fall in world military spending', IMF Working Paper No. WP/93/18, March.

International Monetary fund (1992) *International Financial Statistics Yearbook*, Washington DC: International Monetary Fund.

Leontief, W. and F. Dutchin (1983) *Military Spending: Facts and Figures*, New York: Oxford University Press.

Lowenstein, Ronnie and Richard Peach (1992) 'The impact of the current defense build-down', *Federal Reserve Bank of New York* **17**, 59–68.

Masson, Paul, Steven Symansky and Guy Meredith (1990) 'MULTIMOD mark II: a revised and extended model', International Monetary Fund, Occasional Paper No. 71.

McKibbin, Warwick and Stephan Thurman (1992) 'The impact on the world economy of reductions in military expenditures and military arms exports', Paper presented at the United Nations University Conference on 'Arms reduction and economic development in the post cold war era', Tokyo.

Steinberg, Dimitri (1992) 'Soviet defense burden: estimating hidden defense costs', *Soviet Studies* **44**, 237–63.

Stockholm International Peace Research Institute (SIPRI) (1992) *SIPRI Yearbook*, Oxford: Oxford University Press.

Thomas, R. William, H.O. Stekler and G. Wayne Glass (1991) 'The economic effects of reducing US defence spending', *Defence Economics* **2**, 183–97.

US Arms Control and Disarmament agency (ACMA) (1991) *World Military Expenditures and Arms Transfers 1990*, Washington, DC: ACDA.

11 Effects of a rise in G-7 real interest rates on developing countries

CHRISTIAN E. PETERSEN
and T. G. SRINIVASAN

1 Introduction

Empirical global or 'North–South'[1] models have traditionally focused on trade-sector linkages, particularly when modelling linkages between developed and developing countries. This almost exclusive concern with North–South trade did not matter much as long as the developing countries remained fairly isolated from the financial sectors of industrial countries and official capital flows were the main source of external finance for developing countries. However, there is evidence of increasing financial integration between the North and the South.[2] Industrial country financial market developments now impact on developing countries in new and faster ways. Private portfolio capital flows are becoming increasingly important as a source of external finance for developing countries, and more developing country governments are now opting for flexible or market-determined exchange rates. These new developments in North–South finance have also enlarged the role of developing country policies. The debt crisis of the 1980s has taught us how critical it is for countries to manage their external debt in the event of a prolonged rise in interest rates. Though moderated from their peak levels in the mid 1980s, even as of 1991, the vulnerability of the South remained high: external debt of the South stood at US$1.5 trillion, which was nearly twice the level of Southern exports, and 40 per cent of Southern debt carried a variable interest rate. Currently, short-term interest rates in industrial countries are low compared to their levels in the 1980s, but they are expected to move up as these countries emerge decisively out of the current recession. In this paper, our objective is to sketch the implications of a rise in G-7 short-term real interest rates for the South.

While studying the effects of higher real interest rates, it is important to emphasize that alternative causes which raise the interest rate to the same extent may have dissimilar effects on developing countries. For instance, if the rise in interest rate was prompted by a surge in industrial country aggregate demand in the face of tight monetary conditions, then developing countries would benefit by higher exports, but lose because of increased interest payments and possible portfolio outflows. On the other hand, if the rise in interest rate was attributable to only a monetary crunch in industrial countries, developing countries would face not only a rise in interest rates, but also a fall in external demand with ambiguous direction of portfolio flows.[3] In this paper, we examine the second of these cases: we implement such monetary contractions in G-7 countries that G-7 short-term real interest rates rise by 100 basis points for five years; this process is then gradually reversed over the following three years.

The responsiveness of primary commodity prices to interest rate changes can be an important source of additional external risk for developing countries, particularly for those which export mainly primary commodities. There is reason to believe that a negative correlation exists between real commodity prices and real interest rates in the context of a portfolio adjustment model. As the interest rate rises, holders of commodity stocks will try to switch out of stocks, thereby reducing prices. The empirical magnitude of this negative effect or real interest rates on real commodity prices is not a settled issue. This link, however, is very crucial for many developing countries dependent on commodity exports, as it affects their terms of trade. For the purpose of the present exercise, we have used an interest rate semi-elasticity of 2 for non-oil primary commodity real prices, drawing on research work done at the World Bank.[4]

Another important factor which would affect the outcome for developing countries is the severity of their external financing constraint. The compulsion to stay within prudent borrowing limits imposes additional costs of adjustment for financially constrained economies. We use the instrument of government spending in financially constrained economies to force a cut in domestic absorption, i.e., an increase in the saving rate, such that prudent limits on external debt stocks are not exceeded, when these economies adjust to higher interest rates.

We present results of three simulation experiments in the paper, structured to assess the importance of financial arbitrage in primary commodity markets and the additional costs imposed by the need to maintain external solvency. In the first experiment, real commodity prices are held fixed at baseline levels and the issue of external solvency of developing countries is not addressed. In the second simulation, we allow for changes in real commodity prices. In the third simulation, we also enforce external solvency for those developing countries which are either moderately or severely indebted.

The paper is organized as follows. In Section 2, we summarize the new features of the BANK-GEM model used in the present exercise and explain the specific details of our simulation experiments. More elaborate presentations of the underlying model are given in Petersen *et al.* (1991) and Pedersen (1993). Section 3 has a brief discussion of results for the G-7, consequent to a rise in real interest rates. Section 4 explains the simulated effects on low and middle-income countries (LMICs), summarized in terms of regional and analytical aggregates. Finally, Section 5 presents the main conclusions.

2   Features of BANK-GEM

BANK-GEM stands for World Bank Global Economic Model, built and maintained at the International Economic Analysis and Prospects (IECAP) division. Unlike some other global models which model only pre-defined developing country regions, BANK-GEM models 144 individual countries, the results of which may be aggregated according to any desired grouping criterion.[5] BANK-GEM ensures that projections and policy scenarios are consistent according to basic accounting frameworks,[6] global as well as domestic. Since the features of a proto-typical developing country model are described in detail in Pedersen (1993), we concentrate here only on the recent changes we have made to the model.

2.1   New trade linkage mechanism

In BANK-GEM, as in many other global linkage models, export prices and import volumes are endogenously determined for each country. Export volumes and import prices are determined through bilateral trade share matrices. Up until now, in BANK-GEM, the international trade linkage has been constructed in nominal terms, implying that the underlying elasticity of substitution between products originating from competing exporters is one. One important drawback of this approach is that it does not distinguish between primary commodities and manufactures: the 'law of one price' for commodities does not allow for price competition among exporters of primary commodities. Furthermore, having only one traded good allows for undesirable substitution effects among goods with totally different characteristics. A disaggregation of traded goods, even if it is not carried forward into sectors of production, will at least help represent more accurately movements in the terms of trade facing developing countries. In the new version of BANK-GEM, we have implemented a disaggregated method of trade linkage among countries, by using separate bilateral market share matrices for food and beverages (SITC0,1), raw materials (SITC2,4), ENERGY (SITC3) and manufactures (SITC5 to 9).[7]

We describe the determination of export volumes and import prices in our current disaggregated trade linkage framework as follows. First, behaviourally determined aggregated import volumes for each country are split into four groups of traded goods assuming constant real shares. Then, import volumes for the three traded goods groups other than manufactures are allocated to suppliers (exporters), assuming constant *real* market shares, i.e., an elasticity of substitution of zero. This construction is a consequence of the assumption that the law of one price prevails. Imports of manufactures, however, are allocated among suppliers according to a constant *nominal* market share assumption, i.e., an elasticity of substitution of one. Export prices of food and beverages, raw materials and energy are set in world markets and these are assumed to bear a relation to industrial country export prices of manufactures. Export prices of manufactures are set behaviourally in individual country models. Thus, we are able to construct globally consistent trade volumes and prices at a disaggregated level of four groups of traded goods.

2.2   Exchange rates and interest rates for developing countries

The exchange rate regimes for individual developing countries are modelled according to current exchange rate arrangements as laid out in Table 11.1. For all choices of exchange rate regimes other than a floating one, the individual developing country exchange rate against the US dollar follows from the G-7 currency movements endogenously solved in the G-7 segment of BANK-GEM. For instance, in a francophone African economy, with its currency linked to French franc, national currency movements against the US dollar follow that of the French franc. For those developing countries that have some form of a floating exchange rate regime, we currently follow a PPP rule. In our future work, we plan to improve on this by allowing for forward-looking jumps in exchange rates for these countries.

In the simulation mode, interest rates in the developing countries are modelled according to uncovered interest parity: home interest rate equals the sum of foreign interest rate and the expected rate of depreciation of home currency against the foreign currency. When a country's currency is pegged to a single currency, short-term interest rate variation over baseline in the home country is set equal to the same variation as in the anchor country, as no change is expected in the

Table 11.1   Exchange rate regimes in LMICs, 1993

LMIC Region	Single Currency Pegs			Basket-peg	Floating	Total
	US$	Franc	Other			
Sub-Sah. Africa	5	12	2	12	13	44
South Asia	0	0	0	2	3	5
East Asia	0	0	0	6	3	9
Latin Am. & Car.	7	0	0	0	17	24
East & Cen. Europe	0	0	1	3	5	10
Mid. East & N. Africa	6	0	0	4	2	12
All LMICs	18	12	3	27	43	104

Notes: LMICs as defined here excludes Former Soviet Union and South Africa. Other pegs refer to South African Rand or DM. Basket-peg includes SDR peg. Floating includes managed floats and dual exchange rate regimes, where one rate is floating.
Source: Exchange Arrangements and Exchange Restrictions, Annual Report IMF (1992) and some updates.

exchange rate against the anchor currency. For the basket-peg countries, we use the US as the 'foreign' country. The use of the uncovered interest parity rule in setting interest rates implies that the pegged country's credit-worthiness as perceived by lenders does change after the shock. This assumption may be justified on the grounds that in our final simulations external solvency is imposed on developing countries. For countries that use a floating exchange rate regime we currently assume real interest parity augmented by a risk premium which depends on debt service indicators.

2.2   Simulation specification

The shock analysed here is defined as a 100 basis points increase in G-7 short-term real interest rates during 1993–7, which is then slowly returned to the baseline in the next three years, as the shock diminishes: 75 basis point rise in 1998, 50 basis point rise in 1999 and 25 basis point rise by year 2000. The NIGEM model is used as the simulation framework for assessing the effects of this shock on G-7 countries. The model is solved in forward-looking mode. A fiscal solvency assumption operates in all G-7 countries excluding Canada.[8] This rule adjusts personal taxes in the simulation to track baseline ratios of fiscal deficits to GDP. Exchange rates are allowed to jump initially to meet a terminal period condition that enforces baseline ratios of current-account balances to GDP by 2008. Expected inflation one period ahead is allowed to affect current-period labour-market behaviour. European interest rates follow the German rate. In other words, no realignments of the ERM take place. Long-term interest rates are averages of future 40 quarters' short-term interest rates. The current exchange rate regimes implemented in developing countries are preserved for the entire simulation period.

To investigate the effects of a real interest rate shock under the assumptions above we used some modelling 'fixes' to overcome computational constraints in current PC technology. Since at present BANK-GEM is not solved in forward-looking mode, the exercise has been split into two parts to make better use of forward-looking behaviour embedded in NIGEM. The objective is to make a backward-looking model – BANK-GEM – track the results for G-7 economies of a forward-looking model – NIGEM. This has been attempted by exogenously feeding the results of critical forward-looking variables from NIGEM into BANK-GEM. First, NIGEM (version February 1993) has been simulated from 1993 to 2008 with forward-looking exchange rates, long interest rates and consumer prices, with ERM in place. In the second stage, the shock to the real interest rate as well as the simulation results on G-7 variables critically dependent on the forward-looking solution are exogenously fed into BANK-GEM simulations for the period 1993 to 2002. This approach is open to the criticism that the paths of exogenized variables are insensitive to detailed links between G-7 and developing countries modelled in BANK-GEM. In our future work, we hope to be able to overcome this limitation by implementing forward-looking simulations in BANK-GEM.

3   Effects of higher real interest rates in G-7

Figures 11.1 and 11.2 show the implications for nominal interest rates of the 100 basis point real interest shock relative to the baseline forecast. Lower inflation attenuates the jump in nominal rates. The time profiles on inflation and money supply consistent with the real interest rate shock can be found in Figures 11.3 and 11.4, respectively.

Figure 11.5 shows that adverse effects peak in the sixth year when G-7 GNP falls close to 1 per cent below baseline, and then as the real interest shock is weakened output also returns slowly to baseline. Higher interest rates reduce domestic absorption in all G-7 countries, particularly investment. As a consequence, imports fall bringing down world trade by as much as 1.6 per cent. Lower capacity utilization associated with deflated demand brings down inflation rates rather rapidly in Japan (Figure 11.3). Consequently, nominal interest rates rise less in Japan, creating a negative interest rate differential with respect to the US. The

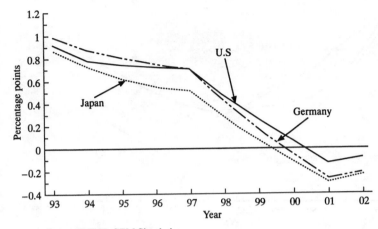

Source: NIESR GEM Simulation.

Figure 11.1　G-3 short-term nominal interest rates

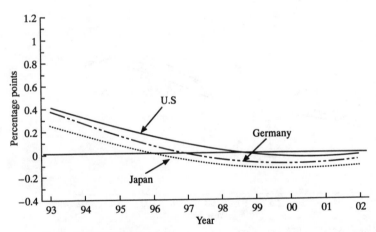

Source: NIESR GEM Simulation.

Figure 11.2　G-3 long-term nominal interest rates

yen appreciates slightly, reaching a 2 per cent appreciation in ten years (see Figure 11.4). Within G-7, however, the economies of the US, the UK and Canada suffer less than average. Here GNP falls between one-half and three-fourths of a per cent, reflecting the lower real interest rate sensitivity of investment behaviour in these economies.

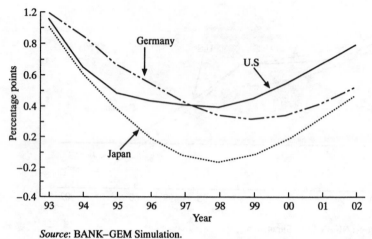

Source: BANK–GEM Simulation.

Figure 11.3   G-3 inflation

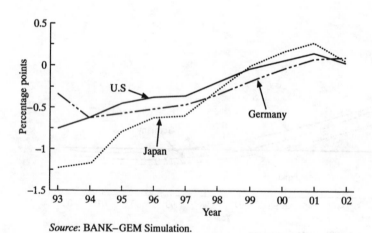

Source: BANK–GEM Simulation.

Figure 11.4   Growth in G-3 money supply

The average export price of manufactures in US dollar terms (MUV) falls by 2 per cent or roughly as much as the fall in the US money supply. Oil prices are assumed to be linked to the export price of manufactures and therefore fall by as much. Other commodity prices fall nearly twice as much as the price of manufactures (see Figure 11.9, below), by

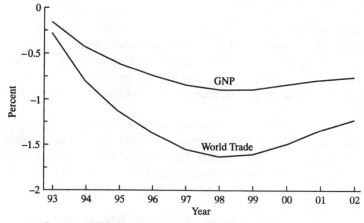

Sources: NIESR GEM simulation and BANK–simulation.

Figure 11.5   G-7 GNP and world trade

assumption, leading to deterioration in the terms of trade for commodity exporters.

4   Effects on developing countries

At least five channels are of importance for assessing the impact of higher interest rates on low and middle-income countries (LMICs). First, less growth in G-7 leads to less exports for the LMICs. Second, domestic interest rates in the LMICs tend to rise. Third, payments of debt service increase. Fourth, real commodity prices tend to fall as investors try to shift their portfolios from commodity-related financial instruments. Fifth, contractionary fiscal policy actions by LMICs might be needed to stay within borrowing constraints on financing of otherwise deteriorating current accounts.

4.1   Initial effects

We now describe the initial effect of the interest shock, assuming constant relative commodity prices and without constraints on external finance. An increase in the G-7 real interest rates lowers demand for LMIC exportables. The NIESR GEM simulation exhibits a medium-term[9] import elasticity of −0.5, that is, a one percentage point increase in real interest rates leads to a fall in the growth rate of G-7 imports of the order of half a per cent. As a consequence LMIC exports and world trade are growing at a rate that is 0.4 per cent less than the baseline rate. The distribution of the export shock among LMIC regions depends on the composition of G-7 import cuts and the relative price inflexibility of LMIC exports of manufactures. Imports in the US are cut by more than the average, leading to a greater than average fall in Latin America's exports. China, on the other hand, by lowering prices is able to gain market shares and therefore sustain less of an export loss.

The rise in G-7 interest rates affects domestic rates in the LMICs. This changes the yield on domestic government bonds sold to the private sector and thereby disposable income. Government bonds are to a large extent variable-rate debt. In the model it is also assumed that private consumption and investment are interest sensitive, hence altering the savings and investment ratios.

The third channel works through increases in interest payments on LMIC debt owed to the G-7 countries. The change in debt service from a temporary interest shock depends crucially on the structure of long-term debt. Figure 11.6 shows the composition of long-term debt, divided between concessional debt, debt carrying a variable interest rate and fixed-rate debt. Of the $1,160 billion of total long-term debt stock owed by LMICs in 1991, variable-rate debt comprises $471 billion. Adding short-term debt, the total variable-rate debt stock is of the order of $691 billion. In the model simulation it is estimated that the average increase in interest payments from 1993 to 1996 is $6.4 billion per year, keeping in mind that nominal interest rates increase by 80 basis points, less than the 100 basis points for the real rates.

It is important to note that the current account for the LMICs deteriorates by an average of $2.4 billion per year through the same period, leading to a build-up of debt stocks above the baseline. Figure 11.7 shows the relationship between interest payments, current account, and debt outstanding in deviations relative to the baseline. Note that, even though interest rates converge to baseline levels by year 2002, the increase in interest payments does not. There are two reasons for this. Debt is permanently raised in these initial calculations. Second, LMIC import compression in the early years of the shock leads to pent-up demand for imported goods, causing a deterioration in the trade balance in later years as the countries catch up with investment and consumption plans. This, through current-account deficit accumulation, leads to a further increase in the stock of debt.

Other external factor flows change in response to higher interest rates. Receipts on foreign reserves holdings rise, thus increaing public-sector factor income. While returns on private foreign assets increase, foreign

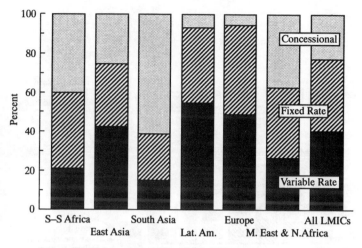

Source: *World debt tables, 1992–93*, World Bank.

Figure 11.6   Structure of long-term debt, 1991

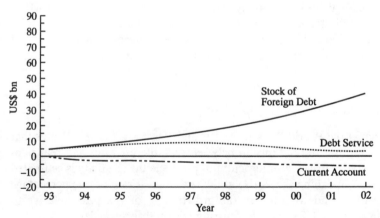

Source: BANK–GEM simulation.

Figure 11.7   Current account, interest payments and stock of debt: initial effects, low- and middle-income countries

investors are requiring a higher return on their equity holdings. As a result, the net effect depends on the stock of private-sector foreign assets, eventual capital flight and the accumulated level of foreign direct investment.

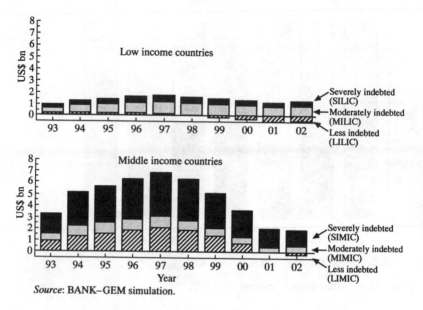

Source: BANK–GEM simulation.

Figure 11.8   Initial effects on debt service payments

On a regional basis it is analytically convenient to classify the LMICs according to indebtedness (severe, moderate, less) and income per capita (low and middle).[10] Figure 11.8 shows the composition of increased interest payments according to these categories. The brunt of the increase is carried by the severely indebted middle-income countries, whose average interest payments go up by $2.7 billion.

4.2   Results with commodity price effects added

Research at the World Bank (Palaskas and Varangis, 1990) indicates that there is a long-run relationship between real interest rates and real non-oil commodity prices. For agricultural products the elasticity is estimated to be −1.7, meaning that a rise in the real interest rate of one percentage point would lead to a fall in the growth rate of the price relative to manufactures of 1.7 per cent occurring with a three-year lag. For metals and minerals the elasticity is estimated to be 2.1.[11] Figure 11.9 depicts the price trajectories. Such a fall in the terms of trade has a major impact on the LMIC current accounts. About 20 per cent of LMIC exports originate from trade in non-oil commodities. Figure 11.10 shows the simulated effects on LMIC current accounts, debt stocks and interest payments. Comparing with Figure 11.7, the long-run effects are markedly different. The current-account impact for the period 1997–2002 is more

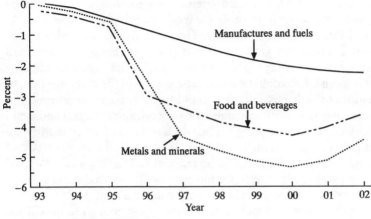

Source: BANK–GEM simulation.

Figure 11.9   World prices

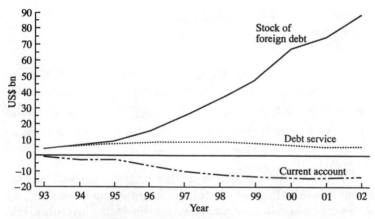

Source: BANK–GEM simulation.

Figure 11.10   Current account, debt service and stock of debt: commodity price effects added, all LMICs

than twice the size of the previous. The stock of accumulated additional debt more than doubles.

4.3   Results with external financial constraints also added

The previous analysis was conducted under the assumption that the LMICs would be able to obtain financing for the incurred current-account deficits. In a world of increased competition for funds this might be unrealistic for the severely and even the moderately indebted countries. As Figure 11.10 shows, debt stocks will not return to equilibrium values in ten years, but continue to grow. At some point mechanisms other than (intertemporal) borrowing must bring debt stocks back onto a sustainable path. This mechanism could be a real depreciation of the exchange rate, to the extent that this is possible, or it could be fiscal policy intervention to alter the savings rate. Both instruments have been applied again and again in debt-ridden countries during the last decade. In the final simulation an external solvency constraint is imposed. It is assumed that the stock of foreign debt ten years hence must be reduced to baseline levels. A fiscal feedback control rule is enacted for this purpose.[12] Government consumption for severely and moderately indebted countries contracts in order to compress private demand and thereby imports are enough to obtain the target value on the stock of debt by year 2002. Furthermore, it is assumed that the policy is implemented gradually over five years. The forward-looking control rule is specified formally as

$$\Delta G = -\phi \cdot \tau \cdot \frac{\Delta D_T}{Y\$_T} \cdot Y$$

where ΔG is the instrumental change in real government expenditures relative to baseline, ϕ is the feedback parameter, τ is a time profile parameter, τ = 0.2, 0.4, 0.6, 0.8, 1.0, 1.0, ..., $\frac{\Delta D_T}{Y\$_T}$ is the *ex ante* ratio of change (relative to baseline) in terminal period debt stock to terminal period baseline GP, with both debt and GDP valued in current US$ terms. Y is real GDP.

Let us for a moment concentrate on the severely indebted middle-income countries (SIMICs), which includes Argentina and Brazil. Figure 11.11 shows the change in government savings (including investments) in per cent of GDP for the case with no fiscal intervention and the case with the external solvency constraint. In the first case the government deficit widens by half a percent of GDP, while in the second case the government savings rate increases relative to the baseline in the second half of the simulation period. This forces the domestic savings rate back towards baseline values, and the current account actually improves relative to baseline after seven periods, see Figure 11.12. The interest payments are then financed by lowering the investment ratio, but in the long run this is reduced less with fiscal adjustment than without. This is in marked contrast to the first scenario, in which the domestic savings rate falls by 0.3 percentage points and stays there, and even though 0.2

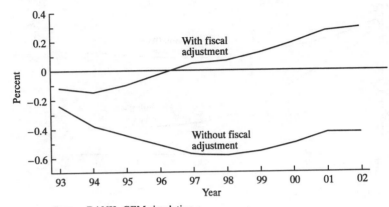

Source: BANK–GEM simulation.

Figure 11.11   Government savings in percent of GDP: severely indebted middle-income countries

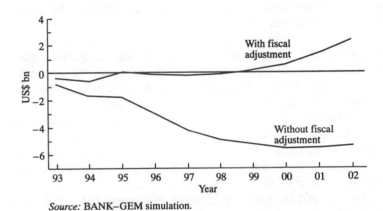

Source: BANK–GEM simulation.

Figure 11.12   Impact on current account: severely indebted middle-income countries

per cent of the savings short-fall is financed through the current account, the domestic investment ratio ends up falling more than in the case with active fiscal policy. In terms of GDP growth both scenarios return to baseline rates. But the price to be paid for external solvency amounts to 1 per cent of GDP. Figure 11.13 shows the trajectories for real GDP in percentage deviations from the baseline.

The bottom line is shown in Table 11.2. The increase in the G-7 real interest rate under the assumption of active fiscal intervention to bring

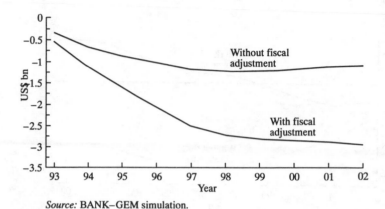

Source: BANK–GEM simulation.

Figure 11.13   Impact on real GDP: severely indebted middle-income countries

debt stocks back to baseline level on a ten-year horizon leads to an average fall in the GDP growth rate by 0.3 per cent for the severely indebted middle-income countries. For the severely indebted low-income countries the growth rate reduction averages 0.2 per cent. On the other hand, low-income countries such as China, with low indebtedness and high price flexibility, will incur little loss. In general, middle-income countries have a higher sensitivity of growth to interest rate variability than low-income countries. Part of the explanation, particularly applicable to severely indebted countries, is the greater proportion of variable-rate debt in their portfolio. Another reason, applicable to countries that are not severely indebted, is their greater integration into the world trading system. Table 11.3 illustrates this point by depicting a measure of openness for each of the regions, defined here as the sum of exports and imports as a share of GDP.

We can now invert the mapping of analytical regions and turn back to geographical aggregates. World GDP is estimated to grow 0.2 per cent slower during 1993–6 as a result of a 1 per cent increase in the real interest rate. On a ten-year horizon average world growth would be 0.1 per cent lower. The same holds true for the G-7 countries. But the developing countries are hurt more. LMIC growth is 0.3 per cent lower for the medium term and suffers 0.15 per cent for the decade average. The LMICs are as such affected one-and-a-half times the fall in G-7 GDP. This is in start contrast to the results of a G-7 fiscal shock (from another simulation, the results of which are not discussed in detail in this paper), in which the LMIC growth effects are estimated to be only 0.7 times the G-7 growth effects. An interest shock has twice the effect. Figure 11.14 summarizes

Table 11.2   Change in average growth rate, 1993–2002

	Less indebted	Moderately indebted	Severely indebted
Middle income	−0.11	−0.22	−0.31
Low income	−0.01	−0.12	−0.20

Table 11.3   Regional openness

	Less indebted	Moderately indebted	Severely indebted
Middle Income	78.0	57.7	41.9
Low income	30.9	29.8	41.4

Notes: Openness is defined as the sum of exports and imports as percent of GDP, average 1993 to 2002 baseline projections.

the GDP impact at a regional level. Latin America, as expected, is hurt the most, but also North and West Africa are impacted on severely due to high debt burdens. Eastern and Southern Africa mostly carry concessional debt at fixed rates. Their GDP short-fall is of the same order of magnitude as the world average. East Asia as a whole is hurt less than the G-7, mostly because of the resilient Chinese economy. Other countries in the region show greater sensitivity, of the same order of magnitude as the G-7 countries themselves. While South Asia is impacted on little if the external solvency constraint is not imposed, credit constraints bring the impact in line with the world average.

5   Conclusions

An adverse interest rate shock has significant consequences for LMIC growth performance, as was empirically well established during the 1980s. For a five-year rise in real interest rates of 100 basis points, we estimate that for LMICs as a whole growth rates will be reduced by 0.3 per cent per year in the medium term. Latin America is hurt the most, with reductions in growth rates of more than 0.5 per cent. Also North and West Africa are hurt seriously, with growth rate reductions of the order of 0.4 to 0.5 per cent. Asia, on the other hand, is more resilient in facing up to interest rate shocks.

The nature of the policy shift in the North is important in relating overall growth rates in the North to that of the South. Our earlier study of the effects of fiscal contractions in the North showed that, though the

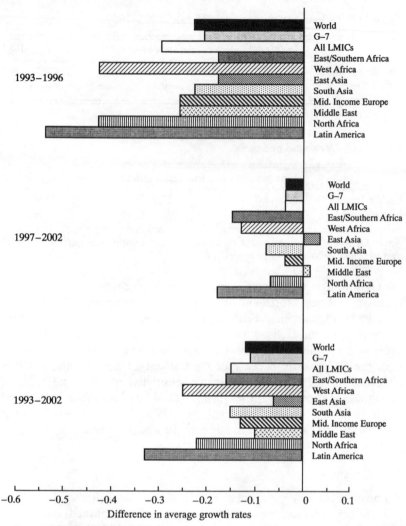

Source: BANK–GEM simulation.

Figure 11.14   Impact on growth of a rise in real interest rates of 100 basis points

LMIC growth rate followed that of the North downwards, it did not fall by as much, reducing only by some three-quarter of the fall in Northern growth. The present study of the effects of monetary contractions in the North, in contrast, indicates that LMICs suffer more than the North – the reduction in the LMIC growth rate is one-and-a-half times that of the North. Fiscal adjustment in the North, targetting government deficit reduction, lowers interest rates, which alleviates some of the negative impact of reduced exports from the South to the North. In contrast, an interest rate rise will lower trade as well as increase the debt burden of the South.

The impacts on developing country external accounts are amplified when we take into account movements in real commodity prices consequent to a real interest rate shock. When secondary effects stemming from terms-of-trade losses are incorporated, the debt stock of the LMICs could swell by almost $100 billion in the course of ten years, even if the interest shock only has a five-year duration. Unless adjustments are made to LMIC policies that increase the savings ratio the situation can clearly become unsustainable. On the other hand, prudent fiscal adjustment policies can bring the stock of foreign debt back to reasonable levels, but at a loss of up to 1 per cent of GDP in the short term relative to a 'muddling through' policy. However, prudent policies will eventually bring about higher investment to GDP ratios, that, together with lower debt, will make the South more resilient to future shocks.

NOTES

Views expressed in the paper are not attributable to the World Bank.

1 The terms 'South' and 'developing countries' will be used interchangeably in this paper.
2 For more details on this new trend see Global Economic Prospects, 1993, The World Bank.
3 Ambiguous because, while speculative capital will flow out, equity capital flow may come in due to diminished demand prospects in industrial countries.
4 See Palaskas and Varangis (1990) and Alogoskoufis and Varangis (1992).
5 BANK-GEM uses G-7 country models of NIGEM of the National Institute of Economic and Social Research together with the Bank-built developing country models for all other countries. The primary focus being low and middle-income developing countries (up to US$7,910 in GNP per capita in 1991), 92 LMIC models are specified in detail, the rest, including 'high income' non-OECD countries, receive a simplistic treatment.
6 See McCarthy et al. (1989), Riordan (1990) and Riordan (1991) for expositions of the Global Accounting Framework underlining the model, and the DEC Analytical Database, which serves as our main data source.
7 Data used for constructing bilateral trade flow matrices for the four-fold classification of goods for 144 countries have been obtained from the UN. We are grateful to Fred Campano at the UN and Ben Guerts of the Dutch Planning Office in helping us with this.
8 Canada is excluded for the simple reason that in NIGEM Canadian public sector accounts are not modelled in as much detail to permit this as in other G-7 countries.

9 'Medium-term' refers to the average impact of the first four years of the shock. The greatest impact on growth variables is typically in the second year.

10 For a mapping of countries to these groups according to World Bank, *Global Economic Prospects and the Developing countries*, 1993.

11 Palaskas and Varangis, p. 25 estimates a relationship between real interest rates and real commodity prices that can be summarized as follows:

$\dot{P} = -1.7(r_{-3} - r_{-5})$ for agricultural products

$\dot{P} = -2.1(r_{-3} - r_{-4})$ for metals and minerals.

12 This is an integral control rule targetting baseline current account.

REFERENCES

Alogoskoufis, G. and P. Varangis (1992) 'OECD fiscal policies and the relative prices of primary commodities', Policy Research Working Papers, WPS 955, World Bank, Washington DC.

McCarthy, F. D., B. Laury, E. J. Riordan and J. P. Zhou (1989) 'Global accounting framework: the basic system', in F. D. McCarthy (ed.), 'Developing countries in transition', vol. I, World Bank Discussion Paper, No. 63, World Bank, Washington DC, pp. 12–128.

NIESR (1993) *The National Institute World Model*, The National Institute of Economic and Social Research, London.

Palaskas, T. B. and P. Varangis (1990) 'Primary commodity prices and macroeconomic variables', Policy Research Working Papers, WPS 314, World Bank, Washington DC.

Pedersen, L. (1993) 'A macroeconomic developing country model: first step of a World Bank global economic model', International Economic Analysis and Prospects Division, The World Bank, Washington DC.

Petersen, C. E. (1991) *MAXSIM, An Econometric Software Package: User's Guide*, International Economic Analysis and Prospects Division, The World Bank, Washington DC.

Petersen, C. E. and K. N. Pedersen (1991) *MAXSIM, An Econometric Software Package: Reference Manual*, International Economic Analysis and Prospects Division, The World Bank, Washington DC.

Petersen, C. E., K. N. Pedersen, E. J. Riordan, R. A. Lynn and T. Bradley (1991) 'BANK-GEM: a World Bank global economic model', presented at the Project LINK Conference, Moscow, 23–7 September 1991.

Riordan, E. J. (1990) 'Global accounting framework: DEC analytical database. Progress toward a consistent database for analysis and modeling', in F. D. McCarthy (ed.), 'Problems of developing countries in the 1990s', Vol. I, World Bank Discussion Paper, No. 97, World Bank, Washington DC, pp. 148–230.

—— (1991) 'DEC analytical database: report on methods and data sources', International Economic Analysis and Prospects Division, The World Bank, Washington DC.

World Bank (1993) *Global Economic Prospects and the Developing Countries*, International Economics Department, The World Bank, Washington DC.

12 Quantifying North–South interdependencies with MCM simulations

JAIME MARQUEZ

1 Introduction

This paper uses the Federal Reserve Board Staff's Multicountry Model (MCM) to characterize interactions between developed and developing countries. Interest in these interactions stems from the increasingly important role of developing countries in world trade and finance markets. These interactions have been studied before but existing analyses rely on highly aggregative models, a reliance that carries a loss of information.[1] For example, Muscatelli and Vines (1989) and Soludo (1992) find that a fiscal expansion in all industrial countries lowers income for the bloc of developing countries. If this finding does not apply to *each* developing country, how can it be used for designing national policies?

The MCM is a large-scale, structural model that recognizes idiosyncrasies in countries' behaviour which are concealed in aggregative models. These idiosyncrasies stem from differences in legal systems and endowments of natural resources which are reflected in key parameters of a model: the degree of nominal rigidities, the substitutability between domestic and foreign products, the substitutability between money and bonds, and the responsiveness of output to changes in factor supplies. In addition, the MCM contains equations for Mexico and other developing country blocs which allows assessing both the loss of information associated with treating developing countries as a bloc and the role of external indebtedness in the international transmission of policy changes. Finally, the model's parameters are econometrically estimated. The alternative of assuming the values of these parameters recognizes country idiosyncrasies by chance and not by design.

I begin the analysis in Section 2 by describing the structure of a country model in the MCM. In Section 3, I use model simulations to quantify

North–South interdependencies. Specifically, I consider four scenarios: a fiscal contraction in the North, a fiscal contraction in the South, and two US fiscal contractions that differ in the stance of US monetary policy. The first two scenarios help quantify North–South interdependencies as such; the US fiscal scenarios serve to quantify the role of external indebtedness in US–Mexico interdependencies.

The simulation results reveal several findings of interest. First, a fiscal contraction in the North lowers income in the South except in Mexico, which underscores the loss of information associated with treating developing countries as a bloc, Second, a fiscal contraction in the South induces a small but sustained income loss in the North that, again, varies across industrial countries. Third, a US fiscal contraction with money targetting, by lowering US interest rates, reduces Mexico's external-debt service and stimulates its GDP despite the contraction in the US import market. Implementing this US fiscal contraction with interest rate targetting eliminates the beneficial effects of lower interest rates, accentuates the reduction in US real GDP and reduces Mexico's income.

2   Description of the model[2]

The MCM has in excess of 1,250 equations grouped into thirteen countries and regions: Canada, France, Germany, Italy, Japan, the United Kingdom, the United States, the Rest of the OECD (ROECD), Mexico, four Asian Newly Industrialized countries (NICs: Hong Kong, Singapore, South Korea and Taiwan), OPEC, the Soviet bloc and the Rest of the World (ROW). Table 12.1 shows a compact representation of the typical country model. The equations are grouped into eight sectors: domestic expenditure, government finance, international trade, monetary sector, aggregate supply, labour supply, prices and international finance.

The *domestic expenditures* sector explains real consumption and real investment. Consumption expenditures (equation (1)) (durable and non-durable) depend on real personal disposable income and the real interest rate; inflationary expectations are formed adaptively. Personal disposable income (equation (2)) equals labour income, net interest receipts and government transfers in excess of personal taxes.[3] Investment expenditures (equation (4)) (residential and non-residential) depend on gross output and real interest rates.[4] Real government purchases are treated as exogenous; real net exports are determined in the international trade sector.

The *government finance sector* determines nominal government expenditure, tax receipts, the government deficit and government debt.

Nominal government expenditures (equation (10)) equal the value of government consumption plus net transfer payments and interest payments on government debt. Government revenues (equation (9)) recognize differentials in tax rates across personal income, corporate profits and oil consumption.[5]

The *international trade sector* explains multilateral merchandise trade, non-factor services and factor services. Merchandise exports are disaggregated into non-oil and oil; non-oil exports (equation (13)) depend on foreign real income and relative prices. Oil exports are exogenous for all countries and regions except Mexico and OPEC. Mexico's oil exports equal the excess of oil production over oil demand. OPEC's oil exports equilibrate world demands and supplies of oil, which implies that (1) OPEC is the only significant net exporter of oil at the margin and (2) OPEC sets the price of oil and acts as the residual oil supplier.

Merchandise imports are also disaggregated into non-oil and oil. Non-oil imports (equation (16)) depend on real income and relative prices. Oil imports (equation (17)) equal the excess of oil requirements over the exogenously given level of oil production. Oil requirements consist of change in oil inventories and oil consumption (equation (29)); the latter depends on real income and relative prices. Non-factor services are explained in a manner analogous to non-oil merchandise trade. Exports of non-factor services (equation (14)) depend on foreign real income and relative prices; imports of non-factor services (equation (18)) depend on domestic real income and relative prices.

Finally, factor services are disaggregated, whenever possible, according to their source – portfolio or direct investment. Factor receipts (equation (19)) depend on the stock of claims on foreigners, interest rates and foreign income. Factor payments (equation (20) depend on the stock of liabilities to foreigners, the interest rate on those liabilities and domestic income.

The *monetary sector* explains real moneyholdings and interest rates. The nominal money supply in G-7 countries, France excluded, and the NICs is taken as given. For France and the ROECD, the money supply adjusts to peg their currencies to the DM. For Mexico, changes in the money supply depend on the balance of payments and the government deficit. The model does not have monetary sectors for OPEC, the Soviets and the ROW.

Assuming that real money holdings depend on real income and the nominal short-term interest rate, the model determines the nominal short-term interest rate using the equilibrium condition in the money market (equation (21)).[6] Short-term interest rates for France and the ROECD obey an open interest-parity condition *vis-à-vis* Germany. Finally,

Table 12.1   Prototype country model in the MCM: compact representation

Domestic expenditure

$$C = C(YD/PC, is - E\%\Delta PQ) \tag{1}$$
$$YD = L \cdot W \cdot (1 - \tau) + CAPRET \cdot (1 - \tau') + TR \tag{2}$$
$$CAPRET = f(is, il, YV, K) \tag{3}$$
$$I = I(Q, is - E\%\Delta PQ) \tag{4}$$
$$\Delta INV = F[C(-1) + I(-1) + G(-1), is - E\%\Delta PQ] \tag{5}$$
$$Y = C + I + G + \Delta INV + X - M \tag{6}$$
$$YV = PC \cdot C + PI \cdot I + PG \cdot G + PINV \cdot \Delta INV + PX \cdot X - PM \cdot M \tag{7}$$

Government finance

$$GDEF = EXP - T \tag{8}$$
$$T = L \cdot W \cdot \tau + CAPRET \cdot \tau' + CO \cdot \tau'' \tag{9}$$
$$EXP = PG \cdot G + TR + is \cdot GDEBT(-1) \tag{10}$$
$$GDEBT = GDEBT(-1) + GDEF \tag{11}$$

International trade

$$X = XNO + XO + XS \tag{12}$$
$$XNO = X(Y^*, PXNO/P^*) \tag{13}$$
$$XS = XS(Y^*, PXS/P^*) \tag{14}$$
$$M = MNO + MO + MS \tag{15}$$
$$MNO = M(Y, PMNO/P) \tag{16}$$
$$MO = CO + XO - QO \tag{17}$$
$$MS = MS(Y, PMS/P) \tag{18}$$
$$XSF/FA = XSF(is, is^*, Y^*) \tag{19}$$
$$MSF/FL = MSF(is, is^*, Y) \tag{20}$$

Monetary sector

$$MA/PC = MA(Y, is) \tag{21}$$
$$il = i(is, E\%\Delta PQ, il_{us}) \tag{22}$$

Aggregate supply

$$Q = Y + MO \tag{23}$$
$$Q = Q(K \cdot CU, L, CO) \tag{24}$$
$$QPOT = Q(K, LF, CO) \tag{25}$$
$$QPOT = YPOT + MO \tag{26}$$
$$K = K(-1) + I \tag{27}$$
$$CU = CU(Q/QPOT, L/LF) \tag{28}$$
$$CO = CO(Q, PO/PQ) \tag{29}$$

Labour supply

$$LF/POP = LF[W(1-\tau)/PG] \tag{30}$$
$$U = (LF - L)/LF \tag{31}$$
$$\%\Delta W = W(U, E\%\Delta PQ, Q/L) \tag{32}$$

Prices

$$Pj = Pj(PQ, PMNO), j = C, I, G, INV, XS, MS \tag{33}$$
$$PMNO = S \cdot PXNO^* \tag{34}$$
$$PQ = P(PO, W, QPOT/Q, Q/L) \tag{35}$$
$$PO = S \cdot PO^* + \tau'' \tag{36}$$
$$P = YV/Y \tag{37}$$

$$PSNO = PXNO\,(PQ,\,S\cdot PXNO^*) \tag{38}$$
$$PX = (PO\cdot XO + PXNO\cdot XNO + PXS\cdot XS)\,/X \tag{39}$$
$$PM = (PO\cdot MO + PMNO\cdot MNO + PMS\cdot MS)\,/M \tag{40}$$

International finance
$$S\cdot PQ_{us}/PQ = S\,[(il - E\%\,\Delta PQ) - (il_{us} - E\%\,\Delta PQ_{us})] \tag{41}$$
$$FA = FA\,(-1) + CAPOUT \tag{42}$$
$$CAPOUT = CAO\,(Y^*,\,is,\,is^*) \tag{43}$$
$$FL = FL\,(-1) + CAPIN \tag{44}$$
$$CAPIN = CAI\,(I,\,is,\,is^*) \tag{45}$$

Mnemonics:

C = Personal consumption
$CAPIN$ = Capital inflow
$CAPOUT$ = Capital outflow
$CAPRET$ = Return to capital
CO = Consumption of oil
CU = Capacity utilization
EXP = Government expenditures, nominal
FA = Foreign assets
FL = Foreign liabilities
G = Government purchases
$GDEBT$ = Government debt, nominal
$GDEF$ = Government deficit
I = Private fixed, gross investment
il = Long-term interest rate
INV = Inventories
is = Short-term interest rate
K = Capital stock
L = Employment
LF = Labour force
M = Imports of merchandise and non-factor services
MA = Monetary aggregate
MNO = Merchandise, non-oil imports, real
MO = Non-factor service imports, real
MS = Non-factor service inputs, real
MSF = Factor income payments
P = GDP deflator
PC = Deflator for consumption
PG = Deflator for government purchases
PI = Deflator for investment
$PINV$ = Deflator for inventory investment
PM = Deflator for imports of merchandise and non-factor services
$PMNO$ = Deflator for non-oil imports
PMS = Deflator for non-factor service imports
PO = Price of oil, domestic
POP = Population
PQ = Deflator for gross output
PX = Deflator for exports of merchandise and non-factor services
$PXNO$ = Deflator for non-oil exports

PXS = Deflator for non-factor service exports
Q = Gross output
QO = Domestic production of oil
$QPOT$ = Potential gross output
S = Exchange rate, local/US dollar, nominal
T = Government revenue
TR = Government transfers
τ, τ', τ'' = Tax rates
U = Unemployment rate
W = Wage rate
X = Exports of merchandise and non-factor services
XNO = Merchandise, non-oil exports, real
XO = Oil exports, real
XS = Non-factor service exports, real
XSF = Factor income receipts
Y = Real GDP
YD = Disposable income, nominal
$YPOT$ = Potential real GDP
YV = Nominal GDP
$*, us$ = foreign country, United States

long-term nominal interest rates (equation (22)) are determined with a term-structure relation augmented for inflationary expectations; for non-US countries, the term structure also includes the US long-term interest rate.

The *aggregate supply* sector determines labour requirements and potential output. To determine labour requirements, the model uses a Cobb–Douglas production function (equation (24)) where gross output (equation (23)) depends on employment, oil and capital adjusted for capacity utilization; for some countries, the model includes a time trend to capture neutral technological change. For given levels of capital, oil and real GDP, the production function is normalized on labour to yield labour requirements. Potential output is determined by substituting the full-employment levels of labour and capital into the production function (equation (25)). Thus developments affecting investment or the labour force influence potential output in the MCM. For developing countries, the production function is also Cobb–Douglas but with oil and capital as the sole productive factors. Thus this function only determines potential output.

For industrial countries, the *supply of labour* (equation (30)) depends on the after-tax real wage. Given the rate of inflation, the growth in productivity, and the level of unemployment, the model uses a Phillips curve to determine the growth rate of nominal wages (equation (32)). For developing countries, nominal wages depend on consumer prices and the gap between actual and potential GDP.

The *price sector* explains the price of gross output, the non-oil export price and the deflators for domestic spending. The price of gross output (equation (35)) depends on wages, the price of oil, growth in labour productivity and the gap between actual and potential output. The price of non-oil exports (equation (38)) depends on the price of gross output and the foreign non-oil export price expressed in local currency. Finally, the expenditure deflators (equation (33)) depend on the prices of gross output and non-oil imports to recognize that domestic and foreign products vary in importance across expenditure categories.

The *international-finance sector* explains exchange rates and changes in the external asset position. Based on Edison and Pauls (1993), the model assumes that an increase of 100 basis points in the US real, long-term interest rate differential raises each bilateral, real dollar rate by 5 per cent *vis-à-vis* the currencies of the G-7 except France (equation (41)). The currencies of France and the ROECD are pegged to the DM; the Mexican peso–US dollar rate follows the Mexico–US price differential; the dollar exchange rate for the NICs follows the open interest-parity condition *vis-à-vis* the United States; and the currencies of OPEC, the ROW and the Soviets are pegged to the US dollar. Finally, changes in claims on foreigners depend on foreign real GDP and differences in rates of return (equation (43)). Changes in liabilities to foreigners depend on domestic economic activity and interest rates (equation (45)).

3   Empirical findings

3.1   Estimation results

Given the simultaneous nature of the MCM, parameter estimation is carried out with instrumental variables using data through 1987. Selecting the functional form involved trade-offs between simplicity, consistency with the properties of the error term (normality, serial independence and homoskedasticity) and simulation properties. Table 12.2 shows the estimated long-run coefficients for selected equations. Inspection of these estimates suggests important differences in the structure of market interactions among these countries.[8]

3.2   Simulation results

For this paper, the G-7 countries and the ROECD constitute the North; Mexico, OPEC, the NICs and the ROW (except the Soviet bloc) constitute the South.[9] To quantify North–South interdependencies, I rely on dynamic simulations under four scenarios:

Table 12.2 Selected long-run coefficients of the MCM

	Canada	France	Germany	Italy	Japan	United Kingdom	United States	ROECD	Mexico	NICs	OPEC	ROW	Soviet
Consumption (mpc)													
Durable	0.666	0.179	{0.856	}	0.133	0.181	0.149	1.000	0.762	0.738	1.000	0.954	residual
Non-durable	0.773	1.300	0.600		0.539	1.000	0.953						
Non-oil imports													
Income elasticity	1.758	2.060	1.000	1.890	0.882	2.271	2.580	1.270	0.932	1.178	0.162	0.501	2.025
Price elasticity	−1.780	−0.551	−1.500	−0.313	−0.402	−0.649	−0.583	−0.583	−0.244	−0.671	−0.482	−0.303	−0.470
Non-oil exports													
Income elasticity	1.000	1.349	1.767	1.000	1.500	1.784	1.000	1.235	1.641	3.008		0.661	1.350
Price elasticity	−0.850	−0.280	−0.629	−0.970	−0.910	−0.549	−2.420	−0.949	−1.309	−1.216		−0.706	−0.108
Money demand													
Activity elasticity	1.126	1.186	1.850	1.000	1.240	4.080	0.913	0.100	1.506	1.590			
Interest elasticity	−0.105	−0.017	−0.018	−0.062	−0.050	−0.091	−0.006	−0.103	−0.007	−0.034			
Aggregate	M1	M3	M3	M2	M2	M4	M2	M2	M2	M2			
Long-term rates													
Short rate	0.639	0.848	0.236	1.000	0.401	0.353	0.864	0.348					
Expec. inflation			0.364		0.369	0.319	0.766						
US long-term rate			0.022			0.018		0.305					
Production function													
Labour	0.767	0.712	0.608	0.430	0.808	0.347	0.722	0.619	0.431	0.254		0.778	
Capital	0.196	0.210	0.334	0.368	0.153	0.600	0.235	0.577	0.569	0.572		0.203	
Oil	0.037	0.078	0.058	0.202	0.039	0.053	0.043	0.043		0.174		0.019	
Oil consumption													
Income elasticity	1.000	1.000	1.000	1.000	2.150	1.000	1.410	1.000	0.660	1.000	2.167		9.289
Price elasticity	−0.623	−0.680	−0.203	−0.489	−0.164	−0.472	−0.676	−0.062	0.000	−0.057	0.000	−0.100	−0.100

	Wages	Unemployment	Inflation	Capacity pressure	Domestic price (CPI for LDCs)	Labour	Oil	Import price
Wages	−0.430	−0.466	−0.567	−0.489	−0.440	−0.707	−1.285	−2.989
Unemployment	1.000	1.000	1.000	1.000	0.942	0.994	1.000	
Inflation							1.102	1.000
Capacity pressure							2.715	3.110
Domestic price (CPI for LDCs)								
Labour	0.493	0.679	0.686	0.652	0.549	0.887	0.842	0.939	0.373
Oil	0.036	0.090	0.061	0.177	0.029	0.190	0.077	0.590	
Import price							0.722	0.001	1.284

A1: A contraction of government consumption of each Northern country by 1 per cent of its real GDP.

A2: A contraction of government consumption of each Southern country by 1 per cent of its real GDP.

A3: A contraction of US government consumption by 1 per cent of US real GDP, with money targetting.

A4: A contraction of US government consumption by 1 per cent of US real GDP, with interest rate targeting.

These shocks are implemented at once (no phasing-in) and sustained from 1982(2) to 1987(4).

A1   North's fiscal contraction. A fiscal contraction in the North lowers the region's own real income by 1 per cent relative to baseline for the first year (Table 12.3). These losses diminish subsequently because the resulting downward pressure on interest rates stimulates private spending, which compensates for the decline of government purchases. After six years, the North's real income is 0.3 per cent above baseline; these crowding-in effects are faster in Germany and the United States than in Japan.

The reduction in the North's GDP spills over to the South as a decline in the demand for Southern products. This transmission channel is important because exports of the South constitute a large share of its GDP and are destined, by and large, to the North.[10] As a result, the initial 1 per cent reduction in the North's real GDP induces a 0.3 per cent reduction in the South's GDP. Income losses for the South reach a maximum of 0.7 per cent after three years and diminish afterwards as the crowding-in effects in the North gain importance. After six years, real income in the South is 0.3 per cent above baseline.

The results also indicate that the South's GDP contraction is not common to all developing countries. Indeed, Mexico's real GDP expands because of the stimulative effects of lower interest rates. Specifically, the decline in US nominal interest rates lowers the LIBOR rate (three-month dollar deposits) and reduces the interest rate that Mexico pays on its external debt. The resulting decline in interest payments improves the balance of payments, increases the money supply, and reduces Mexican interest rates. This reduction in interest rates stimulates Mexico's aggregate demand which more than offsets the loss of exports. Muscatelli and Vines (1989) and Soludo (1992) find an inverse relation between fiscal expenditures in the North and income in the South. The MCM predicts that this inverse association applies to Mexico and not the South as a whole.

A2 South's fiscal contraction. A contractionary fiscal policy in the South lowers the region's income by 1.5 per cent in the first quarter and by 6.1 per cent after six years (Table 12.4). This relatively large fiscal multiplier is dominated by the decline in ROW's real GDP (not shown) which reaches 8.1 per cent after six years and has a weight of 52.8 per cent in the South's aggregate.[11] The decline in ROW's GDP is due to the absence of both a monetary sector and automatic stabilizers in that country's model, two limitations due to lacking data. For Mexico, the fiscal contraction reduces real GDP by 1.5 per cent in the first quarter and by 3.1 per cent after six years, despite the reduction in domestic *nominal* interest rates. The fiscal contraction creates an excess capacity that lowers prices, raises *real* interest rates, and exacerbates the decline in aggregate demand induced by the fiscal contraction.

The contractionary fiscal policy in the South spills over to the North as a lower demand for Northern products. This contraction in the South's import markets is reflected in a deterioration of the balances of trade for the G-3 countries. The resulting income loss of the North, though sustained, is not large because a relatively small share of their exports are destined to the South.[12] Moreover, this income loss is not uniform across countries. Specifically, Japan's income losses exceed the North's average because nearly half of its exports are destined to the South. The reduction in US income is smaller than that of Japan despite devoting nearly as much exports to the South because exports are more important in Japan, as a share of GDP, than in the United States. Germany's income loss is similar to that of Japan despite having a smaller share of exports flowing to the South because of third-country effects: Germany exports to countries that export to the South.

A3 US fiscal contraction – monetary targetting. A contraction in US government purchases, assuming money targeting, lowers US real GDP by 0.9 per cent in the first quarter (Table (12.5). This contraction diminishes over time because the decline in both interest rates and the dollar stimulate private spending offsetting the fiscal contraction. Economic activity in Japan experiences a small decline because the appreciation of the yen and the contraction of the US market are not offset by the stimulative effects of lower Japanese interest rates. Similarly, Germany's real income is largely unaffected by the contraction in US government purchases.

Lower US real income reduces imports from developing countries. But unlike the case of a North-wide fiscal contraction, income in the South increases. This increase in South's GDP is due to increases in ROW's and Mexico's GDP. ROW's income increases because its currency

Table 12.3 Global fiscal contractions: fiscal contraction in the North

	1982(1)	1982(2)	1982(3)	1982(4)	1983(1)	1983(2)	1983(3)	1983(4)	1984(4)	1985(4)	1986(4)	1987(4)
GNP/GDP (%)												
US	0.0	−1.0	−1.0	−1.0	−0.9	−0.8	−0.7	−0.7	−0.6	−0.4	−0.1	0.1
Japan	0.0	−1.3	−1.4	−1.5	−1.5	−1.5	−1.4	−1.4	−1.2	−1.1	−1.1	−1.0
Germany	0.0	−1.1	−1.2	−1.2	−1.1	−1.0	−1.0	−1.0	−0.8	−0.5	−0.2	0.2
North	0.0	−1.0	−1.1	−1.1	−1.0	−1.0	−0.9	−0.9	−0.6	−0.4	−0.1	0.3
Mexico	0.0	0.0	0.0	0.1	0.1	0.1	0.1	0.1	0.2	0.3	0.3	0.4
South	0.0	−0.3	−0.2	−0.3	−0.4	−0.5	−0.6	−0.6	−0.7	−0.5	−0.2	0.3
Short rates (+/−)												
US	0.0	−1.5	−1.5	−1.4	−1.3	−1.3	−1.3	−1.3	−1.7	−1.9	−1.9	−1.8
Japan	0.0	−0.5	−0.5	−0.5	−0.5	−0.6	−0.6	−0.5	−0.5	−0.5	−0.5	−0.5
Germany	0.0	−0.3	−0.5	−0.7	−0.8	−0.9	−1.0	−1.0	−1.2	−1.4	−1.4	−1.4
Mexico	0.0	−1.8	−2.1	−1.9	−1.7	−1.7	−1.5	−1.4	−1.6	−0.8	0.4	1.4
Long rates (+/−)												
US	0.0	−0.6	−0.6	−0.7	−0.7	−0.7	−0.8	−0.8	−1.2	−1.4	−1.6	−1.6
Japan	0.0	−0.2	−0.2	−0.3	−0.3	−0.3	−0.3	−0.3	−0.4	−0.4	−0.5	−0.4
Germany	0.0	−0.2	−0.2	−0.2	−0.2	−0.3	−0.3	−0.3	−0.4	−0.5	−0.6	−0.6
Expected inflation (+/−)												
US	0.0	0.0	−0.1	−0.2	−0.3	−0.3	−0.4	−0.5	−0.5	−0.5	−0.4	−0.2
Japan	0.0	0.0	−0.1	−0.1	−0.1	−0.2	−0.2	−0.2	−0.2	−0.2	−0.2	−0.2
Germany	0.0	0.0	0.0	−0.1	−0.1	−0.1	−0.2	−0.2	−0.3	−0.4	−0.5	−0.5
Unemployment (+/−)												
US	0.0	0.8	0.7	0.6	0.6	0.5	0.4	0.4	0.3	0.1	−0.1	−0.3
Japan	0.0	1.4	1.5	1.5	1.5	1.4	1.3	1.2	0.9	0.8	0.6	0.4
Germany	0.0	1.4	1.5	1.4	1.2	1.1	1.0	1.0	0.7	0.3	−0.1	−0.4

Trade bal bn US$ (+/−)												
US	0.0	1.4	4.4	5.8	6.8	6.8	7.1	7.3	7.9	9.0	11.3	14.9
Japan	0.0	1.7	1.7	1.6	1.2	0.7	0.4	0.4	0.1	0.5	0.6	2.1
Germany	0.0	1.6	0.9	0.4	−0.1	−0.3	−0.4	−0.4	0.2	1.5	4.3	8.7
Mexico	0.0	0.0	0.0	−0.1	−0.1	−0.1	−0.1	−0.1	−0.1	−0.1	−0.1	0.0
Consumer prices (%)												
US	0.0	0.0	−0.1	−0.2	−0.2	−0.4	−0.5	−0.6	−0.9	−1.1	−1.3	−1.4
Japan	0.0	−0.1	−0.2	−0.2	−0.3	−0.3	−0.4	−0.4	−0.6	−0.8	−1.0	−1.1
Germany	0.0	0.0	−0.1	−0.1	−0.1	−0.2	−0.2	−0.3	−0.6	−1.0	−1.5	−2.0
Mexico	0.0	0.0	−0.1	−0.2	−0.2	−0.3	−0.4	−0.5	−0.8	−1.1	−1.5	−1.7
Exchange rates (%)												
US – G-10 fx/$	0.0	−2.0	−1.8	−1.5	−1.1	−1.0	−0.7	−0.7	−1.9	−3.4	−4.8	−6.1
Japan – $/Yen	0.0	1.9	1.7	1.5	1.1	0.8	0.6	0.6	1.4	2.3	3.2	4.3
Germany – $/DM	0.0	2.1	1.8	1.4	1.0	0.9	0.7	0.6	1.8	3.3	4.7	6.2
Mexico – $/Peso	0.0	0.0	0.0	0.0	0.0	0.0	−0.1	−0.1	−0.1	0.0	0.1	0.3

Note: Per cent (%) and absolute (+/−) deviations from baseline

Table 12.4 Global fiscal contractions: fiscal contraction in the South

	1982(1)	1982(2)	1982(3)	1982(4)	1983(1)	1983(2)	1983(3)	1983(4)	1984(4)	1985(4)	1986(4)	1987(4)
GNP/GDP (%)												
US	0.0	0.0	-0.1	-0.1	-0.1	-0.1	-0.1	-0.1	-0.1	-0.1	-0.1	-0.1
Japan	0.0	-0.1	-0.2	-0.3	-0.4	-0.4	-0.5	-0.6	-0.7	-0.7	-0.6	-0.6
Germany	0.0	-0.1	-0.2	-0.3	-0.3	-0.4	-0.4	-0.5	-0.6	-0.5	-0.3	-0.2
North	0.0	-0.1	-0.1	-0.1	-0.2	-0.2	-0.2	-0.2	-0.3	-0.2	-0.1	0.1
Mexico	0.0	-1.3	-1.4	-1.6	-1.8	-2.0	-2.1	-2.1	-2.4	-2.7	-2.7	-3.0
South	0.0	-1.5	-2.2	-2.8	-3.4	-3.8	-4.2	-4.5	-5.4	-5.8	-5.9	-6.1
Short rates (+/−)												
US	0.0	-0.1	-0.1	-0.1	-0.1	-0.2	-0.2	-0.2	-0.3	-0.4	-0.5	-0.5
Japan	0.0	0.0	-0.1	-0.1	-0.1	-0.2	-0.2	-0.2	-0.3	-0.3	-0.3	-0.3
Germany	0.0	0.0	-0.1	-0.1	-0.2	-0.2	-0.3	-0.3	-0.5	-0.7	-0.8	-0.9
Mexico	0.0	-1.1	-1.3	-1.1	-0.8	-0.6	-0.5	-0.8	-1.0	-0.3	1.2	-5.0
Long rates (+/−)												
US	0.0	0.0	0.0	-0.1	-0.1	-0.1	-0.1	-0.1	-0.2	-0.3	-0.3	-0.4
Japan	0.0	0.0	0.0	0.0	-0.1	-0.1	-0.1	-0.1	-0.2	-0.2	-0.2	-0.2
Germany	0.0	0.0	0.0	0.0	-0.1	-0.1	-0.1	-0.1	-0.2	-0.2	-0.3	-0.3
Expected inflation (+/−)												
US	0.0	0.0	0.0	0.0	0.0	0.0	0.0	0.0	-0.1	-0.1	-0.1	-0.1
Japan	0.0	0.0	0.0	0.0	0.0	0.0	0.0	0.0	-0.1	-0.1	-0.1	-0.1
Germany	0.0	0.0	0.0	0.0	0.0	0.0	0.0	0.0	-0.1	-0.2	-0.2	-0.3
Unemployment (+/−)												
US	0.0	0.0	0.0	0.1	0.1	0.1	0.1	0.1	0.1	0.1	0.0	0.0
Japan	0.0	0.1	0.2	0.3	0.4	0.4	0.5	0.5	0.6	0.6	0.4	0.3
Germany	0.0	0.1	0.3	0.4	0.4	0.5	0.5	0.5	0.6	0.4	0.2	0.0

Trade bal bn US$ (+/−)												
US	0.0	−1.2	−1.7	−2.1	−2.7	−3.1	−3.5	−4.1	−5.3	−5.6	−6.2	−7.8
Japan	0.0	−0.8	−1.4	−1.9	−2.4	−3.1	−3.5	−4.1	−5.6	−6.9	−8.2	−9.3
Germany	0.0	−0.3	−0.6	−1.0	−1.4	−1.7	−1.8	−2.1	−2.7	−3.5	−3.8	−3.5
Mexico	0.0	1.1	1.0	1.1	1.1	1.1	1.1	1.0	1.1	1.0	0.8	0.9
Consumer prices (%)												
US	0.0	0.0	0.0	0.0	0.0	0.0	−0.1	−0.1	−0.1	−0.2	−0.3	−0.3
Japan	0.0	0.0	0.0	0.0	0.0	−0.1	−0.1	−0.1	−0.2	−0.3	−0.4	−0.5
Germany	0.0	0.0	0.0	0.0	0.0	0.0	0.0	−0.1	−0.2	−0.3	−0.5	−0.8
Mexico	0.0	−0.1	−0.3	−0.5	−0.8	−1.1	−1.5	−2.0	−4.2	−6.9	−10.5	−14.6
Exchange rates (%)												
US − G-10 fx/$	0.0	−0.1	−0.1	−0.1	−0.1	−0.1	−0.1	−0.1	−0.2	−0.5	−1.0	−1.5
Japan − $/Yen	0.0	0.0	0.0	0.0	0.0	0.0	0.0	0.1	0.1	0.3	0.5	0.8
Germany − $/DM	0.0	0.1	0.1	0.1	0.1	0.1	0.0	0.1	0.2	0.5	1.1	1.6
Mexico − $/Peso	0.0	0.0	0.1	0.3	0.6	0.9	1.3	1.8	4.1	7.2	11.1	15.6

Note: Per cent (%) and absolute (+/−) deviations from baseline

Table 12.5 US fiscal contraction: monetary targetting

	1982(1)	1982(2)	1982(3)	1982(4)	1983(1)	1983(2)	1983(3)	1983(4)	1984(4)	1985(4)	1986(4)	1987(4)
GNP/GDP (%)												
US	0.0	−0.9	−0.9	−0.9	−0.8	−0.7	−0.7	−0.6	−0.5	−0.4	−0.1	0.1
Japan	0.0	−0.1	−0.1	−0.1	−0.1	−0.1	−0.1	−0.1	−0.0	−0.1	−0.1	0.0
Germany	0.0	0.0	0.0	0.0	0.0	0.0	0.0	0.0	0.0	0.0	0.1	0.1
North	0.0	−0.5	−0.4	−0.4	−0.4	−0.3	−0.3	−0.3	−0.2	−0.1	0.0	0.2
Mexico	0.0	0.0	0.0	0.1	0.1	0.1	0.1	0.1	0.2	0.3	0.4	0.5
South	0.0	0.0	0.1	0.1	0.1	0.1	0.1	0.0	0.0	0.2	0.4	0.9
Short rates (+/−)												
US	0.0	−1.4	−1.4	−1.3	−1.2	−1.2	−1.1	−1.1	−1.5	−1.7	−1.8	−1.7
Japan	0.0	−0.1	−0.1	−0.1	−0.1	0.0	0.0	0.0	0.0	−0.1	0.0	0.0
Germany	0.0	0.0	−0.1	−0.1	−0.1	−0.1	−0.1	−0.1	−0.1	−0.1	−0.1	−0.1
Mexico	0.0	−1.7	−1.9	−1.7	−1.5	−1.5	−1.3	−1.2	−1.4	−0.7	0.5	1.5
Long rates (+/−)												
US	0.0	−0.6	−0.6	−0.6	−0.6	−0.7	−0.7	−0.7	−1.1	−1.3	−1.4	−1.5
Japan	0.0	0.0	0.0	0.0	0.0	0.0	0.0	0.0	0.0	0.0	0.0	0.0
Germany	0.0	−0.1	−0.1	−0.1	0.0	0.0	0.0	0.0	−0.1	−0.1	−0.1	−0.1
Expected inflation (+/−)												
US	0.0	0.0	−0.1	−0.2	−0.2	−0.3	−0.4	−0.4	−0.5	−0.5	−0.4	−0.2
Japan	0.0	0.0	0.0	0.0	0.0	−0.1	0.0	0.0	0.0	0.0	0.0	0.0
Germany	0.0	0.0	0.0	0.0	0.0	0.0	0.0	0.0	0.0	−0.1	−0.1	−0.1
Unemployment (+/−)												
US	0.0	0.8	0.7	0.6	0.5	0.4	0.4	0.4	0.2	0.1	−0.1	−0.3
Japan	0.0	0.1	0.1	0.1	0.1	0.1	0.1	0.0	0.0	0.0	0.0	−0.1
Germany	0.0	0.0	0.0	0.0	0.0	0.0	0.1	0.0	0.0	0.0	0.0	−0.1

Trade bal bn US$ (+/−)												
US	0.0	2.6	5.7	7.2	8.4	8.5	9.0	9.5	10.6	11.5	13.9	17.7
Japan	0.0	0.7	0.5	0.1	−0.5	−0.7	−0.9	−1.0	−0.6	−0.3	−0.1	0.5
Germany	0.0	0.9	0.8	0.6	0.4	0.3	0.2	0.1	0.4	1.1	2.4	4.4
Mexico	0.0	0.0	0.0	−0.1	−0.1	−0.1	−0.1	−0.1	−0.1	−0.1	−0.1	0.0
Consumer prices (%)												
US	0.0	0.0	−0.1	−0.2	−0.2	−0.3	−0.4	−0.5	−0.8	−1.0	−1.2	−1.3
Japan	0.0	0.0	−0.1	−0.1	−0.1	−0.1	−0.1	−0.1	−0.1	−0.1	−0.1	−0.1
Germany	0.0	0.0	0.0	−0.1	−0.1	−0.1	−0.1	−0.1	−0.2	−0.3	−0.3	−0.5
Mexico	0.0	0.0	−0.1	−0.2	−0.2	−0.3	−0.4	−0.4	−0.7	−1.0	−1.2	−1.3
Exchange rates (%)												
US – G-10 fx/$	0.0	−2.3	−2.2	−1.9	−1.4	−1.3	−1.0	−0.8	−1.5	−2.5	−3.5	−4.6
Japan – $/Yes	0.0	2.5	2.3	2.0	1.5	1.4	1.0	0.8	1.4	2.4	3.3	4.3
Germany – $/DM	0.0	2.3	2.1	1.8	1.4	1.3	1.0	0.8	1.5	2.4	3.3	4.3
Mexico – $/Peso	0.0	0.0	0.0	0.0	0.0	0.0	−0.1	−0.1	−0.1	−0.1	−0.1	0.0

Note: Per cent (%) or absolute (+/−) deviations from baseline

Table 12.6 US fiscal contraction: interest rate targetting

	1982(1)	1982(2)	1982(3)	1982(4)	1983(1)	1983(2)	1983(3)	1983(4)	1984(4)	1985(4)	1986(4)	1987(4)
GNP/GDP (%)												
US	0.0	-1.1	-1.2	-1.4	-1.6	-1.7	-1.9	-2.1	-3.1	-4.8	-7.4	-10.8
Japan	0.0	-0.1	-0.1	-0.1	-0.1	-0.2	-0.2	-0.2	-0.3	-0.6	-0.8	-1.3
Germany	0.0	0.0	-0.1	-0.1	-0.1	-0.1	-0.2	-0.2	-0.4	-0.6	-0.9	-1.6
North	0.0	-0.5	-0.5	-0.6	-0.7	-0.8	-0.8	-0.9	-1.4	-2.1	-3.2	-4.8
Mexico	0.0	0.0	0.0	0.0	-0.1	-0.1	-0.1	-0.1	0.0	0.0	-1.0	-1.5
South	0.0	-0.2	-0.4	-0.5	-0.8	-1.1	-1.5	-1.8	-3.9	-6.8	-11.3	-17.9
Short rates (+/−)												
US	0.0	0.0	0.0	0.0	0.0	0.0	0.0	0.0	0.0	0.0	0.0	0.0
Japan	0.0	0.0	0.0	0.0	0.0	0.0	0.0	0.0	0.0	0.0	-0.2	-0.2
Germany	0.0	0.0	0.0	0.0	0.0	0.0	0.0	0.0	0.0	-0.1	-0.3	-0.5
Mexico	0.0	-0.2	-0.2	-0.2	-0.2	-0.3	-0.3	-0.5	-0.9	-1.5	-4.3	-9.6
Long rates (+/−)												
US	0.0	0.0	0.0	0.0	0.0	-0.1	-0.1	-0.1	-0.3	-0.6	-1.0	-1.6
Japan	0.0	0.0	0.0	0.0	0.0	0.0	0.0	0.0	0.1	0.1	0.0	0.0
Germany	0.0	0.0	0.0	0.0	0.0	0.0	0.1	0.1	0.1	0.1	0.1	0.2
Expected inflation (+/−)												
US	0.0	0.0	-0.1	-0.2	-0.3	-0.5	-0.6	-0.8	-1.5	-2.4	-3.6	-5.5
Japan	0.0	0.0	0.0	0.0	0.0	0.0	0.0	0.0	0.1	0.1	0.0	0.0
Germany	0.0	0.0	0.0	0.0	0.0	0.0	0.0	0.0	0.1	0.2	0.1	0.2
Unemployment (+/−)												
US	0.0	0.9	0.9	1.0	1.1	1.1	1.2	1.3	2.0	3.0	4.5	6.4
Japan	0.0	0.1	0.1	0.1	0.1	0.1	0.2	0.2	0.3	0.5	0.6	1.1
Germany	0.0	0.1	0.1	0.1	0.1	0.2	0.2	0.2	0.4	0.6	0.9	1.6

Trade bal bn US$ (+/−)											
US	0.0	4.9	7.8	9.3	11.0	12.5	14.6	16.8	26.7	42.4	63.1	95.8
Japan	0.0	−0.7	−1.2	−1.8	−2.2	−2.9	−3.6	−4.6	−9.1	−17.1	−28.9	−45.1
Germany	0.0	−0.2	−0.5	−0.9	−1.4	−1.7	−2.0	−2.4	−5.1	−10.1	−20.7	−35.7
Mexico	0.0	0.0	0.0	0.0	−0.1	−0.1	−0.1	−0.2	−0.1	−0.2	−0.6	−0.9
Consumer prices (%)											
US	0.0	−0.1	−0.2	−0.4	−0.5	−0.7	−0.9	−1.1	−2.3	−4.0	−6.6	−10.3
Japan	0.0	0.0	0.0	0.0	0.0	0.1	0.1	0.1	0.3	0.4	0.3	0.4
Germany	0.0	0.0	0.0	0.0	0.0	0.0	0.1	0.1	0.3	0.6	1.0	1.5
Mexico	0.0	0.0	−0.1	−0.2	−0.3	−0.4	−0.5	−0.7	−1.7	−3.4	−6.5	−11.7
Exchange rates (%)											
US – G-10 fx/$	0.0	0.2	0.7	1.3	2.1	2.9	3.8	4.9	9.8	16.8	27.0	44.4
Japan – $/Yen	0.0	−0.2	−0.7	−1.4	−2.2	−3.1	−4.1	−5.1	−10.0	−16.8	−26.5	−43.8
Germany – $/DM	0.0	−0.2	−0.6	−1.3	−2.0	−2.8	−3.7	−4.7	−9.5	−16.3	−26.6	−43.7
Mexico – $/Peso	0.0	0.0	−0.1	−0.2	−0.2	−0.2	−0.4	−0.4	−0.7	−0.8	−0.4	1.2

Note: Per cent (%) or absolute (+/−) deviations from baseline

is pegged to the dollar which is depreciating. Mexico's real GDP expands because of the declines in both its terms of trade and interest rates. The decline in its terms of trade is induced by deflationary forces in the United States, that, by lowering Mexico's import prices, reduce consumer prices, wages, and export prices. The decline in Mexican interest rates stems from the reduction in US interest rates which reduces the LIBOR rate, lowers Mexico's debt service, improves the balance of payments, and increases the nominal money supply. In addition, Mexico's imported deflation raises the real stock of real money.[13]

A4   US fiscal contraction – interest rate targetting. A US fiscal contraction with (short-term) interest rate targetting induces a substantial contraction in US real GDP (Table 12.6). This fall in aggregate demand lowers prices and raises real interest rates, dampening aggregate demand further. These deflationary pressures appreciate the dollar and, by reducing net exports, compound the decline in real GDP which has significant spillover effects on both Germany and Japan. Specifically, after six years, real income in Germany and Japan declines by 1.3 per cent and 1.6 per cent, respectively. These income changes were virtually absent in the case of US money targetting, a result underscoring the importance of monetary policy in quantifying international interdependencies.

The importance of the US policy mix is also apparent for Southern countries which, unlike in the previous scenario, experience substantial declines in real income. The sharpest decline in real GDP is for ROW (not shown) given that (1) ROW's currency is pegged to the US dollar, which is appreciating, and (2) the ROW sector lacks a money market which would, by lowering interest rates, dampen the loss of income.

For the first four years, Mexico's real GDP is largely unaffected by the change in the US policy mix; for the last two years, Mexico's real GDP declines. The initial period of relative GDP stability is the result of two mutually offsetting effects. First, the decline in US GDP lowers Mexican exports and real GDP. Second, the deflationary pressures in the United States lower Mexican import prices, which then reduces all other Mexican prices. This imported deflation raises the real money supply, lowers interest rates, and stimulates aggregate demand by enough to offset the loss of exports. After four years, the reduction in US GDP is very large, which induces losses of exports that are not offset by the accompanying deflation.

NOTES

I have benefited from comments by Beatriz Armendariz de Aghion, William Helkie, Cathy Mann, the participants in the CEPR Conference on North–South Interactions, the editors of this volume, and an anonymous referee. The views expressed in this paper are solely the responsibility of the author and should not be interpreted as reflecting those of the Board of Governors of the Federal Reserve System or other members of its staff.

1 Examples of aggregative models include Marquez and Pauly (1987), Beenstock (1988), and Currie *et al.* (1988).

2 The last documented version of the MCM appears in Edison *et al.* (1987). Since then, the MCM has been updated to allow more countries, extend the estimation sample, and recognize the simultaneity in parameter estimation. The development and implementation of the 1992 version of the MCM was a joint effort with William Helkie; details of the changes are available on request.

3 Data constraints for developing countries limit the degree of disaggregation in the components of domestic expenditures and preclude explaining both personal disposable income and its components. For example, the model explains Mexico's aggregate consumption with real, per-capita GDP instead of disposable income.

4 Mexico's investment also depends on merchandise non-oil imports to recognize (1) the complementarity between domestic and foreign capital and (2) the role of foreign exchange constraints on investment.

5 Again, data limitations for developing countries preclude such a differentiation of taxes.

6 For Mexico, the demand for real balances depends on real GDP and the interest rate differential with respect to the United States (currency-substitution effect).

7 Mexican capital outflows depend on the US–Mexico differential in short-term nominal interest rates. Mexican capital inflows, in real terms, depend on Mexico's gross fixed investment. This formulation says that foreign investors are motivated to invest in Mexico by the same factors that motivate Mexicans to invest domestically.

8 Mexico has experienced substantial changes in the post-sample period, such as the introduction of the Brady plan, the implementation of adjustment policies, and the prospect of participating in a free-trade agreement with Canada and the United States. These changes affect the economy as a whole and I do not know how specific parameter estimates might change, if at all, in response to extending the sample period.

9 The weights for constructing these aggregates are the average shares for each country's GDP in the group's constant dollar, constant price, real GDP. The weights for the Northern countries are 3.7 per cent for Canada, 4.1 per cent for France, 7.6 per cent for Germany, 2.7 per cent for Italy, 15 per cent for Japan, 5.3 per cent for the United Kingdom, 42.6 per cent for the United States, and 19 per cent for ROECD. The weights for the Southern countries are 5.3 per cent for Mexico, 11.1 per cent for NICs, 30.8 per cent for OPEC, and 52.8 per cent for ROW.

10 The shares of non-oil exports destined to the North are 64 per cent for the NICs, 87.6 per cent for Mexico, 86 per cent for ROW and 82 per cent for OPEC.

11 The previous version of this paper, circulated at the conference, shows detailed responses for all the countries in the MCM.
12 The average shares of non-oil exports destined to the South are 14 per cent for Canada, 30 per cent for France, 22 per cent for Germany, 29 per cent for Italy, 47 per cent for Japan, 30 per cent for the United Kingdom and 42 per cent for the United States.
13 These declines in interest rates, however, are self-correcting because they lower the government's interest payments and budget deficit, and thus contract the money supply.

REFERENCES

Beenstock, M. (1988) 'An econometric investigation of North–South interdependence', in D. Currie and D. Vines (eds.), *Macroeconomic Interactions between North and South*, Cambridge: Cambridge University Press.

Currie, D., D. Vines, T. Moutos, A. Muscatelli and N. Vadalis (1988) 'North–South interactions: a general equilibrium framework for the study of the strategic issues', in D. Currie and D. Vines (eds.), *Macroeconomic Interactions between North and South*, Cambridge: Cambridge University Press.

Edison, H., J. Marquez and R. Tryon (1987) 'The structure and properties of the FRB multicountry model', *Economic Modelling* 4, 115–315.

Edison, H. and D. Pauls (1993) 'Re-assessment of the relationship between real exchange rates and real interest rates', *Journal of Monetary Economics* 31, 165–88.

Marquez, J. and P. Pauly (1987) 'International policy coordination and growth prospects of developing countries', *Journal of Development Economics* 25, 89–104.

Muscatelli, A. and D. Vines (1989) 'Macroeconomic interactions between the North and the South', in R. Bryant, D. Currie, J. Frenkel, P. Masson and R. Portes (eds.), *Macroeconomic Policies in an Interdependent World*, Centre for Economic Policy Research, London.

Soludo, C. (1992) 'North–South macroeconomic interactions: comparative analysis using the Multimod and Intermod global models', Brookings Discussion Papers in International Economics, No. 95, The Brookings Institution, Washington DC.

Discussion

BEATRIZ ARMENDARIZ DE AGHION

In this paper Jaime Marquez describes the latest version of the Federal Reserve Board's Multicountry model (MCM), and illustrates its usefulness by simulating the impact that the US macroeconomic policy would have on Mexico. His main finding is that fiscal contraction in the US – in particular when the US authorities target money supply – will have both a negative and a positive effect on the Mexican economy. Negative because as a result of fiscal contraction the US will experience a recession which will, in turn, decrease demand for Mexican exports. Positive because fiscal contraction lowers interest rates in the US and this decreases Mexican foreign debt services. The latter effect is shown to offset the former, and hence the author concludes that Mexico would benefit from fiscal contraction in the US.

Marquez' contribution to the debate on increased economic interdependence between Mexico and the US is a timely one, particularly because of: (a) falling US interest rates and LIBOR in recent years, and (b) the recent ratification by the US Congress of the North American Free Trade Agreement (NAFTA).

However, since the data used to estimate the parameters goes only to 1987, the paper's main result can be questioned on two grounds. First, the analysis excludes the debt reduction (Brady deal) Mexico obtained from its external creditors in 1989; and thus the beneficial effect from a lower interest rate in the US is greatly exaggerated. The reason is that under such a debt reduction agreement, 46.7 per cent of the Mexican external debt has been converted into 'par bonds' at a *fixed interest rate*.[1] Second, the analysis excludes NAFTA, and thus the potentially large negative effects of a US recession on Mexican exports is clearly underestimated. Had the analysis considered both Brady and NAFTA, a contractionary policy in the US would be seen to prove more harmful than beneficial to the Mexican economy.

The inclusion of NAFTA in the analysis may prove to be a particularly fruitful exercise, particularly when other very important analytical considerations from international trade theory are taken into account. If, for example, gains from trade under NAFTA are very substantial (because trade creation is stronger than trade diversion) then a contractionary policy in the US will prove even more harmful to Mexico, and will thus reinforce the negative effect. More generally, the more Mexico benefits from larger economies of scale and scope under NAFTA, the harder hit it will be by a US recession.[2] Although such considerations may deserve a separate study, I am sure the Board's MCM might easily include them in order to improve its predictive power on the Mexican economy.

NOTES

1 See Van Wijnbergen (1991).
2 Empirical studies on trade and industrial structure abound. See for example, Smith and Venables (1987) for the case of Europe and Harris and Cox (1983) for the case of Canada.

REFERENCES

Harris, R. and D. Cox (1983) *Trade, Industrial Policy and Canadian Manufacturing*. Toronto: Ontario Economic Research Council.
Smith, A. and A. Venables (1987). 'Trade and industrial policy: some simulations for EEC manufacturing', paper presented at a Conference on Empirical Studies of Strategic Trade Policy, Cambridge MA.
Van Wijnbergen, S. (1991) 'Mexico and the Brady Plan', *Economic Policy* 6, (12), 13–56.

13 The consequences of US fiscal actions in a global model with alternative assumptions about the exchange regime in developing countries

RALPH C. BRYANT and
CHARLES CHUKWUMA SOLUDO

1 Introduction

This paper contributes to empirical knowledge about the macroeconomic linkages between the economies of the developing countries (the 'South') and the OECD industrial countries (the 'North')[1] Our analysis focuses on policies of fiscal contraction carried out by the United States. These policies are of topical interest in their own right and are also representative of other shocks originating in the North to the aggregate demand of Northern economies. We emphasize the consequences of US fiscal contraction for Southern economies, and in particular how these effects can be dramatically different depending on the exchange rate regime implemented by Southern governments.

The paper relies on empirical simulations conducted with the Brook-I version of the IMF's MULTIMOD model. This version of MUL-TIMOD, which incorporates more detail about the financial and external-debt aspects of developing country economies than the more familiar versions, is an adaptation by the authors of exploratory work initiated by Symansky (1991a)[2]

Our analysis also addresses an issue that has received scarcely any attention in previous empirical research. We ask whether the effects of policy actions and non-policy shocks on the Northern economies themselves can be significantly influenced by the decisions of Southern governments about the management of exchange rates. Studies focusing on the Northern economies have of course considered the different consequences of alternative exchange regimes operated by Northern governments. What has not been studied is whether alternative choices of exchange regime in the South can significantly influence macroeconomic outcomes in the North. The simulations with

MULTIMOD reported here suggest that such effects may be non-negligible.

Our paper addresses another issue with important policy implications. We contrast the consequences of fiscal actions that are implemented simultaneously with their announcement versus the consequences of fiscal actions that are pre-announced and phased in gradually over time. Our simulations highlight the conclusion that the effects in the United States itself and in other OECD economies will vary significantly depending on how a fiscal-policy action is announced and actually implemented. No less important, the transmission to Southern economies of Northern fiscal actions depends on how suddenly or gradually they are executed and on whether or not the policy actions are anticipated.

Section 2 of the paper describes the Brook-I version of MULTIMOD and its modelling of Southern economies. Section 3 focuses on the consequences for Southern economies of an immediately implemented fiscal contraction in the United States. Section 4 takes up the issue of whether macroeconomic outcomes in Northern economies can be significantly influenced by the choices of Southern governments about exchange rate management. Section 5 analyses the differing effects of immediately implemented versus pre-announced, phased-in US fiscal actions. Section 6 contains concluding remarks.

2   Modelling of Southern economies and North–South interactions in the Brook-I version of MULTIMOD

The global, policy-simulation model developed by the staff of the IMF, known as MULTIMOD, and a closely related model developed by a team of economists at the Canadian Department of Finance and the Bank of Canada, known as INTERMOD, are noteworthy among the small number of analytical efforts that have been made to capture some of the key linkages between Northern and Southern economies.[3]

The version of MULTIMOD used for this paper, referred to as Brook-I, follows the lead of Symansky (1991a) in incorporating more detailed financial and debt equations in the submodel for the developing country region. When creating the Brook-I version of MULTIMOD in the fall of 1991 and early 1992, the authors transported the model source code used for Symansky (1991a), written for TROLL mainframe software, into Fortran source code. We conduct our model simulations with the PC SIM Fortran software programme originally developed for running the INTERMOD model on personal computers.[4]

The Brook-I version of MULTIMOD contains submodels (separately specified blocks) for eleven countries/regions. Eight represent the industrial countries, one each for the United States, Japan, Germany, France, the United Kingdom, Italy, Canada and the Small Industrial Countries (SIC, an aggregate of the non-G7 OECD countries). The remaining countries in the world are grouped into three blocs: an aggregate of the four newly industrialized East Asian economies (Asian NICs), an aggregate of the high-income oil-exporting countries, and a large aggregation of all other developing countries (also referred to as debt-constrained countries, made up of Africa, Latin America, Asia-Pacific and some Middle East and European developing countries). The modelling of the combined Asian NIC economies is analogous to a typical industrial-country block. The oil-exporters bloc has little 'domestic' structure and is included primarily to ensure a completely identified and internally consistent system of world trade and capital flows. The macro structure of the debt-constrained developing country region – hereafter referred to as the DC region – includes equations for financial flows and debt-related variables, thereby permitting an analysis of policy issues involving the DC region's external debts.[5]

MULTIMOD can be described as a dynamic Mundell–Fleming model that incorporates rational, model-consistent expectations in both goods and financial markets. Changes in policy today – or expected changes in policy tomorrow – have immediate effects on so-called 'jumping' variables, for example the exchange rate, interest rates, output prices, wealth, and debt prices. Traded-goods prices and volumes, exchange rates, and interest rates, all of which are endogenous in the model, are the principal channels, in the first instance, through which external factors affect domestic economies. The model contains the standard savings-investment channels of the typical industrial country, and is fairly large (with some 570 equations including identities).

The Brook-I treatment of trade flows between North and South – disaggregated into the three components of manufactured goods, oil and primary commodities – is identical with that used in the more familiar variants of MULTIMOD. We therefore do not repeat the descriptions available elsewhere (Masson et al., 1990; Soludo, 1992).

Financial linkages between North and South in the model focus on debt prices, capital flows, and their implications for growth in the Southern economies. Two assumptions underlie the modelling of the relationship between external debt and domestic monetary conditions. First, it is assumed that in the domestic markets of the DC region, after-tax rates of return on private capital and government liabilities are equalized. Second, the expected returns on DC government external debt and DC government internal debt are equalized. It is hypothesized that the returns are equalized both by financial-market arbitrage and the endogenous tax behaviour of the DC governments. Governments of the DC region are assumed to have the power to tax or inflate away differences in returns. They therefore face the same marginal lending rate in both domestic and international markets. The incomes of DC residents are taxed to make payments on all government liabilities, and the existence of one domestic interest rate is therefore assumed. Perfect capital mobility adjusted for default risk on DC region external debt is assumed to hold *vis-à-vis* the rest of the world. Accordingly, an arbitrage relationship sets the DC domestic interest rate equal to the world interest rate adjusted for default risk. As a further simplifying assumption, as in Symansky (1991a), DC governments are assumed not to be able to issue new debts (external or internal), and are thus constrained to operate a balanced budget from year to year. In contrast, private residents in the DC region can incrementally (subject to market conditions and incentives) incur new external debt or, alternatively, accumulate foreign assets.

Changes in the DC region's external financial position influence DC economic activity through two main channels in the model. One channel is through the effect that external-debt prices (changes in the secondary-market discount on 'old' external debt) have on the domestic rate of return. The other linkage is through the relationship between debt service and taxation. Investment in the DC sector is modelled as a gradual adjustment of the capital stock to an optimal level. A decline in debt-servicing requirements for the DC region reduces the tax burden on DC residents, raises the after-tax rate of return, and thus encourages DC investment. For example, debt forgiveness, which reduces outstanding contractual obligations of the DC government, will lead to a rise in the discounted market price of DC government debt (a decline in the default risk and the domestic cost of financing) and hence to a reduction in both current and future taxes, and thence to an increase in the after-tax return on investment. Both of these effects lead to an increase in investment and growth in the model (Symansky, 1991a, p. 11).

The outstanding amount of 'old' DC government debt owed to foreign creditors increases with interest obligations and decreases with interest payments and buy-backs of the debt. The secondary-market price of the old debt is defined as the discounted value of expected payments on the debt (interest payments and buy-backs) divided by the current stock of debt. The default risk premium is defined as the percentage of the present value of obligated payments not made on the debt, or one minus the debt price.

In a critically important financial equation for the DC region in the Brook-I version of MULTIMOD, the DC governments are assumed to choose the amount of interest payments on their old debt to foreign creditors that will be 'voluntarily' paid in the current period. This equation, in effect a 'reaction function' of the DC governments, assumes that voluntary interest payments to foreign creditors are set higher the larger is the capacity output of the DC region. The voluntary interest payments are also assumed to be a function of the size of the contractually obligated interest payments. More precisely, the specification of the equation is

$$DPIP_t = \alpha(DYCAPV\$_t) + \beta(UR_t)(DPDT_{t-1}) + \text{residual}$$

where $DPIP$ is the amount of voluntary interest payments measured in US dollars, $DYCAPV\$$ is the real capacity output of the DC region expressed in terms of nominal, US-dollar values, UR is the average contractual US-dollar interest rate to be paid on the debt, and $DPDT$ is the value of the 'old' external debt measured in US dollars.[6]

Given the preceding reaction function and the other financial equations in the DC sub-model, the secondary-market price of DC old external debt can rise in two ways: through an increase in DC potential output, which increases debt servicing and the present value of future interest payments, and through debt reduction negotiated by DC governments and foreign creditors, which by assumption lowers the stock of DC debt more than it reduces the present value of future interest payments.

The debt features of the DC region sub-model appear to capture some key linkages between the debt price, capital flows, and domestic economic activity. For example, any shock that impacts on the debt price or debt interest payments affects the default risk and the domestic interest rate, and thus domestic investment and growth in domestic output.

The financial aspects of the DC-region sub-model of the Brook-I version of MULTIMOD are a promising initial attempt to incorporate the debt constraints facing Southern economies into a global macro-economic model. But much more research needs to be done before one can be confident of the most appropriate method of modelling these constraints. In our experiments with the model, we have found that the behaviour of the DC region – and even the behaviour of interest rates and exchange rates in the industrial-country sectors of the model – is sensitive to the detailed specification of the DC debt and financial equations. For example, modest changes in the parameters of the DC-government reaction function shown above can substantially alter conclusions about the effects on the DC region of Northern fiscal and monetary policies.[7] Only after further research will it be possible to judge whether this sensitivity is a misleading artifact of the model's specification or an accurate reflection of real-life behaviour.

Policy analyses with the Brook-I version of MULTIMOD can be carried out under alternative assumptions about the exchange regime implemented by the DC region. For this paper and also for Soludo (1992), we simulate in effect two variants of the Brook-I model. One variant assumes that the DC region maintains a flexible exchange rate against all other currencies. Together with the assumption of capital mobility between the DC region and the rest of the world, this assumption entails treating the DC money supply as exogenously specified by DC governments. This variant of the model is referred to here as FLEX. In the second variant, referred to as FIX, the money supply of the DC region is endogenized and the DC bilateral exchange rate against the US dollar is assumed to be pegged at an unchanged value.

The FIX and FLEX variants of the model represent polar-case assumptions about the choice of exchange regime for developing country economies. For most developing countries, the exchange regime actually used in real life tends to be an intermediate hybrid of the pure fixed and pure floating cases. We believe a comparison of the simulation results with the FIX and FLEX variants of the model provides useful insights because the two sets of results probably bracket the implications of alternative DC exchange regimes for North–South macroeconomic interactions.

3   The fiscal consequences in the South of an immediately implemented fiscal contraction in the United States

For the first of our two illustrative US fiscal contractions, labelled UGIM, we assume that at the beginning of 1993 the US government announces and immediately implements a very large, permanent cut in real US government expenditures equivalent to 3 per cent of US real GDP.[8] The cut is not expected when it is announced, but thereafter the maintenance of the cut is assumed to be fully credible. This shock, of course, is primarily of interest for diagnostic purposes. In practice, the US government has not contemplated fiscal contractions nearly as large or as sudden as an immediately implemented 3 per cent of GDP. (Section 5 of the paper contrasts this UGIM fiscal contraction with an equivalently sized US fiscal contraction that is instead pre-announced and then subsequently phased in gradually over a period of three years.)

US monetary policy and monetary policies in all other OECD countries are assumed to be unchanged in the sense that the target paths for countries' money stocks are kept unchanged from the baseline target paths. As is typically done in all versions of MULTIMOD, the fiscal policy of each government is constrained by an intertemporal fiscal closure rule designed to enforce the long-run intertemporal budget constraint facing each government.[9] All simulations are conducted over a period of fifty-three years (beginning in 1993 and ending in 2045).[10]

To economize on space, we omit any tables summarizing the simulation results. Instead, we present a selective overview of the results using charts constructed in a common format. All the curves in the charts represent deviations of a variable from its path in a baseline simulation. For most variables the deviations are expressed in percentage terms (e.g., GNP/GDP, consumption, and exchange rates are shown as per cent deviations from baseline). The remaining variables are presented in the form of level deviations (e.g., interest rates are expressed in percentage-point deviations from baseline).

Each chart has a legend indicating the simulation from which each curve is taken and the name of the variable plotted (the acronym used in the model). The title of each chart also typically indicates the variable or variables plotted. The simulation labelled UGIMFIX uses the UGIM assumptions summarized above and pertains to the model variant in which developing countries use the FIX exchange regime. The UGIM-FLEX simulation uses the same UGIM assumptions but uses the model variant that permits the DC-region exchange rate to fluctuate freely under the FLEX regime. For easy interpretation of the charts, curves pertaining to a simulation prepared with the FIX regime for the DC region are always plotted with solid lines and hollow symbols. Curves from a simulation prepared with the FLEX regime for the DC region are always plotted with dashed lines and solid (filled-in) symbols. When a chart shows a single variable, comparing the outcomes under the FIX and FLEX simulations, the symbol for the FIX simulation is typically a hollow square and the symbol for the same variable in the FLEX simulation is a filled-in square. If the chart shows two different variables (and hence has four curves in total, two from a FIX and two from a FLEX simulation), the square symbol is used for one of the variables and a diamond symbol for the other (hollow or filled-in depending on whether the curve pertains to the FIX or FLEX exchange regime for developing countries).

The UGIM fiscal contraction, as simulated by the Brook-I version of MULTIMOD, has qualitatively familiar consequences for the US economy and other Northern economies. US output falls sharply in the initial year, but then begins to recover as the negative income effects of the government-spending reduction begin to be offset by increases in other spending on domestic output induced by lower interest rates, lower prices, and a depreciation of the US dollar. With the domestic economy initially weaker and the dollar depreciating in exchange markets, the US current-account balance improves. The transmission of the US fiscal contraction to other OECD countries tends to be 'positive': that is, foreign outputs initially fall in response to the fall in US output and the improvement in the US current balance. Over the medium and long run, US output is significantly above rather than below baseline, while foreign outputs also tend to rise above baseline. (We discuss consequences in the North in more detail below.)

The effects on the DC region of the US fiscal contraction depend critically on the exchange regime implemented for that region. With the FIX regime, the DC currency remains pegged to the depreciating US dollar; against a weighted average of all foreign currencies, the DC currency initially experiences an effective *depreciation* of some 3.5 per cent (Figure 13.2). In sharp contrast, when the DC currency is allowed to float in the FLEX regime, the DC currency appreciates against the US dollar (behaving in a manner qualitatively similar to the yen, the DM, and other OECD-country currencies). The extent of the initial appreciation against the dollar in the FLEX regime is some 10 per cent (Figure 13.1), significantly larger than the appreciation against the dollar of the yen and the currencies of the European Monetary System (EMS). As a result, the DC currency experiences a sizeable effective *appreciation* against all currencies combined (Figure 13.2).

The DC region's export prices and import prices are strongly influenced by the very different outcomes for the region's exchange rates. Figure 13.3 shows the effects on the price indexes for total exports and total imports (*DPXT* and *DPIT*). For the FIX regime, under which the DC currency undergoes effective depreciation, both export and import prices rise in local currency. Export and import prices decline sharply in local currency under the FLEX regime, reflecting the effective appreciation of the DC currency.[11]

In response to the fall in aggregate demand in Northern economies, DC export volumes fall – slightly under the FIX regime and more significantly under the FLEX regime (curves with the diamond symbol in Figure 13.4). The differing effects under the two regimes are of course attributable to the different exchange rate movements. Because the DC currency depreciates under the FIX regime, the expenditure-switching effects from the depreciation work to offset the negative income-absorption effects. The effective appreciation of the DC currency under the FLEX regime sets in motion expenditure-switching effects for DC exports that work in the same direction as, rather than offsetting, the

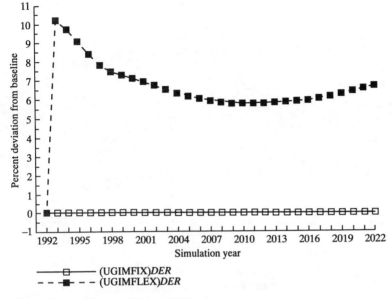

Figure 13.1   DC region bilateral US$ exchange rate

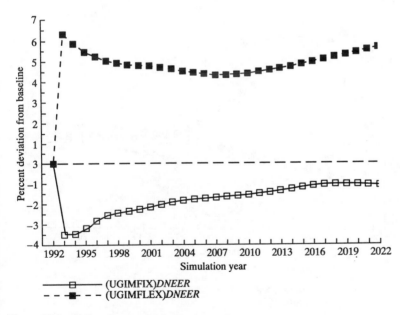

Figure 13.2   DC region nominal effective exchange rate

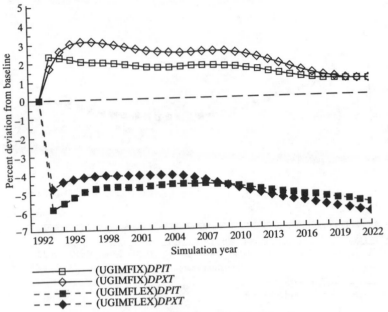

Figure 13.3　DC export and import prices (local currency)

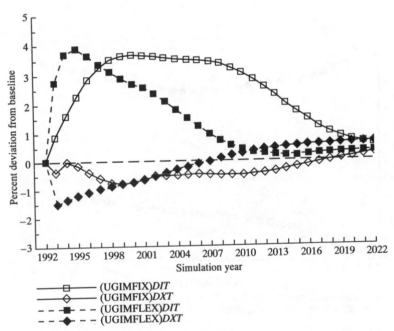

Figure 13.4　DC region real exports and real imports

income-absorption effects due to the fall in Northern aggregate demand. The volume of real imports into the DC region (Figure 13.4, curves with the square symbol) increases sizeably under both exchange regimes, though the increase is much larger and faster under the FLEX regime because of the relative-price effects due to the appreciation of the DC currency.

Under the FIX regime, real GDP in the DC region *increases* sharply in the first two years (Figure 13.5). This movement in output is in the opposite direction from what happens initially to output in the United States and, by and large, in the rest of the North. Under the FLEX regime the DC region behaves much more like other non-US regions: output falls in the first two years (by relatively modest amounts), before gradually rising above baseline in response to the crowding-in effects of lower domestic interest rates and prices on investment expenditures. Movements in the DC price level (Figure 13.6 shows the absorption deflator) are even more disparate under the two exchange regimes than the movements of DC output. Prices rise markedly above baseline for the first four years under FIX and then thereafter gradually fall back toward baseline. Under FLEX, the local-currency price level falls below baseline, fairly sharply at first and then much more gradually.

The DC region's capital stock (Figure 13.7) and hence also its capacity output rise progressively above baseline over time. The increases are initially larger under the FIX regime, but ultimately become larger under the FLEX regime. The evolution over time of both the capital stock and capacity output are, of course, predominantly influenced by real investment.

Even under the FLEX regime, though initially less so than under FIX, real consumption and real investment in the DC region are above baseline after the US fiscal contraction. The contrasting paths of DC output under the two exchange regimes (Figure 13.5), in particular the initial fall in output under FLEX, is importantly attributable to the different evolutions of DC trade flows. The DC-region trade balance initially worsens, especially in real terms, under both exchange regimes, but the 'deterioration' is markedly larger under the FLEX regime (Figure 13.8). The DC current-account balance (likewise shown in Figure 13.8) also moves in the deficit direction, again by larger amounts under the FLEX than under the FIX regime. The DC region, benefiting from lower world interest rates, pays less in debt service for each dollar of its external debt. At the same time, however, the improved outlook for the DC-region economy facilitates new net inflows of capital from abroad. This external financing permits the enlarged trade and current-account deficits, which in turn entail inward transfers of real resources from the rest of the world.[12]

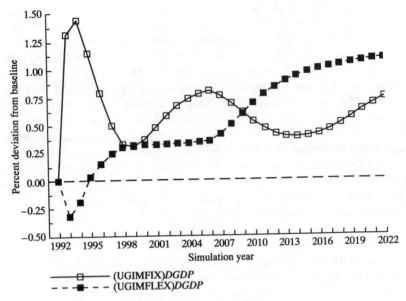

Figure 13.5   DC region real gross domestic product

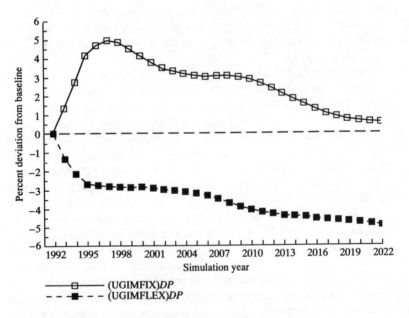

Figure 13.6   DC region price level (absorption deflator)

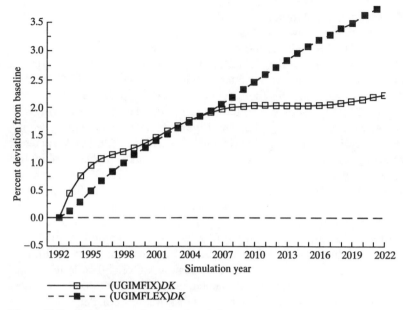

Figure 13.7   DC region real stock of capital

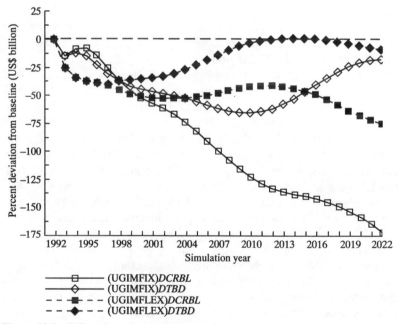

Figure 13.8   DC trade and current-account balances

Some financial consequences of the US fiscal contraction for the DC region are shown in Figures 13.9–13.12. The improved outlook for the DC region's economy and the decline in OECD interest rates induce falls in the default risk premium on 'old' DC external debt (*DRP*, shown with square symbols in Figure 13.9) and a corresponding rise in the secondary-market price of that debt (Figure 13.10). Domestic interest rates in the DC region (*DRS*, shown with diamond symbols in Figure 13.9) fall, in part reflecting the general decline in world interest rates. DC governments, behaving as discussed earlier, choose to make higher 'voluntary' interest payments on their existing debt (Figure 13.11), which raises the confidence of foreign creditors. As shown in the figures, these financial variables behave significantly differently under the FIX and FLEX regimes. As seen implicitly in Figure 13.8 and explicitly in Figure 13.12, the net inflow of 'new' foreign capital to the DC region and hence the decline in the DC net foreign asset position is initially larger under the FLEX regime. Over the longer run, however, the current-account deficit and the net inflow of new foreign capital are simulated as substantially smaller under the FLEX than under the FIX regime.

It is not straightforward to give a summary appraisal of the welfare consequences for the DC region stemming from the US fiscal contraction. The short-run consequences differ from those in the medium and long runs. And the effects are decisively influenced by the choice of exchange regime for the DC region.

With the DC currency floating against all currencies, the US fiscal contraction dampens DC output and income in the short run as well as causing prices to decline relative to baseline. In the medium run, on the other hand, output and income rise above baseline while the price level continues gradually to decline. In the long run, the increases in output and income under the FLEX regime are even greater than those simulated for the FIX regime. In the short run, the DC region can attain higher levels of output, income, and consumption from operating the FIX regime. Pegging the DC currency to the US dollar yields a gain in competitiveness in world markets because the DC currency thereby depreciates against all currencies except the US dollar. This gain in competitiveness, is, however, a two-edged sword since it represents an unfavourable change in the DC region's terms of trade. Over the longer run, real investment and the real capital stock are higher under the FLEX than the FIX regime. Eventually, output and even absorption itself may be higher under the FLEX regime.

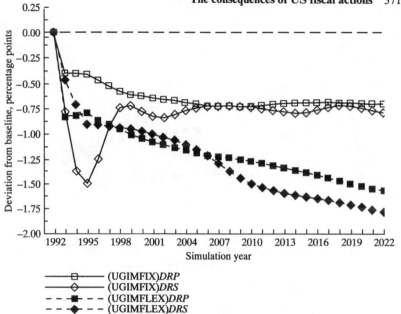

Figure 13.9 DC nominal interest-rate variables

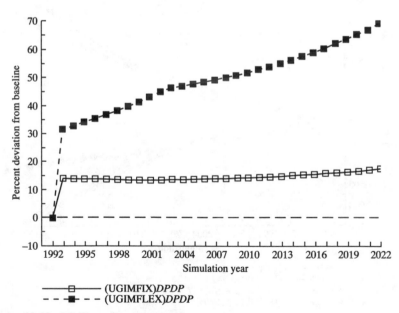

Figure 13.10 Market price of DC 'old' external debt

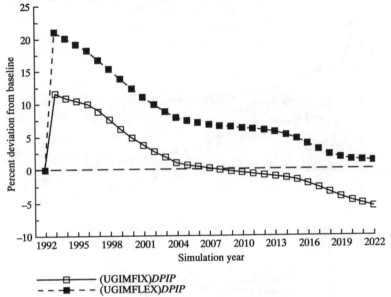

Figure 13.11   Interest payments on DC 'old' external debt

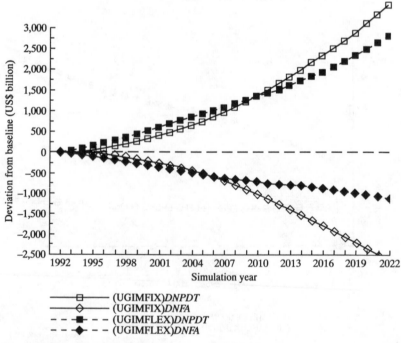

Figure 13.12   DC net foreign assets

4   Consequences for Northern economies of the choice of exchange regime by Southern governments

It is a natural next step to use the UGIMFIX and UGIMFLEX simulations to ask whether the DC region's choice of exchange rate arrangements is consequential for Northern economies. As observed already, the FIX and FLEX regimes represent polar extremes rather than realistic, intermediate cases. Furthermore, it has not yet been demonstrated that the Brook-I version of MULTIMOD – or, indeed, any version of MULTIMOD – accurately summarizes the key features of macroeconomic interactions between industrial and developing economies. Conclusions based on a few simulations from this single model must therefore be framed with caution. At the very least, however, the simulations done for this paper provide considerable food for thought and convince us that macroeconomic feedback effects running from the South to the North deserve more study than they have hitherto received.

When we compare the simulated effects on Northern macroeconomic variables of the UGIM assumptions for a cut in US government expenditures, we find numerous variables for which the effects are similar regardless of whether the DC region operates the FIX or the FLEX exchange regime. For example, the initial fall in US real GNP in the first year and the subsequent rebound in the second year are slightly larger in the UGIMFIX than in the UGIMFLEX simulation (Figure 13.13). Yet the differences are not large enough to warrant attention in realistic policy discussions. The movements of the US dollar/Deutschmark exchange rate (and other bilateral exchange rates between the dollar and other key currencies) are similarly close under the FIX and FLEX assumptions about the DC-region exchange regime (Figure 13.16). Most analysts would treat the small differences between the two simulations as negligible to a first approximation.

For other US variables, however, the differences between the two simulations may not be negligible. Two examples are sufficient to make the point. For the US price level, measured by the absorption deflator (Figure 13.14), the simulation with the DC-region FIX regime leads to a small fall of US prices below baseline in the first year, with a substantial fall in year 2 and a further modest fall in year 3. When the DC region implements the FLEX regime, however, US prices rise above baseline in the initial year and then fall below baseline in years 2 and 3 by much less than when the DC region has a FIX regime. The difference is readily attributable to the effects of exchange rates on US domestic prices. When the DC currency as well as other currencies appreciate against the dollar

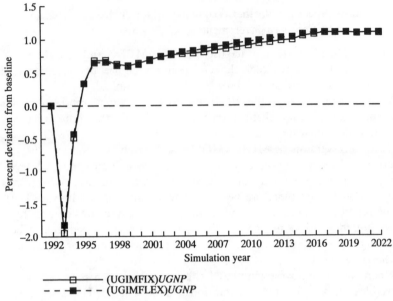

Figure 13.13   US real gross national product

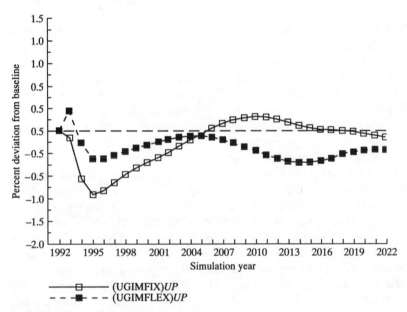

Figure 13.14   US price level (absorption deflator)

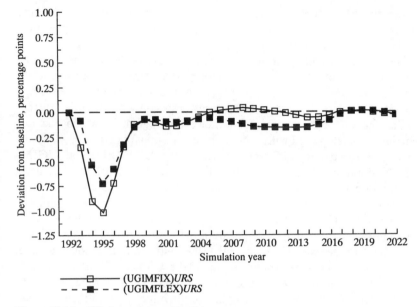

Figure 13.15   US short-term nominal interest rate

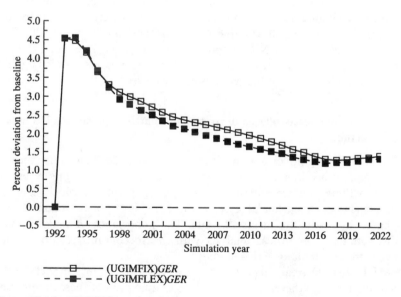

Figure 13.16 $/DM bilateral exchange rate

under the FLEX regime, the larger effective depreciation of the dollar puts upward pressure on domestic prices relative to the case in which the dollar does not depreciate against the DC currency.

The differing exchange rate movements of the dollar against the DC currency presumably also are a major part of the explanation for the different movements of the US short-term nominal interest rate (Figure 13.15). Nominal (and real) US interest rates fall nontrivially further under the DC FIX regime than under the regime in which the DC currency floats upward with other currencies against the dollar.

Even more striking differences between the UGIMFIX and UGIMFLEX simulations appear for the transmitted effects of the US fiscal contraction to variables in other industrial countries. German nominal interest rates exhibit a similar pattern to US interest rates, with the decline in the German short rate being three times larger when the DC region implements the FIX rather than the FLEX regime (Figure 13.17). For the FIX regime, German real GDP initially falls below baseline, exhibiting the 'positive' transmission of the US shock that is typically expected. When the DC region follows the FLEX regime, however, German real GDP *rises above* baseline in the initial year and rises further in the second (Figure 13.18).

Differences in the transmission of the US/policy action to Japanese real GDP are less striking, with the effects of the FIX and FLEX regimes somewhat different but both smaller than in the case of transmission to Germany (Figure 13.19). More sizeable differences are observed for the transmission to real GDP in the Asian NICs region (Figure 13.20). The first-year fall in Asian NIC output is about twice as large when the DC region pegs to the dollar as when the DC currency floats upward against the dollar together with the Asian NIC currencies.

5   Pre-announced, phased-in versus immediately implemented US fiscal actions

When analysing policy actions, it is important to distinguish unexpected actions that are immediately implemented at the time of announcement from actions that are announced prior to the period in which they are implemented. A particular case of the latter is a policy action that is phased in gradually, in installments. The importance of making these distinctions in empirical analysis with macroeconometric models has been stressed in many earlier studies.[13]

MULTIMOD treats expectations in a forward-looking, model-consistent manner and therefore lends itself to examination of these differences. We also focus on these distinctions here because the issue of whether to

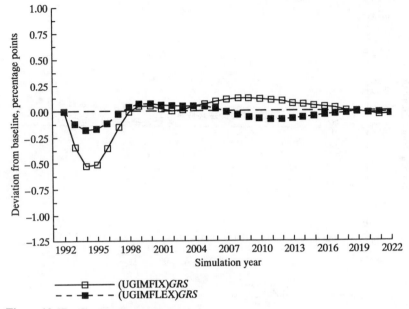

Figure 13.17   German short-term nominal interest rate

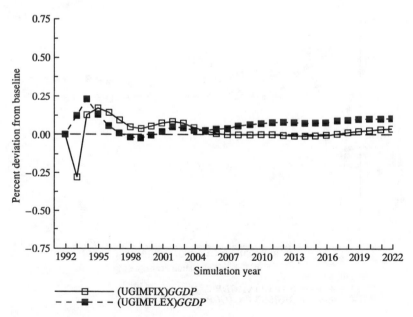

Figure 13.18   German real gross domestic product

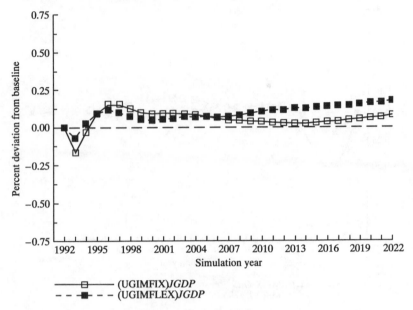

Figure 13.19   Japanese real gross domestic product

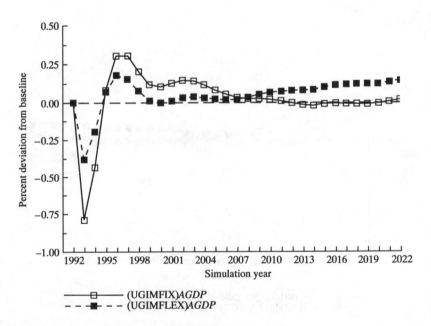

Figure 13.20   Asian NICs' real gross domestic product

reduce budget imbalances rapidly or instead gradually has received priority attention in recent policy discussions in the United States (and increasingly in Germany).[14]

For comparison with the preceding analysis, we thus consider a second specification of a US fiscal contraction, labelled UGPH ('PH' for phased-in rather than 'IM', immediately implemented). The US government is assumed to announce a programme of reductions in government spending equivalent to 3 per cent of GDP at the beginning of 1993; implementation of the cuts, however, does not begin until 1994 and even then the cuts are implemented only gradually. Specifically, real government expenditures are changed by the following percentages of baseline real GDP: 0 (1993), −1 (1994), −2 (1995), −3 (1996). After 1996 the 3 per cent-of-real-GDP cut is maintained indefinitely. Except for the pre-announcement and gradual phasing in of the cuts in UGPH, the UGIM and UGPH contractions are identical.[15]

We continue to summarize the simulation results with standardized charts. Each of the following charts now plots four curves for the same variable. The two new simulations are labelled UGPHFIX and UGPH-FLEX (corresponding to the two model variants in which the DC region operates a FIX or a FLEX exchange regime). These new simulations are contrasted with the UGIMFIX and UGIMFLEX simulations already studied. Because the differences between the two fiscal contractions are important primarily in the short and medium runs, the subsequent charts show only a ten-year time period (1993–2002) rather than the longer thirty-year period used earlier. As before, curves with solid lines and hollow symbols denote the simulations in which the DC region operates the FIX exchange regime, while curves with dashed lines and filled-in symbols denote the simulations with the DC-region FLEX regime. The results for the UGIM simulations continue to be plotted with a square symbol. Results for the new UGPH simulations, in contrast, are plotted with a circle symbol. To contrast the two types of fiscal contraction, the reader should thus focus on the difference between the curves marked with squares and those marked with circles (hollow squares versus hollow circles for the DC FIX regime, or filled-in squares versus filled-in circles for the DC FLEX regime).

A key difference for the United States itself between the immediate and phased-in simulations is sharply evident in Figure 13.21: whereas US output and incomes in 1993 fall sharply in response to the unexpected, full-dose cut in government spending (UGIM), output and incomes actually *increase* in 1993 under the UGPH cuts begin to be made in 1994, moreover, the resulting falls in output and incomes tend to be considerably dampened relative to those in the UGIM simulation. In

MULTIMOD, a gradual phasing-in of a fiscal contraction substantially mutes the negative, Keynesian consequences for output and incomes that one traditionally associates with fiscal contraction. This cushioning of output from a phased contraction is a consequence of 'crowding-in' responses, especially to the depreciation in the external value of the dollar. If expenditure cuts are fed in gradually to the economy, crowding-in responses to the initial cuts are already operating powerfully in the later years when the further gradual cuts are being implemented. Anticipations of a programme of phased-in fiscal contraction, which in the UGPH simulation go to work before any cuts are actually made, reinforce this cushioning of output and incomes while the programme is being implemented. The effects on real absorption (Figure 13.22) show a similar pattern to those for real GNP.

The 'price' the US economy pays for the cushioning of output and incomes during implementation of the phased-in fiscal contraction is to postpone the time when the economy begins to reap substantial benefits from the higher national saving associated with the fiscal contraction. For both the UGPH and UGIM simulations, US real GNP eventually moves significantly above and thereafter remains above baseline. But the economy gets to that point much sooner when the fiscal medicine comes as a surprise and is taken in one large dose.[16]

The two different styles of fiscal contraction lead to obviously different outcomes for the US budget deficit in the early years of the simulations (Figure 13.23). The initial depreciation of the dollar in 1993 is twice as large for the UGIM as for the UGPH assumptions (the latter again, of course, attributable solely to anticipations). The pattern of depreciation in the second through fourth years is also quite different (Figure 13.24 plots the dollar/DM exchange rate; the patterns for other major currencies are qualitatively similar).

Our main concern in this paper is with the effects of Northern fiscal actions on Southern economies. We thus now provide some selective evidence to show that, even for the DC region, the consequences differ appreciably depending on whether a US fiscal contraction is implemented immediately or phased in gradually after being pre-announced.

If the DC currency is pegged to the dollar, the DC effective exchange rate depreciates by significantly less when the US fiscal contraction is phased in than when it is implemented all at once (Figure 13.25, UGPHFIX versus UGIMFIX). If the DC currency floats upwards against the dollar, the effective appreciation of the DC currency is slightly muted for the phased-in contraction (Figure 13.25, UGPHFLEX versus UGIMFLEX). The differences in exchange rate movements give rise to correspondingly different movements in the local-currency prices of DC-region exports

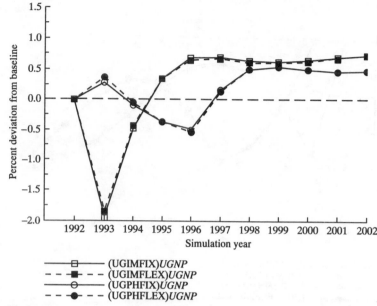

Figure 13.21   US real gross national product

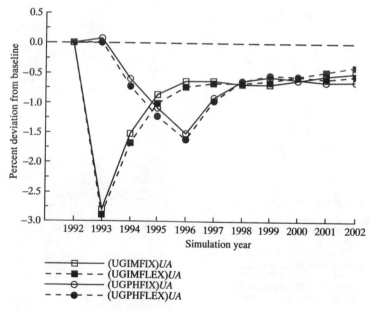

Figure 13.22   US real absorption

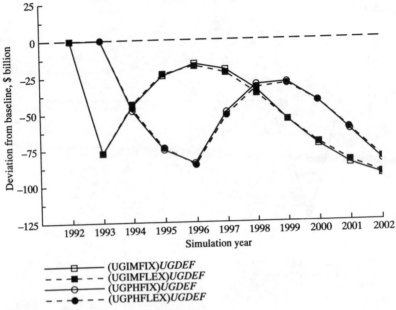

Figure 13.23   US government budget deficit

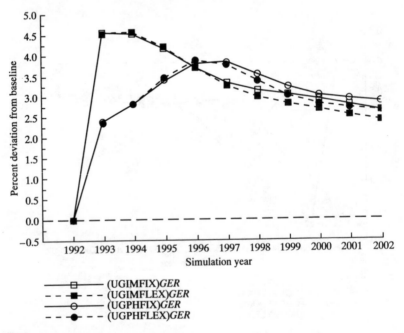

Figure 13.24 $/DM bilateral exchange rate

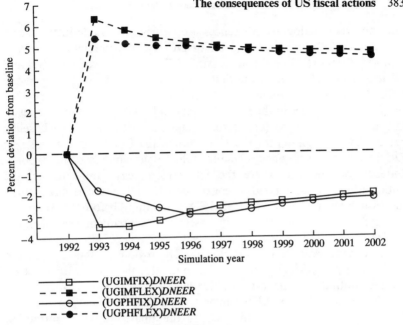

Figure 13.25   DC region nominal effective exchange rate

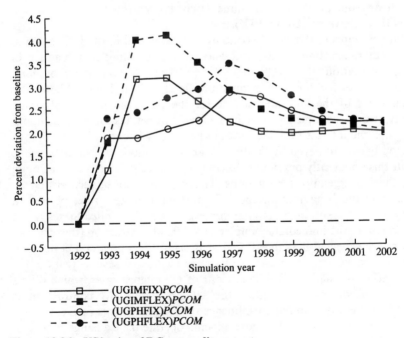

Figure 13.26   US$ price of DC commodity exports

and imports. Analogous differences are clearly observable in the world dollar prices of commodities (a major DC-region export) and of oil (an important import). For the most part, dollar prices of commodities and oil tend to rise further in the first few years in the UGIM than in the UGPH simulations (Figures 13.26 and 27).[17] Given the tendency for outputs and incomes in the United States and other OECD economies to fall less below baseline (or, in some cases, even to rise above baseline rather than fall below) for the UGPH than the UGIM simulations, the DC region also experiences smaller falls in the volume of its exports. Indeed, for the case where the DC region pegs to the dollar, the anticipations of the phased-in contraction in 1993 even permit a small increase in DC real exports (UGPHFIX simulation) before the volume of exports declines modestly below baseline in subsequent years (Figure 13.28).

The consequences for real GDP in the DC region are shown in Figure 13.29. The phased-in US contraction mitigates the downward pressure on DC output for the case where the DC governments operate the FLEX regime (UGPHFLEX versus UGIMFLEX). Analogously, if the DC governments peg to the dollar, the phased-in US contraction significantly diminishes the surge in output that would otherwise occur with an equivalent-size but immediately implemented US contraction (UGPHFIX versus UGIMFIX).

Interest rates in the world economy generally, and in the DC region in particular, are importantly influenced by the timing and manner of implementation of the US fiscal action. The DC domestic short-term interest rate for the four simulations is shown in Figure 13.30. The behaviour of the DC interest rate for the phased-in fiscal contraction may at first seem puzzling: if the DC region operates the FIX exchange regime, the interest rate does not fall below baseline in either the first or second year, and even by the third year is only modestly below baseline. But this apparently puzzling behaviour is primarily due to the phasing-in of the US expenditure reductions. This inference can be seen clearly by studying the behaviour of the US short-term interest rate, plotted in Figure 13.35. Although nominal interest rates in the United States fall in response to the immediately implemented fiscal contraction (the 'normal' response expected in conventional analysis of fiscal policy), US nominal interest rates actually *rise* above baseline in the first several years in the phased-in simulations. The behaviour of US interest rates, which differs greatly according to whether the UGPH or UGIM contraction is implemented, is a dominant influence on the movements of DC interest rates – especially if the DC governments operate the exchange regime in which the DC currency is pegged to the dollar.[18]

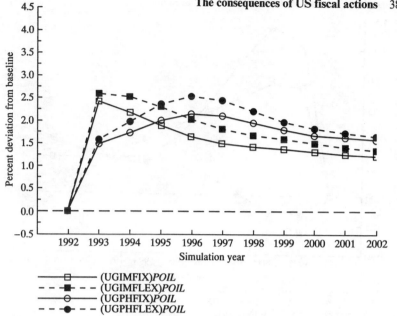

Figure 13.27   World nominal price of oil (in US$)

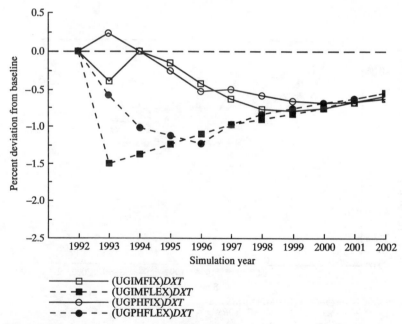

Figure 13.28   DC region real exports (volume)

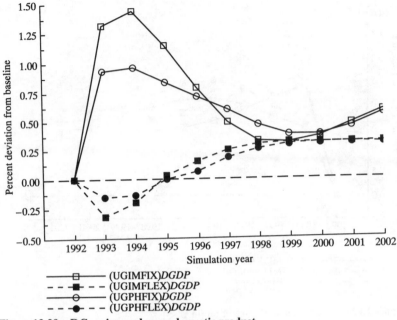

Figure 13.29   DC region real gross domestic product

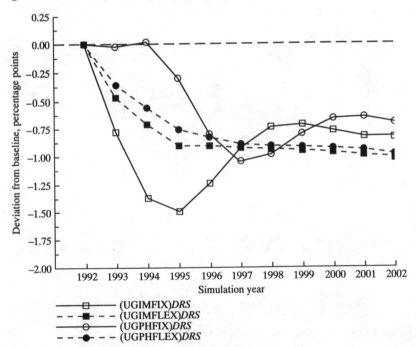

Figure 13.30   DC short-term nominal interest rate

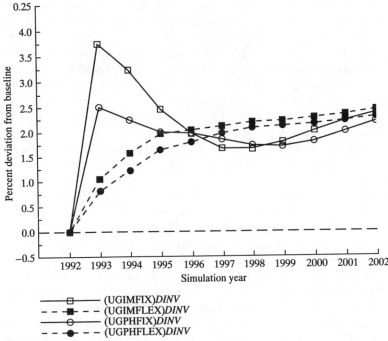

Figure 13.31   DC region real investment

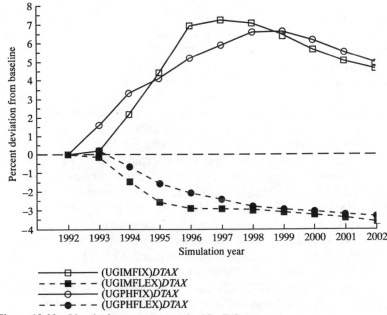

Figure 13.32   Nominal tax revenues raised by DC governments

Further examples of the different consequences of the two styles of US fiscal contraction for the DC region are presented in Figures 13.31 (real investment) and 13.32 (tax revenues raised by the DC governments). It remains true, of course, that the divergent implications of the FIX and FLEX exchange regimes are more important issues for the DC region than the different effects of the two types of US fiscal contraction. But one cannot study Figures 13.25–13.32 closely without coming away with a healthy appreciation for the point that, for many DC variables and hence probably also for DC welfare, the details of how the United States attempts to reduce its swollen budget deficit are of more than passing interest.

If the reader turns back to Figures 13.21–13.24, which report the effects on some key US variables of all four simulations discussed in this section, it is apparent that it makes little if any difference – for those US variables – whether the DC governments operate a FIX or a FLEX exchange regime (or, presumably, any intermediate regime). At the same time, as observed in the course of discussing Figures 13.17–13.20 for the UGIM simulations, the DC choice of exchange regime can have non-trivial consequences for other Northern variables. We conclude our discussion here by presenting a few additional charts for variables outside the DC region, all of which indicate differences not only between the UGIM and UGPH simulations but also between the simulations for the DC-region FIX and FLEX regimes.

US real imports and US absorption prices exhibit the FIX versus FLEX differences to be expected on theoretical grounds. If the DC currencies appreciate against the dollar along with other currencies, the average relative price of US imports is higher than if the DC currency is pegged to the dollar; consequently, US real imports are somewhat lower in the FLEX than the FIX simulations (Figure 13.33). For analogous reasons, the somewhat greater effective depreciation of the dollar when the DC-region operates the FLEX regime works more strongly to offset the downward pressure on US domestic prices in the UGIMFLEX than in the UGIMFIX simulation, and places somewhat more upward pressure on US domestic prices in the UGPHFLEX than in the UGPHFIX simulation (Figure 13.34). As already noted, US nominal interest rates (Figure 13.35) are non-trivially higher in the FLEX than the FIX simulations. As a result, real investment expenditures in the United States experience less upward movement – the differences are modest in size, but probably not small enough to be labelled trivial – in the FLEX than in the FIX simulations (Figure 13.36).

Transmission effects of a US fiscal contraction to other Northern economies and to the Asian NIC economies, again for some but not for all

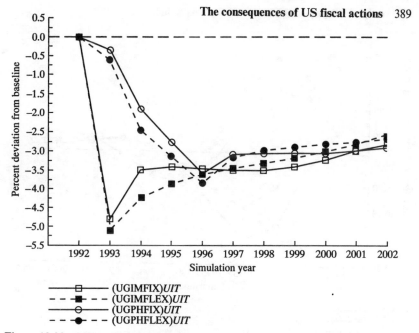

Figure 13.33 US real imports (volume)

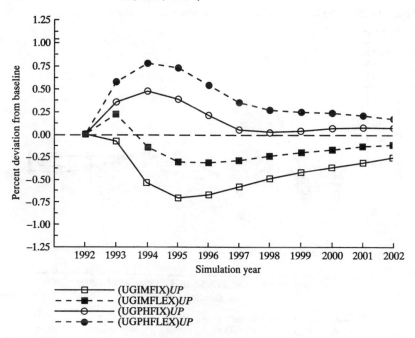

Figure 13.34 US price level (absorption deflator)

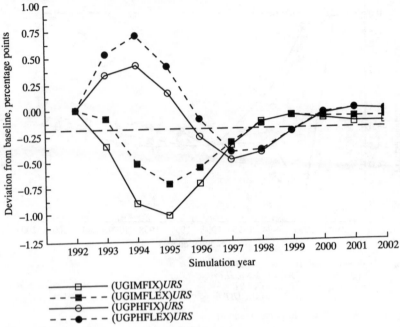

Figure 13.35   US short-term nominal interest rate

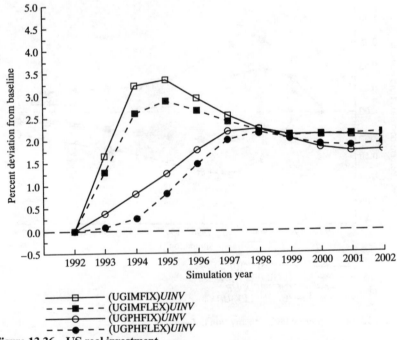

Figure 13.36   US real investment

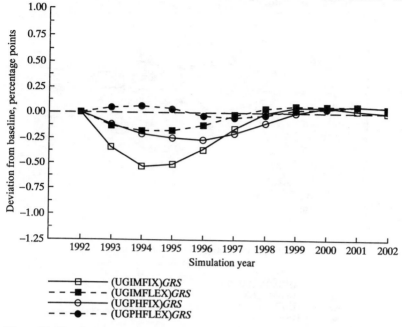

Figure 13.37 German short-term nominal interest rate

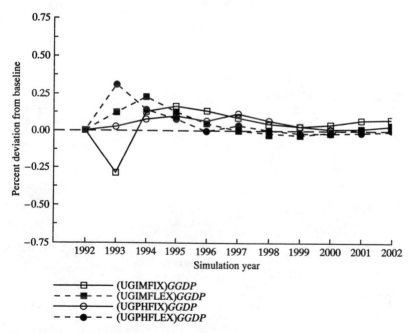

Figure 13.38 German real gross domestic product

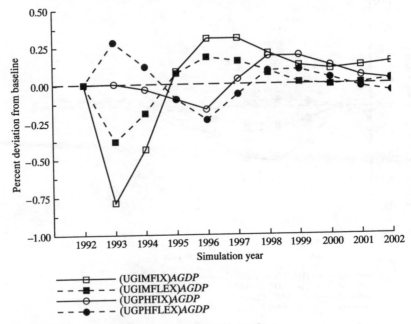

Figure 13.39   Asian NICs' real gross domestic product

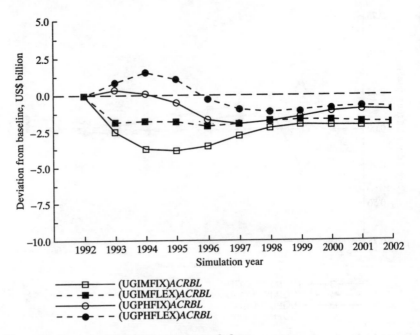

Figure 13.40   Asian NICs' current-account balance

variables, are affected in noticeable ways by the Southern governments' choice of exchange rate arrangements. Figures 13.37 and 38 show the results for the four simulations for the German short-term interest rate and German real GDP (reinforcing the impressions already obtained from Figures 13.17 and 18). The differing qualitative patterns and quantitative effects of each of the four simulations on the real GDP and on the current-account balance of the Asian NIC economies can be studied in Figures 13.39 and 40.

6 Concluding remarks

The empirical evidence summarized in this paper stems from exploratory research. The MULTIMOD model, and especially the Brook-I version of MULTIMOD, is still under development – most especially in its treatment of the economies of developing, Southern nations. Considerably more research needs to be done with MULTIMOD, and with other systemic models of the global economy, before it will be possible to make reliable empirical generalizations about the macroeconomic linkages among Southern and Northern economies.

Notwithstanding the preceding caveat, our research highlights the point that the specification in multicountry models of the financial and debt features of developing economies can have critically important effects on estimates of the macroeconomic behaviour of developing country regions, and possibly significant effects even for the behaviour of the global economic system as a whole. Several of the conclusions we emphasize here on the basis of simulation evidence from MULTIMOD, moreover, are likely to be born out by further research.

Our analysis confirms the conclusion, already clear from numerous other studies of developing counties, that the choice of exchange rate arrangements by Southern governments can have significant welfare consequences for Southern economies. We have not tried in this paper, of course, to draw specific welfare inferences about exchange rate management. Our view is that such inferences require an explicit, careful focus on policy-loss functions and a more geographically disaggregated perspective, focusing on individual developing-country nations. Although our analysis is general and therefore quite limited in applicability, we do believe it establishes helpful presumptions about the types of macroeconomic effects that future research should try to identify.

Our evidence here confirms the important differences in effects between fiscal actions that are simultaneously announced and implemented versus fiscal actions that are pre-announced and phased in gradually. We have shown that these differences are significant not only for the country originating the actions but also for foreign economies, not least the economies of developing nations.

One more controversial and more tentative conclusions pertain to the non-negligible effects on some Northern macroeconomic variables of Southern choices about exchange-rate management. The evidence on this issue from the Brook-I version of MULTIMOD is suggestive, but far from definitive. Even on this point, however, we believe our findings are, at the least, sufficient to justify further research.

NOTES

1 Although this topic is the focus of the current book and a related earlier volume (Currie and Vines, 1988), the subject has received much less attention than the cross-border transmission of economic policies among the industrial nations themselves. For overviews of the empirical evidence on macroeconomic interactions among the OECD countries, see Bryant et al. (1988); Bryant et al. (1989); Bryant et al. (1993); and Bryant and McKibbin (1994).

2 Basic references for MULTIMOD are given below. Soludo (1992) discusses some of the background and some additional simulations conducted with the Brook-I version of MULTIMOD.

3 For the basic references on MULTIMOD, see Masson et al. (1988, 1990) and Symansky (1991b). For INTERMOD, see Helliwell, Meredith et al. (1990) and Meredith (1989). Helliwell and Masson (1990) and Soludo (1992) compare the properties of MULTIMOD and INTERMOD, with special emphasis on the developing-country submodels.

4 The Fortran-based PC SIM software stems originally from mainframe simulation programmes developed in the late 1960s and early 1970s at the Bank of Canada and the University of British Columbia (UBC). A PC version of the programme was begun by Philip Bagnoli at UBC and subsequently completed in 1988 at the Canadian Department of Finance, Ottawa. In addition to support from the preceding organizations, additional financing came from the Canadian Social Sciences and Humanities Research Council. Several modifications to the software were made by Philip Bagnoli and Ralph Bryant in 1991–92 with financing from the Brookings Institution, supported by grants from the MacArthur and Ford Foundations.

5 Bayoumi et al. (1995) report simulation results using still another variant of MULTIMOD containing further disaggregation of developing-country regions. That version does not, however, use the financial and debt equations developed in Symansky (1991a) and incorporated in the Brook-I version.

6 When contractual, obligated payments of interest on the old external debt exceed (are less than) the 'voluntary' payments that DC government choose to make, 'interest arrears' on the old debt increase (decrease). Any 'new' debt incurred by private residents of the DC region is assumed to be fully serviced at market interest rates.

7 In the Brook-I version of MULTIMOD used for simulations in this paper, the values of α and β in the DC-government reaction function have values, respectively, of 0.018 and 0.67. To illustrate the worrisome sensitivity: if

one specifies a value of 0.015 for α and a value of 0.33 for β, these changes are sufficient to reverse the signs of the effects of a US fiscal contraction on the dollar exchange rate, private capital flows, and real GDP of the DC region.

8 The size of the cut in real expenditures, measured in constant dollars, rises gradually in line with growth in baseline real GDP in order to maintain the cut at 3 per cent of real GDP throughout the simulation period.

9 The intertemporal rules in all the industrial countries are such that tax rates adjust over time in order to prevent stocks of government debt from rising or falling without bound relative to GDP. Each country's tax rate adjusts endogenously so that the simulated debt–GDP ratio eventually approaches an exogenously specified target ratio. In the simulations for US fiscal contractions in this paper, the target debt–GDP ratio and the values of several coefficients of the tax-rate reaction function for the United States alone are changed to specify an eventual fall in the US debt–GDP ratio of about 10 percentage points. See Bryant (1993) for a discussion of these changes in the US target debt–GDP ratio and the coefficients in the US tax-rate reaction function. The intertemporal fiscal rule enforced for the DC region constrains DC governments not to issue new debt, but rather to adjust taxes to ensure budget balance year by year. This rule of course sharply limits the flexibility assumed for fiscal policy in the DC region. Although it is logically necessary to find some way of enforcing governments' intertemporal budget constraints in models with forward-looking expectations, the question of the most appropriate specification for these 'closure rules' is still an unresolved issue in macroeconomic modelling.

10 The procedure used to solve MULTIMOD in the PC SIM software programme is an application of the Fair–Taylor extended-path technique (Fair and Taylor, 1983). Ideally, the 'terminal conditions' used in the process of generating model solutions – in this study, the values for 2046 and beyond for key variables in equations with forward-looking behaviour – should not significantly influence the computed simulation values for early and even middle periods of the simulation. That desirable characteristic does not hold fully for the MULTIMOD simulations reported here. To reduce the risks that this technical problem could materially affect the inferences drawn from the simulations, we do not report simulated data for years after the decade of the 2020s.

11 The US dollar price of the DC region's commodity exports rises under both the FIX and FLEX regimes (indeed by slightly more under the FLEX regime). But the increase for the FLEX regime is only by some 2 to 4 per cent; given the large appreciation of the DC currency against the dollar under the FLEX regime (Figure 13.1), the local-currency price of commodity exports falls.

12 The declines in OECD interest rates following fiscal contractions in the United States or in all OECD countries tend to be smaller in MULTIMOD than in several other multicountry models (see, for example, Bryant and McKibbin, 1995, Figures 28 and 35). Moreover, the incremental capital inflows in the MULTIMOD simulations entail algebraically lower values for the DC region's net foreign assets (higher levels of external debt), which tend to raise debt-service payments (despite the lower interest rate per dollar of debt).

13 See, for example, Masson and Blundell-Wignall (1985), Haas and Masson (1986), Taylor (1988), McKibbin (1991) and Bryant *et al.* (1989).

14 For discussion, see for example Bryant (1993) and McKibbin and Bagnoli (1993).

15 Identical assumptions are also made about the definition of unchanged monetary policies and about the operation of intertemporal fiscal closure rules. All the simulations discussed in this paper assume that the US fiscal actions are regarded, when announced, as fully credible. (It is possible to use models such as MULTIMOD to study policy actions that initially may be interpreted as imperfectly credible, but that type of analysis is beyond the scope of this paper.)

16 We do not have space here to dwell on the medium- and long-run consequences for the US economy. Different models give somewhat different estimates of the size of the long-run gains in output resulting from fiscal contraction (MULTIMOD's estimates tend to be smaller than other models). Models also differ on the details of timing when immediately implemented contractions are contrasted with contractions that are pre-announced and phased in gradually.

17 The world dollar price of commodities is an interesting exception in the initial year. The *anticipated* effects of the phased-in contraction are strong enough in 1993 to cause commodity prices to rise even more in 1993 than they rise for the immediately implemented contraction. For the second, third, and fourth years, however, the UGIM commodity prices move above the UGPH prices.

18 In the US, Japanese, German, and Canadian submodels of MULTIMOD (all versions), the behaviour of nominal interest rates over short horizons depends importantly on interactions between the money-demand function and the 'money targetting' interest rate reaction function of the monetary authority. MULTIMOD allows endogenous short-run deviations of the simulated value of the money stock away from the target money path; but if such deviations occur, the monetary authority leans against the deviations through its interest rate reaction function. In the UGPH simulations, the price level appearing in the money-demand function for the United States rises above baseline by more than the real-transactions variable in the US money-demand function falls below baseline. (Indeed, as seen in Figure 13.21, the real-transactions variable is even above baseline in the initial year.) Hence money demand rises initially, which in turn leads to a rise in the short-term interest rate (via the monetary authority's reaction function) to restrict the tendency of the money stock to rise above baseline. In the UGIM simulations, the price and activity variables in the money-demand function fall unambiguously below baseline, causing a decline in short- and long-term interest rates.

REFERENCES

Bayoumi, Tamim, Daniel Hewitt, and Steven Symansky (1995) 'MULTIMOD simulations of the effects on developing countries of decreasing military spending', Chapter 10 in this volume.

Bryant, Ralph C. (1993) 'Consequences of reducing the US budget deficit', Memorandum, The Brookings Institution, Washington DC 26 January

1993). Brookings Discussion Paper in International Economics, No. 104 (February 1994).

Bryant, Ralph C., John F. Helliwell and Peter Hooper (1989) 'Domestic and cross-border consequences of US macroeconomic policies', in R. C. Bryant, D. Currie *et al.* (eds.), *Macroeconomic Policies in an Interdependent World*, Washington DC: International Monetary Fund, Brookings Institution, and Centre for Economic Policy Research. Unabridged version available as Brookings Discussion Paper in International Economics No. 68, Washington DC: Brookings Institution.

Bryant, Ralph C., Dale W. Henderson, Gerald Holtham, Peter Hooper and Steven A. Symansky (eds.) (1988) *Empirical Macroeconomics for Interdependent Economies*, Washington DC: Brookings Institution.

Bryant, Ralph C., Peter Hooper and Catherine L. Mann (eds.) (1993) *Evaluating Policy Regimes: New Research in Empirical Macroeconomics*, Washington DC: Brookings Institution.

Bryant, Ralph C. and Warwick J. McKibbin (1995) 'Macroeconomic effects on developing countries of shocks in the OECD: evidence from multicountry models', Chapter 8 in this volume.

Currie, David A. and David Vines (1988) *Macroeconomic Interactions between North and South*, Cambridge: Cambridge University Press.

Fair, Ray C. and John B. Taylor (1983) 'Solution and maximum likelihood estimation of dynamic nonlinear rational expectation models', *Econometrica* 51, 1169–85.

Haas, Richard and Paul R. Masson (1986) 'MINIMOD: specification and simulation results', *IMF Staff Papers* 33, 722–67.

Helliwell, John F. and Paul R. Masson (1990) 'The effects of industrial country fiscal policies on developing countries in the 1980s', *Revista di Politica Economica* 80, 195–231.

Helliwell, John F., Guy Meredith, Philip Bagnoli and Yves Durand (1990) 'INTERMOD' 1.1: A G-7 Version of the IMF's MULTIMOD', *Economic Modeling* 7, 3–62.

Masson, Paul R. and A. Blundell-Wignall (1985) 'Fiscal policy and the exchange rate in the big seven: transmission of US government spending shock,' *European Economic Review* 28, 11–42.

Masson, Paul R., Steven Symansky, Richard Haas and Michael Dooley (1988) 'MULTIMOD: a multi-region econometric model', In Staff Studies for the *World Economic Outlook*, Research department of the International Monetary fund.

Masson, Paul R. Steven Symansky, and Guy Meredith (1990) *MULTIMOD Mark II: A Revised and Extended Model*, IMF Occasional Paper No. 71, Washington, DC.

McKibbin, Warwick J. (1991) *Global Linkages: Macroeconomic Interdependence and Cooperation in the World Economy*, Washington DC Brookings Institution.

McKibbin, Warwick J., and Philip Bagnoli (1993) 'Fiscal deficit reduction: an evaluation of alternatives', Brookings Discussion Paper in International Economics No. 101, Brookings Institution, Washington DC.

Meredith, Guy (1989) 'Model specification and simulation properties', Working Paper No 89-7, Ottawa: Working Group on International Macroeconomics, Department of Finance.

Soludo, Charles C. (1992) 'North–South macroeconomic interactions: comparative analysis Using the MULTIMOD and INTERMOD Global models', Brookings Discussion Papers in International Economics No. 95, the Brookings Institution, Washington DC.

Symansky, Steve (1991a) 'Closure rules and new developing country region for MULTIMOD', paper presented at the conference on 'Global interdependence: theories and models of the linkages between OECD and non-OECD economies', held in Seoul, South Korea.

(1991b) 'Changes to MULTIMOD since July 1990' Occasional Paper No. 71, International Monetary Fund Reseach Department,

Taylor, John B. (1988) 'The treatment of expectations in large multicountry econometric model', Chapter 7 in Bryant et al. (1988).

Index